MASTERS OF MAHĀMUDRĀ

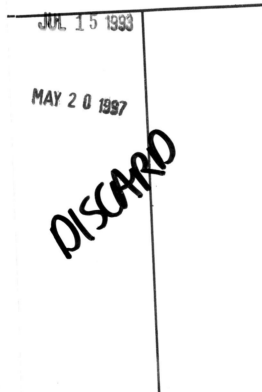

SUNY Series in Buddhist Studies

Edited by Kenneth K. Inada

MASTERS OF MAHĀMUDRĀ

Songs and Histories of the Eighty-Four Buddhist Siddhas

Translation and Commentary by
Keith Dowman

Illustrations by
Hugh R. Downs

State University of New York Press

The cover illustration is of the Mahāsiddha Jālandharipa, The Ḍakinī's Chosen One.

Published by
State University of New York Press, Albany

Printed in the United States of America

For information, address State University of New York Press, State University Plaza, Albany, N.Y., 12246

Library of Congress Cataloging-in-Publication Data

Abhayadatta.

Masters of Mahamudra.
(SUNY series in Buddhist studies)
Bibliography: p.
Includes index.
1. Siddhas—Biography. 2. Tantric Buddhism—India.
I. Dowman, Keith. II. Downs, Hugh R. III. Title.
IV. Series.

BQ342.A2313 1985 294.3'925'0922 [B] 85-20771
ISBN 0-88706-158-3
ISBN 0-88706-160-5 (pbk.)

Invocation and Dedication

A man attuned and at peace with all others, whose words are revelation with personal relevance to each listener, and whose very posture and gesture are meaningful communication; a man who knows his own mind and everyone else's and whose constant infectious humor elevates his friends and guests to stars in the cosmic dance: he is the Lama. In the beginning I pay homage to one such man called Kanjur Lama. He was born in Eastern Tibet, became a respected savant at Riwoche Monastery in Amdo, and ended his life as a refugee in Darjeeling, India, at the age of eighty-four. May this invocation of the Lama give us direct perception of his Mind, and may the merit of this work fulfill his intent that all sentient beings be released from the wheel of life and attain The Great Perfection, or The Magnificent Stance (Mahāmudrā).

Contents

List of Illustrations

Preface

Mahāmudrā is a name of the highest tantric path to Buddhahood, and it is the ultimate goal itself. The eighty-four masters of Mahāmudrā were the original founding fathers of the Mahāmudrā tradition who formulated its techniques of meditation, and also the founders' lineal successors who practiced those techniques. They all attained the realization of Buddhahood. These masters were called *mahāsiddhas*—Great Attainers—and they lived in India between the eighth and twelfth centuries.

At the core of this work on the masters of Mahāmudrā is an adaptation of the Tibetan text called *Legends of the Eighty-four Mahāsiddhas* (*Grub thob brgyad bcu tsa bzhi'i lo rgyus*), and this text can be appreciated on three levels. Firstly, the legends of the historically pre-eminent *siddhas*—Nāgārjuna, Saraha, Lūipa, Virūpa, to name a few—are stories of magical power and knowledge. These exemplify the astonishing and entertaining didactic stories belonging to the Buddhist lineages of Indian Tantra transmitted by Guru to disciple down the centuries. Secondly, most of the legends can be perceived as allegories in which every anecdote is an analogy and every act a metaphor composed to instruct the tantric initiate in his or her life-praxis and meditation. Some of the short lesser known siddhas' legends consist only of basic biographical information and meditation instruction shorn of the hermetical sheath of allegory. Thirdly, since the legends were written down shortly after the death of the last of the eighty-four, there is history to be sieved from them, despite the orthographical depredations of scribes and wood-block carvers. Thus we have eighty-four authentic tantric legends, eighty-four paradigms of tantric meditation technique, and eighty-four personalities, some historical, some archetypal, who lived in India between the eighth and twelfth centuries.

The eighty-four chapter headings are the names of the siddhas of the legends. The first component of the material under each title is one or two stanzas of the italicized "song of realization" translated from a short Tibetan text called *Vajra Songs: The Heart Realizations of the Eighty-four Mahāsiddhas* (*Grub thob brgyad bcu rtogs pa'i snying po rdo rje'i glu*) compiled by a scholar named Vīra Prakāśa. These songs reveal the nature of the siddhas' realization and the path that they traversed to reach it, all couched in the formal imagery and technical terminology of the Mahāmudrā tradition. Beneath this verse, in twelve point type, is the legend itself. The legends have been adapted from the stilted mnemonic style of the Tibetan manuscript to give a fluent idiomatic rendering into English while maintaining fidelity to the original meaning. At the heart of the legend is the siddha's meditation instruction (*upadeśa*) in verse. These italicized verses are free translations rendered with the special care and attention given them in the oral transmission that the lineage-Lamas insisted upon. The legends were narrated by an Indian scholar, or *paṇḍita*, Abhayadatta Śrī, to a Tibetan monk, Mondup Sherab, probably in the twelfth century. The identity of these principals and the editions of their texts are discussed in Appendix I.

The introduction to this work is also an introduction to the Buddhist Tantra, which reaches its climax in Mahāmudrā. This background should give the reader insight into the context and techniques of Mahāmudrā meditation and also into the concepts and terminology of the meditation instruction in the legends. The first part of the commentary that follows each legend, like the introduction, is written primarily for those readers interested in the legends as paradigms of meditation technique, and accordingly it has been entitled Sādhana, which means "the endeavour and method of intentional existential praxis" (see Glossary). The material for this section, which dwells mainly upon the definitions of words and on the meanings in the instruction, was compiled from a variety of sources: from the oral transmission of the Tibetan texts of *The Legends* by the Nyingma scholar Bhaga Tulku, the incarnate Lama of a monastery in Arunachal Pradesh, India; from elucidation of the text by Taklung Tsetul Rimpoche, and by the lay scholar Se Kusho Chomphel Namgyel; from the oral transmission of similar meditation practices, specifically Mahāmudrā instruction from the late Gyelwa Karmapa and other Kahgyu Lamas, the creative and fulfillment stages of meditation taught within the Nyingma school, and Dzokchen instruction (the Nyingma equivalent of Mahāmudrā); from reading the root-tantras of the siddhas' lineages—particularly the *Saṃvara, Guhysamāja, Hevajra* and *Caṇḍamahāroṣaṇa tantras*, the meditation liturgies (*sādhanas*) of Vajra Yoginī in many of her forms, and the *dohā* songs of the siddhas. But no amount of oral and literary transmission, academic study and analysis, can simulate the effects of meditation practice, least of all tantric meditation that is taught eliptically and on many levels simultaneously. Authority to practice (T. *lung*), initiation into the *maṇḍala* (*dbang bskur*), and transmission of practical techniques of meditation (*khrid*), are only the initial stages of learning the essential preliminaries, wherein a vision is developed. The work of identifying and actuating the psychic realities that are indicated by the complex inter-related symbolism of the iconography of a deity, for example, and realizing experientially the various states of awareness evoked in the poetry of the tantras and their sādhanas, can only be done through meditation in the laboratory of the mind under optimal conditions—ideally a mountain hermitage. Thus the commentary reflects experience in a tradition of meditation similar to the siddhas' tradition gained by the commentator during twelve years of practice.

Western initiates seeking an understanding of the nature of mind through the medium of Tantra are not usually hampered by problems of motivation or capacity to meditate. Rather, misinterpretation of symbological meaning and iconography and failure to penetrate the true significance of terminology, ideas and concepts—problems in the realm of hermeneutics—probably form their biggest obstacle. Thus study of literal translations of tantric texts without commentaries in a language that has personal meaning for the student, or without oral transmission from a teacher who has gained realization of the goal of the Tantra through the techniques described, is counter-productive if not a real danger to sanity. Justification for interpretive commentary, and indeed interpretive translation, is found in Tibet and China during the early periods of transmission of the doctrine, when the essential formulae of Tantra were re-stated in the cultural idioms of those countries. With such successful precedents in mind, the language of the introduction to this work, and of the commentary, sometimes introduces western concepts quite alien to traditionalist Tibetan scholars. For example, readers familiar with homeopathy can gain insight into the methods of Tantra through the theory epitomized in the Latin dictum *similia similibus curantor,* with its connotations of "the poison is the panacea" and "the smaller the dose the higher the potency." Again the phrase *coitus interruptus* is effective insofar as it is familiar to the western ear, its experientially assimilated connotations evoking a notion very close to that intended in the relevant tantric meditation. As a final example, the images of adepts walking through walls, flying in the sky and eating rock, and so on, so familiar to the eastern mind, but ridiculed by western rationalists, are best discussed in the context of "mind over matter" (when they are not understood analogically). Although in eastern Buddhist thought mind is not conventionally opposed to matter, the efficacy of such a concept justifies its use. Further, why should the western aspirant become burdened by eastern concepts and thought patterns when he already possesses adequate conceptual baggage, which anyway he must detach himself from, if not eradicate, along the path? Thus, although the basic doctrinal formulae in the commentaries are those transmitted for twelve hundred years and more, the commentary herein reflects personal experience in a language comprehensible to the intelligent lay reader.

After Sādhana, under the heading Historiography, all the material relevant to the task of establishing the historical identity of the siddha, his place in a lineage, and the period of his existence, has been gathered together. Concerning the more prominent siddhas, legends and anecdotes from other sources have been included to elucidate these identity problems, but limitations of space have kept legends from other sources and discussion of conflicting arguments and alternative theories to a minimum. Where no reference to a siddha exists outside our legend the only point of discussion is his or her name. The siddhas' names used throughout are those Sanskrit forms confirmed by etymological analysis, and these have replaced Apabhraṃṣa and Tibetan forms together with numerous corrupt forms found in the various editions of *The Legends* and other Tibetan sources, but these have been selectively listed in this commentary. In general, despite the multiplicity of names, paucity of historiographically valid material has allowed only partial success in solving the multitude of historical problems relating to the siddhas and their times. Discovery of new sources, besides an exhaustive scrutiny and re-evaluation of known Tibetan sources, is essential before the lineage tree (p. 390–1) can be a definitive indicator of the siddhas' lifetimes and their lineal relationships. The Tibetan sources that have provided the lineal information are discussed in Appendix I.

The siddhas' epithets given in the eighty-four chapter headings as a mnemonic aid are translations of their names, or descriptive epithets sometimes based on a false etymology found in the legend itself, or they have been borrowed from other Tibetan sources. The suffix *pa* in the siddhas' names is at once the contraction of Sanskrit *pāda* (T. *zhabs*), an honorific form applied to saints and siddhas, and the Tibetan masculine denominator. To indicate that a siddha's status is derived mainly from the exemplary sādhana attached to his name and not from his place in a lineage, the title Mahāsiddha becomes merely Siddha. The feminine form of *mahāsiddha* is *mahāsiddhā*, of *siddha siddhā*, details that were not rendered into Tibetan.

The Glossary of Sanskrit Terms defines the italicized Sanskrit words found throughout the text. Words used only once in parenthesis have not been glossed. Since the siddhas spoke sanskritic languages—Prakrit or an Apabhraṃṣa dialect—Sanskrit has been the preferred language of technical terminology. But since Tibetan is the language in which the legends have come down to us, while Sanskrit forms have been used in the text, in the notes both Sanskrit and Tibetan, or sometimes only Tibetan forms, are given according to their relevance. To locate the definitions of Sanskrit and Tibetan words omitted from the glossary, the index will direct the enquirer to the note where the principal definition is found, or through the note to the place in the text to which the note refers.

The transliteration of Tibetan words rendered phonetically in the text can be found in the index. Wherever they occur, transliterated Tibetan words are indicated by T. in a single entry, and in the first instance of a series of Tibetan definitions. The numbers in italics in parenthesis after a siddha's name refer to the number of his legend. To assist in easy reference a Glossary of Numeral Terms, the irksome mnemonical phrases that appear so frequently in Buddhist literature—which do, however, carry a numerological value—has been included with Tibetan and Sanskrit equivalents where appropriate.

Line-drawings of twenty of the siddhas have been provided by Hugh R. Downs. The inspiration for these original drawings was derived from examples and descriptions in his private collection of traditional art and related literature. There are standard iconographies in Tibetan art representing the various styles of enlightened human beings—*yogins*, scholars, monks, (*bhikṣus*) and so forth. Traditionally, when searching for models, an artist would consult his iconographic examples, literary descriptions and his own notes, and then his creation though based on a traditional model would none the less be an original expression to fulfill a specific purpose. Since far greater latitude is permitted in rendering historical figures than in representing precise metaphysical principles in iconography, a subtle progressive modification of siddha images has occurred. For this reason, and due to the conscious alteration of particular images to suit the needs of specific lineages, and, of course, simple error, we possess a wide variety of depictions of the eighty-four mahāsiddhas. It is the responsibility of the artist to sift through this material and find the ideal for the moment and the need. Hugh R. Downs undertook a traditional apprenticeship in Tibetan drawing and painting under the guidance of his Guru, the Sherpa yogin Au Leshe, an experience he describes in his photographic and literary essay *Rhythms of a Himalayan Village.*[1] His representations show most vividly the power and force of the siddhas' manner of being, while stressing both the ascetic element in their paths to enlightenment and the esthetic and sensual refinement of their life-styles. The captions below the illustrations are derived from a series of Tibetan line-drawings of unknown provenance that were amongst those used by the artist as models.

I am indebted to a large number of people whose assistance at some time during the past ten years has facilitated the writing of this book. Particularly, the debt of gratitude accumulated over the years to my Lamas is such that the merit derived from anything here of any worth automatically accrues to them: to Lama Kalzang for publishing the text that inspired me, to Chatral Rimpoche for editing that text, to Dunjom Rimpoche for blessing the work and transmitting authority to translate it, to Bhaga Tulku for the oral transmission, to Taklung Rimpoche and Se Kusho Chomphel Namgyel for helping with difficult passages, and to those others who provoked insight into the siddha tradition. Further, my thanks go to Roger Dean, Donald Lehmkuhl, Noel Cobb, Peter Cooper (Ngawong Tenzin), the late Peter Hansen, Georgie Downes, Keith Redman, Ted Woucester, and particularly my wife Meryl, for their practical assistance and supportive energy and encouragement. My thanks also to Tony Luttenberger, Fred Lane, Stuart Hammil and many others who gave me space and indulgence during an itinerant working existence. Mimi Church's work on the siddhas' biographies in both primary and secondary sources, together with her invaluable reinforcement and enthusiasm, receive special thanks. Finally, Michele Martin's appreciation of both the theory and practice of this work provided an ideal editorial ambience for the book's publication, and for that I am most grateful.

Keith Dowman
Chabahil Ganeshtān
Kathmandu
Nepal

December 1984.

Introduction

The evolution of Tantra into the dominant spiritual power in Indian life coincided with the growth of a terrible, destructive menace on India's north-west frontier. At the beginning of the eighth century, when Arab power was supreme from Morocco to Sindh, in India the numerous inheritors of imperial Gupta glory were engaged in internecine conflicts, and Indian culture was in a state of decay. The old dispensation was vitiated, society taking refuge in inflexible caste rules and regulations; and as form and procedure governed social life, so ritual dominated religion and scholasticism the academies. There was no vital, united society to meet the threat of the fanatical Islamic armies who wreaked burning, pillage and massacre, and who were a new kind of enemy, compelling Islam or the sword. As a stream of Buddhist refugees brought tales of the destruction of Buddhist Central Asia to India, Tantra was increasing its influence, particularly in Oḍḍiyāṇa, the front-line state, and also in eastern India, where a new power, the Buddhist Pāla Dynasty, was emerging. Was it coincidence that India took refuge in Tantra with its uncompromising non-dualist metaphysics, its school of spontaneous liberation, and its fierce flesh-eating, blood-drinking deities, during a period of incipient doom? Is it a further coincidence that, after rejecting Tantra for centuries, the West finds it increasingly acceptable as the notion of mankind's extinction become credible?

Nearly four centuries passed between AD 711, when Sindh (S. Pakistan) was conquered, and the end of the twelfth century when the Buddha's Tree of Enlightenment was finally desecrated by Turkish soldiers. Some critics maintain that the final blossoming of pure Hindu civilization between the eighth and twelfth century was the most magnificent achievement of India's cultural history. During that period Tibet embraced Buddhist Tantra and the main part of the Buddhist tantric canon was translated into the Tibetan language, thus saving it from incineration in the great Indian libraries. Java was colonized and the great *stūpa* at Borobodur was built. Although most of the artistic achievement at home was destroyed by the Muslims, the scripture of the Pāla Empire (Bengal, Bihar, Orissa and Assam), the ruins of the great academies built by the Pāla Emperors, and the temples of Khajuraho, bear witness to the genius of tantric art. "Tantra" describes the ethos of Indian culture of this time;[2] the men who embodied that ethos and the aims and ideals of the culture, the generators and directors of the creative energy that converted the people and transformed society, the guides and exemplars on the path of Tantra, these men were called siddhas. The eighty-four siddhas, whose lives and practices are described in these legends, were the siddhas who practiced the Buddhist Tantra, as opposed to the Tantra of devotees of Śiva (*śaiva*s) or the Tantra of the worshippers of the Great Mother (*śākta*s).

The number eighty-four is a "whole" or "perfect" number. Thus the eighty-four siddhas can be seen as archetypes representing the thousands of exemplars and adepts of the tantric way. The siddhas were remarkable for the diversity of their family backgrounds and the dissimilarity of their social roles. They were found in every reach of the social structure: kings and ministers, priests and *yogin*s, poets and musicians, craftsmen and farmers, housewives and whores. However, the greatest names amongst the eighty-four—Tilopa, Nāropa, Saraha, Lūipa, Ghaṇṭāpa, Ḍombipa, etc.,—were sadhu siddhas, mendicant yogins living with the people on a grass-roots level of society, teaching more by psychic vibration, posture and attitude— *mantra, mudrā* and *tantra*[3]—than by sermonizing. Some of these siddhas were iconoclasts, dissenters and anti-establishment rebels fulfilling the necessary function of destroying the rigidity of old and intractable customs and habits, so that spontaneity and new vitality could flourish. Obsessive caste rules and regulations in society, and religious ritual as an end in itself, were undermined by the siddhas' exemplary free-living. The irrelevance of scholastic hair-splitting in an academic language, together with a host of social and religious evils, were exposed in the poets' wonderful mystical songs written in the vernacular tongues. They taught existential involvement rather than metaphysical speculation, and they taught the ideal of living in the world but not of it rather than ascetic self-mutilation or monastic renunciation. The siddhas are characterized by a lack of external uniformity and formal discipline.

Under the generous patronage of the Pāla Emperors in the eastern Indian empire, where the majority of the siddhas lived, the revolution became the establishment. The great academies of Vikramaśīla and Somapurī were built, and the ancient monastic establishment at Nālandā was extensively enlarged. The militancy of the siddha-poets decrying empty ritualism, charlatanism, specious philosophizing, scholasticism, hypocrisy and the caste system,[4] is less apparent during Nāropa's period in the eleventh century. The attitudes and precepts of Tantra became more socially acceptable after generations of siddhas in positions of temporal power had influenced people and events on many levels. From the beginning, Tantra's flexibility permitted initiates like Līlapa to retain their secular status, wealth and pleasure, and this principle of tolerance and inclusiveness was a significant factor in the appeal of the doctrine; as the millennium approached the increasing hedonism could be used as a path to spiritual liberation. However, the ideal of spiritual anarchism, the attitude that precluded attachment to religious forms, prevailed, and in its esoteric, yogic form, Tantra remained the preserve of initiates into the lineage, and no institutionalism compromised their spirit of existential freedom.

Tantra took centuries to come out if its closet. Its history up to the era of the siddhas can only be conjecture, but it appears that originally, in the guise of fertility cults, it belonged to the pre-Aryan, tribal worshippers of the Mother Goddess, and later, also, to the low castes and out-castes of Hindu society. A corpus of sympathetic and imitative magic for a variety of mundane purposes such as healing became part of the various tantric cults. Then over the centuries, as they became "sanskritized" and more sophisticated, these cults assimilated brahmanical deities, their rituals and the principles of mantra. Later still, Upanishadic philosophy, Patañjali's *Yoga-sūtras* and principles of mahāyāna Buddhist philosophy were assimilated, and a crucial transformation was accomplished—a body of ritual magic became a soteriological system with liberation from human suffering as its aim. Whether the *Kāpālikas*, or a similar sect of primitive *śaiva* Tantra, or heretical Buddhist monks, formed the first lineage of Tantra as we know it, is not known, but in the fourth or fifth century, a need arose for order and consistency in the system, and this could only be achieved by committing to palm leaf manuscript what until then had been purely oral transmission. The *Mañjuśrīmūlakalpa*[5] contained a body of mahāyāna lore and also the basic father-tantra maṇḍala of the Five Dhyāni Buddhas; but the *Guhyasamāja-tantra*[6] is considered to be the first of the root-tantras describing yoga techniques as well as the maṇḍalas, mantras and rites associated with the propitiation of a particular deity and his retinue, in this case Guhyasamāja. This tantra was probably compiled in the sixth or seventh century, not reaching its final form until Indrabhūti "revealed" it in the eighth century. The eighth and ninth centuries saw the revelation of most of the major tantras, particularly the mother-tantras, incorporating many elements from the *śākta*, Goddess-worshipping cults.

When the scriptural tantras were written down, Tantra could no longer be kept secret. There were many reasons for secrecy, perhaps the most important being the need to avoid the hostile propaganda of brahmin orthodoxy. One of Tantra's appeals was its catholic tolerance in initiating members of all castes and both sexes, a practice that militated against the priestly supremacy of the brahmins. Practices such as meat-eating, drinking liquor, and in some *śākta*-influenced tantras, sexual intercourse between untouchables and twice-born initiates, were abhorrent to the brahmins. One of the achievements of the siddhas was to make Buddhist Tantra socially acceptable, but although the exoteric forms of Tantra comprised the religion of the masses, the orthodox have retained their hostility until this day. In the same way that Buddhism had attracted India's greatest minds to its past forms, amongst the siddhas were men with the ability to write great commentaries on the tantras, in the process interpreting ambiguity in terms consistent with mahāyāna ethics and principles, excising all traces of gross practices that carried a stigma.

Before describing the yogas and the teaching of these spiritual adventurers and multi-facetted adepts called siddhas, it will be helpful to define several Sanskrit words that remain untranslated throughout the work, words that have no English equivalents. The first word is siddha itself. Literally a siddha is a practitioner of Tantra who is successful in attaining the goal of his meditation. This achievement is known as *siddhi*. *Siddhi* is two-fold: magical power (mundane), and the Buddha's enlightenment (ultimate).[7] Thus siddha could be rendered "saint," "magus," "magician," "adept;" but these words are feeble, failing to evoke the originality of the siddhas' tantric life-style. For the uninitiated Indian the word siddha evokes magical power above all; if a yogin can walk through walls, fly in the sky, heal the sick, turn water into wine, or even levitate and read minds, he deserves the title siddha. If that same yogin has a crazy glint in his eye, smears himself with ashes, moves himself or others to tears with his song, calms street mongrels by his presence, tears a faithful woman from her family, wears a *vajra*—a symbol of immutability—in his yard-long hair-knot, eats from a skull-bowl, talks with the birds, sleeps with lepers, upbraids demagogues for moral laxity, or performs with conviction any act contrary to convention while demonstrating a "higher" reality, then he is doubly a siddha. Common people impressed by appearances have no conception of the siddha's esoteric aim—Mahāmudrā—and cannot know that a siddha may also be an inconspicuous peasant, an office worker, a king, a monk, a servant or a tramp.

The Sanskrit word sādhana can be translated as "spiritual discipline." It can also be rendered "psycho-experimental techniques of personality transcendence and ecstasy," or "the activity of an integrated body, speech and mind motivated by the Bodhisattva Vow." More specifically, sādhana is "the *yogin*'s practice of his Guru's precepts," or "an initiate's meditation liturgy." Obviously, then, sādhana is a vital concept for a *tantrika* (a practitioner of Tantra). In fact, sādhana is his whole life, and to the degree that his life is not integrated into his sādhana he breaks the pledge he swore at the time of his initiation, which was based on his intention to selflessly devote his entire being to the non-dual, gnostic enlightenment experience and to others. The Tibetan form of the word sādhana (T. *sgrub thabs*) simply means "the method of accomplishing [success]." The forms of the mahāsiddhas' sādhanas are as varied as their personalities, although in the limited sense of sādhana most of their meditation techniques belong to what is known as the creative and fulfillment modes of meditation.[8]

The invariable goal of these siddhas' sādhanas is *mahāmudrā-siddhi*. *Siddhi* has already been defined as "power," and power is of two types: mundane and ultimate, ordinary and supreme. The latter is synonymous with *mahāmudrā-siddhi*, which is nothing less than the Buddha's enlightenment. The easiest way of dealing with the vague and overworked word "enlightenment" is to define it as the attainment of the ultimate mystical experience of the oneness of all things, the non-dual cognition of ultimate reality, clear light, gnostic awareness—the dissolution of the individuated personality in the universal mind. The Buddha's enlightenment is specifically defined as coincident with a vast, empathetic, self-sacrificial, social sensibility—love, in fact. That is *mahāmudrā-siddhi*. The mahāyāna explains "Buddha" in terms of three "bodies" or rather three modes of being: being as empty space and awareness, being as instructive visionary enjoyment, and being as compassionate apparition; a fourth mode of being is spontaneous being, integrating the other three, and this can be called Mahāmudrā—the Great Seal, Magnificent Symbol, Sublime Stance, Absolute Reality. While the term Mahāmudrā is usually found embedded in highly abstruse metaphysical jargon, in the mother-tantra it is synonymous with an essential symbol for ultimate reality, the vulva, and it is useful to bear that meaning in mind. *Mahāmudrā-siddhi* is invariably accompanied by mundane *siddhi*, though not *vice versa*, and mundane *siddhi* is conventionally defined as attainment of the eight great *siddhis*, the six extra-sensory powers and the four transformative modes of action.[9]

The great powers, are enumerated differently in the various traditions, sometimes as seven, sometimes as eight. The *siddhis* that Nāgabodhi attained from Nāgārjuna in these legends were the power to pass through matter, power to wield the enchanted sword of awareness, the powers of creation and annihilation (materialization and de-materialization), the powers to dispense the pill of third-eye vision and the eye-salve of omniscience, the power of speed-walking, and power to perform the alchemy of immortality. The language of this list may be interpreted literally or figuratively, according to faith and understanding. Thus the power to walk through walls can be explained literally as a siddha's magical feat to induce faith in the credulous, or figuratively to demonstrate, for instance, the nature of reality as a dream, an illusion, an hallucination, where all things are experienced as light and space. All these *siddhis* must be understood in the light of the basic precept "all is mind;" for the siddha there is no body/mind, matter/spirit duality. Lastly, what makes these *siddhis* great is their use as technical aids to *mahāmudrā-siddhi* in sādhana, though it is stretching a point to include the Lama's vaunted power of speed-walking in the above list.

The six extra-sensory powers are mental powers of the same order as the great *siddhis* but they are couched in psychological terminology. Thought reading and memory of past lives need no explanation; clairaudience is "the divine ear" by which all languages including those of birds and animals can be understood, from near and far; clairvoyance, "the divine eye," as astral vision, especially implying intuition of another's suffering; ability to perform miracles includes manipulation of the elements, flight, and walking on water, and so on; finally, ability to arrest and extinguish emotivity, which leads to *nirvāṇa*. These, again, are all powers that can be used to expedite *mahāmudrā-siddhi* for oneself or others. Fleeting knowledge of such powers as clairaudience and thought-reading is accessible to beginners in concentration meditation, for instance; but to evoke such powers at will during post-meditation experience, however, is an actual sign of success in sādhana.

The transformative modes of action—pacification, enrichment, control and destruction—employ the eight great *siddhis*, the extrasensory powers and every possible skillful means to calm the mind, one's own or another's, endow it with enriching qualities, control or manipulate it for beneficial purpose, or eliminate it. The means of effecting these four techniques of altering consciousness should arise spontaneously out of a siddha's realization, for he is powerless if action depends upon discursive thought. The immediate intuition and accomplishment of these four modes are represented by four Ḍākinīs, who must be propitiated.

Saṃsāra has herein usually been left untranslated. "Wheel of life," "round of rebirth," "cycle of confusion," "transmigratory existence," are succinct phrases that are adequate, but poor in connotation. Exoterically, saṃsāra is the frustrating cycle of rebirth through the human realm, heaven and hell, and the animal and spirit realms, determined by one's own previous actions, or *karma*. Esoterically, saṃsāra is the whirligig of mind, toned by various and successive complex emotional states, conditioned by thought, described in terms of the penetrating psychology of the six realms. In psychological terms, saṃsāra is "anxiety," which all will admit to more or less, although only acute anxiety is recognized as a state that should be treated—by a priest, a psychiatrist, or an analyst. Psychosis, paranoia and delusions of grandeur, schizophrenia and neurosis, are all terms germane to description of the realms of saṃsāra; according to Buddhist analysis, all of humanity is to some degree psychotic, or at best alienated, until release is attained. Whether viewed in terms of transmigration, the unsatisfactory human condition, anxiety or neurosis, saṃsāra is what all people sometimes, and some people always, wish to escape. Buddhism is primarily concerned with techniques of escape from saṃsāra to nirvāṇa; where the word "release" or "liberation" is used in a Buddhist context, it always refers to release from saṃsāra. The siddhas developed their own methods of release, which can be characterized as quick, democratic, demanding and dangerous. And *nirvāṇa?* Nirvāṇa is a continuum of emptiness.[10]

The literal meaning of the word Tantra is rarely implied in common usage. It means "thread," "continuity" or "warp and woof." It refers to the one essential, immutable and continuous element in life, and that is emptiness or "such-ness,"[11] the ultimate, indeterminate, existential reality inherent in ordinary consciousness. "Tantra" is used herein to indicate the ethos of a way of life determined by a body of practices described in a canon of texts which themselves are called tantras. Since only the self-evident and sensational elements of Tantra—ritualism, sex and magic—are widely known, the common associations of the term are unbalanced and misleading. Of the four classes of Buddhist Tantra (there is no space here to deal with the similar but different Hindu Tantra),[12] the two lower levels are predominantly ritualistic and to a large extent concerned with attainment of temporal goals and magical powers. The higher levels of Tantra do involve ritual meditation, but in the supreme Tantra (*anuttarayoga-tantra*) which leads to *mahāmudrā-siddhi*, ritualism *per se* is rejected. The eighty-four paradigms of tantric practice given in these legends describe non-ritualistic meditation. Although sex is renounced in orthodox Buddhism, in Tantra it is accepted as a valid means by which Mahāmudrā can be attained. The delusion that all tantric yoga is sexual yoga is fostered by the tantras' frequent use of sexual analogy, metaphor and symbol to describe psychic processes.

To understand the metaphysical content of the siddhas' teaching it is useful to look at the scriptural tantras. All tantric literature is based upon what are known as the root-tantras. Each of these texts deals with practices associated with a particular deity. Thus the deities Guhyasamāja, Cakrasaṃvara, Hevajra, Mahāmāyā and Yamāri, as the most important deities associated with the siddhas, each pertain to a root-tantra that describes a maṇḍala in terms of a divine entourage of psychic powers that comprise the Guru's mind, the creative and fulfillment modes of meditation, subsidiary rites (fire sacrifice, extensive feasts and offerings), detailed description of symbology and ingredients for symbolic offerings, and other sections specific to the individual tantra.[13] Lack of definitions and explanations necessitated the vast commentarial literature that grew up subsequently. But the root-tantras and their commentaries are practical manuals, and nowhere do we find a structured metaphysical model of mind and the universe, or an analysis of the soteriological functions of *tantra-yoga*. Metaphysical definitions must be deduced from the tantras' symbology and maṇḍalas, and so on.

In a non-dual philosophy absolute reality is everyday experience, which is unutterable: thus the siddhas' disdain of speculative metaphysics. Nevertheless, this ineffable absolute, represented as *yantras*, *maṇḍalas* and deities, was their obsession, and the dynamo generating superhuman power, energy and realization. They had no concept of it and no knowledge of it; it cannot be conceived and the temporal mind cannot comprehend it. It is indefinable, indeterminable and without location.[14] *Tathatā* is perhaps the most evocative word for it. It means "that-ness" or "such-ness," "the absolute specific," the universe in a grain of sand. It is the ungraspable essence that our poets and musicians have sought, and their intuition of it makes them western tantrikas. It has no cause and no root, and is therefore said to be "unborn" or "pure potential."[15] It is the cosmic totality and a sesame seed; a seed or an egg is often used to symbolize it.[16] But anything that is said about it is simply poetry—with a connotation of self-indulgence—or it is for didactic purposes, calculated to make an aspirant recognize it. Most people only experience a flash of it or a vague intimation. Since reality is utterly indeterminable, there is no truth in any concept of absolute truth whatsoever,[17] and the relative phenomena that are inseparable from it are a lie, until they are recognized as reality (see *19*).

Paradoxes appear constantly in the tantras. They function as Zen koans, concepts used to destroy all conceptual thought. Conceptual knowledge is one of the twin veils that occlude reality; whereas paradox is the most apposite expression of it. One statement of the paradox that is only resolved existentially appears constantly in the siddhas' songs of realization (at the head of each legend). If the siddhas' experience is a continuum of space, if all things are emptiness (*śūnyatā*), if there is only clear light, where are sensual objects, the material universe? This paradox is answered by the single most important formula in mahāyāna metaphysics, "emptiness is form and form is emptiness."[18] Emptiness is nothing if not form, and the absolute specific is certainly not nothing; when all things dissolve into space and are seen as space, substance remains as a rainbow, or better, as a hologram. The very attractive mahāyāna proposition that nothing exists outside the sensual and mental realms, affirms that absolute reality is to be found within the common light of day, that emptiness *is* form. Constant peak experience of the absolute specific implies non-dual perception, union of subject/object, knower/known, self/other. This ultimate tantric mystery is Mahāmudrā, and the sexual analogy of lovers achieving a sense of complete oneness while still in their own separate bodies is probably the best, if not the only, image capable of expressing this paradoxical mystery.

Attainment of this union in Mahāmudrā, entails elimination of the barriers between oneself and other people. Suddenly the social field opens up as the siddha empathizes totally with his fellow beings, and since he has attained the powers of mind-reading and prescience (as a direct result of uniting self and other) he is capable of guiding them in their sādhanas. And also, simultaneously with the attainment of the ultimate mystical experience, the siddha is imbued with compassion ("suffering together"), and automatically he acts spontaneously to fulfill the Bodhisattva Vow, which is the commitment to serve others without prejudice in whatever way necessary. Loving kindness, sympathetic joy, compassion and equanimity, the four boundless states of mind, constitute a preparatory meditation that cultivates the feeling of oneness with all beings; the Mahāmudrā union generates these social virtues, and feelings such as love induce that union. The siddhas of the legends were renowned for their spontaneous effusion of emotion, whether it was for a beautiful woman or a starving puppy, and the songs[19] of the *siddhācāryas* are full of profound sentiments of love for woman.

The dual elements of the Mahāmudrā union are skillful means and perfect insight,[20] the first being the male co-ordinate and the second the female. Thus the Guru embodies the skillful means necessary to achieve the pure pleasure of enlightenment, and the Ḍākinī brings perfect insight and wisdom, the pure awareness and the ecstasy. Contrary to Hindu Tantra, as a rule these poles are not characterized as passive and active; stasis lies in separation and alienation (failure to recognize union), while dynamic energy ("being in love") is the result of union. Means and insight, comprising the radical duality, are interpreted differently in different sādhanas, and also at different levels of progress and for different ends. In general, however, skillful means is designated "compassion" and perfect insight "emptiness." Compassion in this context is not to be defined as pity, or even as divine love; compassion here is the Bodhisattva's sensibility responding spontaneously to the demands of the outer world with an immense variety of skillful means. These means are expressed by the entire pantheon of tantric deities, particularly the wrathful deities that represent conformations of psychic forces transmuting negative energies into the elixir of pure pleasure. These deities' faces are represented as masks in the Tibetans' painted scrolls to indicate that there is no attachment to the violent emotions that the faces depict. Acting out of compassion the siddha emanates a fierce form of anger, for example, to destroy fear; and detachment from that emotion makes him invulnerable—a *vajra* siddha, or *vajrācārya* as they say in Nepal.

The co-ordinate of male compassion is female emptiness. The complete definition of perfect insight, to repeat a vital definition, is "penetrating insight into the nature of all things as emptiness," and, therefore, perfect insight and emptiness relate as similar aspects of the one indeterminate absolute, or to rephrase it, emptiness has the cognitive capacity of pure, non-dual awareness[21] spontaneously self-aware of its "unborn" manifestations. When compassion and emptiness unite, whatever the specific manifest form of the siddha's skillful means, it is rendered self-aware, empty and absolutely specific: this is the Ḍākinī's blessing.

These metaphysical concepts must be understood with Saraha's maxim in mind: there is no truth in any concept of truth. Yet as functional thought-forms they are fine tools by which the siddhas' legends and precepts can be interpreted. Compositions of them can also be enjoyed as finely spun webs of metaphysical speculation, for their complexity, internal logic, refinement of definition, and proximity to existential reality, has rarely been equalled elsewhere. These tantric formulae embody the accumulated wisdom of two millennia of Indian experiment in the laboratory of the mind. Tantra was the final blossoming of the yoga of knowledge (*jñāna-yoga*); since the twelfth century most Indian spiritual movements, influenced by Islam, have been cults of faith and devotion (*bhakti-yoga*). The Muslims' iconoclastic zeal, horror at finding sex and god confounded, and their militant intent to eradicate Buddhist centers of learning—the monastic academies—resulted in the annihilation of the higher Buddhist Tantra in India, although the Tibetans inherited much of it; the lower tantra lived on in folk tradition and Hindu Tantra.

Even from this metaphysical analysis it should be clear that the siddhas enjoyed their sādhana. The psychological types who needed a simple life took to the road, but they lacked the radical ascetic intent that led some of their contemporaries, the *paśupata śaiva* yogins, for example, to torment their bodies or minds in destructive self-abnegation (*tapasya*). The siddhas practiced purification, of course, but guilt was eradicated by initiation, and sin was only failure to practice meditation and any tendency to take an extreme view. Life was an audio-visual spectacular, a dance of ephemeral energy configurations that some called Mahāmāyā, the female personification of Magnificent Illusion. "Live as a child lives," "the world is full of natural happiness. Dance, sing and enjoy it!" "Enjoy the pleasures of your senses, but" and here was the crunch which distinguished the siddha from the neurotic sensualist, "don't be attached to them. While drawing water, don't get wet!"

Thus enjoyment was both the result of sādhana and also the means. Amongst the eighty-four siddhas there were many individuals whose object of meditation was sensually delightful, like flowers, bird-song, music, and also sexual intercourse. The result of sādhana is pure pleasure,[22] and this, as its adjective implies, is quantitatively different from the heightened sensation of sensual experience. Pure pleasure is the feeling tone of the Buddha's mode of being as empty space, and it is essential to grasp the nature of this ultimate plane of being and its relation to the two relative planes. The ultimate existential mode of experience that is emptiness, the *dharmakāya* is all-inclusive, and the words which characterize it are expressive of the inexpressible, an inconceivable non-duality: pure awareness, emptiness, pure pleasure, all-pervasive space,[23] and clear light. The relative modes of visionary enjoyment, the *saṃbhogakāya* and apparitional incarnation, the *nirmāṇakāya*, are the duality that unites as the ultimate Mahāmudrā mode. The male co-ordinate of skillful means corresponds to the mode of visionary enjoyment and discriminating esthetic delight, where guidance is found in the form of ubiquitous, divine archetypes and symbolic indications; the essential nature of this mode of being is radiant light. The female coordinate of perfect insight corresponds to the mode of apparitional incarnation in which the Ḍākinī dances her magical display with tantalizing brilliance; in her essential nature she is manifest compassion. These three modes may also be visualized as interpenetrating spheres, or as the center, the radius and the circumference of a maṇḍala. That is the doctrine of the Buddha's three modes of being, and it is essential to an understanding of the siddhas' metaphysics.

Now, possessing the equipment necessary to read and understand the instruction and gain more than superficial pleasure from the legends as mystical fables, we will look at the legends' structure and at the actual meditation practice of the siddhas. In general, the structural pattern of the legends is diagnosis, prescription and cure. We find a sick man aware of his sickness, disgusted with his life. He is contrite and willing to do whatever is necessary to effect a cure. A Guru inevitably appears, and after the disciple requests instruction, the Guru grants initiation and precepts; the meditation guidance is usually given in terms of the creative and fulfillment modes of meditation. The disciple performs his sādhana and attains *mahāmudrā-siddhi*, and in the process the original disease is cured. The siddha achieves Buddhahood in his lifetime, and in his own body he attains the Ḍākinī's Paradise.

Without exception the legends stress the importance of the Guru. The Guru should not be viewed simply as an extraordinary human being with certain special knowledge to be transmitted, although this will be the preconception that the supplicant brings with him. It is essential, incidentally, that the disciple approaches the Guru as a supplicant; for, bound by his own tantric commitment, the Guru can only give precepts to those who approach him with respect, and who request initiation and instruction at a propitious moment and an appropriate juncture. But initiation radically alters the Guru/disciple relationship, destroying all the initiate's preconceptions. The heart of the initiation is the Guru's revelation of himself as the Buddha and the initiate's experience of identity with this Guru/Buddha. Thereafter, the initiate's basic practice is to reproduce this ultimate experience of oneness and to assimilate it fully into his everyday life. Identifying the Guru/Buddha's body with all human beings and all appearances whatsoever, and his speech with all human speech and all sound whatsoever, and his mind with all-pervasive, pure, non-dual awareness, he effectively identifies himself with the Guru. So, although the initiate will always retain respect for the human individual in whom the Buddha manifested at initiation, gradually his notion of the Guru expands to include all beings without exception, including himself. The siddha is a man with such a vision.

Many siddhas had incarnate Ḍākinī Gurus, and many more had no human Guru at all. The root-tantras can be classified as father, mother or non-dual tantras: father-tantras stress the creative mode of meditation and skillful means; mother-tantras emphasize fulfillment meditation and perfect insight; and non-dual tantras treat both equally. Mother- or *yoginī-tantra* was very popular amongst the siddhas—the names of Cakrasaṃvara and Hevajra appear most often in the legends—and thus the Ḍākinī, generally in the form of Vajra Vārāhī, Cakrasaṃvara's consort, appears frequently in their mindscape. Sometimes a Wisdom Ḍākinī[24] appears in the realm of visionary enjoyment (*saṃbhogakāya*) to initiate a yogin at the propitious moment. If his capacity for creative imagination is sufficiently developed he sees her in a vision before him, otherwise he may hear a voice or simply see her and hear her in his mind's eye—the result is the same. Sometimes the Ḍākinī is embodied; the mundane or worldly Ḍākinī[25] often appears as a whore or a dancing girl to the itinerant yogin—in Tibet and Nepal, and perhaps India, drinking establishments and brothels were identical, and the hostess would be the madam. This identification of woman with the Ḍākinī shows the thorough-going non-duality of Tantra—every woman *is* the Ḍākinī; even though she may lack experiential recognition of it and never have heard the name, still she is the tantrika's Ḍākinī: even without beauty and intelligence, every woman is an immaculate, entrancing Ḍākinī, the embodiment of wisdom. For one siddha the Ḍākinī was his mother, and for another she was a young girl. The Ḍākinī Guru is clearly most capable of empowering a yogin to practice the fulfillment mode of meditation by uniting with him as insight to his skillful means, and this happens frequently. Other siddhas were initiated by Bodhisattvas—Mañjuśrī, Lokeśvara or Tārā—some appearing in divine form in the sphere of visionary enjoyment (*saṃbhogakāya*) and others as incarnate emanations (*nirmāṇakāya*).

Very frequently in the legends the Guru meets his disciple in a cremation ground.[26] Cremation grounds are replete with all kinds of symbolic meaning. First, it is the death-bed of the ego; unconsciously we make our way there walking the streets in a pall of *angst*, loneliness and self-hatred. It is the obvious place to meet one's Guru. The tantric yogin celebrates the cremation ground as an ideal place to meditate upon the precious human body, the transitory nature of existence, upon death and karmic retribution, and upon emptiness itself. It is also a good place to keep warm on bitter winter nights. Thus Guru and disciple meet in empathy. And here the initiate dies to the world of confusion and is reborn into the world of light. Jackals and hyenas lurk in the shadows, shrieking and howling, crows and vultures wheel overhead hoping, like the jackals, to taste human flesh. While the funeral pyres crackle and flame as the sparks fly upwards, the Dākinī in the gut *cakra* ignites and melts concrete thought-patterns and all the rigidity of the head center which, in the form of the elixir of immortality, drips down into the Ḍākinī's skull-cup. All phenomenal appearances take on an ethereal radiance, and sentient beings seem like apparitional phantoms in ecstasies of delight in the fertile ambience of sepulchral scenery. Further, here in the cremation ground the initiate can find the appurtenances of the yogin's life-style: a skull to use as a cup, a femur for a thigh-bone trumpet, human bones for a necklace, coronet, bracelets, and so forth. Just as bones are the infrastructure of the human body, so emptiness pervades reality. Thus the siddhas of the legends were initiated and instructed in the cremation ground.

It is clear that the initiation is not merely a formal rite showing the disciple a carrot and welcoming him into the club. The initiation, which is also an empowerment, should ideally reveal the Buddha-nature, the nature of mind, the indeterminate absolute; and the specific qualities of the deity into whose maṇḍala the initiate is led must also be disclosed. This implies an extremely sensitive recipient, and a very perspicacious and powerful transmitter. Most of the siddhas who had no previous meditation experience before they met their Gurus were experiencing an acute sense of loss, a spiritual vacuum brought about by extreme pain, mental or physical, and they were thus ripe for a radical change in mind (Greek: *metanoia*). At the bottom of the pit of samsaric suffering there is a point of recognition of one's own limitations and delusions that previously were such an integral part of the mind that they could not be viewed objectively and accepted for what they were, and coincident with this humbling recognition is a new sense of fresh potential and high expectation of the precious human body. Thus a rebound out of the pit is incipient in hell itself, and it is the Guru's function to deflect the rebound away from the trap of rebirth into another realm and off the wheel of life altogether. In *The Tibetan Book of the Dead*[27] such "traps" are described as different colored lights that attract the consciousness of beings, according to their karmic propensities, in between death and rebirth. Further, remorse and contrition are essential elements in the pre-initiation syndrome, as they are in the Christian experience of "meeting Christ" and "rebirth." The greater the sense of revulsion, shame, self-hatred and nihilistic distress, the more receptive the initiate is likely to be, and the more radical the "turning around in the seat of consciousness." The Guru must always arrive on the scene at the propitious moment, and if he is indeed the Guru he will.

Following initiation comes instruction, which may have only a tenuous connection to the specific content of the initiation. But the Guru's instruction is more than conveyance of concepts to be put into practice. First, in the flush of the mystical experience of initiation the Guru/Buddha's word is essentially empty sound and pure pleasure; pure awareness of this constitutes the most important aspect of "secret teaching."[28] Second, listening to the Guru's instruction with an open mind, symbolic overtones can usually be heard, and this level of guidance, transcending concepts, is direct and penetrating. Danger, however, lies in interpreting these symbolic indications through the filter of a deluded mind, rather than allowing intuition to assimilate them immediately. Third, the precepts enshrining specific meditation instruction is what is to be practiced as sādhana. Most of the siddhas' practices can be subsumed under the heads of creative and fulfillment modes, but Tantra, defined in contra-distinction to hīnayāna and mahāyāna is "the path of multiple means,"[29] and in this phrase lies an ocean of possibilities.

Interpreting "multiple means" broadly, Tantra or *vajrayāna* (the path of practice where the *vajra*, or thunderbolt, is symbolic of ultimate, empty reality) includes the practices of hīnayāna (the lesser path), such as one pointed concentration (*śamatha*), guarding the doors of the senses (*vipaśyanā*), a strict personal discipline, and much more; the practices of mahāyāna, the Bodhisattva's path, such as meditation on emptiness, contemplation of the four boundless states of mind, arousal of the *bodhicitta* of compassion, and so forth, together with the vast variety of tantric practices. These tantric practices primarily include, for example, visualization of deities and recitation of mantra, physical yoga and manipulation of *prāṇa* (breath), complex alchemical rites, formless meditation, and pilgrimage. But Tantra is also the path of multiple means because it employs the entire gamut of human activity as the basis of meditation, as the siddhas' sādhanas demonstrate. The king meditates on his throne, the farmer in his fields, the lecher meditates in bed, and the widower in the cremation ground. Further, the yogin sitting in contemplation may be confronted by horrible neurotic confusion and startlingly perverse concepts: any and every mind-state whatsoever is the means to its own transformation. Thus the infinite variety of imperfect human personalities is also the multiplicity of means to attain *mahāmudrā-siddhi.*

It is useful here to introduce the metaphor of alchemy to explain the mechanics of tantric meditation. The yogin is an alchemist who must transmute the base metal of a confused mind into the gold of pure awareness. The quality of the base metal in the yogin's possession is irrelevant. His philosopher's stone that turns all into gold is full awareness of a homeopathic dose of the poison that caused the original confusion. If lust is the dominant mind-poison, then meditation upon a controlled experience of desire, in the light of the Guru's initiation and instruction, shows him the emptiness of all desire, and realizing the ultimate nature of his mind he realizes the ultimate nature of the entire universe, and thus attains *mahāmudrā-siddhi.*

The panacea, then, is the *nature* of neurotic personality, and the principle of the cure is "like cures like" (*similia similibus curantor*—the axiom of homeopathy). This innovative and considerably dangerous technique was justified by the Buddha's prophecy that his doctrine would endure for five hundred years in its pure form, five hundred in a modified form, and that thereafter, in the *kaliyuga*, the age of strife, the black or iron age, man would be unable to follow the discipline, or find the compassion, to practice the ways of either the hīnayāna *arhat* or the mahāyāna Bodhisattva, and the way of the siddha would be revealed. In the *kaliyuga* the impatient disciple wants results immediately, unwilling to wait for literally aeons of successive rebirths before attaining nirvāṇa. The time-consuming practice on the lesser paths is the process of purifying the mind, eradicating vice and passion and cultivating virtue and clarity. One basic principle of Tantra is that good and evil, virtue and vice, and pleasure and pain, are equally delusive when there is still clinging to the good and pleasant and rejection of the vicious and ugly; but everything is of equal value as raw material in the process of transmutation. The danger that an initiate will abuse this precept, asserting in justification of hedonism and immorality the rationale that vice and passion have the same ultimate quality as virtue and clarity, is minimized by the initiate's sworn obedience to his Guru and by the commitments he pledges to his Guru at initiation. These commitments are called *samayas*, and for the initiate to break his *samayas* is to throw himself, with his Guru, into hell. Risking the danger of the tantric path is justified by the proven efficacy of tantric techniques. Proof enough is the existence of a pure lineage that today is still transmitting the precepts which transform ordinary consciousness into a siddha's awareness.

In this alchemical meditation—*rasāyana*—what in other systems of meditation are treated as obstacles are friendly helpers on the path. Neurotic attitudes and frustrating features of the environment are the means by which such conditions are transcended. Lusts, attachments, deceits, fascinations and fixations are the meat of meditation, and the uninvited guest, irritating impingement of sound, paranoid delusion and mental chatter, all assist the yogin in becoming a siddha. Still, those siddhas who became most renowned—Lūipa, Saraha, Tilopa, Nāropa, Virūpa and Nāgārjuna—who initiated lineages that, through Tibet, are still alive today, were renunciate yogins who abandoned home and family ties, their palaces and academies, security and comfort, fame and wealth, and the institutional fabric of existence, to practice in conditions of deprivation. All eighty-four performed the same alchemical meditations, but those who removed the principal and proximate causes of gross and acute fascination and attachment, and the strongest agencies of the mind's structuring and conditioning, achieved most. The value of renunciation is manifold, but with regard to the friendly helpers mentioned above, they are most helpful if they come one at a time allowing sufficient attention to be given to each. Further, homeopathy and homeopathic doses are most effective in a pure environment with a sensitive psycho-organism.

The Legends of the Eighty-four Mahāsiddhas, as a compendium of the various psycho-experimental techniques that constitute sādhana, is virtually unique. The meaning of "the path of multiple means" becomes clear, and the terminology of the creative and fulfillment techniques, which most siddhas practiced, is defined. In creative meditation the yogin begins by identifying with the field of emptiness; out of emptiness arises a seed-syllable[30] that is the quintessential euphonic corollary of the form of the principal deity of the maṇḍala to be created. Employing the faculty of creative visualization, out of the seed-syllable arises the deity and his entourage of divine beings and their consorts visualized within a palace surrounded by symmetrical walls and gates. Then, by means of *mudrā, mantra* and *samādhi*, these three, the deities of the maṇḍala are realized; through symbolic gestures of the hands, recitation of the creative mantra of the deity and visualization of the deities' forms, in a samādhi of identification with the Guru's mind, the yogin vitalizes the psychic functions that the deities, their crowns, ornaments and emblems, etc., represent. Further, this basic process of visualization and recitation culminates in the emanation of lights from the yogin's head, throat and heart centers to the corresponding centers in the Guru-Buddha in the sky above, to be reabsorbed with the vitalizing power of the Buddha's three modes of being. In this way the yogin is identified with the deity; and insofar as the deity, replete with symbolic representations of the Buddha's awareness and qualities, is a statement of non-dual absolute reality, at this point there is no distinction between the maṇḍala, the Guru's Body, Speech and Mind, and the yogin's experience.[31] Further elaboration of the visualization includes offerings to the deity, rites of confession, restoration of the *samaya* pledges, praise and adoration, and other similar functions. Finally, the vision is dissolved back into the emptiness out of which it arose. Creative meditation induces realization of the nature of relative truth:[32] all phenomenal appearances are illusion; what appear to be concrete isolates are functions of our sensory apparatus; there is no essential soul or *ens* that persists independent of the psycho-physical conglomerate; the universe is a system of interdependent relationships.

Fulfillment meditation includes "higher" techniques of meditation, which result in understanding of ultimate truth.[33] But since relative and ultimate truth are two sides of the same coin, creative and fulfillment stages both lead to the same goal. Fundamentally, fulfillment meditation techniques entail the perception of emptiness in form, or the dissolution of form into emptiness: the dissolution of the creative stage vision into emptiness is technically a fulfillment stage practice. Examples of fulfillment mode yogas are dream yoga, the yoga of the mystic heat, Mahāmudrā meditation, the yoga of the apparitional body, the yoga of resurrection, clear light meditation, and the yoga of uniting skillful means and perfect insight to create the seed-essence of pure pleasure.[34] The system of visualization vital in fulfillment meditation is that of the subtle body. This imaginary subtle body consists of psychic nerves—*nāḍī*; their focal points or energy centers—*cakras*; the energy that runs in the nerves—*prāṇa*; and the essence of *prāṇa*, known as "seed-essence" or *bindu*. A central channel, or nerve, runs from the sexual center to the fontanelle, and the left, *rasanā*, and right, *lalanā*, channels run parallel joining the central channel, the *avadhūti*, at the gut center. Converging from all parts of the body like physical veins, subsidiary nerves enter the central channel at the five focal points of psychic energy[35]—the sexual, gut, heart, throat and head centers. Visualization of this system allows the yogin to manipulate the energies relating to the various centers for different mundane purposes, but the highest aim is to inject all energy into the central channel and up to the head center where ultimate liberation is achieved. The key to this system relates right and left channels to skillful means (male) and perfect insight (female) respectively, and the central channel to their union—Mahāmudrā.[36] In an important sexual yoga, with or without a sexual partner, red and white seed-essence, *bodhicittas*, are mixed in the sexual center to rise up the central channel as *kuṇḍalinī*. This is the yoga of uniting pure pleasure and emptiness.[37]

Many legends state that the Guru's precepts instruct in both creative and fulfillment modes of meditation, but in the verse of instruction, which is like a jewel in the plain narrative setting of the legend, it is unclear how the instruction relates to the different modes. In such cases assume that "creative" and "fulfillment" modes indicate principles of meditation, the first that "emptiness is form" and the second that "all things are emptiness." For example, the skull-cup symbolizes the first principle, and its emptiness the second. Since creative meditation employs the extroversive energy of desire and procreation and relates to the father-tantra, while fulfillment employs the introversive energy of aversion and the death-wish and relates to the mother-tantra, the "creative mode" indicates radial energy, and the "fulfillment mode" focal energy. Further, insofar as virtually all Buddhist meditation is derived from the two fundamental techniques that the Buddha Śākyamuni taught—extroversive insight meditation, and introversive concentration meditation[38]—the "creative mode" signifies predominant use of the former principle and the "fulfillment mode" of the latter. Mahāmudrā is attained by uniting creative and fulfillment modes: by practicing simultaneous meditation upon form and emptiness; by practicing insight and concentration techniques simultaneously; by fusing centripetal and centrifugal energies; by uniting skillful means and perfect insight. Thus male and female principles, realized by creative and fulfillment modes respectively, are united.

To complete this practical exposition of the *anuttarayoga-tantra* by means of the triadic structure of vision, meditation and action,[39] something more should be said of action, the siddha's existential praxis. The nature of this praxis is rarely analyzed because it has no specific form. Generally, in legend and song, it is described in terms of the eight great *siddhis* and through metaphor and symbol, but only to motivate and inspire the neophyte. When the Guru does include it as a subject of instruction, as in the siddhas' *dohās*, the siddha's behavior is characterized as unlimited and spontaneous, selfless and compassionate. After the initiate's experiential realization of pure awareness and emptiness in a mystical experience of union has determined constant, involuntary emanation of compassionate action, there are no restraints whatsoever upon the scope of the siddha's activity. With the experientially based conviction that the relative world is all vanity, and that any mundane ambition is a futile waste of the opportunity afforded by this precious human body to attain spiritual liberation, together with a realization of the unity of self and others and the resultant benign empathy, the siddha cannot but act for the benefit of himself and others simultaneously. Thus insofar as the Bodhisattva Vow permeates his being, the siddha is driven to action uninhibited by any social or moral norm. The effusion of selfless love and the constant awareness of what is necessary override, and eventually eliminate, the conditioned restraints that inhibit manifestation of the full potential of human activity.

The Bodhisattva Vow, or rather the experience of oneness with all sentient beings that determines the quality of a siddha's action, is not to be considered the cause of his activity, nor are his actions to be seen as a function of ordinary karmic cause and effect. On the contrary, stressing the siddha's freedom from the effects of past karma his behavior is characterized as "spontaneous" (free of any connotation of impulsiveness). "Spontaneous action"[40] can be conceived as a mode of the integrated physical, verbal and mental capacities of the psycho-organism operating in total responsiveness to the situation of which it is the central and principal part. Metaphorically, it is a case of the tail wagging the dog; the Guru/siddha responds immediately to the ultimate needs of his circle (his maṇḍala) despite the obfuscations of self-interest, desire or ambition uppermost in his disciples' consciousness. The siddha has no choice but to respond selflessly to the stimulus provided by the highest function of interaction with his disciples, the function of release from human limitations. Thus he acts to liberate the people he encounters from the confines of their emotional and mental prisons. Since the siddha's personal karma has no place in determining the nature of his action, and because his action is a reflex of beings seeking their own salvation, it is styled "no-action,"[41] a concept that the Taoist expresses as *wu wei*. Further, insofar as the siddha acts spontaneously, free of thought or effort, totally absorbed in awareness of the moment, his action is said to be unmotivated and aimless.[42] As the siddha contemplates the river's flow with an intrinsic but detached awareness, his actions make no ripples—that is the Buddha's Karma. Ego-motivated action is an attempt to divert the river's flow for personal or social advantage, and such action creates a concatenation of cause and effect that eventually returns to impinge positively or negatively upon its perpetrator—that is karma.[43] The siddha's action is in such harmony with the natural flow that he may appear to be the agent of a supernatural authority, or he himself may be identified as that authority with the elements at his command. He may be perceived as a magician who can order the stars and set the planets in their courses, or at the very least he may be seen as the conductor of nature's symphony.

It is pertinent at this point to stress that the siddha's vision does not itself induce a siddha's actions. Intuition that the phenomenal world as we perceive it is a lie, that moral and social values are mind-created and therefore purely utilitarian, that "truth" is relative to hypothetical, metaphysical criteria, are insights that must be based in perpetual experiential identification with empty awareness through a twenty-four-hour-a-day meditation practice.

Only then does "action" become "non-action". Meditation is the bridge between vision and action.

If the siddha's action is concomitant with Mahāmudrā, what then of his craziness, his flaunting of social convention and his uninhibited emotivity? To a large extent those very prejudices, preconceptions and other limitations of his critic's blinkered vision which the siddha rejoices to see eradicated, determine the perception of him as crazy. For instance, when the critic interprets the siddha's act, or gesture, as a crazy irrelevancy, as the *non-sequitur* of a madman, it is probable that he is failing to intuit the level of response upon which the siddha is operating, and that his discursive analysis is precluding the soteriological effect in his own mind through which those open to the siddha's transmission of meaning by symbolical action or gesture benefit. Similarly, when a moralist of the Confucian type castigates a siddha for violating social conventions such as the rules of pure eating, or for immoral behavior such as sexual transgression, from the Buddha's point of view there is less virtue in the moralist's inflexible social and moral prescriptions than in the siddha's "sinful" attempts to induce awareness, with all the social and moral benefits that accrue, wherein enlightenment is the ultimate goal. Thus on the short-cut path of Tantra, disregard of social and moral discipline is the corollary of the compassionate skillful means employed by the adept to eradicate obstacles to liberation.

Although the siddha's activity should not, therefore, be perceived as "crazy" on account of transgression of moral and social parameters, according to Maitripa uncontrolled emotivity as a result of inadequate training is authentic divine madness.

The thought-free yogin is like a child,
Like a bee in a flower garden tasting every bloom,
Like a lion roaring in the jungle,
And like the wind blowing where it listeth.
If his mind is trained in attention and discretion
His behavior is immaculate;
If there are no checks upon his mind's effusion
The yogin behaves like a divine madman.[44]

Certainly, after the siddha's enlightening experience of ego-loss and the irrevocable identification with empty awareness, there is no possibility of modifying his behavior patterns: spontaneity is the siddha's mode. But from Maitripa's experience, if the neophyte is trained to discipline the emotions, and discretion and prudence are cultivated before Mahāmudrā meditation bears fruit, then the effusion of emotion can be utilized rather than the yogin being a creature of it. While the dance, or persona, of the crazy, thought-free yogin should be part of every siddha's repertoire, as it was in the case of the famous Tibetan siddha Drukpa Kunley[45] for example, exclusive reliance upon this didactic style with its social limitations and lack of flexibility, would appear to be the mode of a siddha of lesser attainment. But within the tradition there is no distinction made between the Mahāmudrā attainment of a Nāgārjuna (*16*) and a Mekopa (*43*). Finally, tangential to this topic, Maitripa's verses indicate the fine line, or the lack of any boundary at all, between Mahāmudrā and madness. But for Maitripa and all the siddhas on Tantra's short-cut path to the Buddha's enlightenment, commitment was so complete, doubt in the efficacy of the path and access to the goal so inconceivable, that the dangers involved were considered in much the same way as we approach the danger to life when crossing a busy highway.

All the siddhas who attained *mahāmudrā-siddhi*, the active expression of which has been discussed above, "finally attained ultimate liberation in the Ḍākinī's Paradise."[46] In some legends however, the final line stating that the siddha attained the Ḍākinī's Paradise "in his own body" introduces some ambiguity. It can be inferred that his body dissolved into light and his demise (*parinirvāṇa*) was a magical spiralling into the empyreum. Alternatively, the statement could be a recapitulation of his life since his enlightenment; in his ultimate mystical experience he attained the pure land where his existence was felt to be a constant dance with the Ḍākinīs, who represent the empty awareness of his pleasure. Further, the phrase rendered as "Ḍākinī's Paradise"[47] is ambiguous in itself and could be translated simply as "sky" or "space." For the Mahāsiddha Padmasambhava, the Ḍākinī's Paradise was his homeland of Orgyen (Oḍḍiyāṇa, the Swat Valley), which was also conceived as a Dharmakāya Buddhafield. The majority of the siddhas who did not attain the Ḍākiṇī's Paradise were those who only accomplished mundane *siddhis* and, attaining immortality, or extraordinary longevity, remained on earth working for humanity. These were the *nāth* siddhas, who were to become recognized as the progenitors of the great *haṭhayoga* tradition of *śaiva-tantra.* The belief that they are still alive today is shared by millions of contemporary Hindus, who will probably direct the enquirer to the Kumaon district in the Himalayas to find Gorakṣa (*9*), Cauraṅgi (*10*) and the other immortals, still meditating in secluded caves.

The legends convey the lore of eighth-twelfth century India and also the timeless ethos of Hindu spirituality. But their psychological core has a universal appeal and application that transcends culture, religion and race. Aspects of Tantra can be found in the mysticism of every culture, and the systematic formulation of mysticism (insofar as mysticism can be systematized) that is Tantra is touching responsive chords in contemporary western society. The western mystical mind that is potentially responsive to the tantric message of the siddhas is likely to show a strong repugnance to materialistic attitudes, the social and professional rat-race, and the tedium of repetitive routine. As to a suitable predisposition, he or she may be suffering nervous anxiety, about to undergo a psychological breakdown or to enter analysis, or may be a perfectly healthy poet, craftsman or contemplative; but the mind should already be free of emotional and conceptual constraints that hinder faith in the irrational and trust in the Guru. The potential initiate should be intelligent enough to grasp simple metaphysical concepts and sufficiently introverted and self-disciplined to sit in contemplation. If he has no knowledge of the sanctity of sex he should at least be free of prudish or prurient attitudes; and also, if he has contempt for scholasticism and pedantry, and a healthy disrespect for intellectual analysis, and if he has some disdain for secular authority, institutional discipline, social convention and sacred cows, his attitude is congruous with that of the progenitors of the lineage. The image of the empty bucket, right-end up, free of leaks, demonstrates the nature of mind that is then ready for the Guru's teaching.

A major obstacle on the path of Tantra (which is viewed by its adherents as a middle path) that particularly afflicts the western mind deeply conditioned by a rational and scientific education, is a rooted belief in the law of the excluded middle. This law of reasoning that insists upon a categorical positive or negative answer to any question, ignoring the middle ground, is of crucial importance in the technological world, but it is a radical impediment to development of gnostic vision. It entails taking an "extreme" stance, when according to *madhyamika* metaphysics *mahāmudrā-siddhi* is only accessible when all extreme thought patterns have been eradicated, or to be less extreme, when such thought patterns have become *dominated* by a vision that experientially reflects reality never as this or that, never as the negation of this or that, never as a synthesis of this and that, and never as an absence of this and that. Reality, in fact, is the excluded middle: it is indeterminable. In Europe it was heresy to think in these terms during the political domination of the Church, when many thousands of men and women were martyred for daring to conceive non-dualistic metaphysical doctrines that expedited union with the divine.

However, what is lacking in conventional education and Cartesian, mainstream cultural thought patterns in the West, can be more than outweighed by actual gnostic experience achieved fortuitously, or by use of psychedelic substances. Many religious cultures, including the Indian but excluding the Tibetan,[48] use psychotropic drugs as initiatory keys and as aids in psycho-experimental techniques of release from saṃsāra and alleviation of neural disorders, and in the West psychedelics have played an important part in fomenting interest in the tantric path. Social acceptance of human sexuality as a means to an end besides reproduction is another contemporary phenomenon conducive to a mind-set receptive to Tantra. However the fact that only one of the siddhas made a chemical preparation his sādhana (Vyāli, *84*) and only one used sexuality as the principal means to his enlightenment (Babhaha, *39*), places psychedelic chemicals and sex in clear perspective in the Buddhist Tantra. Even casual association with Tibetan Lamas, the contemporary bearers of the siddha tradition, makes it difficult to avoid the inference that although psychedelics and sexual freedom may be important indicators of our liberation from the anti-mystical, and therefore anti-tantric, straight-jacket of Judao-Christian thought and ethics, they are not passports to the Buddha's enlightenment.

Although a Westerner may possess the requisite receptivity, attitudes and experience conducive to optimal potentiation of tantric precepts, he must find a Guru to instruct him. He may find that a divine Bodhisattva or a divine Ḍākinī appears to him propitiously, but the instruction received from such an agency can only be very simple and direct unless much preliminary work on the mind has been completed and unless a very strong working relationship is established with the divine agency. A mundane Ḍākinī may grant informal initiation and succinct, sensitive advice, but where is the Western Ḍākinī who can give practical guidance based upon a thorough understanding of the tantras and experiential knowledge of techniques? The principal bearers of the siddhas' tradition today are Tibetan Lamas, who through our good fortune are now seeking refuge in hospitable countries around the globe, due to the destruction of their theocracy in Tibet, and because they find they can fulfill a need where they settle. The Tibetan school that has retained the siddhas' ethos as well as the transmission of an uncorrupted though modified teaching tradition, is the Kahgyu school. To this school belongs the Tibetan classic *The Hundred Thousand Songs of Milarepa*,[49] which expresses the siddhas' teaching as interpreted by Milarepa and his Guru Marpa who received instruction from Nāropa and Kukkuripa in the eleventh century. There are several competent Lamas in the West today who have received Milarepa's transmission through the lineage of the late Sixteenth Gyelwa Karmapa. The Sakya school has transmitted the Mahāmudrā teaching of the siddha Virūpa, in particular. The Nyingma school bases its doctrines upon the Mahāsiddha Padmasambhava's precepts. There is hardly an Indian-originated Tibetan lineage that does not include a name found amongst the eighty-four mahāsiddhas. Although the cultural impact of Tibet over a thousand years must have altered the tenor of the Indian tradition, since in general the Tibetan schools are characterized by an overwhelming reluctance to question Indian doctrines, departure from the Tantra of the siddhas has been minimal.

The Lamas will teach the siddhas' sādhanas, but very few will initiate an untutored western aspirant and grant him precepts spontaneously. Very few can jump the cultural chasm, diagnose an individual's problem and prescribe the cure. Most will insist upon a lengthy period of preparation in the disciplines of hīnayāna and mahāyāna, and, also, essential preparatory tantric meditation practice.[50] However, the siddhas' tradition is by no means dead, and the next generation in the West can enjoy the fruit of this generation of Lamas' work. Since need, ability and aspiration are present in a favorable environment, there is no reason why countless American and European siddhas should not flourish in a latter-day blossoming of the tantric tradition transposed to the West.

Notes to the Introduction

1. Hugh R. Downs, *Rhythms of a Himalayan Village*, Harper and Row, San Francisco, 1980.
2. It is always dangerous to generalize about India—a subcontinent—and Indians—diverse races and tribes. "Tantra" describes the dominant ethos of pre-Muslim India.
3. See Glossary of Sanskrit Terms.
4. RS II: intro., and Das Gupta 1969: 51-61.
5. Bhattacharyya N., 1982: 62-63.
6. Bhattacharyya B., 1931: intro., and Wayman 1977: Pt. 2, ch. II, A.
7. *Sādhāraṇa-siddhi*, T. *thun mong gi dngos grub*, and *parama-siddhi, mchog gi dngos grub*. See p.5-7.
8. *Utpattikrama*, T. *bskyed rim*, is the creative stage of meditation and *utpannakrama* or *niṣpannakrama, rdzogs rim*, is the fulfillment stage. See p. 19ff.
9. See Glossary of Numeral Terms.
10. *Śūnyatā*, T. *stong pa nyid.* To render *śūnyatā* into English, emptiness has been preferred to voidness or The Void to avoid the negative connotation of a vacuum, which is to be abhorred. Experientially, *śūnyatā* has the "feeling" of fullness, the essential, overwhelming, all-pervasive awareness of an instant of perfectly clear experience (T. *klong*) that desubstantiates and de-concretizes both oneself and the world and is coincident with the conviction that life is a dream and all phenomena illusion. Both voidness and emptiness lack the connotation of the bliss (T. *bde ba*) that accompanies perfect insight (*shes rab*) into phenomena as illusion (*sgyu ma*) and space (*dbyings*), and also of completion (*rdzogs pa*) and consummation (*zung 'jug*).
11. *Tathatā*, T. *de bzhin nyid.* The stem of this onomatopoeia is also the stem of the synonym for Buddha, Tathāgata, Thus-Gone, and of Buddhahood, *tathāgatagarbha.*
12. It is evident from the history of the early lineages of Buddhist and Hindu Tantra, if these terms are at all applicable, that there was a broad measure of agreement in metaphysics, terminology and tech-

niques—they even held teachers in common. But there was a fundamental conceptual discrepancy in their notions of the nature of being. The Buddhists saw the absolute as no-essence, egolessness, selflessness (*anātman*, T. *bdag med pa*) while the *śaivas* and *śāktas* conceived of an individuated absolute, "the soul" (*ātman, bdag po*). A corollary of this discrepancy is their different conceptions of the female principle. The Buddhists see the Ḍākinī as empty awareness (e.g. *Nairātmā*, T. *bDag med ma*) and the *śāktas* as pure energy (*Śakti*). Provoked by the social ostracism dealt them by the brahmins in India the Tibetans stressed these distinctions to the point of mutual exclusion of the two traditions. But there is little doubt that the contemporary situation in Nepal, where the Newars see themselves as one fold of tantrikas following either the Buddhist or the *śaiva* path, obtained in India until the Muslims destroyed the monastic base of Buddhism and the Buddhist option ceased to exist. More useful than the Tibetan standpoint is the expedient, simplistic view that the Hindus are practitioners of the exoteric, mundane-oriented Tantra while the Tibetan Buddhists are bearers of the esoteric, transcendental soteriology. The Vedāntins, certain *śākta* cults and *śaiva* lineages, particularly the *nāths*, all with Buddhist origins, are the exceptions that prove the rule.

13. See Bhattaccaryya N., 1982: ch. 2 for a general introduction to the tantras, and Dr. Snellgrove's translation of the *Hevajra-tantra* as a specific example.
14. T. *rjod med, spros bral* and *gnas med.*
15. T. *rgyu med* (causeless), *gzhi med* (groundless) and *skye med* (unborn).
16. T. *thig le nyag cig*, the universal seed, is the term employed in Dzokchen.
17. An axiom attributed to Saraha.
18. From the *Heart Sūtra* (*Hṛdāya-mahāyāna-sūtra*; Conze 1959: 162–3): this is the quintessence of the entire *prajñāpāramitā* corpus of literature which forms the philosophical basis of Tantra.
19. *Caryāgītī*; see glossary.
20. *Upāya*, T. *thabs*, and *prajñā, shes rab*. This indivisible duality (*yuganaddha*, T. *zung 'jug*) describes the nature of all male-female attributions, of which compassion and emptiness are the first.
21. *Jñāna*, T. *ye shes*. In India, *jñāna* (pronounced *gyān*) has come to mean wisdom, the sage's discursive utterances; but the Tibetan *ye shes* refers only to immediate, gnostic, sensory awareness.
22. *Mahāsukha*, T. *bde ba chen po.*
23. *Dhātu*, T. *dbyings*. "Inner space" is more evocative; but "outer" space is not excluded from it.
24. *Jñāna-ḍākinī*, T. *ye shes mkha' 'gro*. Wisdom Ḍākinīs are Buddha

Ḍākinīs and, therefore, may manifest in any of the three modes of being.

25. *Loka-ḍākinī*, T. *'jig rten mkha' 'gro*. Mundane Ḍākinīs perform positive, useful functions on the path, but they are not fully enlightened beings; they may be allies and spiritual friends (T. *grogs mo*), but not initiators into Mahāmudrā.

26. Eight cremation grounds (*aṣṭaśmaśāna*, T. *dur khrod brgyad*) are enumerated in sacred geography. The number eight refers to the psychological categories of the eight forms of consciousness (*aṣṭavijñāna*): the five sensual, and intellectual, emotional and seed consciousnesses. Each cremation ground has a pond, a tree, a *stūpa* and a protectress in proximity. Boudhanāth, in the Kathmandu Valley, is one such cremation ground, and the Cool Garden Cremation Ground (Śītavana T. *bSil ba'i tshal*) is located on a hill four miles north-east of Bodh Gaya in Bihar, according to contemporary Tibetan sources.

27. *Bar do thos grol* (Evans-Wentz 1957), *Liberation by Hearing [the nature of] the Intermediate State [between death and rebirth]*, a revelation of Orgyen Lingpa, one of the great tertons (treasure-finders) who lived in the period of the Nyingma revival in the 14th century. In this *anuttarayoga* for the living, death is to be understood as rebirth on the wheel of life, death as the unawareness and egoism of samsaric existence.

28. T. *man ngag*. There is no precise Sanskrit equivalent; *upadeśa*, T. *gdams ngag*, refers to any and all of the Guru's precepts.

29. T. *thabs sna tshogs gyi lam*.

30. The monosyllabic root or seed mantra (*bīja-mantra*, T. *sa bon gyi sngags*) that is the primary cause of the deity's appearance, the creative mantra (*bskyed pa rkyen gyi sngags*) that creates the conditions of the deity's appearance, producing the constellation of psychic realities that the deity's iconography represents, and the action-mantra (*karma-mantra, T. las kyi sngags*) that activates the deity's powers, are the three forms of mantra employed successively in creative meditation. It is one of the mysteries of Tantra that the mantra and the vision of the deity are identical to the deity as "felt" formless archetype. See Dowman 1984: 28, 192.

31. Thus the two stages of visualization and recitation termed approach and identification (T. *bsnyen sgrub*) are completed. Dowman 1984: 199 n. 57, 245.

32. *Saṃvṛtisatya*, T. *kun rdzob bden pa*, "the truth that all is vanity." Ultimate and relative truths are different perspectives of vision upon the same ineffable absolute that is the substance of experience in Mahāmudrā and Dzokchen, where creative and fulfillment meditations are united (T. *bskyed rdzogs zung 'jug*).

33. *Paramārtha-satya*, T. *don dam bden pa*.
34. T. *rmi lam, gtu mo, phyag chen, sgyu lus, grong 'jug, 'od gsal, thabs dang shes rab zung 'jug bde chen thig le*.
35. See Glossary of Numeral terms.
36. For a description of the initiation, instruction and practice of this yoga, see Dowman 1984: 38-43, 231ff., 246ff.
37. For Nāropa's instruction in this yoga see Guenther 1963: 76-79. See also *39*.
38. *Vipaśyanā*, T. *lhag mthong*, and *śamatha*, T. *zhi gnas*. Creative and fulfillment techniques employ the principles of these meditations, not the actual practice described in the sūtras.
39. The four aspects of the Mahāmudrā doctrine (*q.v.*).
40. T. *lhun gyi grub pa'i bya ba*. In Buddhist logic there is an unambiguous distinction between primary cause (T. *rgyu*) and secondary, conditional causes (T. *rkyen*); spontaneity has no primary cause but is affected by conditional circumstances.
41. T. *bya bral*. The image that gives insight into this concept is of the siddha so totally relaxed, so removed, detached from his "performance" (T. *spyod pa*), that he can passively watch the functions of his body, speech and mind as we would watch a movie: that is the Buddha's detachment. In another sense, since in Mahāmudrā there is no beginning, middle or end of any *dharma*, no creation or cessation, there is no manifestation and therefore "no-action;" there is only "pure potential" in an ineffable union of ultimate and relative. See Dowman 1984: 243.
42. T. *dMigs med*, literally, "without image;" in formal meditation the image, T. *dmigs pa*, is the object of meditation, such as a candle flame or a visualization.
43. The Tibetan equivalent of the Sanskrit *karma* that is applied to Buddhas and sentient beings alike, is *las* for sentient beings and *'phrin las* for Buddhas. *Las* means "action" or "work," while *'phrin* is an honorific prefix. Different schools perceive the Buddha's karma in different ways. Gautama's final action, his death, was, according to some scriptures, effected by his thoughtless killing of an insect in a past life, but upon his parinirvāṇa his karmic depths were exhausted. The spontaneous action of Mahāmudrā leaves no trace. Thought, voice and action patterns (*saṃskāra*) determined by moral or immoral actions of body, speech and mind in this lifetime have been eradicated, allowing the siddha free, spontaneous responsiveness in the immediate situation, but racial and genetic karma, karma from past lives—and intra-uterine *karma*?—may still be functional.
44. Maitripa, *lTa ba sgom pa spyod pa 'bras bu'i dohā mdzod*.
45. Drukpa Kunley ('Brug smyon Kun dga' les pa), the patron protector

of Bhutan, was a great scholar, a poet and an adept in Dzokchen, but folklore portrays him as a crazy itinerant yogin. He exemplifies the mahāsiddha capable of wearing many masks, his mask of craziness granting the latitude to exceed moral and social norms that permitted communication with disciples who otherwise would have remained outside the pale of the Dharma. As Drukpa Kunley himself sang (Dowman 1980: 98):

Dancer in the indestructible stream of magical illusion,
Power-holder . . . Hero . . . Little Yogin . . . Vagabond . . .
Light-traveller . . . Champion . . . Diviner . . .
Yogin tasting the one flavor of all things—
These are some of the masks I wear.

46. T. *mThar lus de nyid kyis mkha' spyod du gshegs so*: "finally, in his very body, he attained the Ḍākinī's Paradise." Although there are few variations of this line in the Tibetan, the English was rendered in every possible variant translation.
47. *Khecara/ī*, T. *mkha' spyod*, which is also a synonym of *mkha' 'gro*, Ḍākinī.
48. This is to exclude the homeopathic, alchemical *bdud rtsi chos sman* and similar herbal panaceas distributed by the Lamas during Long-life (T. *tshe-grub*) and Gaṇacakra (*tshogs 'khor*) rites, because their efficacy depends as much upon sympathetic magic as upon the potency of the constituent herbal and other organic and non-organic substances.
49. Chang 1970.
50. T. *sngon 'gro*, pronounced "ngondro." The same basic preparatory meditations are an obligatory part of all the four Tibetan sects' meditation training that lubricates the psychic functions employed in creative and fulfillment yogas. Firstly there is discursive meditation upon the precious human body, impermanence, karma and karmic retribution; and secondly, the Five Hundred Thousands (T. *'bum lnga*), a hundred thousand of prostrations, recitations of the Bodhisattva Vow, recitations of Vajrasattva's mantra, creations of the universal maṇḍala and practices of the Guru-yoga visualizations and mantras. This formal preparation may be replaced by other suitable preparatory exercises, but this format is tried and tested and guaranteed to bring results.

1

THE MAHĀSIDDHA LŪIPA THE FISH-GUT EATER

A wild dog with honey rubbed on its nose
Madly devours whatever it sees;
Give the Lama's secret to a worldly fool
And his mind and the lineage burn out.
For a responsive man with knowledge of unborn reality
A mere glimpse of the Lama's vision of pure light-form
Destroys mental fiction like an elephant berserk
Rampaging through hostile ranks with a sword
lashed to its trunk.

Long ago, in the island kingdom of Śri Laṅkā, a young prince ascended the throne of his fabulously wealthy father. The court astrologers had calculated that the kingdom must be given to the deceased king's second son if it was to remain strong and its people content. In his palace, where the walls were plated with gold and silver and studded with pearls and precious stones, the young king ruled his two brothers and all the people of Śrī Laṅkā. However, possessing nothing but contempt for wealth and power, his only desire was to escape his situation. When he first attempted to escape, his brothers and courtiers caught him and bound him in golden chains, but finally he succeeded in bribing his guards with gold and silver, and at night, disguised in rags, he escaped with a single attendant. He rewarded his faithful accomplice generously before leaving his island kingdom for Rāmeśvaram, where King Rāma reigned, and there he exchanged his golden throne for a simple deer-skin and his couch of silks and satin for a bed of ashes. Thus he became a yogin.

The king-turned-yogin was handsome and charming, and he had

no difficulty in begging his daily needs. Wandering the length of India, eventually he arrived in Vajrāsana, where the Buddha Śākyamuni had achieved enlightenment, and there he attached himself to hospitable Ḍākinīs, who transmitted to him their feminine insight. From Vajrāsana he travelled to Paṭaliputra, the king's capital on the River Ganges, where he subsisted on the alms he begged and slept in a cremation ground. Begging in the bazaar one market day, he paused at a house of pleasure, and his karma effected this fateful encounter with a courtesan, who was an incarnate, worldly Ḍākinī. Gazing through him at the nature of his mind, the Ḍākinī said, "Your four psychic centers and their energies are quite pure, but there is a pea-sized obscuration of royal pride in your heart." And with that she poured some putrid food into his clay bowl and told him to be on his way. He threw the inedible slop into the gutter, whereupon the Ḍākinī, who had been watching him go, shouted after him angrily, "How can you attain nirvāṇa if you're still concerned about the purity of your food?"

The yogin was mortified. He realized that his critical and judgemental mind was still subtly active; he still perceived some things as intrinsically more desirable than others. He also understood that this propensity was the chief obstacle in his progress to Buddhahood. With this realization he went down to the River Ganges and began a twelve year sādhana to destroy his discursive thought-patterns and his prejudices and preconceptions. His practice was to eat the entrails of the fish that the fishermen disemboweled, to transform the fish-guts into the nectar of pure awareness by insight into the nature of things as emptiness.

The fisherwomen gave him his name, Lūipa, which means Eater of Fish-guts. The practice which gave him his name also brought him power and realization. Lūipa became a renowned Guru, and in the legends of Dārikapa and Ḍeṅgipa there is further mention of him.

Sādhana

It is appropriate that the first of the eighty-four legends should repeat the elements of the story of the first Buddha, Śākyamuni, in a tantric guise. Lūipa is a king who renounces his throne for the sake of enlightenment. Like Śākyamuni he escaped in the night with a single attendant to become a yogin, and Śākyamuni, too, probably employed a deer-skin (*kṛṣṇasara*) as a mat, a throne, and a shawl. Deer-skins indicate renunciate status; the Bodhisattva Avalokiteśvara wears one around his torso. But Lūipa was born into the *kaliyuga* when it was no longer possible to practice the fierce discipline and simple practices that Śākyamuni taught. In order to eradicate the subtle defilement that the Ḍākinī indicated and to resolve the dualistic mental constructs that are the root cause of saṃsāra, to attain freedom from saṃsāra in this lifetime a radical short-cut method was required, and in Lūipa's case, as with many of the siddhas, a Ḍākinī was at hand to provide it.

Lūipa was a master of the mother-tantra, and his Gurus were Ḍākinī Gurus, mundane Ḍākinīs, embodiments of the female principle of awareness.[1] The Ḍākinī who indicated his sādhana was a publican and whore-mistress, for liquor shops doubled as brothels. The "royal pride" she discerned in his heart can be rendered more precisely as "racial, caste and social discrimination,"[2] and with her putrid food she pointed at a method which can best be described as the path of dung eating. Cultivate what is most foul and abhorrent, and consciousness is thereby stimulated to the point of transcendence; familiarize yourself with what is most disgusting and eventually it tastes no different from bread and butter. The result of this method is attainment of the awareness of sameness[3] that is at the heart of all pride, all discrimination and prejudice, and transmutes these moral qualities, that are the mental equivalent of fish-guts, into emptiness. To elaborate the Ḍākinī's parting sally: so long as you fail to perceive the inherent reality of emptiness in every sensual stimulus, every state of mind, and every thought, you will remain in dualistic saṃsāra, judging, criticizing and discriminating. To attain the non-duality of nirvāṇa find the awareness of sameness in what is most revolting, and realize the one taste of all,[4] which is pure pleasure.

More light is shed on Lūipa's practice by considering what fish meant in his society. First, fish is the flesh of a sentient being and therefore anathema to the orthodox brahmin; but left-over fish-guts is fit only for dogs, the lowest life-form on the totem pole. Such a practice, if indeed Lūipa performed a literal interpretation, would have made him unclean in the eyes of his former peers, untouchable and unapproachable. Self-abasement and humiliation is the corollary of "dung eating;" destroy every vestige of those associations with former birth, privilege and wealth, and in an existential pit discover what there is in human being that can inspire real pride, divine pride, that is inherent in all sentient beings. Second, fish is a symbol of spirituality and sense control, and Lūipa's Saṃvara sādhana, which is not described here, involves transformation of his universe into that of a god in his paradise, and attainment of control of his energies (*prāṇa*) and thus of his senses.

Historiography

Our legend is the only source to assert that Lūipa was born in Śrī Laṅkā, to which the text's Siṅghaladvīpa must refer. But there were several kingdoms in the sub-continent called Siṅghaladvīpa, one contiguous to Oḍḍiyāṇa which other sources give as Lūipa's birthplace. In Bu ston's account,[5] Lūipa was son of King Lalitacandra of Oḍḍiyāṇa. When the prince encountered Śavaripa, Saraha's disciple, he was immensely impressed by this siddha and begged him for instruction. He received initiation into the *Saṃvara-tantra.* The initial part of his sādhana was completed when he joined a circle of twenty-four Ḍākas and Ḍākinīs in a rite of offering in a cremation ground which climaxed in consumption of the corpse of a sage. With a final blessing from his Guru he left Oḍḍiyāṇa and began a mendicant sadhu existence. That period ended when, feeling the need for sustained one-pointed meditation practice, he sat down to meditate beside a pile of fish-guts by the banks of the River Ganges in Bengal (Baṅgala), where he remained until he had attained *mahāmudrā-siddhi.* His subsequent encounter with the king and minister who became Dārikapa and Ḍeṅgipa portray Lūipa as an outrageously honest and fearless exploiter of personal power, and also an adept wielder of the apt phrase bearing tantric truth. Consistent with this facility with words, the Sakya school's account of Lūipa's life[6] asserts that he was a scribe (*kayasṭha*) at the court of the Mahārāja of Bharendra, Dharmapāla. Begging alms at Dharmapāla's palace Śavaripa recognized the scribe Lūipa as a suitable recipient of his Saṃvara lineage; his extraordinary talent was evident in the versified letters he wrote to the king's correspondents, a task requiring acute, one-pointed concentration. Tāranātha's account[7] differs significantly from Bu ston's in that Lūipa was a scribe to the King of Oḍḍiyāṇa, and was initiated into Vajra Vārāhī's maṇḍala.

The most significant piece of information in these legends is that Lūipa worked at the court of the Mahārāja of Bharendra, Dharmapāla. The only king who had the right to call himself Mahārāja of this kingdom was the great Pāla Emperor Dharmapāla, who gained it by right of conquest. Since the Sakya legends have been given the greatest historiographical credence of all the siddhas' legends, it is tempting to accept this crucial identification and place Lūipa as a younger contemporary of Dharmapāla (AD 770–810). If Lūipa was initiated in his youth at the end of the eighth century or the beginning of the ninth, his Guru Śavaripa's lifetime can be calculated, together with the dates of Dārikapa and Ḍeṅgipa, and also Ḍombi Heruka (*4*) who Lūipa taught.[8] Kilapa (*73*) may also have been his disciple.[9] But if Lūipa was born in the eighth century he cannot be identified with Mīnapa/Macchendranāth, an identification that has been attempted due to several coincidences:[10] the stem of both their names means "fish;" they are both associated with Śrī Laṅkā and Bengal; they both conceived *yoginī-tantra* lineages (Lūipa—Saṃvara, Mīnapa—Yoginī-kaulā), and they are both known as *adi-guru*. Whereas Mīnapa was the originator of *nāth śaiva* lineages, from which he gained his *adi-guru* status, Lūipa has no Hindu associations, although his sādhana has a *śākta* ethos.

Lūipa's first place in the eighty-four legends could reflect the belief of the narrator, or the translator, that Lūipa was First Guru (*adi-guru*) of the Mahāmudrā-siddhas in either time or status. The other claimant to this title is Saraha.[11] Regarding time, Lūipa was born after Saraha, but although Lūipa's Guru was Saraha's disciple, their lifetimes probably overlapped. Regarding status and personal power, whereas Saraha's reputation lies to a large extent in his literary genius, Lūipa's name evokes a sense of the siddha's tremendous integrity and commitment, the *samaya* that creates the personal power demonstrated in his legends. Both Saraha and Lūipa were originators of *Saṃvara-tantra* lineages, but it was Lūipa who received the title of Guhyapati, Master of Secrets, to add to his status of *adi-guru* in the lineage that practiced the *Saṃvara-tantra* according to the method of Lūipa; he received direct transmission from the Ḍākinī Vajra Vārāhī.[12] If Lūipa obtained his original Saṃvara revelation in Oḍḍiyāṇa, the home of several of the mother-tantras, he would have been one of the siddhas responsible for propagating this tantra in Eastern India. But whatever the tantra's provenance, Lūipa became the great exemplar of what Saraha preached, as confirmed in his own few *dohā* songs, and his sādhana became the inspiration and example for some of the greatest names amongst the mahāsiddhas: Kambala, Ghaṇṭāpa, Indrabhūti, Jālandhara, Kṛṣṇācārya, Tilopa and Nāropa were all initiates into the *Saṃvara-tantra* according to the method of Lūipa. Marpa Dopa transmitted the tantra to Tibet, where it has remained the principal yidam practice of the Kahgyu school until today.

Although the Tibetan translator rendered "Lūipa" as The Fish-gut Eater (Nya lto zhabs), the root of the word is probably Old Bengali *lohita,* a type of fish, and Lūipa is thus synonymous with Mīnapa and Macchendra/Matsyendra. Lūhipa, Lohipa, Lūyipa, Loyipa, are variants of the name.

2

THE MAHĀSIDDHA LĪLAPA THE ROYAL HEDONIST

In the fastness of the Four Boundless States,
A yogin-king reigns like a royal snow-lion.
The lion is crowned with his turquoise mane's five plaits;
The yogin's crown is his five-fold insignia of Buddha's awareness.
The lion's ten claws pull an ox's flesh from its bones;
The yogin's ten perfections cut through negative powers.
With this realization Līlapa gained his freedom.

Reclining upon his lion-throne one day, a South Indian king was visited by a wise yogin. The king took pity on the yogin. "You must suffer greatly wandering from country to country in such a miserable state," said the king.

"I suffer not at all," replied the yogin. "You are the one who needs pity."

"Why do you say that?" asked the king, bemused.

"You live in dread of losing your kingdom, and you endure constant fear of your subjects' anger. So you suffer. As for me, I cannot be burnt though I leap into fire; I will not die if I swallow poison; and I am free of the suffering of old age and death itself. I possess the alchemists' secret teaching on immortality."

The king was profoundly impressed by the yogin, and with newly acquired faith, he said, "Obviously it is impossible for me to copy your itinerant life-style, but if it is practicable for me to meditate while sitting on the throne in my palace, I beg you, please, give me the necessary instruction."

The king prostrated in humble supplication, and the yogin granted his request. The king received initiation and empowerment of the deity Hevajra and instruction upon the practice of Hevajra's meditation, and then he entered a trance, a samādhi of one-pointedness.

Thereafter the king meditated upon his lion-throne, reclining upon cushions of silk, surrounded by his queens and ministers and entertained by the court musicians playing various kinds of instruments. He became famous as Līlapa due to his evident fondness for sensual pleasure and his fascination with beautiful form.

Līlapa's meditation instruction was to concentrate unwaveringly upon the ring he wore on his right hand. After his concentration had become fixed, he was instructed to visualize Hevajra surrounded by his retinue of divinities within the ring. When he had succeeded in transfixing that vision, by uniting creative and fulfillment modes of meditation realization spontaneously unfolded. With the dawning of this understanding he attained the power and realization of Mahāmudrā together with many other qualities, such as extrasensory perception.

Līlapa's story demonstrates that when the Guru's instruction and the disciple's highly motivated aspiration and karmic propensities coincide, there is no need to renounce the enjoyment of sensual pleasure to attain liberation. Līlapa became known throughout the world for his wonderful acts of selflessness. Finally, he attained ultimate liberation into the Ḍākinī's Paradise.

Sādhana

There were many reasons for the success of vajrayāna in India. Social trends assisted: the decline in power of the brahmins and increasing popularity of the lower castes' deities, and the decline of ascetic monasticism and a tendency towards hedonistic pleasure, were both causes and effects. In this social climate vajrayāna was inherently attractive, and not least in its attraction was the marriage of sensual pleasure and the prestige of religious ordination. In vajrayāna the monistic trend of Indian philosophy reached its inevitable end, where the nature of all human activity was accepted as divine, the same in quality and quantity as the supreme essence itself. But as the legend points out, in order for the aspirant to realize himself as a god, and his environment as paradise, certain conditions must obtain. He must first find a Guru with whom he has rapport and who can prescribe a relevant practice; his motivation must be correct, which means directed towards gnostic realization and selfless service rather than pleasure oriented; and his karma must be sufficiently mature, meaning that his disgust with his present situation must be intense. Evidently Līlapa was fortunate in the coincidence of propitious conditions, for immediately after his initiation he became absorbed in a one-pointed samādhi,[13] which is very difficult when life has been spent in frivolous distraction or worldly preoccupation.

In order to achieve one-pointed concentration, even for most tantrikas, it is necessary to retreat to a cave, to physical solitude and silence. But with a successful initiation and a perceptive Guru's instruction, together with the other conditions mentioned above, renunciation can become a state of mind, and "the cave" can become a retreat from worldly attachment into the cave of emptiness. This cave of emptiness is not a hole deep in the mind from which the *sādhaka* can look out at the world going by, for emptiness is not separate from form, as the *Hṛdāya-sūtra* says, implying that the one-pointed samādhi is absorption in the object, the ring in Līlapa's case.

Fixation of concentration is the initial stage in Līlapa's creative mode practice, fixed concentration indicates attainment of the center of the maṇḍala out of which the deities and their retinue emanate. Further, when the vision of the deities of the maṇḍala is transfixed, when every detail is in place and in focus, when the two central deities in union, and the sixteen *yoginīs* of the retinue, shine radiantly in their own colors, this is an indication that the aim of the creative stage is achieved. The creative mode of meditation teaches the insubstantiality of form, that form is emptiness. The legend does not clarify the nature of Līlapa's fulfillment meditation, but if it is the simplest form of that mode, meditation upon emptiness itself, then the converse realization of "form is emptiness" arises—which is "emptiness is form." With the union of creative and fulfillment modes, reality is the play of *māyā*, the dance of the Ḍākinī in all her various moods and guises, the variety of divine-human potential, and the ideal expression of this vision is the Hevajra maṇḍala. Although Saṃvara, Heruka, is the pivot of the maṇḍala, representing the component elements of the psycho-organism,[14] his Consort and retinue, the Ḍākinīs, are where his awareness lies. The *Hevajra-tantra* is, therefore, a mother-*tantra* or *yoginī-tantra*, and Mahāmudrā is its ultimate attainment.

In Līlapa's song of realization, the snow-lion is a mythical king of beasts. The female gives the nectar of immortality as milk, a nectar that can only be collected in a jade bowl. The male's turquoise mane of five plaits symbolizes the five modes of pure awareness: mirror-like awareness, awareness of sameness, discriminating awareness, all-encompassing awareness of space and all-accomplishing awareness. His ten claws are likened to the ten perfections: moral conduct, generosity, patience, sustained endeavor, concentration, perfect insight, skillful means, aspiration, inner strength and pure awareness. The invulnerable fortress of the yogin's mind is composed of the four boundless states of mind: compassion, loving kindness, sympathetic joy and equanimity.

Historiography

There is no encouragement in our legend to identify Līlapa (Līlapāda, T. sGegs pa'i zhabs) with the great Līlavajra (T. sGegs pa'i rdo rje), although Līlapa is probably a contraction of Līlavajrapāda. According to Tāranātha,[15] Līlavajra, the great *ācārya* of Oḍḍiyāṇa, was born in Ṣiṣa (or Sirsa) in Maṇidvīpa (in the northwest?), ordained in Oḍḍiyāṇa where he spent most of his life, but taught in Baṅgala at Nālandā and also at the foremost tantric academy in India, Vikramaśīla. His Gurus were Lalitavajra the Great, Anaṅgavajra, and Mañjuśrīmitra, and he lived therefore in the second half of the ninth century.[16] Līlapa is identified as following a pupil of Saraha, probably Nāgārjuna,[17] living therefore in the first half of the ninth century. Guṅḍaripa (Godhuri, *55*) may have been his disciple, as also a Kukkuripa.

3

THE MAHĀSIDDHA VIRŪPA
ḌĀKINĪ-MASTER

Mine is the spontaneous reality disposed by the Magnificent Symbol.
Just abiding in things as they are, not thinking, not achieving, no self,
Saved from the pit of nihilism by self-aware existential experience,[18]
Saved from the heavens of eternalism by absolute detachment,
This reality is consummation of perfect awareness and pure delight.

When King Devapāla was reigning over the ancient empire of Bengal, Virūpa was born in the eastern province of Tripurā. Early in his life he was ordained as a Buddhist monk in the great monastic academy of Somapurī, where he joined over a thousand monks in their study and meditations.

While he was still young, Virūpa was granted the initiation and empowerment of the Ḍākinī Vajra Vārāhī, the Sow-faced Ḍākinī. Constantly striving for results from his meditation he recited Vajra Vārāhī's mantra ten million times, and then again ten million, over a twelve year period. But he did not receive so much as a dream-omen to signify progress, and his mind was troubled. One day he became so depressed that he threw his rosary into a latrine. "What do beads have to do with happiness?" he asked himself. In the evening of that auspicious day, at the time of evening worship, just as the realization came to him that he had no rosary, a Ḍākinī appeared and put his rosary into his hand. She then gave him this advice in a vision: "Most Fortunate Child, do not be troubled. With my blessing continue your practice. Rid your mind of the habit of thinking of things as either this or that, and abandon all wandering and critical thought. Strip your mind of mental fiction."

> *The innate purity that is the nature of mind,*
> That *is the essential Vajra Vārāhī.*
> *She exists within,*
> *So do not look elsewhere,*
> That *is foolish and childish.*
> *The nature of mind, a wish-fulfilling gem,*
> *Stripped of all mental fiction,*
> That *is the most satisfying achievement.*

Virūpa practiced the spiritual discipline of Vajra Vārāhī for a further twelve years, and he gained the supreme realization of Mahāmudrā. Since he had thus attained power over life and death, he became accustomed to drink alcohol and to eat the meat that his servants bought and cooked for him. One day his servants caught some pigeons that roosted in the monastery, rung their necks and prepared them for the table. Noticing that the pigeons had disappeared, an observant monk rang the bell that called an assembly.

"Which one of us priests has been eating pigeon?" he cried.

"Surely none of us would kill pigeons," replied the venerable monks who had assembled. "Such a thing is unthinkable!"

During the subsequent cell-to-cell search, a monk peering in through Virūpa's window saw him sitting down to a meal of pigeon pie and wine. In further assembly the monks ordained that Virūpa should be expelled from the monastery.

Virūpa took off his religious habit and together with his begging bowl he laid it before the image of the Buddha in the monastery temple. For the final time he prostrated before the Buddha he had worshipped for more than twenty-four years, and then he left. At the monastery gate he was stopped by a monk who asked him where he was bound.

"You have expelled me from the monastery," replied Virūpa. "I follow the road that can provide for me."

Close by the monastery of Somapurī was a large lake, and the surface of the lake was covered with lotus leaves. Approaching the lake Virūpa placed one foot upon a leaf, and seeing that it did not

Virūpa turned back the river and stopped the sun.

submerge he set off across the lake flitting from one leaf to the next, and with the name of Buddha on his lips he reached the other shore. When the inmates of Somapurī saw this miracle they were filled with remorse. They came to Virūpa and prostrated before him, touching his feet with the deepest devotion.

"But why did you kill our pigeons?" they humbly asked.

"It was an illusion like all temporal phenomena," replied the master. He instructed his servants to bring him the pieces of pigeon wing and then holding them aloft he snapped his fingers and the pigeons came to life and flew away, bigger and better than before. This miracle was observed by all present.

Thus Virūpa abandoned the life of a monk and became a yogin. He performed his next miracle on the banks of the River Ganges. He had besought the goddess of the river, Ganga Devī, for something to eat and drink, but she refused. Her refusal angered Virūpa, and with a harsh command he parted her waters and crossed to the other bank.

In the town of Kanasata, Virūpa entered a tavern. His hostess served him a flagon of alcohol and a plate of rice, which he vastly enjoyed. Then he demanded more to drink, then more and more until the tavern was dry. When the hostess asked him to settle his bill he pledged her the sun, thrusting his magical dagger, his *phurba*, between light and shade, transfixing the sun in the sky. For the next two and a half days Virūpa continued drinking, consuming five hundred elephant-loads of spirits. By this time the King of Kanasata, unaware of Virūpa's presence, was terrified; his ministers were helpless, unable to discover the cause of this disaster to their country. Finally the sun goddess herself appeared to the king in a dream, revealing that it was Virūpa's debt to a woman in a tavern that bound her. The king paid the debt, and Virūpa vanished.

Virūpa travelled on to the country of Indra, a land inhabited by brahmin extremists. Here he happened upon a monolithic image of Mahādeva, the Great God Śiva, which stood six hundred and eighty feet high. The brahmin custodians demanded that Virūpa bow down to this image.

"It is not proper for an elder brother to bow down to his junior," the master told them.

The King of Indra, who by chance had come to worship at that time, supported his priests. "You will be killed if you refuse," the King threatened.

"It would be a sin for me to prostrate to this deity," Virūpa insisted.

"Let the sin be upon me!" said the King.

Virūpa placed his palms together in homage and the great stone image cracked down the middle, and a voice from heaven resounded, "Master, I hear and obey!"

"Swear your allegiance to the Buddha!" commanded the master.

Swearing an oath to protect the Word of Buddha, the fractured image became whole again. The offerings which Śiva's devotees had brought him were then offered to Virūpa, who gave them to the local devotees of Buddha, and it is said that those offerings have sustained the Buddhists to this day.

From Indra Virūpa wandered on to Devīkoṭṭa in Eastern India. The people in the vicinity of Devīkoṭṭa had all become flesh-eating witches. It was their practice to station one of their number on the road outside the town to cast spells upon unwary travellers, so that they could easily be captured come nightfall. Virūpa, and also a brahmin boy who had passed by earlier, were bewitched on the road into town, where they both hoped to find food and lodging. The boy found food, and then he was directed by a helpful Buddhist to a temple at the end of town where he could sleep.

"All the people around here are witches," the Buddhist warned him. "There are no human beings left. They all make trouble, but you can sleep in that temple over there."

Virūpa found the boy in the temple and blessed him with a protective mantra before going to sleep. Meanwhile the witches had gathered to perform their rite of blood sacrifice. They had obtained animal flesh but none of the "great meat" of human beings. The sorcerer who had bewitched the two travellers on the road informed the assembly of his success, and immediately two of their number were sent to fetch the victims. Despite their persistent efforts the brahmin boy under the protection of Virūpa's spell could not be moved, but Virūpa had laid down to sleep on a wooden plank and he was transported to the witches' circle upon it. Plying him with alcohol, they prepared their feast and then, inciting themselves to kill him, clasping their knives in readiness they began laughing with increasingly hysterical abandon. At this Virūpa himself began to laugh, but he laughed the terrible twelve-toned laugh of Heruka, a sound that made the witches' laughter seem like that of children at play, and they all lost consciousness in mortal fright. When they regained their senses the yogin extorted a vow from them that they take refuge in the Buddha and henceforth follow his teaching.

"If you retain the faith that I have instilled in you," Virūpa told them, "you will come to no harm. But if you fail to renew your pledge daily, and if you neglect your practice of the Bodhisattva Vow, you will lose a cup of blood from your veins without damage to your body. And if you revert to any other god for refuge, turning away from the Buddha's law, this discus will sever your heads from your bodies, and the Demon of the North will suck your veins dry."

It is said that even today the Discus and the Demon are visible as constellations of stars in the sky. With the witches of Devīkoṭṭa converted into oath-bound protectors of the Buddha's Word, Virūpa moved on to another country, but it was on a return visit to Devīkoṭṭa some years later that Mahādeva, the Great God Śiva, and Umādevī, his consort, created an illusion of a city of four and a half million households with which to honor Virūpa and worship him with offerings. The food for the feast to celebrate his coming was brought from the Thirty-three Sensual Paradises and all the palaces of the gods.

Virūpa left behind him these autobiographical verses:

In the great monastic academy of Somapurī
I was ordained, and lived a life of quiet discipline.
By the virtue of my past actions a divine emanation
Bestowed upon me initiation, blessing and precepts,
But I practiced my instruction with a deluded mind,
And for twelve years, yes, twelve, I lacked even
a dream-omen.
Finally, bored, I threw my rosary into a latrine
with a curse,
But a Ḍākinī vouchsafed me a vision of instruction,
Which gave me new strength, and I carried on
To realize the intrinsic perfection of the wheel of life.
Then after training myself in the yoga of a thought-
free mind,
The Somapurī monks of the Mahāsāṅghika Order,
Utterly deluded, expelled me from the monastery,
And in order to dispel their misconception
I entered a trance and walked upon water.

I turned back the Ganges and ate forbidden fruit;
I pledged the sun as my troth and indulged my senses;
I cracked the brahmins' image and reduced their pride;
And after I had converted the witches of Devīkoṭṭa
Mahādeva recognized my many powers and qualities,
Creating a city to make offerings to honor me.
If you cannot believe these stories of mine,
Why respect the Buddha's Dharma?

Virūpa lived for seven hundred years, and then, finally, he attained ultimate liberation in the Ḍākinī's Paradise.

Sādhana

There is nothing esoteric or obscure about Virūpa's meditation practice. He practiced the ordinary creative mode of meditation upon the Ḍākinī Vajra Vārāhī, the common form of the Guru's spiritual consort, who is also the consort of the deity Hevajra; he visualized her form while reciting her mantra. The obstacles he encountered afflict every beginner in tantric meditation. It appears that his meditation was impeded by the tension of his striving, by thought-forms[19] intruding upon his concentration, and by his preconceptions as to the nature of the Ḍākinī, the nature of reality in general and the results of his meditation. The instructive vision that broke the vicious circle[20] in which he was trapped for twelve years was of the Ḍākinī as an indeterminate[21] inner reality; this vision detached him from the thoughts that occluded his mind and led to his achievement of a thought-free state. This second occasion of the Ḍākinī's appearance was brought about through Virūpa breaking the pattern of his conscious striving and his conditioned thought-patterns by throwing away his rosary and giving up, simply relaxing into the nature of his mind[22] which is nothing but the Ḍākinī herself. The pure nature of mind is called a wish-fulfilling gem because mind's nature is the emptiness out of which all things arise merely by the conception of them, through the functions of sense perception or by thought.

Historiography

The monastery in which Virūpa spent twenty-five years as a monk, Somapurī, was one of the great monastic academies established in Eastern India by the Pāla dynasty of Baṅgala (Bengal and Bihar). The Pālas were munificent patrons of the Buddhist Tantra in general and of the siddhas in particular. Tāranātha claims that King Devapāla (810–840) built Somapurī,[23] but it was probably built earlier by Dharmapāla (770–810), who was a contemporary of Virūpa. The monastery's exact location is uncertain; Ompur in Bengal is a possible site. The *mahāsāṅghika* order, to which most of the monastic followers of the mahāyāna belonged, was the order that Śāntarakṣita established in Tibet.

Virūpa seems to have wandered extensively in eastern India. His birthplace Tripurā (Rādhākiśorapura, the old capital of Tripurā District, Assam,[24] and Devīkoṭṭa (Bangarh, Dinajpur District, Bengal)[25] were names of Mother Goddess shrines (*śākta-pīṭhas*) in the inaccessible jungles of eastern India, where local tribal devotees of the Mother performed human sacrifice, as in Kāmarūpa.[26] Virūpa is credited in this legend with converting these tribals to Buddhism; it was in Virūpa's era that Devīkoṭṭa became one of Cakrasaṃvara's twenty-four principal power-places.[27] The story of Virūpa in Devīkoṭṭa is, perhaps, a confused report of the Thugs[28] practice of waylaying travellers and sacrificing them to Kālī (with the garrotte, not the knife) and the human sacrifice of the Mother's tribal devotees.

'Witch' is a translation of the Tibetan *phra men* (*veṭāla*) that is more correctly a ghoul, a resurrected flesh-eating corpse, but in Tibetan literature such figures are more often low forms of Ḍākinī, powerful, negatively-charged female beings skilled in black magic and particularly in casting spells. In Tāranātha's story of Virūpa in Devīkoṭṭa,[29] *ḍākinī* and *phra men* are used interchangeably. In that legend Virūpa is given a lotus and a cowrie (both sexual symbols), which mark him as the *ḍākinīs*' prize. With the help of a Buddhist he flees to Śrī Parvata mountain where Nāgabodhi teaches him the psycho-experimental techniques of the deity Yamāri (Yamāntaka), the principal of many classes of minor spirits and a dominant archetype that controls neurotic and disordered powers of the psyche through an awareness of the ultimate insubstantiality of apparently discrete entities. Virūpa returns to Devīkoṭṭa armed with Yamāri's powers and thwarts the *ḍākinīs*' attempts to consume him, binding them to the Buddha-dharma. No mention is made in our legend of Virūpa's undoubted interest in Yamāri. To Virūpa is ascribed discovery of the *Rakta-yamāri-tantra*, and also authorship of a liturgical ritual sādhana associated with the same tantra.

The manner in which Virūpa converts the inhabitants of Devīkoṭṭa and also Mahādeva in Indra, and the phraseology employed, is reminiscent of the legends of Virūpa's contemporary siddha, Padmasambhava, converting the Bonpos and the gods of Tibet. Such power to bind the mind to the Buddha's truth is demonstrated only by Buddha emanations (*nirmāṇakāya*). The psychological assumptions are that first the master's threat has sufficient force to deter the convert from breaking his vows to practice refuge in Buddha and the Bodhisattva Vow; and secondly, that once such basic exercises have born fruit, realization of the nature of all things as void automatically fulfills the vow, rendering any conscious formula superfluous.

A clear impression of Virūpa's travels, and the variety and number of his magical exploits, can be gained from Tāranātha's *Seven Lineages.*[30] But the historiographical inadequacy of this text with its contradictions of the older sources, and evident mixture of sources, becomes abundantly apparent. However the following pieces of information are relevant to our legends: Virūpa is described within the context of the lineage of the Yoginī Caṇḍikā (T. *gTu mo*, "The Mystic Heat"); he is also known as Śrīdharmapāla; the monastery from which he was expelled is given as Nālandā; the land of his excessive drinking scenario was Orissa; and there are similarities between the story of the split image of Śiva in our legend and Virūpa's activity at Somanāth, the internationally famed monolithic statue of Mahādeva in Saurāṣṭra, which was destroyed in AD 1015 by Muslim invaders. According to Tāranātha, after Ḍombi Heruka his chief disciple was Oḍḍiyāṇa-born Kāla Virūpa, who earned his epithet Black (Kāla) because he was fated to kill a brahmin and a cow, and like Oedipus to have sexual intercourse with his mother. There is no space here to describe and compare all the legends and anecdotes concerning Virūpa. He is one of the siddhas for whom there is no lack of legendary material.

Virūpa's principal Guru was certainly Nāgabodhi, Nāgārjuna's disciple, from whom he received the Yamāri mantra on Śrī Parvata.[31] A survey of Tibetan sources,[32] however, lists these Gurus of Virūpa: Āryadeva, the disciple of Nāgārjuna; Asaṅga, while Virūpa's disciple is Śāntarakṣita; Dharmamitra, Virūpa's preceptor at Nālanda; and Dharmapāla, a Nālandā siddha—but there were several Dharmapālas, none of whom achieved pre-eminence. We know that Ḍombi Heruka was Virūpa's chief disciple, and if Virūpa, therefore, lived during the latter part of the eighth century and the first part of the ninth, besides Nāgabodhi both Āryadeva and Dharmapāla could have taught him.

The lineage of *Vārāhī's Six Topics* (*Phag mo gzhung drug*) tells us that a Virūpa took instruction from Lakṣmīṅkarā and taught Maitripa.[33] At the end of the ninth century a Virūpa was taught by Anaṅgavajra[34] and received the *Mahākarūṇika-tantra* from Kambala, and this Virūpa II could have been taught by Lakṣmīṅkarā, Indrabhūti's sister. However, Maitripa, a contemporary of Nāropa, was taught by Virūpa, and it could have been this Virūpa the Younger who received *Vārāhī's Six Topics* from Lakṣmī the Great of Kashmir. This eleventh century Virūpa also taught Vyāḍhalipa (see p. 59) and Marpa the Translator; he could also have been a *nāth*, whose Guru Nāngopa was taught by Vairāgināth, a name of Āryadeva.[35]

Virūpa is revered as the First Lama, or *adi-guru*, of the "path as goal"[36] school and lineage, which is the Sakya sect's *summum bonum*, their equivalent of Mahāmudrā. During the latter part of the Sakya ascendancy in the thirteenth and fourteenth centuries, beautifully crafted bronze sculptures of Virūpa were cast in Sakya in Western Tibet; with the exception of statues of Nāgārjuna three dimensional representations of the siddhas are quite rare.

There is no etymology to explain why Virūpa, "He of manifold forms," was called such. The name was not translated into Tibetan, and since the Tibetans do not pronounce the letter *v*, he is known to them as Birūpa, Bi ru byed pa(?), Birwapa, Bhirbapa, etc. The epithet "Master of Ḍākinīs" is taken from the caption of a Tibetan line-drawing.

4

THE MAHĀSIDDHA ḌOMBIPA THE TIGER-RIDER

The philosopher's stone
Turns iron into gold;
The innate power of the Great Jewel
Converts passion into pure awareness.

Ḍombipa was a king of Magadha. He was initiated by the Guru Virūpa into the maṇḍala of the Buddha-deity Hevajra. Through practice of the meditation rites of Hevajra he experienced the deity's reality and attained his realization and magical power.

The enlightened king regarded his subjects as a father treats his only son, but his people had no idea that their king was an initiate of the mysteries. However, they all agreed that he was an honest man with an innate propensity to treat his subjects kindly.

The king conceived a scheme to drive fear and want from his kingdom. He summoned his minister, charging him in this way: "Our country is plagued by thieves and bandits, and due to past neglect our karma has burdened us with much poverty. To protect us from fear and want, cast a great bronze bell and hang it from the branch of a strong tree. Whenever you see danger or poverty, strike the bell." The minister fulfilled the king's command, and while the king reigned, Magadha was free of crime, famine, plague and poverty.

Some time later a wandering band of minstrels arrived in the city to sing and dance for the king. One of the minstrels had a twelve year-old daughter, an innocent virgin untainted by the sordid world about her. She was utterly charming, with a fair complexion and classical features, and to glance at her was to fall in love. She had all the qualities of a *padminī*, a lotus child, the rarest and most desirable of all girls. The king decided to take this girl for his spiritual consort, and in secret he commanded the gypsy to give her to him.

"You are the great king of Magadha," the man replied. "You rule eight hundred thousand households in such luxury and style that you are left completely ignorant of the other side of life. We are low-caste wretches, reviled and shunned by all. How could you even think of such a thing?"

The king insisted. He gave the minstrel the girl's weight in gold and took her to serve as his mystic consort. For many years he kept her hidden, but in the twelfth year her existence became known. "The king is consorting with an outcast woman," was the rumor that spread like wild-fire across the kingdom, and despite his previous benevolence the king's conduct was not tolerated by the establishment. He was forced to abdicate. Entrusting his kingdom to his son and ministers he departed for the jungle with his low-caste mistress, and in an idyllic hermitage in solitude they continued practicing their tantric yoga for a further twelve years.

Meanwhile the kingdom was misgoverned. The quality of life diminished as virtue ebbed to a low level. A council agreed to request the old king to return to govern, and a delegation was sent into the jungle to find him. When they eventually found the hermitage, from a distance they saw the king sitting under a tree while his consort walked upon lotus leaves to the middle of a pond, where she drew cool nectar from a depth of fifteen fathoms before returning to offer it to her lord. The watchers were amazed, and returned immediately to the city to report what they had seen. Then another delegation was sent with the people's invitation, and the king accepted it, agreeing to return.

The king, in union with his consort, came riding out of the jungle on the back of a pregnant tigress, brandishing a deadly snake as a whip. After the people had overcome their fear and astonishment they begged him to take up the reigns of government again.

"I have lost my own caste status by consorting with an outcast woman," the king told them. "It is not proper for me to resume my original position. However, since death ends all distinctions, burn us. In our rebirth we will have been absolved."

A great pyre of cow-head sandalwood was constructed, and after the king and his consort had mounted it, it was fired. The huge pyre burned for seven days, and when it was cool enough to approach,

Ḍombi Heruka moves at will on the back of a tiger.

the people caught sight of the two of them shimmering, as if covered in dew drops, in the spontaneously arisen illusory form of the Buddha-deity Hevajra in union with his consort, in the heart of a fully-blown lotus. At this point the last vestiges of doubt were removed from the minds of the men of Magadha, and they began to call their king the master Ḍombipa, which means Lord of the Ḍombī.

Stepping out of the fire the king addressed the ministers and all of his people of the four castes. "If you emulate me, I shall stay to govern you. If you will not help yourselves, I shall not remain to govern you."

The people were shocked, and remonstrated, saying, "How is that possible?" "How can we give up our homes and families?" "We are not yogins!"

Then the king addressed them again. "Political power is of little benefit and the retribution is great. Those who wield authority can do little good, and more often than not the damage that flows from their actions leads to misery for all in the long run. My kingdom is the kingdom of truth!"

He spoke, and in that instant of immortality he arrived in the Ḍākinī's Paradise, where he remains for the sake of perfect awareness and pure delight.

Sādhana

In India it is universally believed that the sound of a bell has the power to exorcise demons and to purify the mind; a bell is always sounded before entering a temple. The bell that Ḍombipa had erected was multifunctional: it called prudent attention to thieves and approaching natural disasters, for example; it exorcised the area of any demons responsible for plague and famine; and by purifying the minds of the populace it improved their karma; the all-pervasive sound of the bell is also an auditory symbol of female wisdom and emptiness. After this initial anecdote illustrating the king's benevolence, the bulk of Ḍombipa's legend concerns his sexual sādhana and caste problems.

Inter-caste miscegenation was forbidden for the twice-born castes, and the penalty for breaking this taboo was loss of caste, which meant social ostracism. But the evident anti-caste bias of Buddhism in general, and Tantra in particular, does not manifest as social rebellion and zeal to reform society—unless ordination and initiation into an outcast sect is viewed as an anti-caste act—as everybody recognized caste as an immutable, divine dispensation. Rather, for the tantrika, the mind-set, preconceptions and prejudices of caste-consciousness, comprise a paradigm of the social conditioning that must be eradicated if Buddhahood is to be achieved. Just as we can lose our racial prejudice by marrying a partner belonging to another race, the siddhas took consorts from outcast communities to cultivate the awareness of non-discrimination. Further, in the same way that pride is destroyed by entering into the essence of humiliation, passion dissolves by cultivating sexual desire in the framework of a fulfillment yoga and penetrating its essence. It should be said that the popularity of Ḍombi, Śabara and Caṇḍāla consorts depended to some extent upon availability. No matter what the original caste status of a bone-garlanded yogin, few women of high caste would be associated with him. The Ḍombis were wandering minstrels and musicians.[37] The age of Ḍombipa's consort, twelve, signifies maturity, or perfection; sixteen is the actual age when a girl is ripe according to the *Kāmasūtra*, which places *padminī* at the top of a fourfold classification of the ideal girl's physical attributes. *Mudrā*[38] is the term used to describe Ḍombipa's "mystic consort." On the sensual plane she is the "other body,"[39] the *karma-mudrā*, employed in sexual yoga. On the non-dual, ultimate level she is the *jñāna-mudrā*, the "seal of awareness" stamped upon every experience of body, speech and mind.

Ḍombipa's consort was Vajra Vārāhī to his own Hevajra (although another source calls her Cinta,[40] the *sahaja-yoginī* of Hevajra's retinue). The precise nature of their jungle meditation is omitted, but probably it was the yoga of uniting pleasure and emptiness. Practicing a form of *coitus interruptus* and retention of semen, the energy generated is sublimated, vitalizing the psycho-organism's focal points of energy, raising the level of sensual pleasure to the point where dualistic functions of mind are overwhelmed and the non-dual pure awareness of the Buddha shines through. The *kuṇḍalinī* rises from the sexual *cakra*, through the four levels of joy and the four higher *cakras*, to consummate Buddhahood in the fontanelle center (see p. 217).

The vignette of Ḍombipa's purification by fire is a common enough motif in tantric legend (e.g. Padmasambhava's burning with Mandāravā); fire may indicate the fierce passion that is transmuted into pure awareness by meditation upon its essential nature as mind pure in itself; imperviousness to fire indicates a yogin's control of the elements and may signify that his body has become immaterial, in his own vision, like a rainbow body; the halo that surrounds the wrathful deities in Tibetan iconography is the fire of wisdom that burns away the veils of thought and emotion. The "cow-head" sandalwood[41] of the pyre upon which they were burnt is a highly scented, sacred wood usually employed for carving images and anointing saints.

It is interesting to consider the implications of Ḍombipa's final judgement upon political involvement. In his early years as an enlightened king like Līlapa, he used his situation to fulfill the Bodhisattva Vow of selfless service, and, like the Bodhisattva Avalokitesvara, he took upon himself the misfortunes of beings and the negative karma of wielding authority and power. Finally, however, when his people plead incapacity to emulate the master he refuses to rule them and dissolves into the Ḍākinī's Paradise. We may infer from this that the renunciate yogin's path is ultimately superior to living in the world—if the choice is possible. In the same key, Ḍombipa could have claimed that he never indulged in sexual pleasure, his practice with his consort being a highly ascetic practice in which *transcendence* of sexual involvement was the path to *mahāmudrā-siddhi.*

Historiography

Tāranātha's extensive account of Ḍombipa's life[42] begins in Tripurā, in Assam, where Virūpa was born (see p. 50). Ḍombi was the king (or a lord) of Tripurā. His account is substantially the same as our legend until Ḍombi returns to his kingdom at the insistence of his people. After teaching his own people he wandered afar with his consort, demonstrating his magical power for the benefit of others. In Rāḍha[43] he flew across the city mounted on his tiger, threatening the king and citizens with venomous snakes, forcing them to take refuge in the Buddha (thus the descriptive epithet Tiger-Rider). In Karnaṭaka, in South India, he taught five hundred yogins and yoginīs in a cremation ground, and all except one, who violated the *samaya*, gained *siddhi.* Also in the South, he coerced a people who built sacrifical mounds of animals' hearts as offering to renounce animal sacrifice.

Tāranātha lists Ḍombipa's ten disciples:[44] amongst them are Alalavajra, Garbaripa, Jayaśrī, and Rāhulavajra. G(h)arbaripa has been identified with Dharmapa (*48*). Vilasyavajra and Kṛṣṇācārya are also given as Ḍombipa's disciples, but evidence of the Guru's relationships with all these disciples is sparse. Virūpa was undoubtedly Ḍombi's Guru, but it appears that Lūipa also taught him.[45] Far less probable are the references in all but one of the texts of the legends[46] that make Kṛṣṇācārya his Guru, although Ḍombi would have been alive to meet Kṛṣṇācārya. There is room for some confusion in identifying Ḍombipa's lineage as there was a second Ḍombipa of less importance, who was a disciple of Nāropa and Vyāḍhalipa (see p. 285) and taught Virūpa the Younger and Kuśalibhadra the Younger,[47] Atīśa,[48] and 'Brog mi.

Ḍombipa is better known as Ḍombi Heruka. "Ḍombipa" means Lord of the Ḍombī, Ḍombī being his outcast consort's caste name. Heruka is both the name of a form of Saṃvara and Hevajra, and also an epithet of a siddha who embodies those deities' qualities; since Ḍombi *is* Hevajra, according to our legend, the name is most fitting. Ḍombi Heruka wrote few works, but some of significance. His *Śrī-sahaja-siddhi* is an oft-quoted short form of the *Hevajra-tantra*; he revealed the *Kurukullā-kalpa* and *Aralli-tantra*. He also wrote an *Ekavīra-sādhana*. Most of his writing concerned the mother-tantra, and he is to be considered an important exemplar of woman worship (*stṛ-pūja*). He must have been born in the second part of the eighth century and lived a long life through the first half of the ninth.

B.C. Mich.
49016
Det. 48202
ANTHONY WILKINS

5

THE MAHĀSIDDHA ŚAVARIPA THE HUNTER

Ma Scorpio

In the forest of unknowing lurks a deer,
The deer called Alienation;
Drawing back the great bow of means and insight,
Letting fly the single arrow of ultimate truth,
The deer dies—yes, thought dies!
Then the flesh is a feast of non-duality,
The flavor is a taste of pure pleasure,
And the goal, The Magnificent Stance, is accomplished.

On the slopes of the Vikrama Peak in the rugged Mantra mountain chain, lived a hunter called Śavaripa. Śavaripa's karma was cursed. The hunter's survival depends on taking life, and killing animals and eating their flesh for sustenance results in a rebirth such as that of a hunter; he kills to survive and survives to kill. Seeing his plight, the Bodhisattva of Compassion, Lokeśvara, took pity on Śavaripa, and in order to release him from the vicious circle of his karma he emanated an apparitional hunter similar to Śavaripa. The Bodhisattva met the hunter on the road.

"Who are you?" asked the hunter suspiciously.

"I am a hunter like you," the Bodhisattva told him.

"Where are you from?" asked Śavaripa.

"Oh, very far away," was the evasive reply.

"How many deer can you shoot with a single arrow?" Śavaripa was very proud of his extraordinary ability with a bow and arrow.

"Three hundred or so," said the Bodhisattva.

"I'd like to see you try," said Śavaripa, scornfully.

So the next morning the Bodhisattva led Śavaripa out to a wide plain where they found a herd of five hundred deer which Lokeśvara had conjured. "There you are," said the hunter derisively. "How many will you shoot?"

"All five hundred."

"Why not shoot a hundred to start with," Śavaripa suggested, somewhat disconcerted.

So the Bodhisattva shot one hundred deer with a single arrow, and then he asked the hunter to carry one home for him. When Śavaripa could not lift the weight, his pride suddenly broke. When they reached home Śavaripa begged the Bodhisattva to teach him how to shoot as he did. Lokeśvara promised to do so, but he stipulated that Śavaripa should not eat meat for a month. The hunter and his wife became vegetarians, abandoning their life-long habit of killing animals. The Bodhisattva returned after only a week, and discovering that they were obeying his injunction, he told Śavaripa that if he wanted archery instruction he should contemplate loving kindness and compassion for all living creatures in addition to renouncing meat-eating. The Bodhisattva's inducement was sufficient to make the hunter agree unhesitatingly.

When the month had passed and the Bodhisattva returned Śavaripa greeted him eagerly. But Lokeśvara first drew a maṇḍala for the hunter and his wife, and after strewing flowers upon it he invited them to gaze into it. "What do you see?" he asked them.

Looking into the magic circle they saw themselves burning in the eight great hells, and paralyzed with horror they could not speak.

"What do you see? What do you see?" repeated the Bodhisattva.

"Ourselves, burning in hell!" Śavaripa finally exclaimed.

"Aren't you afraid?" he asked.

"Yes, afraid," whispered Śavaripa.

"Do you want to know how to avoid it?"

"Surely," replied the hunter.

"But are you able to do what is necessary?"

Receiving a final affirmation, the Bodhisattva began to explain the basic tenets of the Buddha's doctrine. "The inevitable long-term effect of taking life is rebirth in a human hell. The immediate, short-term effect is strengthened inclination to kill, so that there is an acute danger of compounding your sin, and there is also a strong possibility that your own life will be cut short as you have shortened others' lives. The social effect is dishonor and a vile reputation. On the other hand, by renouncing activity that involves taking life, you can achieve enlightenment. As renunciation becomes a habit and the tendency to kill diminishes, you accumulate immense merit and virtue, and the probability of a long life increases. Finally, your reputation improves and respect and honor accrue.

In that way Lokeśvara taught them the karmic effects of virtue and vice, the ten virtuous actions and their antitheses, showing them the inevitable retribution that results from unpropitious acts and the benefits of a meritorious mode of existence. Gaining insight into the state of pain inherent in the wheel of life, and feeling remorse and disgust for the way he had lived, Śavaripa was inspired to irreversible faith in the path of the Buddhas. Lokeśvara gave him a full-time sādhana to practice, and sent him to the Danti Mountain to meditate. For twelve years Śavaripa meditated upon undirected and unstructured sublime compassion in a thought-free state,and he attained the supreme realization of Mahāmudrā.

Then one day, awakening out of his samādhi of sublime compassion, he sought his Guru, the Bodhisattva Lokeśvara. When he found him the Guru praised his achievement profusely, and then he gave him further instruction. "O lucky man! Your supreme nirvāṇa is not the nirvāṇa of those who with single-minded purpose extinguish root passion and, finally, life itself, like shepherds putting out a grass fire. You must stay on the wheel of life for the sake of all those bound to it. Your aim should be to release an infinite number of people."

Śavaripa returned to his own country and stayed there. He was called by three different names: Śavaripa ("A man of the Śavara tribe"), Mapjigochen ("He arrayed in peacock feathers"), and Ritro Gompo ("Guardian of the mountain hermitage"). He transmits his meaning to those with propitious karma through song and dance, sound and symbol, and he will stay on earth until Maitreya, the Buddha of Love, the next Buddha, appears and teaches the gospel of the new age.

Sādhana

Vajrayāna, the third and final phase of Buddhist development, does not exclude its precursors. On the path of multiple means every conceivable technique, each tailored to suit the individual, leads to the same tantric goal of Mahāmudrā. The doctrine of karma, a

Śavaripa perceives his innate purity.

hīnayāna teaching, clear and straightforward, gripped the simple tribal hunter. The ten virtues are: restraint from killing, stealing and sexual misconduct (body), slander, calumny, cursing and lying (speech), and thinking malicious, covetous and bigoted thoughts (mind). Śavaripa's explanation details four technical forms of karmic effect: maturation of the act, conditioned reaction propensity, conditioned rebound potential, and social effect.[49] Several other types of causal relationship are elucidated in the doctrine of karma, but they are omitted here.

Lokeśvara's precepts that induce a thoughtless trance of sublime compassion[50] belong to the non-dual Tantra, and the result is the transcendent nirvāna (*mahānirvāṇa*) not the hīnayāna nirvāṇa of extinction. After he had attained this supreme nirvāṇa, Śavaripa's sādhana was to emulate Lokeśvara, who emanated his eleven-headed thousand-armed form, called Sublime Compassion, Mahākarūṇika,[51] to aid innumerable beings simultaneously, vowing not to enter the nirvāṇa of extinction until all creatures could accompany him. This is the pure Bodhisattva ideal, found highlighted in a pure tantric context.

Historiography

"Śavaripa" means The Śabara or The Śabara Siddha. The Śabaras were a wild, aboriginal, outcast, hunting and gathering tribe from the Vindhya Hills and perhaps also from the Deccan: thus "Śavaripa, The Hunter." As the Śabaras were well-known to the eastern Indian siddhas, it is reasonable to assume that the Mantra (or Maṇḍa) Range and the Vikrama Peak are in the eastern Vindhyas, which stretch across India south of the Ganges plains. Bu ston took Mantra Vikrama as a corruption of *manavikrama*, "restoration of mind,"[52] but Śavaripa's birthplace would still be in the eastern Vindhya hills. The Śabaras were an untouchable people even lower than the Ḍombis and Caṇḍālas on the social ladder. "The most archaic level of tantric worship is represented in the *Kādambarī* by the wild Śabara tribe of the Vindhya forest whose 'one religion is offering human flesh' to Caṇḍikā and whose chief had shoulders that 'were rough with scars from keen weapons often used to make an offering of blood to Caṇḍikā.' "[53] The Śabaras were also "corpse-workers" in Bengal, but this may have been later.

The Śabara women were most desirable as consorts to the tantrikas, as popular as the Ḍombis or Caṇḍālās. "Śabarī" became virtually synonymous with "tantric yoginī" in the siddhas' *caryāpada* songs. Saraha sang an evocative love song, a tantric analogy, about Śabara and Śabarī lovers. "The Śabara girl is sitting on a high hill. She has peacock feathers on her head and a garland of *gañja* around her neck. Her dear Śabara is mad, intoxicated by love for her."[54] Śabara should not be identified with Śavaripa. The jungle Śabaras wear peacock feathers as their emblem, and *gañja* (marijuana) has special significance for them. Associated with the Śabaras is the image of a yogin crazed with sexual passion for his Śabarī consort, intoxicated from smoking *gañja*, covered in ashes and drinking alcohol from a skull-cup. For Saraha this image is a metaphor for Buddhist tantric practice.

The emanation of Avalokiteśvara in the text should be considered as Saraha. Saraha was Śavaripa's principal, Saṃvara Guru and Śavaripa was known as Saraha the Younger. But another Saṃvara lineage has: Saraha, Nāgārjuna, Śavaripa, and then Lūipa, who was Śavaripa's principal disciple.[55] Jogipa (*53*), Sarvabhakṣa (*75*) and (Bhava) Bhadrapa (see *24*), were also taught by him. Sakara (*74*) should be considered as a disciple of the second Śavaripa, a contemporary of Nāropa, who taught Maitripa. This second Śavaripa is still rather amorphous; it is easy to envision a succession of yogins born in the Śabara tribe. Vibhuticandra, and even fifteenth century Varṇaratna, were taught by "Śavaripa." Both Śavaripas are known to the Tibetans as Śavari dBang phyug (Śavareśvara). The great Śavaripa was born in the last part of the eighth century and died in the middle ninth.

6

THE MAHĀSIDDHA SARAHA THE GREAT BRAHMIN

Remember, friends, sahaja! *the inborn absolute—*
Seek for it nowhere but on the lips of the Guru.
Realize the ultimate nature of the Guru's Word
And mind is deathless, the body unaging.

Saraha was a brahmin. He was born in the east of India in a part of the city-state of Rajñi called Roli. The son of a Ḍākinī he himself was a Ḍāka, a spiritual being with magical powers. Although tutored in brahmin law he followed the path of the Buddhas, and he received instruction in the tantric mysteries from many Buddhist masters. He observed the laws of the brahmins by day and maintained his Buddhist vows at night. Also, he was a drinker, and eventually he ran foul of his fellow brahmins' rigorous orthodoxy. They accused him of drinking, and before their king, Ratnapāla, they demanded that he should be outcast.

"You are a great king," the brahmins told their king, "and you are responsible for the purity of religion in your country. This Saraha, lord of the fifteen thousand households of Roli, dishonors his caste by drinking alcohol. We entreat you to exile him."

"I cannot exile the lord of fifteen thousand households," replied the king.

Later the king visited Saraha privately and upbraided him, telling him that his drinking habit was unacceptable.

"I do not drink," Saraha told him, "and if you doubt it, assemble the brahmins and the people and I will prove it."

When the people were assembled Saraha subjected himself to trial to prove his innocence. "If I am guilty may my hand burn!" he declared, plunging his hand into a vat of boiling oil. He retrieved it uninjured.

Glorious Saraha sees unity in duality.

"Do you still think he's guilty?" the king asked the brahmins.

"He drinks!" they retorted.

Still protesting his innocence, Saraha took up a bowl of molten copper and drank it at one gulp. His throat was unburned.

"We know he drinks!" shouted the brahmins.

"Let one of you jump into this tank of water with me," Saraha challenged. "Whoever sinks is guilty."

A brahmin volunteer jumped into the tank with Saraha, and it was the brahmin who sank to the bottom immediately.

"I do not drink!" Saraha stated categorically. "Weigh the two of us, and whoever is the lighter is guilty." The scale showed that Saraha was heavier.

"If he has this kind of power, let him drink," the king ordained, and together with the brahmins he bowed down before Saraha, begging him to impart the secret of his power.

Saraha than sang three series of didactic songs, one to the king, one to the queen and one to the people. These songs became famous as *The Three Cycles of Dohās.* The Roli brahmins abandoned their traditional practices and entered the path of the Buddhas; the king and his court eventually attained Buddhahood.

Saraha married a fifteen year old girl and, leaving his home, he took her to another country. There they settled in an isolated place, and while the master practiced his sādhana the girl fulfilled his needs and went out begging. One day he asked her to cook him radish curry. With care she prepared it with buffalo milk-curd and then brought it to him, but as he was sitting in meditation she quietly withdrew. Saraha was to remain in samādhi for twelve years, but as soon as he awakened to the outside world he shouted to his wife for the radish curry.

"You sit in samādhi for twelve years and the first thing you ask for is radish curry?" retorted his consort incredulously. "It is now summertime and radishes are out of season."

Saraha was abashed by her words. He decided to move to the mountains to continue his meditation.

"Physical isolation is not real solitude," his consort instructed him. "The best kind of solitude is complete escape from the preconceptions and prejudices of an inflexible and narrow mind, and, moreover, from all labels and concepts. If you awaken from a twelve year samādhi and are still clinging to a desire for your twelve year old curry, what is the point of going to the mountains?"

Saraha listened to his wife. Thereafter he devoted himself to ridding his mind of conceptual thought and belief in the substantiality of objective reality, cultivating the experience of all things as their original, primal purity. Achieving the mystic experience of all things as space he attained the supreme realization of Mahāmudrā.

Saraha lived a life of boundless selfless service to others, until, finally, with his consort, he attained the Ḍākinī's Paradise.

Sādhana

It is possible to infer from the first part of this legend of Saraha that the master is teaching transcendence of both truth and falsehood, and that in his self-ordained ordeal he is demonstrating that all phenomena are delusory and that there is no truth anywhere (see Thaganapa, p. 138). If Saraha is not demonstrating magical power in order to convert the king and his court, what purpose can there be in proving that black is white and that he does not drink, except to humiliate his enemies? Whatever his purpose The Great Brahmin, a Ḍāka-wizard, shows his control over the elements, particularly fire (heat) and earth (weight). In other words the siddha's consciousness penetrated the seeds of karmic manifestation and altered the usual process of illusory emanation at will. In the West this phenomenon is described in terms of "mind over matter" rather than as an example of creative awareness influencing mental phenomena. The notion of a discrete, subjective mind affecting a substantial, discrete object by will is, naturally, very hard to credit; tantric metaphysics make extrasensory phenomena immediately credible. The "laws of nature" should be considered as habits of mentation and modes of illusory manifestation conditioned in man from the beginning. When a yogin enters the sphere of his unconditioned being and reprograms the elemental, materiality-producing forces (solidity, fluidity, heat and motion; "earth, water, fire and air"), which reside in potential in the vital energy (*prāṇa*) of the body, he can create illusions "contrary to nature." Thus Saraha's manipulation of temperature and weight are small effects produced by a profound *siddhi*, the mundane *siddhi* called magical power.

The Three Cycles of Dohās are Saraha's best known works.[56] Each cycle consists of more than one hundred stanzas in the Apabhraṃṣa language, in the *dohā* metrical form. In natural and humanistic simile and metaphor the poet indicates the nature of Mahāmudrā and the manner of attaining it by means of *sahajayāna*, "the vehicle of the inborn absolute." Bengali scholars believe that Saraha initiated a separate school of yoga employing *sahaja* as the means and the end; but no such separate school existed in Tibet. He uses the term *sahaja* in his *Three Cycles of Dohās* and in many of his other *Dohās* (the metrical form has given its name to a genre of verse not always composed in the *dohā* meter) when he is not treating the fulfillment process of meditation in twilight language; it is always used within the context of Mahāmudrā. In Hindu tantric schools *sahajayāna* has come to imply a way of attaining *siddhi* without really trying, a way of attaining god-realization through indulgence in sensual pleasure with the certainty that coincident with every instant of perception is the empty, ultimate ingredient of ecstacy that is *sahaja*. Saraha taught the most pure, uncompromising and formless precepts of the Highest Tantra (*anuttarayoga-tantra*), rejecting most orthodox forms of religious practice and many tantric forms too. It takes a very subtle mind to grasp his meaning and method, and oral and mind transmission is imperative—"Seek for *sahaja* nowhere but on the lips of the Guru," he sings. It is easy (*sahaja*) to fall prey to the glib precept declaring that we need not meditate nor perform any yoga practice at all because the starting point is the goal, and that we are, in reality, Buddhas as we stand; but it is immensely difficult to sustain the belief in oneself as a Buddha in the presence of the Guru. *Sahaja* is only one of the original notions that Saraha sings of in his *dohās*, and it is as much for the content of his songs as for the beauty of imagery and style that he is recognized as one of India's great poets. With his status as poet and as *adi-guru*, or First Guru of the Saṃvara according to Saraha's method, Saraha lays claim to being the pre-eminent mahāsiddha.

The second part of the legend, the anecdote of the radish curry, introduces Saraha's Ḍākinī-guru. It was his wife, the Ḍākinī, who indicated to Saraha the state of being called Mahāmudrā that is a quantum dimension superior to ordinary trance states. The radish curry is a metaphor for the naive, dualistic concepts and preconceptions[57] that we project upon inchoate, non-dual reality, and which cannot be eradicated by passive samādhis. No matter how high a level of consciousness is achieved in the formless realm, and regardless of the intensity or duration of bliss, meditations which take the yogin into the oasis of a pure-land, into a temporary respite from saṃsāra (such as *śamatha*, certain forms of *za-zen*, Transcendental Meditation, and so many more), are red herrings if the goal is Mahāmudrā. It is not explicitly stated how Saraha arrived at the de-conditioned state of experiencing all things as space, but with some imagination we can see Saraha's remarkable Ḍākinī-consort putting her Guru through the mill of tantric brain-washing. One extraordinary example of a non-meditational mode of erasing beliefs about reality from the mind is the method of self-denial imposed by Tilopa upon Nāropa (*20*). Each Guru-disciple couple works to discover the most effective skillful devices to accomplish the same end. Ego defenses inevitably make the process painful. But if it is successful, after complete disorientation, and after the concepts which compose our common-sense view of reality have been eradicated, the mystical experience of primally pure reality should dominate continuously.

Historiography

Other versions of Saraha's legend feature an arrowsmith's daughter who becomes the master's Ḍākinī-Guru and Consort. The potential scope for didactic symbolism in the arrowsmith's craft makes the omission herein of Saraha's initial encounter with his Ḍākinī all the more unaccountable. The arrow that Saraha is usually depicted as holding represents the gnostic awareness that pierces the heart of duality (belief in the ultimate existence of discrete subject and object). "Saraha" translates as "The Archer" (*sara* = arrow, *ha(n)* = to have shot; T. *mDa' bsnun*). If the more popular versions of Saraha's legend are to be believed, then the two parts of our story should be reversed in order, for in other sources King Ratnapāla was provoked into prosecuting Saraha for cohabiting with a low-caste woman, the arrowsmith's daughter. With such a reversal Saraha would deliver his *Cycles of Dohā*s after his ultimate enlightenment.

The historical stature of the Great Brahmin Saraha is reduced by the lack of any substantial biographical data concerning him. As First Guru of the Mahāmudrā and Saṃvara lineages he is the cornerstone of the siddha tradition; but we have no evidence that confirms his dates. However, by establishing that his lineal successors were contemporaries of King Devapāla (AD 810–850), and associating him with the start of the renaissance of Buddhism in the Pāla Empire, particularly at Nālandā, during the lifetime of the second great Pāla Emperor, Dharmapāla (AD 770–810), we can agree with the conclusion of the great Bihari Tibetologist Rāhula Sāṅkṛtyāyana and place Saraha in the second half of the eighth century and the beginning of the ninth.[58] His birthplace, Rajñi according to the legend, was probably in Orissa and not in the South; the Saraha, or Rāhulabhadra (see p. 255), who was Guru of the first Nāgārjuna, was probably born in the South. King Ratnapāla of our legend can only have been a petty Orian *rāja*. Finally, Saraha was probably educated at Nālandā and became abbot there, teaching the greatest of the latter-day Nāgārjunas.

"The Great Brahmin Saraha was the first to introduce Mahāmudrā as the chief of all paths,"[59] although it had existed as part of the praxis of other tantras, and he initiated the *Saṃvara-tantra*; but other than his eternal Mahāmudrā *dohā*s and the rather obscure *Buddha-kapāla-tantra*, he wrote, or revealed, little. There is no work relating to the *Saṃvara-tantra* above Saraha's name in the Tenjur. Saraha's relationship with the South may be a clue to the provenance of the *Saṃvara-tantra*: his Guru in the *Guhyasamāja-tantra*, Viśukalpa, lived there; Saraha's disciple Śavaripa stayed on Śrī Parvata; and Saraha himself is associated with the tantric *pīṭhasṭhāna* of Śrī Parvata. This sacred mountain is the Śrīśailam power place (not Nāgārjunakoṇḍa where the early Saraha could have lived), a haunt of alchemists, Nāgārjuna amongst them. If he did not obtain the *Saṃvara-tantra* in the South, it is also possible that Vajrayoginī revealed it to him in eastern India, in which case his inspiration could have been eastern *śākta* tantrikas. Lūipa, the initiator of the other principal Saṃvara tradition a generation later, could have had the same sources (but see p. 37). It is significant that Saraha's Dzokchen contemporaries in the North-west did not take a *Saṃvara-tantra* to Tibet, although Mahāmudrā was part of their vocabularies. Whatever the *Saṃvara-tantra*'s origin, Saraha's famous lineage—Śavaripa, Lūipa, Ḍeṅgipa, Vajraghaṇṭā, Kambala, Jālandhara, Kṛṣṇācārya, Vijayapāda, Tilopa, Nāropa—provided the tradition that Marpa the Translator took to Tibet, and that Milarepa and a host of Tibetan siddhas used as their means to obtain *siddhi*.

Apart from Viśukalpa, Saraha's Guhyasamāja preceptor, and his consort, the Arrow-making Ḍākinī, we know that Ācārya Haribhadra taught Saraha the *mādhyamika* tradition of Śāntarakṣita and the *prajñāpāramitā* at Nālandā, and also that Buddhajñāna taught him the mahāyāna.[60] His principal disciples were Nāgārjuna and Śavaripa; Sarvabhakṣa (*75*), and perhaps Bhavabhadra, were also taught by him.

7

THE SIDDHA KAṄKĀRIPA THE LOVELORN WIDOWER

My Ḍākinī-woman, my queen, my lady!
The visible form of my pure awareness,
Form not separate from me, nor yet a part of me,
The phenomenal appearance of empty space:
She is beyond compare and beyond words.

In Magadha there once lived a householder of low caste. He married a girl of his own social status and settled down. He was not an immoral man, but caring not a whit for the virtuous life that leads to spiritual freedom, after tasting the delights of connubial bliss he became obsessed with sensual pleasure. He experienced peaks of undreamed ecstasy. However, while he was still more than content with his lot, believing that this world alone could fulfill all his desires, his beloved wife came to her appointed time and died. He carried her corpse to the cremation ground, and there he broke down and lost himself in sorrow. His mind and will paralyzed, he was unable to tear himself away from his beloved's corpse. It was in this state of despair that an enlightened yogin found him and asked him what was wrong.

"Can't you see the state I'm in, yogin?" he cried. "The loss of my wife is the end of this glorious life for me. It's as if I've just had my eyes torn out. No one on earth can suffer more than this."

"All life ends in death; every meeting ends in parting; all compounded things eventually disintegrate. Everyone in this samsaric world suffers; suffering is the nature of this wheel of existence. So why grieve? Why guard this corpse that's no different from a lump of stony clay? Why don't you practice Dharma and eliminate pain?"

"If there is a way out of the confusion of this existence, please show me, yogin," the bereaved man begged.

"The Guru's instruction is the way out," the yogin told him.

"Then please give it to me!"

The yogin initiated him and empowered him in the precepts relating to the insubstantial seed-essence that has neither center nor circumference. Then teaching him how to meditate, the heart-broken lover was instructed to avoid thinking about his dead wife, but to visualize her as a Ḍākinī, as indivisible pleasure and emptiness, without substance and without self. Thus he entered into meditation, and after six years had passed all thought of his dead wife as a woman of flesh and blood had become a state of pleasure and emptiness. The clouds in his mind dissolved, and the experience of the clear light of pure pleasure arose within him. Just like the poison *dhatura* leaving the mind and taking with it all hallucination and delusion, the poison of bewilderment and unknowing left his being, and he saw the reality of unalterable truth.

The *śūdra* householder of Magadha gained *mahāmudrā-siddhi* and became known to the world as Kaṅkāripa. He taught the Buddha's Word to many beings in Magadha before rising into the Ḍākinī's Paradise.

Sādhana

This straightforward story well illustrates how ordinary men are transformed into yogins out of which mahāsiddhas are made, by spontaneously taking advantage of the opportunity that arises in the "bardo" experienced in the aftermath of disaster. The disaster of the premature death of a partner around whom one's world is built is an excellent paradigm, but many kinds of mini-disaster plunge one into the same intermediate state of high receptivity, devoid of preconceptions, ready for anything, a state metaphorically described as "a cremation ground," where *metanoia* is possible—an earth-bound hedonist enters and a sky-bound divine madman exits. The radical distinction between the pleasure of sexual consummation and the pure pleasure of union with the Ḍākinī is made clear here.

Kaṅkāripa was instructed to meditate upon the anthropomorphic representation of the ultimate reality he describes in his rare song of realization. Remove the attachment to one's mundane consort, the attachment that is reinforced by expendable thought and memory, and what remains is a relationship directly analogous to the ultimate two-in-one union of empty space and pure awareness; the Ḍākinī is thus both a woman and "the visible form of pure awareness," and the Ḍākinī's dance[61] is both the play in male-female rapport and the continuous metamorphosis of phenomenal appearances. The Awareness Ḍākinī is so called because her form is inseparable from the pure awareness of the *dharmakāya* out of which she manifests.[62] "The insubstantial seed-essence that has neither center nor circumference,"[63] the name of the initiatory precepts Kaṅkāripa received, is a description of the ultimate Ḍākinī visualized as a zero-point,[64] the cosmic egg containing the potential, and also the ever-changing actuality, of the universe; another lineage calls it "the indestructible sole seed:"[65] this point-instant of pure awareness[66] has, in common with a single point of light in a hologram, the capacity to contain within it the entire interdependent creation. This Ḍākinī is a union of pure pleasure and emptiness; she is not only present in, but actually *is,* every moment of sensual perception.

Dhatura[67] is a powerful hallucinogen otherwise known as Jimson Weed or Thorn Apple. The active parts of the thorny fruit variety create amazingly credible hallucinations in which the subject can lose himself. It is used by devotees of Śiva in their sādhanas, and as an offering; but to my knowledge it is not employed in Tibetan Tantra.

Historiography

The Tibetan form of this siddha's name, Keng rus zhabs, indicates that Kaṅkālapāda (rather than Kaṅkāripa, Kaṅkalipa or Koṅkalipa) is the correct form. Kaṅkāla (and Keng rus) means "skeleton," a synonym of Kapālika and Kapāla, according to the *Skandha Purāṇa*, where the Kaṅkāla sect is given as one of the five *śaiva* sects that lead to liberation.[68] Thus Kaṅkāla would appear to be a *śaiva* name.

The variant forms of Kaṅkāripa's birthplace, Grahura and Maghahura, suggest that either Magadha, ancient S. Bihar, or Gauḍa, could be the correct form (see *7* and *11*).

8

THE MAHĀSIDDHA MĪNAPA THE HINDU JONAH

The fisherman who clung to his hook and line
To be swept into the ocean of his destiny,
To survive in the belly of leviathan
And practice the yoga Śiva taught Umā,
That fisherman was Mīnapa. Once again on dry land
Even rock could not bear the weight of his excellence.

Mīnapa was a Bengali fisherman. His Guru was Mahādeva, and his attainment was mundane *siddhi*, magical power.

At some distance from Kāmarūpa is the Bay of Bengal, where Mīnapa used to catch his fish and sell them in the marketplace with his fellow fishermen. One day, spinning his line of cotton and baiting it with meat, Mīnapa cast his line and hooked a leviathan. The gigantic fish pulled him into the ocean and swallowed him, but since his karmically predestined lifespan had not yet run its course, he lived on in the fish's belly.

During this period, Mahādeva's Divine Consort, Umādevī, asked the Great God for instruction in his Dharma. Mahādeva was loathe to teach her his highly secret teaching where he could be overheard, so he told her he would only instruct her in a place that she should build under the sea. Umā constructed a suitable abode, and taking up residence Mahādeva began his discourse.

Now it happened that the fish in which Mīnapa was trapped came to rest temporarily near Mahādeva and Umā's dwelling, and so it was that India's Jonah received Mahādeva's full transmission to Umā. When the Goddess dozed off and Mahādeva asked her if she was attending, it was Mīnapa who answered in the affirmative. When Mahādeva had finished Umā woke up.

"Please continue," she murmured happily.

"But I've just finished!" Mahādeva told her in surprise.

"I dozed off in the middle," Umā admitted sheepishly.

"Then who answered when I asked you if you were attending," Mahādeva wanted to know.

"I said nothing," Umā told him.

Then with his super-sight Mahādeva saw the giant fish with Mīnapa inside its belly lying alongside. "Surely this man is now my disciple," thought Mahādeva. "He must take the vow."

Mīnapa received initiation and began a twelve year sādhana inside the fish's belly. When a Śrī Tapari fisherman caught Mīnapa's fish, believing that due to its weight there must be gold or silver treasure inside, he cut open its belly and released Mīnapa.

"Who are you?" he stammered, staggering back.

Mīnapa related his story, and when the crowd of astonished onlookers heard the name of the king in whose reign Mīnapa was swallowed by the fish, they calculated that he had lived inside it for twelve years. They named him Mīnapa (Fish-siddha) and bowed down to him, worshipping him with offerings. Dancing for joy Mīnapa's feet sank into the earth, and dancing upon rock he found his feet left footprints as if the rock was mud. He sang this song of explanation to his open-mouthed audience.

Good fortune arisen from my past lives' virtue
And timely devotion to the teaching,
Now results in amazing capabilities.
What a precious jewel is one's own mind!

Thereafter, Mīnapa worked selflessly for others for five hundred years. He was also known as Vajrapāda and Aciṅtapa. First he gained magical powers, and then, progressing along the path, he eventually arose bodily into the Ḍākinī's Paradise.

Sādhana

What did Mahādeva teach Umā? What were Mīnapa's precepts? This is a matter of speculation upon which we will touch below. The message of this legend, however, lies in its stress on the purely fortuitous, accidental events in the miracle of the disciple's attainment of initiation and precept. But neither Indians nor Tibetans have any concept of chance, luck or accidental coincidence. Every event, major or trivial, has as its cause some act in the past of this life, or in a life aeons ago if there is no conceivable relation of the present to this lifetime's karma. The fish, Leviathan, is universally symbolic of the spiritual life (thus the epithet The Hindu Jonah), and Mīnapa's quite unpremeditated ingestion by the fish is the first of his "pieces of luck" caused by his "past lives' virtue." Involuntarily invested with a spiritual body, Mīnapa finds himself, unlike any other siddha, coerced by his Guru into initiation. Mīnapa had the "luck" of the turtle swimming in the cosmic ocean seeking the one ring thrown in randomly, into which he did indeed thrust his head, to gain enlightenment. Finally, in his totally successful saga of spiritual quest, after the numerologically significant twelve years of sādhana, he is allowed once more to touch earth, released from the fluid and uncertain, indeterminate watery sphere, which is so supportive a medium for sādhana that it could hardly be called a prison. The image of the fish-man has further analogical significance for the tantrika: the fish swims effortlessly, unblinking, apparently unsleeping, in its all-pervasive ocean, in it but not of it—fishes never get wet, never toiling but always well fed, never taking life to survive (to the knowledge of the Ganges river-people and the Tibetans), and never in conflict with one-another. To the Tibetans the fish is sacred. Indeed, Fish-lord (Mīnanāth or its linguistic variants Macchendranāth or Matsyendranāth) may have been an epithet of realized yogins employed like Avadhūti or Aciṅtapa.[69]

Historiography

The historical Mīnapa is difficult to identify. But since Mīna, Macchendra and Matsyendra are the same name in different languages and dialects, we assume that we are dealing with only one siddha. This was a Bengali, a fisherman, an *adi-guru* who received tantric revelation directly from Śiva; he taught principally in Kāmarūpa, and was Gorakṣa's Guru. Further, this one siddha, Mīnapa, is found in the lineages of Buddhists, *śaivas* and *śākta*s alike. During this period there was little or no sectarianism, and a siddha could accept initiation and practice the instruction of Buddhist, *śaiva* and *śākta* Gurus concurrently or consecutively. Although this may have led to some exchange of metaphysics and techniques between lineages, doctrines and yogas remained separate.

In Bengal Macchendra is the *adi-guru* of the *kaula*s, the *nāths* and the *kānphaṭa* yogins. The left-handed Bengali *śākta* sect called the *Yoginī-kaula*, or *Siddhāmṛta*, identify Mīna/Macchendra in the form of Bhairava-Śiva as their *adi-guru*. Their important text called the *Kaulajñāna-nirnaya* contains the dharma that Mahādeva taught Umā. Macchendra received the instruction on the *Kaulajñāna-nirnaya* in the manner related in our legend, except that it was Umā in the form of Gaurī who requested it; or, according to a different story, the brahmin fisherman Mīnanāth recovered it from the sea after Śiva's son Kārttikeya, in the form of a mouse, had stolen it and thrown it away. The goal of *kaula-mārga*, the path of *śakti*, is the union of Kula (Śakti) with Akula (Śiva); this is attained with the ritual assistance of a circle of yoginīs (*yoginī-kaula*).[70]

Tāranātha introduces the following variations in his legend of Mīnapa:[71] Mahādeva was teaching Umā on the hill known as Umāgiri on the banks of the Brahmāputra when Mīnapa in his fish lay in the river close by; the teaching consisted of instruction on the movement of psychic energy (*prāṇa*). Then, with material evidently taken from a different source, Tāranātha describes how the fisherman, released from the fish's belly, obtains a "son" and how they go together to the Guru Carpaṭi (*64*) for further instruction and become known as Mīnapa and Macchendrapa respectively. Mīnapa becomes the Guru of Halipa, Malipa and Tibolipa, and the son, Macchendrapa is the Guru of Gorakṣa and Cauraṅgi. It is probable that the introduction of Mīnapa's disciple, Macchendra, was Tāranātha's device to explain away the two names, and to give the *śaiva* and Buddhist lineages separate *adi-gurus*.

In later, Nepali legends, the Bodhisattva Avalokiteśvara Padmapāṇi taught Śiva the science of yoga, and then in human form as Macchendra, listened to Śiva teaching Parvatī (Umā) while in the fish. Then later while Macchendra disported himself with the yoginīs in Kāmarūpa (or Śrī Laṅkā), a famine occurred in Nepal, and since Macchendra was the only siddha capable of bringing rain, King Narendradeva sent his minister, a siddha, to fetch the Guru. Macchendra granted the minister a boon and promised to go to Nepal. Upon his arrival he told Narendradeva that he would return soon as a bumble bee. In due course, one night a bee appeared, and after its capture it rained immediately. The minister created an image of the Guru by mantra, and this image became the protecting deity of Nepal. One of the Kathmandu Valley's principal temples (*Ka:bāhāl*) houses an image of Macchendranāth which is worshipped as Karūṇamāyā, Loknāth, Avalokiteśvara—the Bodhisattva of Compassion.[72] Macchendra is also revered in Nepal as the bringer of the first rice seeds to the Valley. The father-son relationship that exists between Macchendra and Mīna in Nepal (the reverse of Tāranātha's names), is probably that of an older image and younger tradition of worship rather than of a lineal Guru-disciple relationship.

Mīnapa's chief disciple was Gorakṣa (Gorakhnāth), who was the founding Guru of the *nāth yogi sampradāya*, and thus Mīnapa is worshipped as the original human Guru of the *nāth* lineages. Since Gorakṣa probably lived in the tenth century, Mīnapa can be placed in the same period.

The Bay of Bengal is called the Ita or Sītā Sea in *The Legends*; and Śrī Tapari may be the ancient Tamaralipti on the Ganges delta.

9

THE NĀTH SIDDHA GORAKṢA THE IMMORTAL COWHERD

Whatever your birth, high, middle or low,
Resourcefully using your given situation
You reach your goal without impeding the amazing karmic flow.
Seizing my chance I set the seeds of my enlightenment
By performing selfless service to Cauraṅgi with kindness;
Then after Aciṅta administered the nectar of immortality
Gorakṣa gained insight into non-dual reality.
Now here I stand—Cowherd King of the Three Realms.

Gorakṣa was born son of an incense-seller in eastern India during the reign of King Devapāla. When he was old enough he was hired out as a cowherd by his father. One day he was lying down with some other cowherd boys as the cows grazed amongst the trees when the mahāsiddha Mīnapa, also known as Aciṅtapa, approached.

"Do you see the vultures circling over there?" the Guru asked the boys. "A young prince who has had all his arms and legs cut off is lying against a tree, dying. Who will care for him and save his life?"

"I will!" responded Gorakṣa immediately. "But while I go now to see for myself, doing your work for you, you stay here and do mine."

So Mīnapa watched the herd, and the boy ran to find the prince, using the vultures as a guide. The prince was lying against the trunk of a tree as the Guru had described.

"It is as you say," said Gorakṣa, after he had returned.

"How will you feed him?" asked the Guru.

"The owner of my herd gives me food and drink morning and evening," the boy replied. "I'll give the prince half of my food."

"Very good!" the Guru praised him. "Take care of him so that he can perform the four basic functions of life (*caturāṅgi*)—eating, drinking, sleeping and excreting." He then left.

The boy constructed a leaf-covered shelter around the tree. He went daily to take food and to feed the prince, to remove with his own hands his accumulated excrement, and to wash his body. For twelve years he performed these services for the prince, assisting him in every way.

One day, Gorakṣa, now a young man, arrived at the prince's tree as usual and was dumbfounded to see the prince standing upright on his own two legs. He learned that the prince had been practicing a yoga that Mīnapa had taught him, and that the fruit of that practice had now given him regenerated limbs. Levitating into the air the prince offered to teach Gorakṣa how to meditate.

"I do not need your instruction," Gorakṣa told him. "I already have a Guru. It was he who told me to serve you, and I have simply obeyed his instructions." And he returned to mind his herd and to await Mīnapa.

When his Guru appeared, Gorakṣa told him how he had served the prince and what he had seen when he last attended him. The Guru was delighted. He gave Gorakṣa initiation and empowerment and explained the precepts he should practice. Then he moved on to another country. Through his meditation according to Mīnapa's instruction, Gorakṣa attained ordinary, mundane *mahāmudrā-siddhi.* As soon as the signs of achievement appeared he went in search of his Guru, but when he found Mīnapa his Guru told him that he would not attain complete awakening and the purity of Buddhahood until he had liberated one hundred million beings.

Gorakṣa began by initiating and instructing everyone who would listen to him, but Mahādeva reproved him. "Instruct only those who request it," the god ordained. "And do not initiate those who lack faith and understanding." Thereafter Gorakṣa taught only those people whose karma had prepared them for initiation, but even so he liberated multitudes of people. Until this day those who are ready can receive initiation, and at propitious times those who are pure in mind can hear his drum, though to others he remains silent and invisible. His name, Gorakṣa, means Protector of the Herd.

Sādhana

Mīnapa believed that his karma in previous lives created the enlightenment-situation through which he gained *mahāmudrā-siddhi.* In his song of realization Gorakṣa expresses his credo that no matter what our spiritual and social status, regardless of the hand life deals us, it is possible to use the situation to attain our ultimate end, and by so doing to transform even seemingly negative situations into elements of a positive karmic flow that culminates in enlightenment. Of course, the one factor that must be karmically effected is the intuitive realization, or the encounter with the Guru who provokes the realization, that no set of social or personal circumstances holds less potential for attaining a vision of non-duality than any other. No matter who we are, says Gorakṣa in effect, if we extract the full potential from our situation the disciple becomes the Guru. Rather than act to change our condition, he implies that we should change the way we look at the world. Nourishment is derived from the notion that what we are doing is a divinely self-appointed task or is consistent with the Guru's injunction. The Buddhist ethos of "acceptance," and the man who prefers "to suffer the slings and arrows of misfortune" rather than to oppose them, receives a bad press from the Westerner conditioned never to lie down; but insofar as karmic effect is inevitable, opposition to the karmic flow constrains the activist to view the world in a negative light and to miss the miracles that can provide "the nectar of immortality" and "insight into non-dual reality." Gorakṣa accepted the imposition that Mīnapa laid upon him with implicit faith that this initial, preparatory sādhana[73] would be rewarded. To handle another man's excrement is the most demeaning and defiling act a Hindu can perform; and it appears that Cauraṅgi was a most ungracious fellow, unlikely to be free with praise and thanks. But, if an acolyte knows that he is doing his Guru's bidding and that the karmic result will be initiation into an exclusive esoteric community possessing the nectar of immortality, and into the maṇḍala of the gods' Gods (the *anuttarayoga-tantra* Deities) capable of bestowing both mundane and supreme *siddhi*s, twelve years of menial work may seem like heaven itself.

Like his Guru, Mīnapa, Gorakṣa did not attain Buddhahood immediately, as one version of the text erroneously states;[74] he was required to perform selfless service for aeons. One possible reason is that Mīnapa, Gorakṣa and Cauraṅgi, in particular, practiced *śaiva* or *śākta* sādhanas, which omitted some essential Buddhist element, perhaps commitment to the Bodhisattva Vow—their sādhanas are not described. However, since these siddhas were considered to be Buddhist by authorities who lived close to them in time, even if they practiced Buddhist sādhanas separately, their non-Buddhist theory and practice was probably so similar in content and technique, lacking for instance all taint of dualism and the *ātman* hypothesis, that the chief distinguishing factor was their terminology. It is quite possible that the tantric ambience that exists in Nepal today has its roots in the non-sectarian Tantra of the siddhas' India: *śaiva* and *bauddha* tantrikas worship the same god, by different names, in the same temple, and the indigenous Newari people see no substantial difference between *śaiva* and *bauddha* paths. Avalokiteśvara and Śiva are confounded in the lay mind, both deities being known as Loknāth, Lord of the World. Gorakhnāth's status, however, has altered from that of a great *bauddha/śaiva* yogin to the confusing role of a staunch *śaiva* since the arrival in Kathmandu of strictly pro-hindu rulers, the Gorkhālis, with their patron saint Gorakhnāth. The catholic view is that non-dual vision cannot be qualified, that a *śaiva*'s vision is equal to a *bauddha*'s if duality has been resolved. The orthodox (Tibetan) doctrine is that the *śaiva* path cannot lead to *tathatā* and bodhisattvic enlightened action. This view cannot be accepted as the opinion that prevailed amongst Gorakhnāth's contemporaries and peers.

Historiography

Gorakṣa has the distinction of founding the largest sect of yogins in India. His followers, known as *nāths*, *yogis* (*jogis*), *gorakhnāthis*, and *kānphaṭas*, outnumber other tantric lineages by far. They are distinguished by the large ear-rings, usually of bone, that give them the name Split-ears (*kānphaṭa*). They are monastic by vow and practice, and their soteriological aim is to unite with Brahmāṇ through *tantra-yoga*, a heterogenous corpus of yoga techniques derived from Patañjali, and tantric techniques, many shared with the Buddhists. *Haṭhayoga* is their forte. The *nāths* believe that the doctrines taught by Sāḍa-Śiva to Umā and to Mīna/Macchendranāth on the ocean bottom are the origin of their scriptures, the tantras treating "left-handed" worship of Śakti. The *gaṇacakra* rite including the *pañcamākara* offering is a central part of their ritual.

Gorakhnāth is also recognized by the *kāpālikas* as one of their founders, and it is a theory worth considering that Gorakhnāth was the reformer of the *kāpālikas*, who then became the *nāths*. The *kāpālikas* had their origins back in the fourth century, and still practiced low-level *śākta-tantra*, but the Buddhists had developed their formal knowledge and metaphysical interpretation to a high degree of refinement, and Gorakhnāth would have been the Prometheus who stole their tantric fire. Mīnanāth would have performed the same process on the *yoginī-kaula*, an unreformed *śakta* sect, by the assimilation of Buddhist doctrines and methods. Briggs and Lorenzen leave ample room for visionary conjecture.[75]

Gorakṣa or Gorakhnāth (T. *Ba glang srung, Ābhira*), Cow Protector, was taught by both Mīnanāth and Jālandhara, and his disciples were Vairāginātḥ and other *nāths*[76] It is difficult to be more precise as to Gorakṣa's dates than to say that he lived in the tenth century. The King Devapāla of the legend must have been a minor potentate. One last word from Tāranātha, who clearly believes that Gorakṣa was a Buddhist and taught Buddhist disciples: in the 13th century "most of the yogin followers of Gorakṣa were fools, and driven by greed for money and honor became the followers of Iśvara. They used to say that they were not even opposed to the Turuṣkas (Turks). Only the few of them belonging to the Naṭeśvarī-varga remained Insiders (Buddhists)."[77]

10

THE NĀTH SIDDHA CAURAṄGIPA THE DISMEMBERED STEPSON

From time without beginning
The roots of the tree of unknowing
Well-watered by the monsoon of mental habit
Lent growth to a delusion of branches.
Today I cut down the tree of unknowing
With the axe of the Guru's instruction:
Listen, ponder and practice!

Cauraṅgi was the son of an East Indian potentate called King Devapāla. When the boy was twelve years old his mother died of an incurable disease, but before she passed on she summoned her beloved son and gave him her last testament. "All joys and sorrows have their origin in virtuous and vicious action. Even if your life is at stake avoid doing evil." So saying, she died.

The king was induced by his courtiers to take another wife, but from a foreign country. A few days after his marriage he escaped the palace and went into the thick jungle to dispel a secret grief. One day after he had left, the queen climbed to the palace roof for the view, and there she caught sight of her stepson below and immediately became deeply infatuated with him. She sent a messenger to invite him to come to her side, but he refused her invitation. She felt mortally humiliated. "He despises me!" she thought. "He is my worst enemy. I must eliminate him." And she ordered her attendants to murder him.

Her attendants refused to do the vile deed. "He does not deserve to die," they objected. "He is innocent like a child."

So the queen resorted to deception. When the king returned from his jungle retreat he discovered his wife lying across her bed naked, her clothes torn from her body, her body covered in blood from self-inflicted wounds, while she moaned and wailed.

"What has happened to you?" cried the king.

"I have been undone by your son," she whispered pitifully. "He took his will of me and left me like this."

"If he has done this to you then he shall die!" the king ordered in his outrage. He appointed two executioners immediately. "Take the prince deep into the jungle, cut off his arms and legs and abandon him," he commanded.

The palace attendants ordered to execute the prince loved him more than their own sons, and rather than kill the innocent prince they decided to sacrifice one of their own sons. But when they told the prince of their plan he adamantly rejected it. "That is impossible," he told them. "I promised my dying mother that I would commit no sin even if my life was at stake. You must obey my father's command."

So they took the prince into the jungle, cut off his arms and legs from his body and left him to die propped against a tree. At once the yogin Mīnapa, also known as Aciṅtapa and greatly renowned in Devapāla's kingdom, appeared before the prince. In response to the dying boy's plea for help Mīnapa gave him initiation and empowerment and then instructed him in the yoga of pot-bellied breathing. "With the successful conclusion of this practice your body will once again become whole," the Guru told him. He then left the boy under the tree.

Mīnapa walked the distance a human shout carries and found a group of cowherd boys resting while their cows grazed. How one of them offered to serve the prince Cauraṅgi, and the manner of his service, which became a sādhana, is related in the legend of Gorakṣa.

The prince remained in meditation for twelve years. One evening at the end of this period, a party of king's merchants laden with gold, silver and precious stones happened to pitch their tent close to his tree. Fearing the ravages of robbers and bandits, at nightfall they took their treasure to hide it deeper in the forest, and as they passed close to the prince's tree he heard their footfall and called out to them, "Who's there?"

The merchants were afraid that they had camped near a robbers' den. "We are charcoal-makers," they replied apprehensively.

"So be it!" said the prince.

The merchants returned to their camp with their treasure, but when they opened it up, in fear and amazement they found that it had changed to charcoal. "How can this be?" they asked one another in astonishment.

Then the wise one amongst them spoke. "That man who called to us in the forest must be a saint whose very word becomes manifest, a man who can only speak the truth. Let's go and see if he really is such a man."

So they retraced their steps and found a limbless man lying under a tree, and telling him what had happened they asked him to reverse his former statement.

"I can't say whether I am responsible or not," Cauraṅgi told them. "But if I am, then let the charcoal return to its original state."

Back at the camp the merchants found that their treasure was in its original form; amazed, they again returned to Cauraṅgi, this time with gifts to worship him. Then Cauraṅgi remembered his Guru's prophetic words that once his disciple's practice was finished his body would become whole again. He prayed that his limbs be restored, and it was so. On the following morning Gorakṣa found the prince standing on his own two feet. In explanation he sang to Gorakṣa:

My wise and holy Guru
Introduced me to space and knowledge,
And I realized the one value of all things.
What joy to be free of pleasure and pain!

"As earth is the mother of everything that grows, all-pervasive emptiness is the ground of my re-membered limbs."

Cauraṅgipāda, the Immortal, gained every mundane *siddhi* and performed many miracles, but he had an irascible temperament and would teach no one his secret. However, the tree that had witnessed his practice never died. It is said that it still stands today. And that is the legend of Cauraṅgipa, the possessor of the elixir of immortality.

Sādhana

The secret of Cauraṅgipāda's restored limbs and the mystery of immortality have the same metaphysical basis. The key is the yogin's identification with the unitary factor of experience, which is emptiness, space, an aspect of the *dharmakāya*. Caurangi appears to have attained the one taste of all things [78] through the pot-bellied breathing technique,[79] which is not elaborated in the text. Identifying with the empty space of the *dharmakāya* a pure apparitional body can be achieved;[80] simulating the experience of death, the elements are telescoped one into the next until "air" dissolves into the clear light. Then, at least in theory, the yogin is able to manifest whatever form he conceives, and it should be an elementary practice to visualize a complete human body. Although it is not explicitly stated, Caurangi's body must have been an apparitional body. The apparitional body is immortal, impervious to the vagaries of time and decay, because it is knowledge and pure awareness[81] inseparable from the self-manifest appearances of the mind's nature. In the same way that the body's form is determined by a mental conception, "external" objects are also projections of the mind, and if a yogin's mind is identified with the plenum of all-pervasive inner space (*dharmadhātu*) objects must conform to mental images. Insofar as the plane of sound and vibration is the interface between thought and appearances, sound is the creative medium; the "true word,"[82] an absolutely specific sound, is the sound that is necessarily reflected in the realm of three-dimensional appearances. Thus a yogin with *mahāmudrā-siddhi* cannot lie—his thoughts are automatically translated into phenomenal reality. The creative power of mantra, which is nothing if not "true word," is described in many stories about the siddhas. The siddha Buṇḍadatta, the Nepali King Narendradeva's minister, for instance, who induced Mīnapa to grant him a boon by *mantra-siddhi* (the creative power of *mantra*), later created the image of Karūṇamāyā/Matsyendranāth, that now sits in Ka:bāhāl in the Kathmandu Valley, through the power of mantra. The many stories of great Indian masters of *vīṇā* or *sitar* who could make rain by the perfect rendering of a "water" *rāga*, or whose instruments burst into flame when they played a fire *rāga* to perfection, illustrate the relationship between sound and the elements. Belief in such metaphysical phenomena is no less credible than, say, the belief that war is caused by the collective belligerent intention and thought of a nation, or an army and its leaders. The universe is a collective delusion of all mankind; by identifying with the ground out of which that delusion grows, a single powerful mind can alter part of that great delusion. Such is the belief of the siddhas.

Due to the "theft" of the merchants' treasure, one Tibetan commentator translated Cauraṅgi's name as "Member of the Robbers' Band" (*Chom rkun kyi yan lag*). A less imaginative, but more probable translation is "He of the four vital functions" (*Yan lag bzhi pa*): eating, drinking, sleeping and excreting, the four functions remaining to the prince, and, by analogy, to every ascetic dedicated to immobile absorption. Yogins of the *nāth* tradition practicing *haṭhayoga* were termed "limbless" (*anāṅga*) yogins due to their prolonged austerities in solitude. Like a tortoise withdrawing its head and legs, the yogin first withdraws his consciousness and karmic energy from his extremities, and then from the rest of his body, to concentrate it in the central channel; or he arrests outpouring psychic energy and draws energy in through the nine bodily orifices.

Historiography

Cauraṅgipāda was one of the Five Nāths known as the Nāth Lords, although he figures far less prominently than Kāṇhapa, Mīnapa, Gorakṣa or Jālandhara, in both *nāth* and Buddhist traditions. His Guru was Mīnapa, and his Guru-bhai Gorakṣa; neither tradition mentions any significant disciple. He probably lived in the middle of the tenth century.

11

THE SIDDHA VĪṆĀPA THE MUSICIAN

With perseverence and devotion
I mastered the vīṇā*'s errant chords;*
But then practicing the unborn, unstruck sound
I, Vīṇāpa, lost my self.

Vīṇāpa, master of the *vīṇā*, a complex stringed instrument, was born into the royal house of Gauḍa. His Guru was Buddhapa, and he gained his *siddhi* from Hevajra.

The King of Gauḍa had an only son, who was dearly beloved by his parents and the court. Eight nurses indulged his every whim, and musicians were sent to soothe him. As he grew older he became obsessed with the drone of the *tambura*, and as soon as he was able he learned to play the *vīṇā* and became absorbed in it to the exclusion of everything else.

His parents and the court became anxious. "The prince is heir-apparent and should learn the business of government," they complained. "He must be cured of this obsession with the *vīṇā*."

They hoped that the appearance of a highly trained yogin called Buddhapa would wean the prince from music. The prince was indeed struck by the qualities of this holy man, and at their first encounter he prostrated to him and circumambulated him, and they sat down together to talk frankly about life's problems. Very soon Buddhapa realized that the prince was ready for spiritual training, and he asked him how he felt about practicing a sādhana, a method of disciplining the mind on the path to Buddhahood.

"My sādhana is my music, venerable yogin," replied the prince. "I am totally preoccupied with my *vīṇā* and fascinated by the sound of the *tambura*. But if there is a Buddhist sādhana that I could learn without abandoning music I would certainly practice it."

"If you have the motivation and faith necessary to practice, I will teach you a musical sādhana," the Guru promised him.

The Guru Buddhapa initiated the prince with the initiation that mellows the immature mind-stream. His meditation instruction was this: meditate upon the sound of your instrument free of all distinction between the sound struck and the mental impression; cease all mental interference with the sound, all conceptualization and all critical and judgemental thought, so that you contemplate only pure sound.

The prince practiced these precepts for nine years, and all mental obscuration obstructing pure cognition was eradicated from his mind. After experiencing the clear light shining within like a butter-lamp, he attained Mahāmudrā. Various suprasensory capabilities such as prescience spontaneously arose in his mind-stream and he became universally renowned as the yogin Vīṇāpa. He taught the multitudes of people of Magadha innumerable methods of achieving release from the bonds of existence.

At the end he expressed his realization, gave his last testament, and in his very body he passed into the Ḍākinī's Paradise.

Sādhana

The *vīṇā* is a seven-stringed, plectrum-plucked instrument with a second gourd at its upper end, and the *tambura* is a four-stringed, finger-plucked monochordophonic accompanying instrument. In the legend either the translator was confused by the instruments' names, using them synonymously, or, as I have assumed, Vīṇāpa played the *vīṇā* himself while retaining his early fascination for the *tambura*. In Indian classical music the non-technical ear hears the drone of the *tambura* as a cosmic OM out of which rise and fall the melodious vowels of the feminine *vīṇā* and the rythmic consonants of the masculine *tabla* drums. Thus the sound of the *tambura* is analogous to the unstruck sound[83] out of which all sound rises and which is inherent in all sound; and the sounds of the *vīṇā* and *tabla* are analogous to perfect insight and compassionate skillful means, which in consummate union create the unstruck sound. When masters of *vīṇā*, or *sitar*, and *tabla* play together in perfect accord and are of one mind, the unstruck sound sometimes suddenly resounds in the ear, and the essential purpose of the music, and why it is called sacred music, becomes clear. Vīṇāpa's mastery of the intricacies of the *vīṇā*—complex melody, perfection of pitch, speed of progression, and so on—is his accomplishment of the creative process of meditation, wherein the perfection of form is the primary objective, and technical virtuosity is essential; his mastery of the "unborn, unstruck sound" made audible by eradication of concepts, judgements, comparisons and criticism that obscure cognition of the pure sound of the instrument, is accomplishment of the fulfillment process. The unstruck sound is the sound of silence and is the auditory equivalent of phenomenal emptiness. It is absolute sound; it is the potential sound of everything composed and waiting to be composed. Lost in this non-sound, the sense of self becomes infinitely diffused in emptiness. Musicians are lost in space through the infinite powers of dissolution of the unstruck sound, and their sense of self is reinforced by vestiges of magical power adhering to the mind after hearing the unstruck sound only indistinctly.

Vīṇāpa's personal deity (T. *yi-dam*) was Hevajra, so we can assume that his maturing initiation[84] is associated with the *Hevajra-tantra.*

Historiography

Vīṇāpa's Guru Buddhapāda cannot be identified with any certainty. He could be Buddhaśrījñāna, Saraha's famous disciple and the initiator of a Saṃvara lineage. Buddhapa could also be an error for Bhadrapa. Tāranātha has a Saṃvara lineage: Kṛṣṇā, Bhadrapa (Guhyapa), Vīṇāpa, Tilopa, although other sources' Vinayapa for Vīṇāpa make this suspect. Vīra Prakāśa has both Kāṇha and Bhadrapa as Gurus of Vīṇāpa.[85] Tāranātha has another lineage, established in Oḍḍiyāṇa: Aśvapāda, Vīṇāpa (T. *Pi Wam*, "Lute"), Vilasyavajra (Yoginī Cinto), Vajraghaṇṭā.[86] This would give another Vīṇāpa eighth century dates.

Vīṇāpa's birthplace in the legend, Gauḍa, is a reconstruction of the corruption Ghahura/i.[87] Gauḍa was a city-state on the Ganges on the present Bihar/Bengal border. But whether or not a royal musician achieved *mahāmudrā-siddhi* in Gauḍa, Vīṇāpa is the eternal siddha musician.

12

THE MAHĀSIDDHA ŚĀNTIPA THE COMPLACENT MISSIONARY

Like a child nourished by his mother
Growing into the strength of manhood,
An immature mind methodically guided
By the Guru's precepts, develops in the mahāyāna.
And just as a nervous, hepatic or phlegmatic disease
Is cured by a doctor's drugs,
The malaise of belief in "I" and "mine,"
Instantly, is cured by the Guru's instruction.

During the reign of King Devapāla of Magadha, the *bhikṣu* and renowned preceptor Ratnākaraśānti (Śāntipa), a brāhmin by birth, achieved prominence as a teacher of the five arts and sciences at the monastic academy of Vikramaśīla. The fame of his learning spread throughout the continent.

At that time the reigning king of Śrī Laṅkā, called Kapina, was a man whose virtue and merit fulfilled his every desire. Although Indian travellers had brought stories of the Buddha's doctrine to the people of Śrī Laṅkā the doctrine had not been preached on the island, and when the king and his court heard speak of the great preceptor Śāntipa of Vikramaśīla they resolved to invite the great sage to their country. Loaded with gifts, a messenger was dispatched.

The messenger arrived at Vikramaśīla and presented the gifts of the king and the people of Śrī Laṅkā—gold, silver, pearls, fine silk and valuables—to Śāntipa, prostrating before him and then delivering this message. "The king and people of Śrī Laṅkā send their most profound respect. We barbarian people of a small island are enshrouded in the darkness of our ignorance, consumed by the fires of lust and greed, harried by the weapons of anger and hatred, and the light of wisdom is veiled by a distorted perspective. Take pity on us and come to spread the liberating message of the Mahāyāna—the Great Approach to Buddhahood—amongst us. Consider, is it not right and proper that you should come to the island of Śrī Laṅkā for the sake of its people?"

After due consideration Śāntipa accepted the invitation and set off with an entourage of two thousand monks and the *Tripiṭaka*—the three "baskets" of scripture—loaded on oxen and horses. Passing through Nālandā, Oḍantapurī, Rājāgṛha, Vajrāsana (Bodh Gaya) and many other towns, they finally arrived at the shore of the Singhalese Ocean. The Śrī Laṅkān messenger crossed in advance to inform King Kapina of their imminent arrival. The people of Śrī Laṅkā were as happy as Bodhisattvas on the first level of the ten-fold path, and one by one they left their work to gather on the beach. After seven days they caught sight of the canopies and oxen in the boats on the horizon and were intoxicated with joy. When their guests disembarked they covered the ground with silk for the great preceptor to walk upon, bowing low in homage. They offered him vast quantities of incense and flowers and hurried to prepare their guests' every need. Provided with a place to sleep and the necessities of life Śāntipa stayed three years in Śrī Laṅkā teaching the many doctrines and techniques of the *Tripiṭaka*.

When it was time to return to his own land, Śāntipa received thousands of horses and oxen, gold, silver, coral and other precious things from King Kapina and his people. He took the longer, alternative route home, and after passing through the kingdom of Rāmeśvaram, where King Rāmana had built a great temple to Mahādeva after the recovery of his wife from Laṅkāpurī in Śrī Laṅkā, Śāntipa prepared for a seven day crossing of a deserted country. On the fourth day of that crossing he encountered Koṭālipa (Tog tse pa), whose story is recounted elsewhere (*44*).

After his return to Vikramaśīla, Śāntipa grew old and infirm. His students drove him about in a buffalo cart, giving him sweetmeats to eat and serving him soft food, since he had lost his teeth. When he was one hundred years old he entered a twelve year contemplative retreat.

During those same twelve years the peasant Koṭālipa was also in retreat. But while Śāntipa practiced discursive contemplation, Koṭālipa, absorbed in the essential nature of reality, practiced a non-discursive, thought-free meditation to attain *mahāmudrā-siddhi.* When Śāntipa left his retreat hut, he was given homage by his students; when Koṭālipa attained *mahāmudrā-siddhi* many Ḍākinīs came with Indra, Lord of the Gods, and his divine entourage, to pour ambrosia into "the gate of purity" in the crown of the yogin's head, giving Koṭālipa complete contentment. "This is the real Vajrasattva!" declared all the Ḍākinīs. Koṭālipa's blessings bestowed every divine happiness upon them. "Until I received my Guru's instruction I plowed the mountainside," said the yogin. "Through instruction on the technique of plowing the mind I attained *siddhi.*" Indra and his hosts invited him to the Thirty-three Sensual Paradises, but he refused to go. "It is imperative to pay homage to the Guru because the Guru is a source of grace greater than the Buddha," he told them. "As it is said in the scriptures 'the Guru is the Buddha; the Guru is the Teaching; and the Guru is the Community.' I take refuge in the Guru who embodies The Three Jewels, and I pray for his sacred blessings."

With his eye of wisdom Koṭālipa saw that the journey to Vikramaśīla would take six months on foot, so in his awareness-body he transported himself there in an instant. He prostrated before the Guru and his entourage and circumambulated them, until he realized that they could not see his invisible awareness-body, and then he materialized his physical body and repeated his homage.

"Who is this?" Śāntipa enquired.

"I am your disciple," Koṭālipa replied.

"I cannot remember all my innumerable disciples," said the Guru.

"I am the peasant you found digging the mountainside," Koṭālipa reminded him. After these formalities the two masters began to talk casually about their mutual interests.

Later Śāntipa asked his disciple, "And what results have you obtained from your meditation?"

"Following your instruction I gained *mahāmudrā-siddhi* and the existential mode of pure awareness and emptiness—the *dharmakāya,*" replied Koṭālipa.

"Teaching has been my priority and I have neglected spiritual discipline," Śāntipa confessed in reply. "I have never experienced the perfect reality that I teach, while you have rejected teaching in favor of your sādhana, discovering ultimate truth. I have even forgotten the instructions I gave you, so please demonstrate the results of your meditation and return the precepts to me."

Koṭālipa took Śāntipa to a solitary place and revealed the various qualities of the *dharmakāya*, returning the instructions that his Guru had previously given him. Śāntipa spent twelve more years in meditation before he attained *mahāmudrā-siddhi*, and then he served others faithfully before attaining the Ḍākinī's Paradise.

Sādhana

This legend of Śāntipa is free of explicit criticism of the great preceptor's life and mind; but in the light of Saraha's *dohās*, which reduce to worthlessness all scholastic endeavor, discursive meditation, unrealized preaching and so on, it is difficult to avoid a sense of disdain when reading the description of pomp and glory, the great entourages, the lavish gifts, the buffalo cart and the sweetmeats, and the Guru's complacency and condescension. The peasant-siddha Koṭālipa is the real hero of the story, the siddha whose reward for sustaining a thought-free state of mind[88] was ambrosia poured into his "gate of purity,"[89] the fontanelle entrance to the central channel. But there was no disdain for learning in the five arts and sciences[90]—logic, grammar, medicine, mechanical arts and metaphysics and metapsychology—in the ethos of the siddhas; it was the arrogant confusion of existential realization with mere knowledge that was despised in their songs. The yogin with real existential knowledge was known as a Vajrasattva in India, though not in Tibet: the Guru as the Buddha at the center of the maṇḍala embodying the three modes of being and the Five Dhyāni Buddhas. Iconographically Vajrasattva (T.rDo rje sems dpa') carries the scepter (*vajra*)—adamantine empty compassion—at his heart center and the bell (*ghaṇṭā*)—the dance of the Ḍākinī's awareness—on his left knee. Vajrasattva was a popular subject for Pāla sculptors.

The story of Śāntipa belies the jealous opinion that a teacher must be enlightened in order to instruct and bestow precepts. It is sufficient to be familiar with the territory of the mind through personal experience, and to have gained through meditative experience intuitive insight that permits a decisive diagnosis of a disciple's needs, to be able to prescribe a sādhana. A doctor does not have to experience an illness to cure it, and nor does a scientist need to go to the moon to predict the situation a visitor will find and the necessary procedure he must follow to combat hostile conditions. There are innumerable Lamas now teaching in the West, and it is inconceivable that they should all have attained *mahāmudrā-siddhi*. But with fair knowledge of their traditions and some knowledge of techniques, they are quite capable of transmitting the knowledge necessary to practice a sādhana, though not to give effective initiation and empowerment.

Historiography

As history of Śrī Laṅkā the legend is incomprehensible. There is no King Kapina in the lists of Siṅghala kings. The Emperor Aśoka's son is said to have introduced hīnayāna doctrines into Śrī Laṅkā in the third century BC. The growth of mahāyāna and the *vaitulyavāda* sect from the first century AD was halted occasionally by sometimes quite fierce repression of the so-called heretics by kings sympathetic to the Theravādin order. By the sixth or seventh centuries the hīnayāna and mahāyāna were flourishing alongside the Theravāda order, and in the ninth century vajrayāna was introduced, receiving royal sanction and spreading. *Nil-sādhana*, involving "indulgence in women, wine and love," may have been the cause of a general decline in interest in pure Buddhist doctrines; by the turn of the twelfth century preceptors were invited from Burma to re-establish a hīnayāna line of ordination. Indian missionaries were responsible for every innovation in Śrī Laṅkā. Saṅghamitra, for example, a monk from southern India versed in "exorcism and magical formulae," stimulated a mahāyāna revival in the third century. The monks Guṇavarman, a scion of Kashmiri royalty, and Vajrabodhi, taught mahāyanā on their way to the Far East in the seventh century.[91] The Siṅghala chronicles do not mention the names of any siddha missionaries. Lūipa and Āryadeva are said to have been born in Śrī Laṅkā, and Matsyendranāth is associated with the island in some accounts. Thus Śāntipa's claim to fame cannot rest upon his conversion of the Singhalese; he could only have been one of many Indian monks who taught in Śrī Laṅkā.

The Śāntipa, or Ratnākaraśānti, known to Tibet, flourished during the golden era of Vikramaśīla as Keeper of the Southern Gate[92] when Nāropa was Northern Gatekeeper. Tāranātha considered Śāntipa, with Abhayakaragupta, the last of the all-time great teachers comparable to Vasubandhu, thus stressing his devotion to and practice of the basic disciplines of non-tantric Buddhism.[93] But he was a disciple of the skull-cup bearing Nāropa and actually competed against his Guru in friendly magic, transforming water into liquid gold after Nāropa had resuscitated a dead elephant.[94] ("And what can the great scholar do?" Nāropa had asked.) Another of Śāntipa's Gurus was Thaganapa (*19*). Amongst his very many disciples, Atīśa, to whom he is alleged to have given permission to go to Tibet, is prominent, and another of his disciples who took the Dharma to Tibet was Śraddhākaravarman who was destined to become the most prolific and efficient of the great translator Rinchen Zangpo's collaborators, at Tho ling in Western Tibet. Maitripa was a disciple of his who gained the distinction of defeating his Guru in public debate.[95] Koṭālipa must be mentioned as both disciple and Guru. The bulk of Ratnākaraśānti's literary output deals with the *Prajñāpāramitā.*

Śāntipa, the Vikramaśīla Gatekeeper, lived in the eleventh century. If he gave Atīśa permission to leave the monastery he was in office in AD 1040. If he studied with Nāropa it would have been after AD 1049. We can believe that he led a very long life, so he may have been born in the latter part of the tenth century and died in the second half of the eleventh. There is no evidence of a Śāntipa contemporary with the Pāla Emperor Devapāla (AD 810-850).

13

THE MAHĀSIDDHA TANTIPA THE SENILE WEAVER

The worldly weaver weaves warp and woof,
While I, guided by the Guru's precepts,
I weave the strands of my experience:
My thread is the emptiness of fivefold awareness,
My combing stick is the Guru's instruction,
My loom is perfect insight into emptiness,
And the finished fabric is the dharmakāya—
The unity of all-embracing space and
the play of knowledge.

In Seṅdhonagar there lived a weaver with many sons who worked all his life to accumulate wealth. His sons took wives of similar caste, and the tribe of weavers increased in that land. The weaver's wife died when he was eighty-nine years old and becoming increasingly decrepid and infirm, he was fed by his daughters-in-law in turn. But senile, he became an object of scorn and ridicule, and his sons' wives, believing that visitors' revulsion was creating disrepute for the family and a negative karmic situation, decided to build a grass hut for him in the garden. The old man duly retired to the hut, where he was fed as before, and his family was protected from his abuse and their public shame.

Time passed, and it happened that the Guru Jālandhara came to Seṅdhonagar and approached the weaver's eldest son to ask him for food. The son complied, requesting that the Guru wait outside while food was prepared. When all was ready, the Guru went inside and ate what was offered. As he was preparing to leave, his hostess invited him to stay with them that night, and when the Guru objected that it was not his custom to sleep in a comfortable bed inside a house, she offered him a place in the garden, which Jālandhara accepted. A lamp and other preparations were made, and the Guru went outside.

The old weaver, hearing unusual sounds outside his hut, called out, "Who's there?"

"I'm a visiting mendicant," replied Jālandhara, entering the dotard's hut. "Who are you?"

"I'm these weavers' father," the old man told him. "In the prime of my life I was the master of this house and business, but now, in my old age, I am humiliated and reviled by my own sons and daughters-in-law; to prevent others seeing me I am kept hidden away here in the garden. How hollow are life's promises!"

"Everything we do is a passing show; everyone entering existence enters suffering; everything whatsoever is insubstantial, hollow illusion. But nirvāṇa is peace and happiness," quoth Jālandhara. "Do you want instruction that prepares you for death?"

"I do," replied the weaver. And his Guru gave him initiation into the maṇḍala of Hevajra, gave him instruction in meditation, and then went away.

The old man began to practice his meditation precepts. His life proceeded as before except that he maintained complete silence, no longer complaining to his daughters-in-law and their families. After twelve years of practice, unknown to anyone, he had attained various powers. His accomplishment would have remained secret had not his eldest son forgotten to carry food to him due to a celebration upon the completion of a particularly good carpet, and had not the wife taken his meal to him instead at an unusual hour. Inside his hut she saw a great lamp-like effulgence surrounded by fifteen girls holding dishes of fine food and wearing ornaments unknown in the human realm. She ran to her husband and told him to go quickly to his father, but assuming that the old man was dying he began to weep. His friends hurried into the garden, and seeing the same vision as the wife they were astonished. "No human being is capable of such things!" they said. "The old man must be possessed by a demon."

By morning the whole city of Seṅdhonagar had heard the news, and people came to stare, some prostrating themselves. When the old man emerged his body was transformed into that of a sixteen year old youth, and light radiated from him with such intensity that the on-lookers were forced to cover their eyes. His body was like a highly polished mirror, and all manifest appearances were pure light.

He became known as Guru Tantipa, and after performing marvelous selfless acts for the people, finally he went to the Ḍākinī's Paradise in his own body together with a vast host from Seṅdhonagar. It is said that, even today, if you practice the Guru's instructions with faith and devotion it is possible to rejuvenate this very body, in this very lifetime, obtaining supreme *mahāmudrā-siddhi.*

Sādhana

The form of Tantipa's song of realization is to be found frequently amongst the siddhas' songs; the craftsman describes his realization, or the metaphysics of his meditation practice, in terms of his craft, or he describes how this craft, which is his practice, can be seen as yoga. The entire framework of this siddha's existence, the loom, is the Awareness Ḍākinī (*prajñā*); the substance of his experience, the thread, are the forms of the Ḍākinī (*pañcajñāna*: mirror-like awareness, spontaneous fulfillment of purpose, and awareness of the plenum of emptiness). His Guru's instruction, the combing stick, is the means of keeping all experience whatsoever within the framework of empty awareness. And when there is unbroken continuity of spontaneous pure awareness, his being alive, the finished fabric, is the unity of the ubiquitous space of the *dharmadhātu* and the clear light of knowledge[96]—the *dharmakāya.*

Jālandhara promised Tantipa instruction on the way to die, and Tantipa attained a rejuvenated body as the fruit of his practice. The only indications of the nature of his practice are that he maintained silence for twelve years, that he visualized a maṇḍala, presumably of Hevajra, in which Vajrayoginī was his Ḍākinī, and a retinue of fifteen yoginīs actually manifested to worship him. Thus he probably practiced the creative process of Hevajra's sādhana to achieve realization of the *dharmakāya*. Through such attainment the body is automatically transformed into a body of light, since the *dharmakāya* is a union of space and light;[97] and at death when the clear light appears at the end of the tunnel, in which the propensities of karma tempt the mind to take rebirth in any of the six realms, there is only an ecstatic dissolution of light into light, and then an unselfish choice as to where re-incarnation should occur.

In Tāranātha's similar story of Tantipa[98] the weaver lives in Avantī in Mālava; and the old man receives his *mahāmudrā-siddhi* directly from *bhaṭṭarika* Vajrayoginī when she lays her hands upon his head. After his rejuvenation he returns to weaving, singing all the time, and then meets Kṛṣṇācārya (*17*) to whom he gives practical instruction in non-discrimination—how to eat excrement like bread and butter and how to devour human flesh like a wolf. Tantipa is credited with the accomplishment of prohibiting animal sacrifice to Durgā (in Avantī?) by transforming thousands of sacrificial goats into jackals, thus introducing doubt and fear into the worshippers' minds, and then commanding the Goddess to refrain from accepting blood offerings.

Historiography

The evidence supports a north-western or western domicile for Tantipa. Avantī was the ancient Buddhist kingdom, familiar from the *Jaṭaka Tales*, with Ujain as its capital, forming part of Mālava, now Mālwa. Seṅdhonagar is probably a corruption of Sindhunagar, "Indus-ville," which could have been Takṣila (see p. 364). Jālandhara (*46*) is associated with the North-west—by birth (in Turkhara in Turkestan), by name (Jālandhara is the power-place near present Jullunder or Jvālāmukhī near Mandi), and by association with Oḍḍiyāṇa. But Kṛṣṇācārya's legend herein gives Saliputra as Tantipa's home-town, and our identifications are thrown into doubt.

If Jālandhara was born in the middle of the ninth century we can assume that Tantipa was born in the first half of the ninth and that he was an old man by the start of the tenth. Some disciples of Jālandhara were *śaiva* oriented; there is no evidence of *śaiva* influence in Tantipa's legend except that rejuvenation of the body is a practice associated with the *nāths*—*kāya-kalpa* is their generic name for rejuvenation therapies. However, Tantipa is included in the King of Mithilā's 14th century list of *nāth* siddhas as number five.[99]

14

THE SIDDHA CĀMĀRIPA THE COBBLER

I, Cāmāripa, the divine cobbler,
Wrap the leather of preconception and
  conceptual thought
Around the mould of emptiness and compassion;
Then with the awl of intuitive insight
Stitching the continuous thread of existence
Free of the eight mundane obsessions,
I create spontaneously accomplished dharmakāya *shoes.*

In the town of Viṣṇunagar in eastern India there lived a cobbler named Cāmāripa. He belonged to the shoemakers' guild, one of the town's eighteen castes of craftsmen, and he worked the day long making new shoes and repairing the old. But Cāmāripa constantly sought to escape from his work. He felt that he was not made to be a cobbler and dreamt of other things.

One day a monk passed by his shop and, stopping work, the cobbler spontaneously threw down his tools, ran to the monk and prostrated in the dust before him. "I am sick and tired of this life of endless toil, passion and stupidity," he blurted. "I want to follow the Buddha's path, but I have never encountered a spiritual friend, so I've never begun. Please teach me something that will be of benefit in this world and the next."

"If you feel that you are capable of practicing a sādhana, I will teach you," replied the monk, kindly.

"Will you come and eat with us in our poor, outcast home?" implored the cobbler.

"I will come at sundown," replied the monk.

When the honored guest arrived that evening all was prepared, since the cobbler had informed his wife of the impending visit. With the greatest respect they begged the monk to be seated, washed his feet, and then served a humble feast. The wife and daughters offered him his every need, including the pleasure of a massage and comfortable relaxation. The monk was pleased with this generous welcome and gave the cobbler and his wife initiation and instruction. This was their instruction:

Forming the leather of passion and conceptual thought
Around the mould of loving kindness and compassion,
Take the Guru's precepts as your awl
And carefully sew the thread of freedom from
the eight obsessions
To create the shoes of the miraculously accomplished
goal.
These marvellous dharmakāya *shoes*
Cannot be seen by those with deluded vision.

"Form the leather of conceptual thought and preconception on the mould of compassion, and stitch the thread of indifference to joy and sorrow with the awl of the Guru's precepts and your own peak meditation experience. Thus you create the spontaneously accomplished *dharmakāya* shoes. Visualize your work as a meditation."

The cobbler grasped the Guru's apt metaphor and asked, "What signs will arise when I practice like this?"

"First you will feel an even stronger revulsion for saṃsāra, and then later whatever arises will dissolve into its own essential nature." So saying the Guru vanished.

The cobbler abandoned his old home and went to a solitary place to meditate. Signs of accomplishment arose as his Guru had forseen. Describing his realization by analogy to his craft, he put on the shoes of the Guru's instruction, and with a single bound he traversed the ground of ignorance that underlies the six basic passions; after twelve years of practice all the obscurations of his mind were eradicated and he attained *mahāmudrā-siddhi*.

During the twelve years of twenty-four-hour-a-day practice of identifying the images of his craft with his Guru's instruction the cobbler's work was performed by Viśvakārmān, the god of arts and crafts, and his retinue. The people of Viṣṇunagar were ignorant of his practice as well as the degree of his achievement, until one day a man came to inspect the cobbler's shoes and found him composed in meditation while Viśvakārmān worked at the bench. Astonished, he spread the news, and one by one the people came to see for themselves. They begged him to teach them, so he taught them the indispensable benefits of a Guru's instruction and then explained many different doctrines and techniques to them. They called him Cāmāripāda, the Siddha Cobbler, and he became famous by that name.

He performed marvellous deeds for all the people until he went to the Ḍākinī's Paradise in his own body.

Sādhana

Doubt remains as to whether Cāmāripa meditated at his work bench or in the jungle. If the latter, he must have returned to his cobbling at the end of his twelve years for the episode of Viśvakārmān's visitation and the people's discovery of his achievement. If the former, then "his old home" was his pre-initiation state of mind, and "a solitary place" was a cave in the mind free from preconceptions and mundane obsession in accordance with Saraha's Ḍākinī's definition. Thus Cāmāripa would have sat at his work for twelve years using his activity as the Guru's precepts until finally it was "Viśvakārmān" who worked while he watched, utterly detached from his own activity, and at that point of development, free of any mental interference in the work that his fingers performed without defect, he had achieved "his dharmakāya shoes." With this interpretation he renounced nothing but the eight mundane obsessions: praise and blame, loss and gain, pleasure and pain, ignominy and fame.

Leather is to the cobbler's work as conceptual thought and passion are to our minds. "Conceptual thought"[100] is the all-inclusive phrase for discursive thought, judgemental and critical thought, discriminating thought, confused thought, interpretive thought of the past, conflicting thought of the present, and dream and fantastic thought of the future; it also includes the built-in, usually unconscious, dualizing thought process that interprets an ineffable reality and labels its parts according to arbitrary convention. The fractured, desiccated delusions so labelled, each part conceived as an independent, discrete entity, rather than a point-instant of transforming light-form, interdependent in time and space, are the preconceptions[101] that, together with discursive thought, must be transformed by the empty compassion of the dharmakāya. Passion or emotivity[102] is the motive energy of thought; and lust, hatred, pride, envy, fear and sloth, the six basic passions, are all dependent upon ignorance.[103] Ignorance is the inability to "see" a holistic, non-dual reality, accompanied by the all-penetrating conviction that we are all islands, that man, woman, god, and the subjective and objective factors in a perceptual situation, are all discrete isolates, that "I" and "mine" define bottom line realities, and enlightenment is the recognition of such facts. The thread that binds this "leather" into "dharmakāya shoes" is the thread of existence (*tantra*, T.*rgyud*), the constant, the only constant, in the six realms, and that is emptiness (*śūnyatā*). If we can perceive the thread in our discursive thought, in the current obsessive mental chatter about profit and loss, pleasure, pain and so forth, then we have the thread that leads out of the Minotaur's maze. To intuit this thread of emptiness is to gain freedom from the eight obsessions, to become indifferent to joy and sorrow, to attain the impartial equanimity and clarity of pure pleasure. And how is this to be achieved? Cāmāripa's Guru says through the peak experience of (non-dual) meditation, through intuitive insight (*prajñā*), through the Guru's introduction to it at initiation and through practice of his precepts. Practicing Mahāmudrā meditation in solitude, physical or figurative, peak experiences of emptiness will increase in a process of auto-acceleration, so that conscious effort is counter-productive; "relax into the essential nature of your being" is the salient precept, and your dharmakāya shoes are spontaneously accomplished. Cāmāripa taught the indispensable need for a Guru; until he encountered his first and only spiritual friend, he was without the initial induction into the ultimate nature of reality that is the essential, unfailing point of reference.

Historiography

Cāmāripāda, or Cāmāra, (T.lHam mkhan), is the eternal cobbler and appears in all the lists of siddhas, but we have no lineal references. Viṣṇunagar appears in legends *14, 20* and *29.*

15

THE SIDDHA KHAḌGAPA
THE FEARLESS THIEF

Unarmed, the warrior is invariably defeated,
Though he perseveres constantly in the fight;
Armed with the sword "Undying Awareness,"
Victorious over my three-realm adversaries,
I am happy.

Khaḍgapa, born into a low-caste family in Magadha, had abandoned the work of his forefathers, who were simple farmers and householders, for he had become a professional thief. All his energy was concentrated in robbery. One day after he had been unsuccessful in robbing a certain wealthy household in a town in Magadha, he took refuge in a cremation ground, and there he found the yogin Carpaṭi.

"What are you doing here, yogin?" he asked him.

"I am meditating," replied Carpaṭi. "I fear the repetitive cycle of birth and death on the wheel of existence, and so I meditate."

"What do you hope to gain from this meditation?" asked Khaḍgapa skeptically.

"I will attain a higher state of existence and the happiness that is the fruit of absolute certainty," said the Guru. "Even you could attain the same, so why don't you practice the Buddha's teaching?"

"I respect the Buddha's teaching, alright," the thief replied, "but I have no leisure to sit around in cremation grounds meditating. Although sometimes I escape with the goods I steal from the king, his ministers or householders, often they chase me, and there is a struggle. Please give me the *siddhi* of invincibility that will protect me from them."

Carpaṭi gave the thief initiation and empowerment, and then instructed him in this manner, "In a city in Magadha there is a temple called Gaurī-śankar, which has the external appearance of a *stūpa*, while inside is a shrine-room containing a statue of Avalokiteśvara highly charged with the Bodhisattva's grace. Circumambulate this statue day and night for twenty-one days without stopping or sitting down, even eating while you walk, and when you see a snake glide out from beneath the statue pick it up by the head without any fear or hesitation. If you do as I say you will gain the *siddhi* you desire."

The thief followed his Guru's instruction precisely. After twenty-one days a large black snake slid out from underneath Avalokiteśvara's foot, and he seized it by the head. The snake turned into a sword, and he found himself holding the radiant sword of awareness. The defilements of his thief's mind were eradicated and he gained the *siddhi* of the sword, which is one of the eight great magical powers. That is how he received the name Khaḍgapa, The Swordsman.

After his body, speech and mind had been purified of all defiling delusion, Khaḍgapa taught the Buddha's message to all the people of Magadha for twenty-one days. Finally, after expressing his realization he went to the Ḍākinī's Paradise in his own body.

Sādhana

This legend well illustrates the siddhas' amorality. Khaḍgapa's occupation was no obstacle to his initiation. The primacy of non-referential pure awareness is absolute, while the content of awareness is simply color and shape, sound and vibration; and any means whatsoever that can achieve the ultimate consummation is acceptable within the framework of the Bodhisattva Vow. The siddhas who meditated in cremation grounds were accustomed to meeting those at the bottom of, or outside, the social structure—the outcast, criminals wanted and unwanted, addicts, prostitutes, and the insane—for food-offerings could be distributed there, heat from the pyres was freely available in winter, and the mendicants, sadhus and siddhas, welcomed them without any prejudice or disapprobation. The cremation ground was the obvious place for a thief to take refuge from pursuers and melt into the scenery. The Guru's skillful means of apparently fulfilling a supplicant's desire for mundane *siddhi*, in this case protection, in order to induce him to practice a sādhana wherein the original selfish motivation would be lost and transformed into a higher aspiration and goal, is found in several of the legends.

Khaḍgapa's adversaries in the three realms are demonic personifications of the sensual realm of phenomenal appearances, the esthetic realm of pure form which is a mental realm of noumenal and visionary appearances free of emotivity and sensation, and the formless realm where meditative absorption has transported the yogin beyond time and space into heavens of pure consciousness and essences. Even the third realm is within the scope of the ego, so everything within the three realms which constitute saṃsāra is an "enemy" to be pierced by the sword of awareness. The Buddha's three modes of being can be conceived as the infrastructure of the three realms, which are nothing but self-manifestation of the mind's nature. The sword of awareness is carried by Mañjuśrī, the Bodhisattva of Intelligence, and by several protectors of the Dharma. In Mañjuśrī's hand it cuts away the veils of emotivity and objective knowledge that obscure the clear light of the *dharmakāya.* The sword of awareness is also known as "the sword of the wisdom of unbounded knowledge,"[104] which does not signify that the siddha is omniscient but that he knows the element of knowledge that transcends its content, the knowledge of emptiness. Perfect insight has as its object compassion, the Guru's skillful means, whereas pure awareness is the union of perfect insight and compassion, which is the clear light. The sword of awareness is one of the eight great *siddhis*.

The "large, black snake" which Khaḍgapa seizes firmly by its head represents the moral and conceptual defilements that he brings into clear focus. The three weeks of constant application to his sādhana has given Khaḍgapa one week for the purification of each of his "three doors"—body, speech and mind. The snake also represents aversion, anger and hatred; this snake, the cock of desire and greed, and the pig of sloth and stupidity, represent the three basic poisons of the mind.

Historiography

If Carpaṭi (Carpaṭri in the Tibetan texts) was one of the original *nāths* (see *64*), it may be significant that Khaḍgapa attained only a mundane *siddhi,* and that *mahāmudrā-siddhi* is not mentioned amongst his attainments, signifying that he belonged amongst the *śaiva* siddhas. The Gori- or Gora-samakra of the text is probably a corruption of Gaurī-śankar and the "town in Magadha" could be

Varanasī where an ancient Gaurī-śankar temple stands.[105] Gaurī is the name of Umā after she completed her twelve years of austerities (*tapas*); Śankar is a name of Śiva. Perhaps Śiva was confounded with Avalokiteśvara in this Gaurī-śankar temple, as such an identification is frequently made. Since Khaḍgapa's Guru Carpaṭi was a Guru of Mīnapa, we can place Khaḍgapa's life in the first half of the tenth century. Khaḍgapa himself is not mentioned in the *nāth* lineages.

16

THE MAHĀSIDDHA NĀGĀRJUNA PHILOSOPHER AND ALCHEMIST

When an unenlightened man vainly pretends to be a
siddha
He behaves like a rebel who has usurped the king;
When an enlightened man persists in unenlightened folly
He is like an elephant stuck in the mud.

The brahmin Nāgārjuna began his career in the district of Kahora in the eastern kingdom of Kāñcī. In his wild youth he intimidated the twenty-five thousand households of Kahora, recklessly plundering property and invading privacy. His depredations were so severe that the brahmins in council decided to leave the district permanently, abandoning it to its nemesis. When Nāgārjuna heard this he sent a messenger to inform the brahmins that rather than deprive the people of their priests he himself would move to another place, and that he would divide his property and possessions amongst them all. Giving away all that he owned, he entered a self-imposed exile.

Nāgārjuna left Kahora for Nālandā, taking ordination on the far side of the Cool Garden Cremation Ground (at Vajrāsana?). At Nālandā he studied the five arts and sciences, eventually achieving the pinnacle of academic achievement. But he soon tired of discoursing and began to practice meditation, propitiating the Goddess Tārā, the Savioress. When he saw her face in reality, he left the security and the sustenance of the great monastic academy of Nālandā, which housed seven hundred monks, and took to a mendicant life, travelling to other lands and begging in the towns and villages. However, he was not at peace. He would lie down at night thinking, "I am useless to other people in my present state of attain-

Ārya Nāgārjuna, the Second Buddha.

ment. I must gain the capacity to help others." So he went to Rājagṛha intent upon entering retreat to propitiate the Elemental Consorts (*yakṣīs*).

In Rājagṛha he began by propitiating the Twelve Consorts of the Supreme Elemental with mantra. On the first day there was an earthquake; on the second day a vast flood; on the third day a holocaust of fire descended; on the fourth, violent gales blew; on the fifth, a shower of weapons fell from the sky; on the sixth, *vajra* thunderbolts rained down; and on the seventh, Elemental Consorts gathered to attack but failed to distract him from his inviolable heart-commitment. Then, invoked by his samādhi, all the female elementals came to him.

"What do you need? We will give you whatever you want," they told him humbly.

"I need only a daily supply of food to sustain me throughout my retreat," Nāgārjuna ordered. And for twelve years they brought him four handfuls of rice and five handfuls of vegetables every day.

At the end of his twelve years of sādhana he had under his control one hundred and eight Elemental Consorts, and went forth with the intention of serving all sentient beings. His initial plan was to transform the Gandhaśīla Mountain into gold. First he changed it into iron and then to copper, but just as he was about to turn the copper into gold, the voice of the Bodhisattva Mañjuśrī spoke to him. "This action will only cause conflict and strife amongst the people. You will not help human beings like this; you will only succeed in provoking greater evil and sin." The master abandoned his plan and continued on his way, but today the Gandhaśīla Mountain still has a copper-colored, purplish hue.

Then travelling south to Śrī Parvata Mountain, Nāgārjuna came to the banks of a broad river and asked some herdsmen to direct him to a ford. They showed him to a dangerous part of the river bounded by high banks and infested with crocodiles. Just then another herdsman appeared and warned him of the river's danger at that spot. He led Nāgārjuna to a ford, and taking the master on his back he began to wade across the river. In the middle of the current Nāgārjuna created an illusion of crocodiles threatening to attack them.

"Do not fear so long as I am alive," shouted the herdsman. Nāgārjuna dissolved the forms he had created and they reached the other shore safely.

"I am Ārya Nāgārjuna," the master told the man. "Do you recognize me?"

"I have heard of you," replied the herdsman, "but I have never seen you before."

"For carrying me safely across the river I will give you whatever you wish," Nāgārjuna promised him.

"Then please make me a king," said the herdsman immediately.

The master splashed some water upon a *śāl* tree and the tree turned into an elephant upon which the king mounted.

"Do I need an army?" asked the king.

"When the elephant trumpets the army will appear," Nāgārjuna assured him. And it was so. The king was called Śālabandha (or Śālawāhan), and he was to rule over eight million four hundred thousand tax-paying households in the magnificent land called after the city of Bhahitan. He married a queen called Sindhī, and he reigned over his people with benevolence.

Nāgārjuna continued on his way to Śrī Parvata, and upon his arrival he found a cave and settled down to practice his meditation. After some years King Śālabandha became dissatisfied with his life as a king, and remembering his Guru he went to Śrī Parvata to seek solace. He prostrated to Nāgārjuna, circumambulated him and then opened his heart.

"The business of government gives little satisfaction and creates much frustration. I want to renounce my kingdom and stay here always in your presence," the king told him.

"Do not desert your kingdom," advised Nāgārjuna. "Take this Precious Rosary (*Ratnāvalī*) as your preceptor, and it will protect your kingdom. Further, it will give you the nectar of immortality and fearlessness in the face of death."

"If a time comes when I can stay with you, my teacher, I will keep the kingdom and the nectar. If not I want neither," the king responded. Although Śālabandha did not want to return to his kingdom, Nāgārjuna insisted, instructing him on the practice of the alchemy that produces the nectar of immortality, the nectar that would prolong his life for one hundred years, during which period he would rule his kingdom.

Finally the king did as his Guru had ordained, and for one hundred years his kingdom prospered. The birds and creatures of the mountains lived happily, and the master spread the creed of the Buddha. But eventually the evil spirit Sundarānanda grew jealous and portents of doom appeared in the land. The light of the sun and moon diminished, fruit fell from the trees before it was ripe, rains were untimely, and famine ravished the land. An age of sickness and sword began, as meadows turned yellow and forests withered. King Śālabandha interpreted these omens to mean that his Guru was in danger, and abdicating his throne in favor of his son, Cindhakumāra, he went with a small retinue to sit at the feet of his Guru on Śrī Parvata.

"Why have you come, my son?" asked the Guru.

And the king sang this lament:

Why has misfortune befallen us all?
Why has the Buddha's doctrine grown unpopular?
Why are the powers of darkness in the ascendant?
Why have storm clouds of evil eclipsed the white moon,
The compassion of Mahākarūṇika?
Is the Holy Guru, an indestructible diamond,
Also subject to the laws of decay and death?
I have come here because of evil portents:
Please bestow your compassionate grace upon us.

The master replied:

All birth ends in death;
All creation ends in dissolution;
All accumulation ends in dispersion;
And all composite creation is transitory.
So do not let these omens disturb you.
Drink the elixir of fearlessness!

"If you, my Guru, are not alive, what is the use of the elixir of fearlessness?" asked the king in distress.

Then Ārya Nāgārjuna distributed his worldly goods, and the God Brahmā appeared in the guise of a brahmin to beg for the master's head. When Nāgārjuna agreed to give the brahmin his wish, King Śālabandha, unable to tolerate the suffering of his Guru's death, laid his head at Nāgārjuna's feet and expired. The people cursed the brahmin for his wish, but to no avail. Then wanting to give his head to the brahmin, the master could find no one who would decapitate him, so eventually he took a stalk of *kuśa* grass and performed the deed himself, handing his own head to the brahmin. Then the trees withered, and the virtue and merit of men diminished in that land.

Eight of the *yakṣī* female elementals, who Nāgārjuna had propitiated previously, stood guard over the master's body. They stand there still.

After the master's death a light entered Nāgabodhi, Nāgārjuna's spiritual son and successor, and even now that light radiates like moonbeams in the night. It is said that when the teaching of Maitreya, the Coming Buddha of Loving Kindness, encompasses the earth, Nāgārjuna will rise again to serve all creatures.

Sādhana and Historiography

In the Tibetan mystic tradition, Indian saints and siddhas with the same name are conceived as emanations of the same mind-principle, either in a single thread extending across centuries, or as a series of emanations like the Tibetan tulkus. Here that tradition is seen to have Indian antecedents, for in this Indian legend of Nāgārjuna, as in most Tibetan accounts, the two principal bearers of that name, besides lesser Nāgārjunas, have been confounded. The original Ārya Nāgārjuna, born in South India in the second century, sometimes called the Second Buddha, the great philosopher who founded the *madhyamika* system of dialectics, and who revealed and wrote some of the *prajñāpāramitā sūtras* and commentaries, is confounded with the chief of the *siddhācārya* Nāgārjunas, the ninth century master of the *Guhyasamāja-tantra*, the disciple of Saraha. Several of the anecdotes that comprise our legend are to be found in the biography of the early Nāgārjuna that was translated into (or written in) Chinese by the Indian missionary Kumārajīva in AD 405. The following is an essential precis of Kumārajīva's work.[106]

From the beginning Nāgārjuna showed an amazing intellect and capacity for memorization. By age twenty he had achieved academic fame in traditional brahmin studies. He then abandoned learning and threw himself into a search for sensual pleasure. With the help of a wizard's gift of invisibility, with three friends he would invade the king's palace and molest the palace women. In a tragic denouement his friends were killed while he escaped by standing invisibly next to the king. Self-disgust and guilt prompted his renunciation and ordination as a Buddhist monk. He quickly absorbed the *Tripiṭaka* and *Mahāyana-sūtras*, the latter from a mountain hermit, but dissatisfied he wandered throughout India searching for the "missing *sūtras*," perceiving a lack of consistency and order in the extant texts. Able to defeat all-comers in debate, he grew arrogant and, composing his own doctrines, he founded his own school with a basic doctrine of "non-rejection" and "equanimity in the face of all experience." At this point a *mahānāga* took pity on him and invited him into his subterranean library of *sūtras* that the Buddha Śākyamuni had entrusted to the *nāgas* for Nāgārjuna himself. He mastered them all in ninety days, but discovering a further, inexhaustible store, he realized that experiential realization of the *sūtras*' contents was required rather than greater breadth of learning. He entered a samādhi of "the patience of non-being." Awakening from this samādhi he propagated the *sūtras*, defeated all brahmin opposition, and composed the *madhyamika śāstra* and detailed mahāyāna commentaries. His life ended after a brahmin challenged him to a magical contest; he created an elephant that seized and injured the brahmin, who sat on a lotus in a magical lake. When the brahmin revealed his disdain for Nāgārjuna the master locked himself in a room, and when a disciple hewed down the door only a cicada flew out past him.

Other early Chinese sources[107] mention the episode of the Gandhaśīla Mountain; that he wrote alchemical works including tomes on "the preparation of jewels and herbal medicines;" and that his friend, the Śātavāhana king, was associated with his death. The "standard" Tibetan version of Nāgārjuna's biography is contained in Bu ston's *History of the Dharma*,[108] the version expanded upon by Tāranātha.[109] It is full of information absent in Chinese sources, but little of it can be given historiographical credence. For instance, Nāgārjuna's early life is centered in Nālandā; it is reasonable to assume that since Kumārajīva fails to mention Nālandā it was the siddha Nāgārjuna who was related to that academy. A brilliant brahmin youth was sent to Nālandā to pray for an extension to his life that brahmin astrologers had given up for lost unless extensive offerings were made to brahmin priests. At the renowned monastic academy he was released from the astrologers' curse by the Great Brahmin Saraha, who ordained him, initiated him into the maṇḍala of Amitāyus, the Buddha of Long life, and taught him how to recite the mantra of the Conqueror of the Lord of Death. Saraha also taught him the *Guhyasamāja-tantra* and other tantras before he was ordained by Rāhulabhadra, who became his preceptor (see *47*). His career at Nālandā was curtailed by expulsion for "wrong livelihood" after he had procured a gold-producing elixir to feed the community during a famine while he was refectory servitor (see *84*).

However, Bu ston's story of the master's death does shed some light upon obscurities in our legend. Nāgārjuna had taken an elixir of immortality together with the King Antivāhana, or Uḍayānabhadra, names as obscure as Śālabandha (text: Salabhandha), and he had said that they would die together. The king's son, eager to ascend the throne, attempted to decapitate Nāgārjuna, and the master, fulfilling his vow to serve all beings, took a stalk of *kuśa* grass and beheaded himself. *Kuśa* grass was the only means by which he could die because he had killed an insect with a stalk of that grass in a previous life. "I go to Sukhāvatī, but I will return to this body," were Nāgārjuna's last words. The prince took the head two and half miles away from the body, and neither head nor body decaying, each year they drew closer until they eventually met, and again Nāgārjuna worked for the benefit of all beings.

There is little doubt as to the identity of Nāgārjuna's royal disciple. Insofar as the master raised a cowherd (Ābhira) to kingship, even our legend supports the contention that this cowherd king was the founder of the Śātavāhana dynasty, King Śātakarṇi, whose personal name was Gautamīputra. A letter written by Nāgārjuna to King Gautamīputra has come down to us; it is the famous *Suhṛllekha*,[110] a basic discourse on mahāyāna doctrine. In another letter to Gautamīputra, the *Ratnāvalī*, Nāgārjuna explains the theory and practice of the mahāyāna as it applies to kings. The Śātavāhana dynasty ruled the western, and parts of the central, Deccan. Śātakarṇi lived in the last quarter of the first century through the first quarter of the second century. Accordingly the putative dates of Nāgārjuna are AD 60–150. The decline of Buddhism referred to in the king's song of lament in the legend may indicate a change for the worse at the end of Śātakarṇi's life when brahmanical kings succeeded him; it could also refer to the Śaka invasions from the north, to the anti-Buddhist pogroms mentioned by Tāranātha,[111] or, if much later, to the *śaiva* renaissance after Śaṅkarācārya.

The peculiar circumstances of Nāgārjuna's death require some thought. Suicide is quite beyond the Buddhist pale except when a Bodhisattva is giving up his life in fulfillment of his Vow, as in the case of Śākyamuni's previous incarnation who gave his body to a starving tigress. A *vedānta* story focuses the practical ethical quandary that an uncompromising interpretation of the Bodhisattva Vow produces, and which Nāgārjuna resolved by taking his own life. Śaṅkarācārya taught the impeccable doctrine of living only for others and never refusing a request that could be granted; a doctrine acquired, no doubt, from his Buddhist Guru. A *kāpālika* yogin called Ugra-bhairāva, whose Great Vow (*mahāvrata*) was not completed until he had eaten and drunk from the skull of an anointed king or enlightened sage, found an opportunity to ask for Śaṅkara's skull. The Guru could not deny the *kāpālika*'s request, and it was only his disciples' constant vigilance that prevented him from killing himself as Nāgārjuna had done.[112] The conclusion of this story demonstrates *vedānta*'s more accommodating attitude to humanism, while Nāgārjuna, in the immoderate self-sacrificial tradition of the Bodhisattva of the *Jaṭaka Tales*, represents the true idealism that was Buddhism's popular strength as well as its weakness.

Probably the most important of the siddha Nāgārjunas was the disciple of Saraha who was one of Nālandā's crowning jewels during the vajrayāna epoch. He is best known as an adept of the *Guhyasamāja-tantra* and for his principal work known as the *Pañcakrama*, which is a commentary on the five stages of yoga derived from Patañjali's system and synthesized with the *Guhyasamāja*.[113] He taught in the latter part of the eighth and the early ninth centuries. It may have been this Nāgārjuna who visited Kashmir and lived near the site of the Mogul Shalimar Gardens.[114] This is the one Nāgārjuna of the Tibetan lineages, to whom his Guru, Saraha, gave both father-tantra and mother-tantra, Guhyasamāja and Saṃvara, initiations. His Guhyasamāja disciples were Āryadeva and Nāgabodhi who were to become his regents, Śākyamitra and the tantric Candrakīrti. He gave Śavaripa Saṃvara precepts. In our legends Āryadeva (*18*), Nāgabodhi (*70*), Kucipa (*35*), Paṅkajapa (*51*), and Vyāli (*84*) were a Nāgārjuna's disciples. Līlapa (*2*), Rāhula (*47*), and Bhadrapa (*24*) may also have been taught by one of the Nāgārjunas.

It is not clear whether the Guhyasamāja adept was an alchemist, a *rasāyana-siddha* like his great predecessor and like the tenth century Nāgārjuna who Al-buruni, the Muslim traveller and journalist, recorded: "A famous representative of the science (of *rasāyana*—*rasa* meaning gold) was Nāgārjuna, born at Fort Daihak, close to Somnāth (in Sindh). He used to excel at that art and compiled a book which contains the essence of all literature on that subject and is very rare. He lived a hundred years before our epoch (the eleventh century)." It is possible to identify this *rasāyana-siddha* with the Nāgārjuna who was one of the founding fathers of the *nāth* lineage along with Gorakṣa, Jālandhara, Cauraṅgi and Carpaṭi, all of whom lived in the tenth century. *Rasāyana* is an integral part of the *haṭhayoga* sādhana of the *nāths*. Further it is possible that it was the same Nāgārjuna who learned the Tibetan language and collaborated with a Tibetan translator to render the *Ekajaṭā* (T.Ral gcig ma)-*sādhana* into Sanskrit. There is no mention of this mother goddess with one hair-knot, one eye, one tooth and one breast as an indigenous Indian deity. Many goddesses of the Indian tribes had been incorporated into the tantric pantheon as yoginīs of the psychic channels' focal points in the Cakrasaṃvara maṇḍala, for instance, or in the *śākta* tradition as forms of Durgā, Siva's consort. The main reason for identifying the translator of the Ekajaṭā sādhana with the *rasāyana-siddha* Nāgārjuna is that only after the late tenth century would many Tibetans have come to the Pāla Empire where Nāgārjuna lived.

There may have been more than this minimal count of three Nāgārjunas. There may have been another siddha Nāgārjuna called Kañcannara, since he was born in Kāñcī.[115] The task of identifying these saints and siddhas of the same name requires knowledge of Sanskrit, Tibetan and Chinese sources. However, analyzing the composite Nāgārjuna, one important fact emerges: no later emanation reaches the heights of realization attained by the second century propounder of the *madhyamika* tradition.

Finally, the mention of Sundarānanda (Sunandeśvara in the text) raises many questions. Sundarānanda, who casts an evil shadow over Nāgārjuna's royal disciple's kingdom, is Śiva's Bhairāva form, his wrathful tantric form, and Sundarī is a form of Kālī. Sundarānanda and Sundarī are worshipped at Śrī Parvata (Śrīśailam),[116] and it is probable that the early Nāgārjuna's place of meditation was at Śrīśailam. The Vijayapuri Śrī Parvata of the Ikṣvākus,now drowned under the Nāgārjunakoṇḍa Lake in Andhra Pradesh, was not built during Nāgārjuna's lifetime, although there may have been a *vihāra* on the site. Śrī Dhānyakaṭaka at Amarāvatī, where the master is said to have had railings erected around the biggest *stūpa* in the world, was the chief *dharmacakra* in Andhra. The first Nāgārjuna probably stayed at the ancient power place of Śrīśailam, just like his later namesake, who would have found the perfect ambience in which to cultivate his knowledge of *rasāyana*. In the siddha period Śrī Parvata appears to have been a power-place of immense prestige for tantrikas of all persuasions, but predominantly for devotees of Śiva and Śakti. It is the only place in South India that is repeatedly mentioned in these legends.

17
THE MAHĀSIDDHA KĀṆHAPA (KṚṢṆĀCĀRYA) THE DARK SIDDHA

Zealously practice generosity and moral conduct,
But you cannot attain siddhi *supreme without a Guru*
No more than drive a chariot without wheels.
The wide-winged vulture, innately skilled,
Glides high in the sky, ranging far away,
And the Guru's potent precepts absorbed
The karmically-destined yogin is content.

Born in the town of Somapurī Kāṇhapa, also known as Kṛṣṇācārya, was the son of a scribe. He took ordination in the great monastic academy of Somapurī, built by King Dharmapāla. He was initiated into the maṇḍala of the Deity Hevajra by his Guru Jālandhara.

Kāṇhapa practiced his sādhana for twelve years and was rewarded by a vision of Hevajra with his retinue while the earth trembled beneath him. This experience inflated his pride, but a Ḍākinī appeared and warned him against any idea that this vision was anything but a preliminary sign on the path, assuring him that he had not yet realized ultimate truth. Kāṇhapa continued his solitary practice, but one day, wishing to test himself, he placed his foot upon a rock and left his footprint in it. The Ḍākinī appeared again, entreating him to return to his meditation seat. Again, sometime later, he awoke from his samādhi and found himself floating in space one cubit from the ground, and again the Ḍākinī appeared, warning him of pride of achievement and pointing to his meditation seat. Finally it happened that he rose up with seven canopies floating above his head and seven *ḍamaru* skull-drums spontaneously sounding in the sky around him.

"I have reached my goal," he told his disciples. "We will go to the barbarian island of Laṅkāpurī to convert the inhabitants."

He set out for the city of Laṅkāpurī on the island of Śrī Laṅkā with a retinue of three thousand disciples. At the shore of the sea dividing the island from the mainland, wishing to impress his disciples and also the people of Śrī Laṅkā, he left his attendants and began the crossing walking on the water.

"Even my Guru lacks this gift!" he thought to himself—and he sank into the sea. The current washed him ashore, and he found himself looking up at his Guru, Jālandhara, who was floating in the sky above him.

"Where are you going, Kāṇhapa?" asked his Guru. "What's the matter?"

"I was going to the barbarian island of Śrī Laṅkā to save the people from the pitfalls of saṃsāra," Kāṇhapa replied meekly. "But on the way it occurred to me that my power was superior to yours, and the result was that I lost the power I had, and I sank into the sea."

"You do no one any good like that," Jālandhara commented. "You should go to my country of Paṭaliputra, where the beneficent King Dharmapāla reigns, and there look for a pupil of mine who is a weaver. Obey him implicitly, and you will attain the ultimate truth, which you have not yet understood."

Kāṇhapa set out and, obeying his Guru, he found that his powers were restored. The canopies and *ḍamarus* re-appeared in the sky, and he could walk upon water and leave footprints in rock. When he arrived at Paṭaliputra he left his three thousand disciples outside the city and went in search of the weaver. Walking down the main street of the town where the weavers had their shops, one by one he broke the threads of their looms with his gaze. As each began to retie his threads manually he knew he had to look further for his teacher. At the end of the street, on the outskirts of town, however, he found a weaver whose thread spontaneously re-wound itself, and he knew that he need look no further. Prostrating before this man, and circumambulating him, Kāṇhapa then besought him to teach the ultimate truth.

"Do you promise to obey me in all things?" inquired the weaver.

"I do," Kāṇhapa responded.

Then they walked together to the cremation ground, where they

Kāṇhapa (Kṛṣṇācārya) subdues the elemental spirits.

found a fresh corpse. "Can you eat the flesh of the corpse?" the weaver asked.

Kāṇhapa knelt down, took out his knife, and began to sever a piece of flesh.

"Not like that!" said the weaver with contempt, "Like this!" And he transformed himself into a wolf, leapt upon the corpse, and began to tear at it ravenously. Once more a human being he said, "You can only eat human flesh when you can transform yourself in that way."

Then continuing his instruction, he defecated and offered one of the three pieces of his feces to his pupil. "Eat it!" he ordered.

"People will ridicule me if I eat this," Kāṇhapa protested. "I shan't do it!"

Then the weaver ate one piece, the celestial gods ate another, and the third was carried off by the *nāga* serpents to the nether world.

After they had arrived back in the city the weaver bought five penny worth of food and alcohol. "Now call your disciples and we'll celebrate a communal *gaṇacakra* feast," he ordered.

Kāṇhapa did as he was told thinking, "There's not enough food there for even one man. How is he going to feed us all?"

When the communicants were assembled the weaver blessed the offerings and filled the bowls with rice, sweetmeats and every kind of delicacy. The feast lasted for seven days, and still the offerings had not all been consumed. "There is no end to this," Kāṇhapa eventually thought in disgust. "I am going," and he threw away his left-overs as an offering to the hungry ghosts, called to his disciples, and walked off.

The weaver shouted after them:

Ah, you miserable children!
You are destroying yourselves!
You are the kind of yogins
Who separate the emptiness of perfect insight
From the active compassion of life!
What will you gain by running away?
Canopies and ḍamarus *are small achievements—*
Meditate and realize the nature of reality!

Kāṇhapa did not want to listen. He walked on, and travelled to the land of Bhadhokora, which was four hundred and fifty miles east of Somapurī. He stopped, finally, on the outskirts of the city, where he saw a young girl sitting beneath a lichee tree laden with fruit.

"Give me some fruit," he said to the girl.

"I will not," she replied.

The yogin was not to be denied, and he plucked the fruit from the tree with his powerful gaze. The girl sent each fruit back to the tree with an equally powerful look. Kāṇhapa was suddenly angry, and he cursed the girl with a maledictory mantra so that she fell writhing on the ground, bleeding from her limbs.

An indignant crowd gathered, "Buddhists are supposed to be kind," they muttered, "but this yogin is a killer!"

Kāṇhapa recollected himself when he heard these words, and feeling compassion for the girl he removed the curse. But he was now vulnerable to the curse that she called down upon him, and he fell down vomiting and excreting blood in an acute state of mortal anguish. He called the Ḍākinī Bhande to him, and asked her to go to Śrī Parvata Mountain in the south to bring the herbs that could cure him.

The Ḍākinī departed, covering the six months' journey to Śrī Parvata in seven days. She soon found the herbs required and turned back to Bengal. On the last day of the return journey she passed an old crone weeping by the wayside, and failing to recognize the seductress who had cursed her master, she stopped to ask the cause of her distress.

"Isn't the death of the Lord Kāṇhapa sufficient cause to weep?" moaned the crone.

In despair Bhande threw the vital medicine away, only to find Kāṇhapa still critically ill, awaiting his cure. When he asked for the herbs she could only stammer her tale of deception.

Kāṇhapa had seven days to teach his disciples before finally leaving his karmically-matured body for the Ḍākinī's Paradise. He taught them the sādhana called The Severed-headed Vajra Vārāhī.

After her master's death the Ḍākinī Bhande sought the girl whose malediction had caused it. She searched the heavens above, the netherworld below, and the human world in between. Eventually she found her hiding in a *śambhila* tree. She dragged her out of it and cursed her with a spell from which she never recovered.

Sādhana

Kāṇhapa's story is the only legend that can be described as a cautionary tale. The other siddhas who failed to attain the ultimate *mahāmudrā-siddhi*—Gorakṣa, Caurangi, Khaḍgapa, among others—were treated very kindly by the narrator, but Kāṇhapa, who performed a Hevajra sādhana and was recognized by the people as a Buddhist yogin, was heavily censured. He refused to listen to his Ḍākinī advisor; he committed the cardinal sin of disobeying his Guru, the weaver; he was conceited and hasty; he was governed by anger and pride: he came to a nasty end. The weaver attributed his failings to his incomplete meditation; he had not united insight and skillful means. In practical terms, although he may have attained prolonged periods of insight into emptiness in the controlled situation of trance, during his application of skillful means in an uncontrolled situation, when impediments such as inflated discursive thought and strong emotion arose, he lacked the perception of emptiness that would dissolve these obstacles. Thus, when he was provoked by the Ḍākinī under the lichee tree, instead of donning a wrathful mask while maintaining the inner equilibrium and detachment that accompanies an understanding of all phenomena as empty colored space, he was overcome by anger, and his belated contrition, which he could have reserved for a meditation of atonement, led to his death. Insight and skillful means are said to be like the wings of a bird; with only one wing, a bird cannot fly. As to emotion, so to thought; if his arrogant thoughts dissolved immediately they arose due to his perception of their emptiness, he would not have fallen. If he had been able to experience the sensual feast of the *gaṇacakra* as emptiness, his appetite would have been limitless. If he had really eradicated his conditioned prejudice and preconceptions and gained the awareness of sameness, he could have eaten his Guru's excrement. If he had been free of a sense of ego, he could have transformed himself into a wolf and eaten human flesh. Kāṇhapa exemplifies the common phenomenon of the meditator who experiences the highest heavens in his meditative trance, who may have realized the emptiness of all things, and can even arise from his meditation seat and remain in samādhi; but when called upon to act, the realization achieved in meditation vanishes. Likewise, when conditions are favorable he can demonstrate *siddhi* and fulfill his vow to assist all sentient beings, but when the ultimate insight is necessary to dissolve obstacles, due to vestiges of belief in "self" it is not available. Only siddhas have constant realization of the ultimate reality and live their daily lives with insight and skillful means united.

Three Ḍākinīs feature in this legend; every Ḍākinī has the potential to function as a guide or assistant to liberation. The first Ḍākinī, who Kāṇhapa chose eventually to ignore, may have been a human embodiment or a *saṃbhogakāya* emanation. The Ḍākinī under the fruit tree was a mundane Ḍākinī whose positive potential Kāṇhapa never discovered because she touched his ego, provoking him to compete and, fatally attached, he stirred in her a wrath that soon killed him. Clearly it is very difficult to penetrate to the emptiness of a mundane Ḍākinī when she shows the heavy and black side of her ambiguous nature; but if that is achieved she becomes a most loyal ally, guide and savioress. The third Ḍākinī, Bhande (or Bandhe), is his trustworthy friend who performed superhuman feats out of her devotion to him. Her name could mean "Buddhist Nun" (*bandhā*) or "Skull" (*bhandha*), which would associate her with the *kāpālikas*. Kāṇhapa had a male disciple called Bhandepāda (*32*), but it was a Bhadrapāda (*24*) who sought the murderous Bahurī, found her in a tree in Devīkoṭṭa and slew her, according to Tāranātha.[117]

Only in this legend are the practices of flesh-eating, dung-eating and (by implication) a literally performed *gaṇacakra-pūja* mentioned. In these so-called left-handed (*vāmācāra*) practices there is an element of William Blake's "The road of excess leads to the palace of wisdom," but more than that, it is in the basest impurity, in depravity and the lowest forms of life, and in tamasic food and drink, in the outcaste whore, the *kāpālika* ascetic, excrement, corpses, alcohol, drugs, fish and meat, that the ultimate truth[118] becomes accessible. Finding purity in impurity through the experience of the one taste of all things,[119] the ultimate sameness of all phenomena,[120] which is emptiness, is realized. At the heart of depravity and corruption is the seed of innocence, unconditioned mind,[121] which turns the wheel full circle and unites polarities. The seed grows into the flower of liberated bodhisattvic activities like a lotus growing out of the slime of a lake bottom: no slime, no lotus. The image of the lotus is basic and ubiquitous in tantric sādhana.

The stereotype of the flesh-eating, copulating, dung-eating tantrika is the *kāpālika* ascetic, who consciously seeks the bottom of the pit of saṃsāra to find his way to nirvāṇa. The great poet and singer Kāṇhapa sings of the perfected *kāpālika* in some of his many *caryāpada* songs, and even identifies himself as a *kāpālika*. His Guru Jālandhara was acknowledged as one of their great Gurus, but it is unlikely that Kāṇhapa himself actually took the Great Vow (*mahāvrata*) and performed gross *kāpālika* rites. Although he sings "O Ḍombī, I shall keep company with thee, and it is for this purpose that I have become a Kapāli without aversion. . . . I am the Kapāli and thou art the Ḍombī. For thee I have put on a garland of bones . . ."[122] he also sings the subtle metaphysical equations of the *sahajiyas*, and one is tempted to think that the Kapāli (or *kāpālika*) is for him a state of mind, and that he never practiced the literal interpretation. He sings of an uncompromising non-dual reality in which there is only empty space, and, simply by recognizing that, *mahāmudrā-siddhi* is attained. He rejects the intellectual approach, mantra and visualization, brahmin ritual, the *kāpālika*'s attachment to tantric appearances and conventions, and he sings of the real *kāpālika* as the ideal *sahaja-siddha* who has shaken off all prejudices and partiality, all preconceptions and doctrine, and realized "the ultimate principle of emptiness that arises spontaneously with every movement of the mind."[123]

Historiography

Kāṇhapa is also a founder of *nāth* lineages. Compared to others of the Five Nāths he is not of primary importance, but the *nāth* tradition is rich in anecdote concerning him. His status is defined by a story of Gorakhnāth and Mīnanāth giving a feast at which each selects his own dish. Kāṇhapa chose cooked snakes and scorpions and was hooted from the feast. It is said that he was the son of the fisherman Kinwar, who caught Mīnapa's leviathan. The Kāṇipā, one of the twelve main *panth*s, recognize him as *adi-guru*, as also the Augars, who perform twelve years of sādhana *before* initiation, and lastly the Sepala, lesser, snake-charming yogins.[124] It is as if he was patron-saint of the second-class *nāth*s. But he maintained a close relationship with Jālandhara, his Guru, whom he rescued from inhumation.[125]

"The Black One," "The Dark One," are names referring to skin color, not to moral quality. They are epithets given to dark-skinned aboriginals (*adivasis*), or nick-names given to a yogin of any caste-origin with a dark complexion. Different languages and dialects produced different forms of the name: Kṛṣṇa, Kāṇhapa, Kāhnapa, Kāhnūpa, Kānupa, Kānapa, Kānipa, etc., all translated into Tibetan as Nag po pa. Compounded with *acārya* (*paṇḍita* or adept), Kṛṣṇācārya, Kṛṣṇācārin, Kṛṣṇācāri, may become just

Cāryapā; in Tibetan the Nag po spyod pa pa becomes simply sPyod pa pa. Since Tantra was a path that appealed to the outcaste tribals there must have been many Kṛṣṇas down the centuries. But apart from the *nāth* siddha mentioned above, we are concerned principally with the two Kṛṣṇācāryas of the tenth century who were probably Guru and disciple, and who are confounded in our legend. Jālandhara was the Guru of the Father, Son and *nāth* Kāṇhapas. The Father-Guru was an *ācārya*, and it is likely that this Kṛṣṇācārya was responsible for most of the hundred and fifty works under this name, or variants, found in the Tenjur. It is uncertain whether the Father or the Son composed and sung the *caryāpada* songs. The Son, who may have been the *nāth*, could have sung "I am a Kapāli free from aversion." But certainly the Son is associated with dance and small ritual drums known as *ḍamarus*. Tāranātha[126] tells the story of the Son practicing the *Saṃvara-tantra* at Nālandā being induced by a goddess to go to Kāmarūpa in Assam to gain the power of wealth (*vasu-siddhi*). In Kāmarūpa he found a chest containing an ornamented *ḍamaru*, and the moment he picked it up his feet left the ground in dance. Whenever he played loudly five hundred siddha yogins and yoginīs appeared and danced with him. This Kāṇhapa was an adept in the mother-tantra, and chronologically he was a contemporary of the *nāth* founders. But was there another mahāsiddha Kāṇha of this period? In Nepal a Lord Kṛṣṇa taught Dza-Hūm, and a brahmin Kṛṣṇa taught Marpa Dopa. A later Kṛṣṇa, also called Balin (Balinācārya), a disciple of Nāropa, taught the Tibetans the *Guhyasamāja-tantra*.

As Father and Son Kāṇhapa are confounded in the Tibetan lineages it is almost impossible to relate the many disciples to their respective Gurus. Mekhalā and Kanakhalā (*66* and *67*), Kantali (*69*), Bhadrapa (*24*), and Kapālapa (*72*) received Hevajra initiation from a Kāṇhapa. Kuśalibhadra and Vijayapāda with their contemporary Guhyapāda (Bhadrapa, who also received Kālacakra from a Kṛṣṇa,) were links in Kāṇhapa's Saṃvara lineage.[127] Bhandepa (*32*) received the Guhyasamāja. Mahipa and Dharmapa (*36* and *37*) were also Kāṇhapa's disciples; and Tilopa (*22*) received Lūipa's Saṃvara method from a Kāṇhapa. Carpaṭi (*64*) and Kapālapa (*72*) were affiliated with the *nāths*, but the most renowned disciples of the *nāth* Kāṇhapa were Gopicaṇḍ and Bhatṛnāth, who even Tāranātha acknowledges.[128]

18

THE MAHĀSIDDHA ĀRYADEVA (KARṆARIPA) THE ONE-EYED

All Buddhas past, present and future, have one essence;
Intuiting this essence you know your own mind's nature;
Let go, and relax into unstructured reality,
And with constant relaxation you are a yogin.

Āryadeva was miraculously born on the pollen-bed of a lotus-flower. As soon as he was of age he was ordained in the academy of Śrī Nālandā, and eventually he became the abbot there. He was then the preceptor of one thousand monks and the instructor of numerous scholars, but he had not realized his own perfect potential. In order to gain ultimate knowledge he resolved to find the Great Guru Nāgārjuna, whose extraordinary powers and virtue had inspired his profound respect.

He left Nālandā and set off for the South. On the way, on the banks of a broad lake, he met the Bodhisattva Mañjuśrī in the guise of a fisherman, and after bowing down to him and presenting offerings he asked him where Nāgārjuna could be found. The fisherman told him that the master was living in a nearby jungle, preparing an alchemical potion that vouchsafed immortality. Āryadeva followed his directions and discovered Nāgārjuna collecting the ingredients for his elixir. He prostrated before the master and begged for instruction. Nāgārjuna gave him initiation into the maṇḍala of Guhyasamāja, precepts to practice and permission to stay with him and practice his sādhana.

It became these two masters' habit to go to the town near their jungle hermitage to beg for food. Now while Nāgārjuna found great difficulty in begging anything at all, Āryadeva would return to the hermitage laden with all kinds of good things.

"You are being provided for by lustful women," Nāgārjuna told his disciple. "Your food is therefore unwholesome. In the future you will eat only what you can lift on the end of a pin. Enough of these feasts on banana-leaf dishes!"

Āryadeva obeyed his Guru, eating only the single grains of rice that he could lift with a pin. But the women of the town prepared barley-cakes covered with sweetmeat for him, so that he could eat well without breaking the prohibition. He took the cakes to his Guru, who ate them hungrily. When he reported how he had obtained them, he was ordered to remain in the hut in the jungle. Āryadeva obeyed, but this time a tree-nymph brought him delicacies, and she even neglected to cover up her resplendent naked form while she sat and talked. The food she gave him he took to his Guru, along with descriptions of the tree-nymph. Nāgārjuna went to the tree in which the nymph lived and called to her; the nymph appeared, showing her head, but modestly refusing to expose herself fully.

"Why do you show yourself to my disciple but not to me?" he asked her with chagrin.

"Your disciple is utterly free from passion," replied the nymph, "but in you there is still a trace of lust to be eradicated."

It was at this time that Nāgārjuna gave Āryadeva his name, Sublime God.

When Nāgārjuna's elixir of eternal youth was prepared, he anointed his tongue with a few drops and gave Āryadeva the bowl to do the same. Āryadeva threw the entire bowl against a tree, which immediately broke into leaf.

"If you waste my elixir like that," Nāgārjuna protested, "then you must replace it."

Āryadeva took a bucket of water, urinated into it, stirred it with a twig and gave it to his Guru.

"This is too much," said Nāgārjuna. His disciple splashed half the bucket's contents over another tree, which also came into bloom. Nāgārjuna then said, "Now you know that your realization is mature, do not stay in saṃsāra!"

At these words Āryadeva floated up into the sky in exaltation. But at that moment Āryadeva was approached by a woman who had been following him from place to place for some time. She prostrated before him, giving him honor and worship.

"What do you want, woman?" Āryadeva asked her. "Why have you been following me?"

"I need one of your eyes," the woman replied. "I have been following you because I must have one of your eyes."

Āryadeva plucked out his right eye and gave it to her. Thereafter he was known as Āryadeva the One-Eyed (Karṇaripa).

Āryadeva had followed the instructions of his Guru implicitly and the obscurations of his mind had been eradicated, so that merely by hearing his Guru say that he was liberated he was so, and he levitated to the height of seven palm trees. Thereafter, floating in the sky, he taught the Buddha's message to all beings, bringing their minds to maturity. Finally, turning himself upside down, showing the soles of his feet to the sky, he placed his palms together in adoration and prostrated to his Guru. As he reversed himself the gods showered flowers down upon him, and he vanished.

Sādhana

The thread running through this legend is a sense of Āryadeva's humility and modesty. "Lotus-born" Bodhisattvas are born enlightened and they need only go through the motions of learning, both mundane and spiritual, before they recognize their status as Buddhas. There seems to be no other point to the rather obscure anecdote concerning the distribution of Nāgārjuna's elixir than to demonstrate Āryadeva's enlightenment and his ignorance of this fact. The unawareness of his spiritual status, which Āryadeva showed even in Nālandā, is evidence of maturity on the path. "He who calls himself a Buddha is certainly an imperfect student," says Virūpa in one of his *dohās*. Āryadeva's stream of non-dual perception seems to have been free even of the occasional hiccough that allows an objective thought about oneself to slip in and undermine one's power. Insofar as evolution on the path implies a progressive loss of the ego identity that poses questions such as "Who am I?" and "Am I enlightened yet?" the initial diligent striving and fervent aspiration necessary to enter the path gradually dissolves and with it the notion that there is any such attainable state as "liberation," "enlightenment" and "Buddhahood." Thus Āryadeva needed a Guru to tell him that he had achieved all that there was to achieve, which is to say, the recognition of his original condition as nirvāṇa. The metaphysics of sādhana can be conceived as a sacred dream that derives its validity from the power to take the initiate out of his samsaric condition only to return him to his starting point free of all mental obscurations and emotional defilements.

Āryadeva's state of innocence and purity was an irresistible attraction to women. This must have arisen from his inability to conceive of women as external objects, particularly as sexual objects. Nāgārjuna, still not entirely free of lust, had spent twelve years propitiating female elementals; Āryadeva attracted female spirits to serve him without any effort whatsoever. His disinterest in the tree-nymph[129] induced her to display herself to him unsolicited. The woman who followed him may also have intuited Āryadeva's condition, but she wanted to exploit it. In another Tibetan account of this episode the woman was a *śaiva* tantrika who needed the eye for a reason similar to the brahmin's need for Nāgārjuna's head; she required the eye of a learned monk to complete the prerequisites for attainment of *siddhi.* She may have been a *kāpālika.*

Nāgārjuna's alchemical sādhana is called "the alchemy of mercury."[130] Nāgārjuna was one of the foremost *rasāyana* siddhas (see p. 120), and greatness in this yoga can be defined as the initiate's ability to apply the alchemical process at every level of his being. Thus in the alchemy of mercury, on the physical plane a material substance, a herbal or mineral panacea, is produced that will bestow immortality (or transmute base metal to gold, according to the alchemist's precepts). On the level of the subtle body, by a *haṭhayoga* technique analogous to the process of creating the actual alchemical substance, that is to say, through control of the psychic energies that correspond to the "mica" (*abhra*) in the "seed" of the divine woman, and control of the creative seed (*bodhicitta*) of the divine man, an immortal, subtle body is created that is capable of the sensual pleasure and mental abilities of the gross physical body. Finally, on the absolute level, "a body of light" identical to the *dharmakāya* is realized, and this is immortal in the sense that it is beyond creation and destruction and beyond birth and death. To attain this final level is to attain *mahāmudrā-siddhi.* To attain the immortal subtle body, as do the *nāth*s of the legends, is to attain mundane *siddhi* or magical powers. By such a crude delineation of the metaphysics of *rasāyana* it can be seen how the alchemy of mercury is compatible with other *siddha-yoga*s, such as the techniques of the creative and fulfillment processes of meditation.

Historiography

The two great Nāgārjunas each had a disciple called Āryadeva, but the Āryadevas are confounded inextricably just like the Nāgārjunas. These Gurus and disciples are referred to as Fathers and Sons. Both Āryadevas were their Gurus' principal lineage holder (although Nāgabodhi is a rival to the later Āryadeva); both were prolific writers, both elucidating the works of their masters. The early Āryadeva gained immortal fame by elaborating Nāgārjuna's metaphysics and applying its ramifications to the practice of the Bodhisattva; his best known treatise, the *Catuḥśataka*, explained for the first time how the Bodhisattva should act in the light of *madhyamika* insight. As to the eighth-ninth century Āryadeva, it is notable that he wrote nothing on *rasāyana*; it was the tenth century Nāgārjuna who was the *rasāyana-siddha*; the *Catuṣpīṭha-tantra* appears to have been his sphere of practice and commentary.

Tāranātha's following story of Āryadeva concerns the second century mahāyāna philosopher, but has added, tantric elements.[131] Āryadeva was born from a lotus in the pleasure garden of the King of Śrī Laṅkā. He abdicated after reaching the throne and took ordination. He completed study of the *Tripiṭaka*, and on pilgrimage to India he met Nāgārjuna and sat at his feet on Śrī Parvata Mountain (at Śrīśailam), receiving mahāyāna teaching besides *rasāyana* instruction, and he attained magical powers. After Nāgārjuna's death Āryadeva built many monasteries in the South. He remained there until he was called by a message attached to the neck of a crow that had emanated from the heart of a self-manifest image of Mahākāla at Nālandā, begging him to go North and defeat a brahmin tantrika called "The Evil One Difficult to Subdue". (According to Bu ston this brahmin was the great poet Mātṛceta—ca. AD 160—who composed many beautiful Buddhist verses after his conversion.) On the journey he was waylaid by a woman who required his eye for use in her sādhana. Then "with the help of a shameless layman, a cat, and a jar of black oil, he subdued a sister-*paṇḍita*, a parrot, and chalk of the brahmins. He encircled the place of contest with the brahmin with mantra, and tattered rags, etc., so that Mahādeva could not enter into the heart of his opponent." Āryadeva defeated this brahmin, arrested him and imprisoned him in a temple where in a *sūtra* he read a prediction of his own conversion and accordingly converted to Buddhism. Āryadeva then sang the oft-quoted stanza: "Śiva has three eyes but cannot see the truth; Indra has a thousand eyes but is spiritually blind; but Āryadeva, with only one eye, can see the true nature of the entire three realms of existence." Āryadeva's one eye is, of course, the third eye of non-dual awareness.

Āryadeva has one Guru, Nāgārjuna. His principal disciple, and his regent and lineage-holder, was a Rāhula whom he taught at Nālandā and in the South (see p. 255). Udhili, who he taught to fly by an alchemical method (see *71*), was also his disciple. Āryadeva, who lived in the late tenth century, is also known as Vairāgināth or Kaṇheri, which may be synonymous with Karṇari;[132] Vairāgi is also the name of a *nāth* siddha disciple of Gorakhnāth.[133]

19

THE SIDDHA THAGANAPA THE COMPULSIVE LIAR

Inject water into the ear
To release water in the ear;
Contemplate phenomena as a lie
And you see the truth.

Thaganapa was a low-caste liar born in Eastern India and his livelihood depended upon chance work and deception. One day while he was sitting upon a log devising ways of cheating people, a wise monk passed by.

"What are you doing here, fellow?" asked the monk.

"Please don't ask, venerable sir," Thaganapa replied.

But the monk did not need an answer to his question. "Do not tell lies," he said. "If you speak falsely, when your karma matures you will be reborn in hell. The more you lie the more you believe that lying speech is normal speech, and the more your habit of lying is reinforced: those are the propensities karmically conditioned by lying. The effects similar to the cause of lying are that your tongue is furrowed, your breath always stinks, and your speech is ineffectual and unconvincing. Furthermore, the general effect is that your karma makes your fields infertile and the seeds you sow dry and impotent."

Thaganapa had not heard the doctrine of karma applied to lying, and as soon as he heard it he became frightened. "I am called Thaganapa because I am a compulsive liar," he admitted. "I cannot speak so much as a hundredth part of a hair's breadth of truth. I lie to everybody without exception. What can I do?"

"Could you practice a sādhana?" asked the monk.

"I could try," said Thaganapa, doubtfully. "But I've been accustomed to lying for so long that it may not be possible for me to stop."

"There are even precepts for liars, you know," said the monk.

"Then please teach me them," said Thaganapa, relieved.

The monk considered Thaganapa's disposition, motivation and energy level, and decided to give him instruction in the yoga called "removing water in the ear by means of water." This meditation utilizes deception as an antidote to deception. He gave him the initiation which completely matures the immature mind-stream, and then taught him these precepts. "All elements of perceptual experience whatsoever are deceiving from the beginning. Since all that you see, all that you hear, all that you perceive with the six senses, indeed all that you experience, is deceiving, contemplate all things as a lie."

Ignorant of phenomena's delusiveness
You say you lie;
But if knowledge and the knower are deceptive
And the six sense-fields and sense objects deceive you,
Where can truth be found?
By holding deception to be truth
You suffer on the wheel of existence.
Children, ignorant of the universal lie,
Holding the false to be true,
You revolve constantly on the wheel of existence,
Which is like the rim of a water-wheel.
So contemplate all experience
As inherently deceptive:
See all form as inherently deceptive;
Hear all sound as inherently deceptive;
And finally, regard your belief in deception as a lie.

Thaganapa meditated for seven years upon perceptual knowledge as deception, gaining the understanding that all experience of phenomena is delusive fiction. Through this realization he gained perfect detachment. He went to his Guru thinking that he had attained the ultimate goal, but his Guru gave him further instruction. "The elements of experience can never be established as either deception or truth. Reality is uncreated and indeterminate. Meditate upon your experience of all things as emptiness rendered empty by its very nature."

Thaganapa obeyed his Guru and realized the emptiness of all

things. Then able to accept conflicting thoughts and feelings as the path, he gained *siddhi.* He became known everywhere as the Guru Thaganapa, and taught those with good karma the means of "releasing water in the ear by means of water." Finally, he rose into the Ḍākinī's Paradise.

Sādhana

Thaganapa's sādhana in the initial, creative phase is an excellent paradigm of the "like cures like" technique of tantric meditation. Releasing water in the ear by means of water[134] is analogous to detaching oneself from phenomena by visualizing the rope of experience as a snake. Detached, he saw phenomena as a dream, an hallucination, a fairy castle in the sky, the reflection of the moon in water, the image in a mirror, an echo, and so forth, achieving detachment's associated qualities of clarity, control and equanimity. His perception of phenomena as a distortion of reality unworthy of credence, as a lie, was modified in the second part of his practice, the fulfillment stage, so that he came to the understanding that reality was neither truth nor deception, neither this nor that, nothing that could be pinned down and labelled; it was *tathatā*, the ineffable immediacy of the here and now that is best described as emptiness. Completing this practice, even when passion and its accompanying greedy or bitter thoughts, for example, arose in his mind, phenomena would all be emptiness, and the question as to whether it was deceptive or true was irrelevant.

Contemplation of appearances as a lie is a highly efficacious technique using pre-conditioned reflexes to cut the clinging to, and identification with, phenomena. There are many examples of the like cures like method in later legends, most of them showing the siddha meditating upon the particular sensual sphere or object with which he is obsessed. Thaganapa's compulsion was in the mental sphere, and his initial practice would have been discursive, as it is not immediately apparent why "it's all a lie," why phenomena are deceptive. Phenomena are analyzed in terms of the six sense-fields, which consist of the eighteen elements of perception: the six sensory stimuli, the six sense organs and the six types of consciousness (ear, eye, nose, tongue, body and mental consciousnesses). The six sense-fields are the media through which the mind projects its preconceived images of phenomena, and so long as mind is "ignorant," its projections are delusive. Ignorance originally arises through a lack of mindfulness and attention, causing insecurity and fear, and alienation from phenomena and other people, that results in dualistic perception and the conceptualizing and labelling process that concretes such a reality. To the extent that the universe consists of labelled concepts, it is a lie; it is a fictional world distorted by the mind, and the conditioned conviction of our society that it is the only reality is an enormous hurdle on the path to an alternative, greater perspective. "Insanity," in part, is the dominance of subjective realities that have frightened unfortunate individuals who have been de-conditioned fortuitously; and western psychology's answer, particularly the Behaviorists' answer, to this kind of problem is to re-establish the delusory, objective reality. Given the correct guidance, a certain type of psychotic can be led through the *bardo* to a better rebirth, if not liberation.

Historiography

Thagana is derived from *sṭhaga*, "sly." Although this is an uncommon name we have no reason to identify our Thaganapa, who is probably the disciple of Ānandagarbha and the Guru of Ratnākaraśānti in Buddha Śrījñāna's Guhyasamāja lineage,[135] with the *brahmāṇa* ācārya Thagana, or Takkana of Oḍḍiyāṇa who wrote a *dohākośa* and other tantric works[136] and who taught the *prajñāpāramitā* to Karopa, the disciple of Maitripa.[137] Both the siddha and the *brahmāṇa* would have lived in the eleventh century.

20
THE MAHĀSIDDHA NĀROPA THE DAUNTLESS

Like the hosts of the Universal Emperor
Conquering the continents and islands,
The yogin who knows the taste of sahaja
Conquers saṃsāra, and pure pleasure reigns.

Nāropa was the offspring of a mixed-caste union. His father was a dealer in liquor in Paṭaliputra in the east of India, but Nāropa did not follow his father in the liquor business. He became a wood-gatherer, selling his wood in the market-place. He was not happy with this mode of life, and when he heard tell of the great sage Tilopa he decided to leave Paṭaliputra in search of him. He traded a load of wood for a deerskin and set out for Viṣṇunagar, to all appearances a yogin.

At Viṣṇunagar he was informed that Tilopa had recently left that city. Undaunted Nāropa began a search for his Guru that was to last many years. He wandered the length and breadth of India, asking everywhere for news of Tilopa. Finally, by pure coincidence, he met him on the road. Prostrating in the dust and circumambulating him, he addressed him as Guru, inquiring after his health.

"I am not your Guru and you are not my disciple," Tilopa stormed at him, and then he struck him angrily.

Nāropa's faith was unshaken. He went to beg food and brought it back for Tilopa. Tilopa ate it and then beat him again in anger. Nāropa's faith grew. Ignoring Tilopa's obvious displeasure he ate his Guru's trifling left-overs and circumambulated him again. He remained with him, begging food for him in the day and sleeping close by him at night. Twelve years passed in this way, Nāropa serving his Guru without complaint, although he never received a kind word.

Mahāpaṇḍita Nāropa found *siddhi* in learning.

One day Nāropa begged his food at a wedding feast. The host was most generous, giving the mendicant yogin eighty-four different types of curry, amongst which was a rare delicacy. He carried them back to Tilopa, who was delighted with the delicacy.

"Where did you find this, my son?" he asked. "Please bring some more."

Nāropa was as happy as a Bodhisattva on the first level of the path. "I have sat at my Guru's feet for twelve years without so much as a 'Who are you?' " he thought to himself, "and today he calls me his son." He was ecstatic. He returned to the wedding feast four more times to satisfy his Guru's desire for the delicacy, and each time it was given ungrudgingly. But returning a fifth time he thought, "I am ashamed to beg for the same curry again, yet if I do not I will incur my Guru's displeasure. I will steal it." So when the wedding guests were preoccupied, he stole a pot of the curry and walked off with it.

Tilopa was delighted with his disciple's perseverence, calling him "my diligent son." He then bestowed the initiation and blessing of Vajra Vārāhī upon him and instructed him in meditation.

It took Nāropa six months of practice to gain *mahāmudrā-siddhi.* Thereafter he became known throughout the world, and devotees came to worship him from the four quarters of the earth. The light that emanated from his body could be seen at a distance of one month's journey from his hermitage. After working tirelessly for countless disciples he rose bodily into the Ḍākinī's Paradise.

Sādhana

This synopsis of Nāropa's famous story hardly does the Guru justice. It is not that he is characterized as a mixed-caste son of a liquor dealer, a wood gatherer himself, and a man of little intellect, rather than the scion of a royal Bengali brahmin family, of staggering intellectual brilliance, Abbot of Nālandā; it is that after having stolen the curry at the wedding feast the narrator allows him to walk off with it to receive Tilopa's praise, rather than to be pursued by irate guests, roasted in an iron box, and beaten to an inch of his life. "Thrashed like rice and like sesame seed crushed," moaned Nāropa. "This twisted copper kettle of saṃsāra deserves to be smashed," replied his Guru.[138] In the wonderful biography of Nāropa, available in English, the seemingly well-balanced, wise and successful Abbot of Nālandā comes to a mid-life crisis, caused perhaps by the schizoid stress of continuous absorption in the mere academic theory of a non-dual philosophy wherein simple sensual perception is elevated to divine enjoyment, and a state of beatitude is reached through cessation of metaphysical objectification and logical discursiveness. Whatever the cause, a Ḍākinī messenger,[139] Tilopa's sister, appears to him in the guise of an old hag, and tells him that he knows not the meaning of what he reads, and that he must find his Guru. On the road, eleven more visions, mostly of a repulsive nature, gradually undermine Nāropa's conventional prejudices and humanistic values such as honesty, humanity and purity. His Guru is the embodiment of a mind quite free of conceptualization and conflicting thought,[140] and Nāropa can encounter him only when he is as Tilopa is. Even after their meeting, before he can obtain teaching he must suffer twelve further acts of self-denial, twelve acts like the story of his begging at the wedding party, with the death of Nāropa's ego indicated at its conclusion either by the final moral indignity of theft or by a physical beating to the point of death. Destruction of belief in an "I" is the aim of Nāropa's ascetic acts. For instance, in order to obtain instruction in eternal delight[141] Nāropa is ordered to find a girl, who he proceeds to live with for some time in health and fidelity, happiness and love. Later they drift apart, and Nāropa is left demeaning himself as a miserable smith, where Tilopa finds him. Then, in order to gain instruction in the sameness of the one flavor of the six modes of cognition,[142] Nāropa suffers his Guru's chastisement for living with a girl, and beats his penis in anguish. Before Nāropa can attain Mahāmudrā precepts, Tilopa demands the girl for himself and beats her for turning her back on him and smiling at Nāropa. "Bliss is to offer the *mudrā* as fee to the guru," said Nāropa. "You are worthy of bliss eternal, Nāropa," replies his Guru. Nāropa's sādhana is his life with his Guru; his twelve acts are real initiations, and success in practicing his precepts manifests after only six months. Tilopa disappears, finally, after giving Nāropa the most incisive precept in Mahāmudrā: "Do not imagine, think, deliberate, meditate, act, but be at rest. With an object be not concerned." Thereafter Nāropa passes through a period of apparent insanity, playing, laughing, weeping like a child, before settling down at Pulahari and teaching for the rest of his life.

Nāropa's most important precepts were his Six Yogas (the *Nāro chos drug*), precepts relating to six fulfillment yoga practices included amongst the twelve given in his biography. They are associated with Vajra Vārāhi, who was his principal yidam; Saṃvara and Hevajra were his other mother-tantra sādhanas. He also knew the *Guhyasamāja* and the *Kālacakra-tantras*. His importance to Marpa the Translator and to the Tibetan tradition has exaggerated his status in the Indian tradition.

After his ultimate attainment and his Guru's death, Nāropa initiated his consort, Niguma, who became his Awareness Ḍākinī. She translated many texts with Marpa, but is remembered primarily for her six fulfillment stage meditation techniques, similar to but different from Lakṣmīṅkarā's *Phag-mo gzhung-drug*. When she appeared to Khyungpo Naljorpa at *gaṇacakra* rites in Tibet, "she manifested her various aspects dancing, the skin dark, ornaments made of bone, holding in her hands a *khaṭvāṅga* and *kapāla*;" a frightening apparition of a Ḍākinī eater of human flesh.[143]

Historiography

Nāropa is associated with Kashmir where several reputable sources say he was born; with Pulahari (Puṣpahari),[144] his retreat hut quite close to Nālandā, where he taught Marpa; with Vikramaśīla, where undoubtedly he was "Northern Gatekeeper" contemporary with Śāntipa; perhaps he was also associated with Nālandā, where he may have been abbot;[145] and with Ratnagiri monastery near Bhubanesvar in Orissa.

Nāropa is a good example amongst the siddhas of a one-Guru siddha (but see *54* for identification of Kāla-pāda), although he may have had many "straight" teachers in Kashmir, Vikramaśīla and Nālandā. His disciples are many. Marpa The Translator is certainly the most significant, as the essence of Nāropa's sādhana was transmitted through him to Milarepa, Gampopa and a host of great Tibetan yogins. It is said that he consecrated Atīśa as Abbot of Vikramaśīla. He taught the *Saṃvara-tantra* to Śāntipa, the Nepali Phamtingpa and Vāgīśvāra-kīrti, the Kashmiri Bodhibhadra, and to Maitripa, Dharmamati, Manakaśrī, and Kṛṣṇācārya (Balinācārya). He taught Chiterpa and Paiṇḍapatika from Nepal, a mahāsiddha Ḍombipa, Kuśalipa and the Kashmiri Jñānakara. Marpa Dopa and other Tibetans also received instruction from him. His tantric commentary concerns Hevajra and Kālacakra primarily.

The root form of his name is Nāḍāpāda, and the root of it (*nāḍa*) means "roar".[146] He is also known as Naro and Naroṭapa. Finally, Nāropa's biography was written only one hundred years after his death, and it gives the siddha's dates as AD 1016–1100. Since such dates are much later than had been previously conjectured, Grunwedel giving AD 924–1039, for instance, they have been disputed. It is certainly not difficult to believe that he lived through the middle decades of the century; but no evidence is offered in the biography other than the bare statement to that effect.

21

THE SIDDHA ŚYALIPA THE JACKAL-YOGIN

Talented artists paint such terrifying pictures
That gazing at their work we grow afraid;
But look again, and besides the painted form
Unreal reflected image is all that we find.

Śyalipa was a low-caste laborer of Bighapur who lived close to the town's cremation ground. At night jackals would come to ferret amongst the ashes for bones, and their howling put the fear of the devil into the poor man. Night after night they howled, and his fear became an obsession. One day a monk came to his hovel to beg food, and he fell at the monk's feet in obeisance. Then he brought food and drink and spoke of the latest news. The monk was most appreciative and explained the rewards of generosity to him.

"Venerable sir, your discourse upon the benefits of generosity is quite wonderful," said the frightened man, finally. "But if you can, please be so generous as to teach me how to overcome fear."

"What are you frightened of?" asked the monk. "Is it the suffering of life, death and rebirth? What else is there to fear?"

"Fear of saṃsāra is universal," Śyalopa replied. "No, I have a specific fear. I have become terrified of the jackals that infest the cremation ground nearby. Please teach me how to destroy that fear."

"I have precepts and a mantra to help you," the monk told him. "But first you should take initiation."

Śyalipa offered what little gold and silver he had as the initiation price, and after bestowing an empowerment upon him the monk gave him instruction upon "the fear that destroys fear."

"As you fear only the jackals' howl, and you have no fear of enemies, meditate constantly upon all sound as identical to the jackals' howl. Build a hut in the cremation ground and live there with the jackals," the monk instructed.

Śyalipa obeyed, and gradually he came to realize all sound as the union of sound and emptiness. He lost his fear of the jackals' howling and experienced self-liberating terror as fearless pleasure. After nine years of meditation, the defilements of his body and mind had vanished, and he attained *mahāmudrā-siddhi.* Thereafter he wore a jackal skin to signify his attainment of the one flavor of all things, and he became known as The jackal-Yogin, Śyalipa. He taught his disciples many different practices concerning the indivisibility of appearances and emptiness, and finally he rose bodily into the Ḍākinī's Paradise.

Sādhana

Fear was the mind-poison confronting Śyalipa, and rather than run away from it, or apply an antidote such as music or love, he accepted the advice of the monk, his Guru, who advised him to abolish it by discovering its nature. Then in the process of conquering the little fear, he could overcome the chief fear in life, the suffering of birth, existence, death and rebirth. Meditating on his fear of the jackals' howl he eradicated the basic fear that arises in a split mind conceiving the ego and phenomena, self and others, the knower and the known, as alienated, discrete entities. Through a homeopathic tantric technique he destroyed his fear with fear.[147] First, like Thaganapa visualizing all phenomena as a lie, Śyalipa identified all sound as the jackals' howl, thus detaching himself from the specific cause of his fear and cultivating all sound as an echo-like illusion. When all mental interference is removed from the sensory perception of sound, then awareness of the subtle nuances of sound, of the meaning of modulated tone and pitch, of vibration outside the frequency of the ear, and of the entire rich and rewarding universe of sound, is heightened incredibly; just as Vīṇāpa mastered the *vīṇā* when he stopped thinking about it, Śyalipa was likewise rewarded as an auditor of speech and natural sound. But that was a by-product of his sādhana; the principal effect was that his terror became self-liberating in an experience of pure pleasure as he intuited the empty sound of silence in the jackals' howls and eventually in all sound. Intuiting the emptiness of sound in a fulfillment stage practice, uniting sound and emptiness, he became aware of the one "taste" of all sound. To unite sound and emptiness is to unite appearance and emptiness, thought and emptiness, and all things whatsoever with emptiness; if emptiness is perceived in one medium it is perceived simultaneously in all media. Thus Śyalipa attained *mahāmudrā-siddhi*.

In his song of realization Śyalipa uses the metaphor of a painting to show the foolishness of our fears. Examine the source of fear when moved to terror by a painting and what we find is mere shape and color; examine the origin of fear provoked by a terrible sound, and after removing the mental associations, preconceptions and accompanying emotional response, what remains is an empty echo of a particular timbre and pitch. Second, in the same way that the mind creates an horrific image out of the artist's clever manipulation of color and shape in two dimensions, the mind creates appearances out of an inchoate plentitude of energy and vibration. Finite time and spacial limitaiton are productions of the mind, and phenomena are formed as projections of their own limited conceptual images. Insofar as races, tribes and societies have developed differently, there are variations in their visions of the universe. The Tibetan reality, for instance, animistic and spiritualistic, where everything is conceived as a god or a demon in planes of spiritual extension from the mind, is quite different from our scientific, materialistic vision. When European man believed in a flat earth, for him the earth *was* flat; now that we believe in a global earth, the earth *is* round; when Einstein's theory of relativity is a popular notion, curved space will be as ordinary as baked beans; when we believe that phenomena conform to our concepts of them we will identify with the foundation of all things (*ālaya*) that is emptiness and clear light and watch all possibilities manifest as the Ḍākinī's dance, and time and space will have been conquered.

Historiography

Śyalipa is a corrupt form of Śṛgalapāda, from *śṛgala*, which means jackal (T.sPyan kyi pa). Other variations are Śalipa, Śiyalipa, Silāli, etc. Variations of spelling of his home town, Bighapur, are Vishasura, Bishasura, or Balhipur; this town is unidentified. Moreover, we know nothing of Śyalipa's Guru, his lineage or his deity.

22
THE MAHĀSIDDHA TILOPA
THE GREAT RENUNCIATE

The bird that settles on the face of Mt. Meru
Appears to be made of gold;
The sage who knows all as pure potential
Leaves the material world for Buddhafields of Bliss.

The great sage Tilopa was priest to the King of Viṣṇunagar. He received the princely sum of five hundred gold sovereigns each day for his offices and for teaching the Buddha's doctrines to his innumerable disciples. Yet he was very uneasy and distracted in his work. "My life is meaningless," he would think to himself. "Why continue here?" He tried to resign, but his resignation was refused, and his students always obstructed him, imploring him to remain. Finally he decided to escape. He changed his monastic robes for tattered rags, and left this note in his room: "I will never return. Do not attempt to follow me." Then he fled into the night.

Tilopa walked to Kāñcī and took up residence in the town's cremation ground. He lived there for some time, practicing his sādhana and begging food in the town. After he had met Nāropa on the road, his disciple begged for him and served him in whatever way he could. He continued to practice his sādhana, and after many years the defilements of his mind were eradicated, and he attained *mahāmudrā-siddhi*. In the paradise of the gods he ate sumptuously and was served with honor, and he gained *siddhi*s of Body, Speech and Mind. He became universally renowned as the yogin Tilopa, and setting innumerable beings on the path he worked selflessly for others. He rose into the Ḍākinī's Paradise.

Sādhana

Tilopa is an extremely enigmatic figure, as illusive as he is renowned in his lineage. Most of the knowledge we have of him is derived from Nāropa's legends, and to Nāropa he was abstract and insubstantial as the nature of his own mind. A *tabula rasa* to be defined according to our need, Tilopa appeared not to suffer fools lightly, to have cared nothing for either moral or social convention, and to have practiced what he preached uncompromisingly. Almost contemptuous of humanistic values, he seems to have demanded from his disciples an utterly unbiased and impartial mind, above all capable of the vision of indeterminate, ultimate reality. In his song of realization the key phrase that indicates the substance of such a vision is "pure potential,"[148] he sees all things as pure potential, and what begins as pure potential cannot become anything other than that, and this is experientially confirmed in the vision of all things as kinetic space, a ceaseless panorama of transforming illusion devoid of any substantiality whatsoever. Thus the material world becomes Buddhafields of Sukhāvatī, pure lands of pure pleasure, and the beings existing in this pure land, like the golden bird on the golden slopes of Mt. Meru (the protrusive *axis mundi*), naturally partake of the nature of space. To his lineage, Tilopa personifies a one-pointed, unswerving fidelity to that end and to the induction of others into that vision.

The nearest Nāropa comes to substantiating or humanizing his Guru is to describe Tilopa as "a dark man dressed in cotton trousers, his hair knotted in a tuft, and with protruding, blood-shot eyes."[149] The Tibetans like to depict Tilopa as a *yogin-siddha* with a hair-knot, carrying the fish that identifies him. The fish is the fish of spirituality (see p. 78); but more precisely, the fish of the *pañcamākara* in the *gaṇacakra* rite that symbolizes the senses and control thereof. Control implies complete detachment from the objects of the senses, and also, fundamentally, control of psychic energies. Although Nāropa took a long time to realize it, from the beginning his Guru was a state of mind, specifically non-discrimination, and in general a pure awareness of all phenomena and noumena. Thus in his remarks about his Guru, Nāropa tells us more about himself than the human being Tilopa. Nāropa was the pre-eminent disciple who was capable of visualizing his Guru as a metaphysical plane of experience, and Tilopa was the utterly selfless Guru who was able to demand that vision from a disciple. In its shortest and purest form, tantric sādhana demands a Buddha's responses from the disciple from the moment of his initiation, and it

Tilopa abides in the womb of enlightenment.

was this path that Tilopa forced Nāropa to follow. Thus Nāropa progresses along the path with occasional glorious glimpses of his Guru in his peak experiences, each glimpse followed by troughs of ignorance and despair—a pattern much more like lived experience than a gradual, slow but steady progress through the stages of the path. As Nāropa was Tilopa's only known disciple, and our only source of information about the Guru, it is clear why we know so little of him.

Historiography

Our uninformative legend does not mention how Tilopa was initiated; he certainly had no major siddha-Guru. In his *History*, Tāranātha does not mention Tilopa at all. The Tibetan lineages show that he took the *Guhyasamāja* initiation from Nāgārjuna's disciple Nāgabodhi; this must have been an initiation through vision. He received his *Saṃvara* initiations from Vijayapāda and/or Vinayapāda, and/or Vīṇāpāda, and from Kuśalapa. Bhadrapa gave him the *Hevajra* initiation. The mother-tantras were certainly Tilopa's path. The *Kālacakra-tantra* also came through Vijayapāda. But it has been suggested that Tilopa is Kālacakrapāda in the *Kālacakra-tantra* lineage;[150] this dubious proposition is based upon the arbitrary identification of Tilopa with Tsilupa (see p. 171). Could the pre-eminent renunciate Tilopa, who taught only one disciple and wrote nothing of great importance, have been the academic commentator with many disciples who was Kālacakrapāda Senior? It is only possible if Tilopa was a Nālandā *paṇḍita* before his renunciation.

A final deficiency in our Nāropa/Tilopa legends is the implication that Tilopa did not attain *mahāmudrā-siddhi* until the end of Nāropa's twelve year waiting sādhana. It is improbable that Tilopa's irascible treatment of his disciple was a defense against the importunate Nāropa begging precepts before his Guru had realized the meaning of his own sādhana. Certainly Nāropa's biography implies that Tilopa was a realized siddha at the start of Nāropa's quest.

If Nāropa lived AD 1016–1100, Tilopa would have been born during the second half of the tenth century, living through the first half of the eleventh. Nāropa's biography gives AD 1069 as the year of Tilopa's death. Others have claimed he died thirty years earlier. The variants of Tilopa's name—Tillopa, Tillipa, Tailopa, Telopa,

Tailikapāda and Tilopa—are derived from the word *til*, "sesame seed," and the Tibetans render his name as "The Oil Presser" or "Oil Seller" (sNum pa, Mar nag 'tshong mkhan, Til brdung mkhan), epithets that could describe his trade, but which might also refer to a metaphor for his yoga. Dhilipa (*62*) is the oil-pressing siddha. Lastly, the text's Bhigunagara, where Tilopa served the king, must be the Viṣṇunagar where Nāropa sought his Guru (*20*). Viṣṇunagar was a name on the map of the siddhas' India in contemporary southern W. Bengal.

23

THE SIDDHA CATRAPA
THE LUCKY BEGGAR

Whatever the yogin sees is his instruction,
And realization that all he sees is unborn
That is the most excellent Guru.
Innocence is the way to realize non-duality,
For here the effects of virtue and vice are one.

Catrapa, a simple *śūdra* beggar of Seṅdhonagar, always carried a volume of scripture in his hand while begging. One day a wise yogin took an interest in him and questioned him about his life. When the yogin asked him if he wanted to follow a path in his future lives, the beggar asked to be shown the way. He received the initiation and empowerment of the deity Hevajra together with these instructions:

Acknowledge every fault and misdoing,
And meditate upon pleasure unceasingly.
Regard your own body as the result of past action
And your future as the effect of your present state
of mind.
If you meditate constantly in this way
Signs of success will gradually appear
And you will gain Buddhahood in this lifetime.

Catrapa had difficulty in understanding this verse, so the yogin explained further: "Misdoing arises from lack of awareness, and from lack of awareness all kinds of confusion and mistakes arise. With the realization that all life and phenomena are Mahāmudrā, misdoing will no longer occur. Meditation on pleasure day and night is to view all things as a stream of compassion in which pleasure as the intrinsic nature of all experience arises spontaneously. If you are detached from the desires initiated by past, present and future action, your spontaneous activity will guide you to the ultimate goal. Since all pleasure and pain is caused by mental conditions, insofar as you are not now besieged by attachments, your present attitude is determining a happy future disposition. Constant meditation means a continuous, undistracted effort to attend to your mind. In this way mental delusion will be reduced and the goal of Buddhahood will be reached in this lifetime."

Catrapa stayed in Seṅdhonagar practicing his meditation, and after six years he attained *mahāmudrā-siddhi.* He became famous as the yogin Catrapa, and after seven hundred years he entered the Ḍākinī's Paradise.

Sādhana

Catrapa's practice began with the cathartic therapy of confession. Confession empties the mind of all guilt and brings to the surface, and exorcises, actions, words, thoughts and feelings that have conditioned the mind in perverse attitudes that perpetuate negative karma. But after confession has purified the mind, eradicating negative conditioning (the principal result of psychoanalysis), the function of bringing every action to the attention of an absolving awareness is the function of the meditation that is Catrapa's central sādhana. The precept "attend to the nature of your mind" sounds simple, but is actually the most difficult of practices. If achieved, the phenomena that are the mind's skillfully created means of perception[151] are a stream of compassionate emanation in an indivisible union with perfect insight into its emptiness,[152] and the feeling tone is pure pleasure. This cognitive non-duality is depicted iconographically as Hevajra in union with his Ḍākinī Nairātmā, into whose maṇḍala Catrapa was initiated. This union is experienced as Mahāmudrā and the powers of which the mind is capable at this moment are called *mahāmudrā-siddhi.*

With Mahāmudrā achieved there is no need of a human Guru; the non-dual awareness of all things as pure space provides inspiration and blessing, and whatever is perceived instructs the yogin on his course. Catrapa's song then explains that the innocence of a child is the path to non-dual realization, because the child lacks the moral conditioning that induces guilt, discrimination and prejudice. Catrapa is indicating a practice that can appear as craziness when the mind's conditioning is dissolving and compassionate spontaneity is being cultivated. The concepts of virtue and vice and the moral laws of cause and effect govern a conditioned mind structured to function effectively within society; past lives' karma has set seeds of passion and conceptualization that are best controlled by moral constraint and practice of virtue. Tantra introduces a more efficient way of handling passion and thought, and, further, puts the yogin in touch with the source of the Bodhisattva's aspiration. Innocence defined as the absence of moral, and all other conceptual, functions of the mind, is a characteristic of Mahāmudrā; thus, when like a child the yogin does not sin and has no perception of sin, cultivating innocence he induces the non-dual perception of Mahāmudrā.

Historiography

Catrapa, or properly Cattrapāda, means "The Yogin with the Book" (T. Chos khur nas blong), indicating that he must have continued his begging with his book of scripture during his practice. His town of Seṅdhonagar is probably on the River Indus (see p. 103).

24

THE SIDDHA BHADRAPA
THE EXCLUSIVE BRAHMIN

Knowing emptiness, deluded vision is purified;
Contemplating loving kindness, behavior is perfected;
Understanding the unity of multiplicity is meditation;
And the ultimate goal is the ubiquitous one taste.

In the country of Maṇidhara a brahmin lived in the lap of luxury with his many friends. Though he possessed untold wealth he had a constantly anxious mind. One day after his friends had gone to perform their ritual ablutions, leaving him alone in the house, a well-disciplined yogin appeared, begging for food.

"Unclean! Unclean! You defile my house!" shouted the brahmin angrily. "Get out of here before my friends return and see you. They will curse me for allowing you in."

"What do you mean, 'unclean?' " asked the *yogin*, quietly.

"Unwashed, unclothed, carrying a skull-bowl, eating polluted food and born of low caste," the brahmin retorted. "Now go quickly!"

The yogin did not move. "That is not unclean," he protested mildly. "Viciousness in body, speech and mind is uncleanliness. How can you remove the subtle defilements of your mind by your ritual bath? Only by bathing in the Guru's instruction, pure from the beginning, can you become truly pure." And he sang these lines:

Bodhisattvas are the highest beings,
Not priests or kings.
The precepts of the lineal Guru,
Cleansing body, speech and mind,
Alone gives the real, matchless purity;

Washing the body can never do that.
Desirelessness is the best table and repast,
Not milk, cheese and curd.

The brahmin was impressed, and gaining confidence in the yogin he asked for further instruction.

"Give me food and I will teach you," the yogin offered.

"You cannot stay here," said the brahmin, suddenly frightened again. "My friends and household have no faith. I will come to your house and listen to you there."

"I live in the cremation ground," the yogin told him. "Bring liquor and pork with you when you come."

"How can I do that?" the brahmin objected. "We brahmins are forbidden even to speak those words."

"If you want instruction, do as I say," the yogin insisted.

"But I can't come during the day or people will see me. I'll come at night," he compromised.

After the yogin had left, the brahmin disguised himself and went to the market-place to buy liquor and pork. When night fell he made his way to the cremation ground, and finding the yogin he served him meat and drink, taking the portion he was given. Then his Guru initiated him with a transfer of grace, and he offered the Guru a maṇḍala of thanksgiving. As instruction, in order to break his pride of caste, and as a symbolic demonstration of correct vision, he was ordered to sweep the yogin's latrine; as a symbolic demonstration of correct action he was told to plaster the yogin's hut; and the color of the lime was the symbolic object of correct meditation. Finally, to symbolize the goal, his Guru explained the attainment of vision, meditation and action as one.

The brahmin realized the meaning of these symbols and recognized phenomena and existence as delusory figments of mind. He forsook his caste with its prejudices and became a yogin, and after six years of meditation he achieved *mahāmudrā-siddhi* and became renowned as the yogin Bhadrapa. He spent the rest of his life working selflessly for others, and eventually he attained the Ḍākinī's Paradise with five hundred disciples.

Sādhana

Many of the legends touch upon the exclusivity of the brahmins and their rigid, ritual practices and narrow beliefs. Here, the full significance of the brahmins' bigotry is brought home. The source of their intolerance lies in their notions of ritual purity: no outcaste's shadow shall fall upon God's ordained priests; a brahmin's food must be prepared by a brahmin; a menstruating woman, liquor, pork and beef, of course, destroy the brahmin's purity. However, uncleanliness incurred lightly can be purified with ease; a bath in a sacred river washes away all ritual impurity, besides personal sin and misdoing. A bath in Mother Gangā, India's holy river, guarantees rebirth in Śiva's paradise—Śvārga. The notion of ritual impurity is as old as Aryan India. As a system of occupation-related clans outside of which a man could not marry, the caste system probably existed before the white Aryan tribes arrived in India, but the Aryans imposed a race-based class system upon the already existing hierarchy. Their fourfold apartheid was described by color (*varṇa* or caste literally means "color")—white Aryans, brown Dravidians and black tribals (*adivasis*). The racial bigotry of the caste system was opposed by the Buddha himself on the grounds that all equally possess the Buddha-nature, and the siddhas made ritual equality a central issue in their beliefs, not only because so many of them were outcastes and subject to prejudice, but also on compassionate grounds. Thus, although the siddhas were not social activists, their compassion was manifest in personal communication and an insistence that their initiates forsook all notions of caste. Herein "caste" is used as a symbol of all prejudice and preconception[153] and karmic proclivity.[154] The brahmin abandoning his "caste" is ridding his mind of all conceptual obstacles to Buddhahood, and a very painful sādhana it must have been, although that aspect is not stressed in Bhadrapa's legend. With a little imagination the bare bones of Bhadrapa's relation with his Guru can be fleshed out to present a picture of wretched humiliation and mortification of the proud brahmin (see also Ḍeṅgipa *31*). Hypersensitively and hypocritically concerned with the opinions of his peers, he was forced to clean away excrement just like the Living Buddhas (tulkus) and theocrats "re-educated" by the Red Guards in Tibet in the 1960s. A common, skillful device of the tantric Guru bent on enlightening his disciple on the "fast" path, is to concentrate upon the disciple's weaknesses, often publicly highlighting them, until the disciple's emotional attachments are destroyed. Since a blinding negative emotional response in the disciple is virtually inevitable, a very profound faith cemented by the commitments of initiation are essential.

The structure of Bhadrapa's precepts accords with the four aspects of Mahāmudrā doctrine:[155] vision, meditation, action and goal. Although simple, concise, discursive precepts can be given under these heads with decisive results, Bhadrapa's Guru gives him precepts as symbols. The meaning of the first is self-evident; the second, the plastering of the yogin's hut, symbolic of the Bodhisattva-siddha's action, gains its significance from the brahmin's ritual scruples and from his aversion to the low-caste laborer's job of mixing plaster from excrement and mud and painting it with lime. The third, the color white, is symbolic of the sameness of all things, ubiquitous in the same way that color is inherent in paint. Lastly, vision, meditation and action are one in the omnipresent, all-embracing foundation of the universe[156] that is emptiness.

Historiography

From the Tibetan *Saṃvara* and *Kālacakra* initiation lineages,[157] we learn that Bhadrapa is the disciple of Kāṇhapa[158] and the Guru of Vijayapāda, Vinayapāda and Vīṇāpāda (although these three near homophones suggest error in a Tibetan scribe or block-carver's work). This identification would place Bhadrapa in the tenth century. But Śavaripa also had a disciple named Bhadrapa,[159] and there is record of a Bhāvabhadrapa of Vikramaśīla who wrote a commentary upon the *Hevajra-tantra* (the *tantra* of our legend's Bhadrapa) during King Dharmapāla's reign,[160] and who would have been a contemporary of Śavaripa, which would place him in the latter eighth and early ninth centuries. *Bhadra* (T. bZang po) means "good" or "auspicious," and often forms the second part of a compound name as in Bhavabhadrapa, Kuśalibhadra, Dipaṅkarabhadra, Śākyaśrībhadra and Buddhaśrībhadra, and as Ratnākaraśānti is contracted to Śāntipa, Kṛṣṇācārya to Cāryapa, so compound names with *-bhadra* are reduced to Bhadrapa; thus there is much room for misidentification.

25
THE SIDDHA DUKHAṄDHI THE SCAVENGER

Uniting the relative, creative process
With the ultimate, fulfillment mode,
The result of my Mahāmudrā meditation
Arose as pure awareness of the Buddha's Three Bodies.

In the city of Gandhapur there lived a scavenger of rags, a sweeper by caste, called Dukhaṅdhi. He gained his livelihood by scavenging pieces of cloth and patching them together to make passable garments. One day he met an accomplished yogin, who pointed out to him the fatuity of his almost inhuman existence, suggesting that it would be more profitable for him to practice a tantric Buddhist sādhana. The scavenger was doubtful that anyone would teach him, but the yogin immediately offered to give him initiation and instruction.

So it was that Dukhaṅdhi received the initiation and empowerment of the deity Saṃvara and instruction in the unity of creative and fulfillment meditation. He attempted to meditate in the conventional manner, but he was hindered by his preoccupation with stitching rags. He returned to his Guru and told him that his mind was full of thought, and that he found it impossible to visualize the deity or concentrate upon recitation of the mantra. The yogin gave him instruction in the transformation of mental activity into the path itself.

The intrinsic nature of all things is infinite space
So in reality there are no stitches and no stitching.
The intrinsic nature of deity and mantra is TATHATĀ;
Realize deity, mantra, and all thought forms, as
infinite space.

Dukhaṅdhi followed these instructions, and gradually his thoughts of stitches and stitching, together with the deity and the mantra, dissolved into the space that is the nature of all things. Thereby he understood the meaning of uniting creative and fulfillment modes of meditation. After twelve years he gained *mahāmudrā-siddhi*, and he served untold beings before attaining the Ḍākinī's Paradise.

Sādhana

This Dukhaṅdhi, born into the most unfortunate body a human being could possess, has a remarkable name meaning "He who makes two into one" (Dvikhaṅdi, T.gNyis gcig tu byed pa), or "He who unites duality." His legend and song clarify several vital concepts in the technique of Mahāmudrā meditation. The duality he unites is expressed as the creative and fulfillment processes of meditation,[161] the former being the clearly perceived forms of phenomena, the relative world, and the latter being the ultimate, reality of emptiness or such-ness (*tathatā*). The thought of his work[162] is given the same ontological status as his visualization of the deity and recitation of the mantra in the instruction called "transforming mental activity into the path itself."[163] Meditating upon the intrinsic nature of deity (body), mantra (speech) and thought (mind) the relative and the absolute are united, or their union is focused in awareness since they have never been divided in reality.

"Thought of stitches and stitching" can also be interpreted as thought about the technique and practice of one's meditation, which is one of the meditator's major obstacles. He can become as preoccupied in pondering the metaphysical theory of his meditation, the degree of his progress and the nature of the result, as in his meditation itself. It is then that the precepts on transforming thought into the path are so valuable. Such precepts are what gives tantric meditation its reputation as a "fast" and "direct" method, for every obstruction becomes an ally on the path.

In these epitomes of the siddhas' sādhanas, obviously much detail is omitted. Dukhaṅdhi's meditation took twelve years to evolve. The principles of his meditation are very clearly described, but detailed practical instruction is lacking. For instance: in order to meditate upon the intrinsic nature of deity and mantra, the deity, perfectly visualized, must have become the realm of the Buddha's apparitional form; and mantra, recited with perfect concentration, must have become a constant stream of sound. With the deity a living symbol of apparitional being (*nirmāṇakāya*), and mantra the epitome of the entire spectrum of vibration, they become objects of meditation, which the elusive, patchy, beginner's visualization, and the mantric stream only intermittently attended to, can never be. But there is no instruction upon perfecting visualization and mantra.

The result of this meditation is expressed both as the dissolution of all things into infinite space and attainment of the Buddha's three modes of being, which are apparitional being, instructive visionary being, and absolute empty being. These three are the "subjective" equivalents of the "objective" deity, mantra and thought: deity is the apparitional form of Buddha's compassion; mantra or vibration is the medium of enjoyable visionary instruction; and all thought is non-dual empty awareness with a feeling-tone of pure pleasure.

Historiography

The variants of Dukhaṅdhi's name are Dokhaṅdi, Debanta, Dhosanti, Dvakanti, Khaṅdhipa (but see Kantali, *69*) and also the Tibetan rDo khan do. Gandhapur is unidentified, as is Dukhaṅdhi's Guru and lineage.

26

THE SIDDHA AJOGI
THE REJECTED WASTREL

Following my Holy Guru's injunction,
I visualized a zero-point on my nose-tip;
With my mind fixated upon that sphere
The worlds within worlds within it dissolved.

In the great city of Paṭaliputra a wealthy householder was blessed with a son. But this son was a mixed blessing. As he grew up he became so fat that he was unable to walk, eat, defecate or sit up by himself. His parents and family were helpless, for neither encouragement nor threat was of any avail, and finally, thoroughly abusing him, they carried him down to the cremation ground and abandoned him. He had not been there long before a yogin noticed his abject condition, took pity on him, and brought him food. But the boy was unable to sit up to put it in his mouth.

"If you can't get up to eat, how can you possibly do anything at all?" the yogin said.

"I'm completely useless," whined the lad. "That is why my parents left me here to die."

"I wonder if you could practice a sādhana lying down like that," pondered the yogin.

"I think I could," said the boy. "But who would teach someone like me?"

The yogin offered to instruct him. He initiated the wastrel into the maṇḍala of Hevajra and instructed him in a profound fulfillment process of meditation. "Visualize a sphere no larger than a mustard seed on the tip of your nose, your "upper door," and then visualize a hundred million worlds within that seed," the yogin taught him.

"What signs will occur?" asked the boy.

"Meditate as I have instructed you, and you'll find out soon enough," the yogin replied.

The boy meditated, and the hundred million worlds within worlds together with the seed dissolved into a sphere of emptiness, and realization of the emptiness of Mahāmudrā arose in his every moment of experience. After nine years he obtained *mahāmudrā-siddhi* and became famous as the yogin Ajogi, The Wastrel. Then working selflessly for others eventually he attained the Ḍākinī's Paradise.

Sādhana

Ajogi is the ultimate example of the despised and rejected, freakish yogin. Physically and mentally incapacitated, with nothing to do but practice the simplest of yogas lying on his back, nevertheless he became a siddha. The possibilities of transferring such tantric practices into contemporary hospitals and asylums are immense and exciting; modifying the language and application to suit the situation, the least effect of such rehabilitation therapy would be to destroy inertia and enlarge mental capacity, with the possible result of inducing *mahāmudrā-siddhi*. What is lacking in the western asylum environment, however, is aspiration and stimulus to practice. Ajogi was provoked to act by his need for the food and affection provided by his Guru, and by the fear of death as he lay in the cremation ground.

There is no fulfillment meditation technique more simple than that taught to Ajogi. The hundred million worlds within the mustard seed consist of the three successive dimensions of increasingly diminutive microcosmic universes, analogous to the atomic and sub-atomic worlds.[164] A moment's attempt to visualize this mustard seed and its contents will demonstrate the effectiveness of this method of dissolving thought into emptiness. It has an effect similar to imagining non-existence. This technique also demonstrates the principle that once emptiness has been established in any one corner of the mind it becomes constant in the entire mind-stream. The nose as the "upper door"[165] is the entrance to the two psychic channels that join the main right and left channels (*lalanā* and *rasanā*, sun and moon,) between the throat and head *cakras*. Thus the "zero-point" (*bindu*) on the nose-tip represents a union of the right and left channels, as does the central channel, the *avadhūti*, itself.

Historiography

Ajogi (or Ajoki, Adzoki, etc.) is derived from the Sanskrit Āyogipāda (T.Le lo can), "He who makes no effort," "The Lazy Yogin".

27

THE SIDDHA KĀLAPA
THE HANDSOME MADMAN

These people are deluded from the first,
And yet it is such fools that call me mad.
The ambrosial nectar of the Guru's precepts
Instantly cures the disease of delusion.

Kālapa was extraordinarily handsome. Practice of patience and meditation in a previous life had endowed him with a fine body and very attractive features, indeed, so much so that the people of Rājapur, his home town, would stop in the street and stare at him. He became increasingly irritated with this treatment, and decided to renounce the world and go to live in a cremation ground. Soon after he had settled down in his new environment, he began talking with a yogin who sympathized with his predicament and offered to instruct him in a sādhana. He received the Saṃvara initiation and was instructed to meditate upon the meaning of creative and fulfillment meditation. When he realized the co-incidence of these two aspects of meditation experience, he found that he had lost the delusion of any distinction between himself and others. The result of this was a profound effusion of uninhibited action as he expressed his feelings and inclinations without embarrassment.

"Here's another mad saint!" said the people of Rājapur.

But the divine madman sang:

It is only belief in oneself as an island
That creates the delusion of others apart,
And this split is the cause of anxiety.
The wise man who would be free of his suffering
Visualizes his thoughts as a retinue of gods
That vanish into the basic letter A:

Like a rainbow dissolving into the sky.
Birth, life and death have no hold on this madman:
His powerful effusion of uninhibited action is pleasure;
His realization of unimpeded clarity is pleasure;
His meditation on the unobstructed sense-fields is pleasure;
And his goal attained without effort is pleasure.

He levitated to the height of seven palm trees and demonstrated control of the elements in various other ways. Thereafter he became famous as the yogin Kālapa, and ultimately he reached the Ḍākinī's Paradise.

Sādhana

The meaning of creative and fulfillment meditations, in short, is to create a vision of phenomenal appearances that is quite free of mental interferences such as preconception, prejudice, interpretation, dualistic conception, so that the yogin in his environment becomes a god in his heaven; then all experience is fulfilled by penetrating the illusion of appearances to realize the nature of all things as emptiness, and thereby the yogin is released from the wheel of existence. When appearances are understood as a function of mind, all things can be reduced to thought, and thought to "a retinue of gods." The basic letter A: is defined linguistically as the explosive opening of the glottis necessary to allow air to pass through to the vocal chords so that sound can issue, and in that way it is the sound inherent in all sounds. Thus, symbolically, it represents the sound of silence, the unborn sound,[166] and the emptiness into which thought as deities can dissolve. The people of Rājapur, without experience of the doors of perception thrown open, of reality experienced directly, unfiltered by the conditioned mind, called Kālapa's uninhibited action "madness." His thought-free samādhi (*nirvikalpa-samādhi*), the non-dual samādhi that had destroyed the delusion of alienation between himself and people and phenomena, unleashed an effusion of spontaneous action unhindered by any moral constraint, social convention or notion of personal advancement. Such a deep-felt response to human suffering, total empathy in fact, is a Buddha's responsiveness; it is free of all the egoistic motivation that generally distorts communication. Madness from a conventional, social viewpoint can be the utmost sanity in the eyes of a Buddha.

The social situation that drove Kālapa to the cremation ground effects women far more than men in our society, producing neurosis and sometimes psychosis. Like Kālapa, attractive women are viewed as objects of sexual desire, or at least as esthetic feasts for the senses, and they become painfully alienated from people. A certain kind of woman can manipulate the situation to her own advantage, gaining power over her fascinated admirers, but at the cost of all empathy. Other women are hypersensitive to "objectification," and, feeling insulted, become aggressive; others retreat into themselves and pretend, sometimes successfully, to ignore the attention. Either way is painful, creating anxiety that leads to neurosis of the various types found amongst emotionally-involved feminists. Kālapa's initial reaction was a disgusted retreat from society, followed by physical renunciation of the society from which he felt divided. The ambrosial nectar of the Guru's precepts was the cure of his neurosis.

Historiography

Nothing in this legend but the name suggests the identification of Kālapa with Kālacakrapāda (Kāla-pāda). But since Kāla-pāda is one of the great siddhas, scholars have assumed that he is counted amongst the eighty-four and that Kālapa is he. Kāla-pāda Senior is identified with Celuka (Tsi lu pa, *54*); Celuka's principal disciple, Piṇḍopa, or Piṇḍa Ācārya, was called Kāla-pāda Junior, and it is the latter who is identified with our Kālapa.[167] These siddhas belong to the transmission lineages of the *Kālacakra-tantra*. Celuka taught Piṇḍopa at Pulahari, so some pundits have presumed to identify Kāla-pada Junior with Nāropa.[168] Piṇḍopa is said to have memorized the *Kālacakra-tantra* after hearing it only once. This great faculty of memory was obtained in a strange way. In his past life he was dim-witted, and he performed a sādhana to improve his intellect. A *deva* appeared to him in a dream, instructing him to sculpt a statue of Kurukullā Ḍākinī out of coral, to insert it in the mouth of a dead woman's corpse, and to meditate sitting upon the corpse. He meditated for seven years according to this instruction, and then the woman gazed up at him and asked him what he wanted. Instead of asking her for the ability to remember everything he read, he asked her for memory of everything he wrote. Thus he became Piṇḍo Ācārya, a *paṇḍita*.[169] He was also known as Vāgīśvārakīrti, and a siddha of that name was Southern Doorkeeper at Vikramaśīla during this period. His principal disciples were Mahāpuñya (T. bSod rnams pa chen po) who taught the Tibetans, Samantaśrībhadra, Mañjukīrti and the Kashmiri Somanāth.

However, even the identification of Kāla-pāda Junior with Piṇḍopa is disputable. The Tibetan translators Rwa-lo and 'Bro received the *Kālacakra-tantra* a generation after the transmission of Kāla-pāda Father and Son; the Rwa-lo tradition, followed by 'Gos Lotsawa, favors the above lineage: Celuka, Piṇḍopa, Mahāpuñya. But the 'Bro tradition reverses Celuka and Piṇḍopa, calling Piṇḍopa the Kāla-pāda Senior who went to Śambhala to obtain the *Kālacakra-tantra*. As a further complication, Bu ston identifies Kāla-pāda Junior as Bodhibhadra, otherwise known as Nālendrāpa,[170] the disciple of both Celuka and Piṇḍopa, and also of Nāropa; he could also have been Upāṣaka Bodhi (see p. 282). To summarize: in the latter half of the eleventh century and early twelfth, there were at least five great masters of the *Kālacakra-tantra* in Eastern India, particularly at Nālandā: Celuka, Piṇḍopa, Bodhibhadra, Somanāth and Mahāpuñya. Two of these were known as Kāla-pāda Father and Son, Senior and Junior, and they were responsible for establishing the *Kālacakra-tantra* lineage that was transmitted to Tibet.

Kālapa is reckoned as the last of the eighty-four siddhas. If Celuka lived well into the twelfth century it is reasonable to expect that his son out-lived him and it is conceivable that Kāla-pāda Junior saw the downfall of the Sena Empire when the Senas succeeded the Pālas in the year AD 1162.

28
THE SIDDHA DHOBĪPA
THE WISE WASHERMAN

From time immemorial I have washed out stains,
But I cannot make charcoal white.
The Guru's precepts are the supreme dhobī,
For they cleanse our immaculate empty nature.

In the kingdom of Paṭaliputra there lived a family of washermen—*dhobīs*. One day when the young *dhobī* was engaged in his work, a yogin approached him for alms, which the *dhobī* gave unstintingly, at the same time asking him if he needed anything washed. The yogin held out a piece of charcoal.

"Can you take the stain out of this?" he asked.

"I cannot make a piece of black charcoal white," the *dhobī* replied.

"You are right," the yogin agreed, "and by the same token you cannot erase the stains of the three internal poisons by a superficial washing. I possess the supreme secret by which you need only wash once, avoiding forever this endless cycle of cleaning. I am offering to give it to you."

The *dhobī* entreated him to confide his secret. His Guru gave him first the Saṃvara initiation and empowerment, and then the gift of mudrā, mantra and samādhi. The *dhobī* practiced his instructions for twelve years, removing the impurity of his body by mudrā, the impurity of his speech by mantra and the impurity of his mind by samādhi. These were the essential instructions that the yogin gave him:

The water of the fire mudrā erases the stains of the body;
The water of the vowels and consonants erases impurity
of speech;

The union of father and mother deities erases the obscurations of mind.

The *dhobī* meditated upon his body as mudrā, his speech as mantra, and his mind as the union of creative and fulfillment processes of meditation, and the impurities of his body, speech and mind were eradicated, and he gained *mahāmudrā-siddhi.* After that the clothes that he was given to wash were spontaneously cleaned with no exertion on his part whatsoever. When the people saw this they realized that their *dhobī* had gained the powers of the Buddha, and he became renowned as the yogin Dhobīpa. He worked selflessly for all mankind and attained the Ḍākinī's Paradise in his very body.

Sādhana

The stress on cleanliness and purity in many legends may appear contrived unless the Hindu obsession with ritual purity is recalled. The twice daily *snān*, the ritual bath, and successive changes of clothes, are accepted routines of life for the twice-born. Thus Bhadrapa, the brahmin, was left alone to talk about the real nature of cleanliness while his friends went to bathe; and here the *dhobī*s work is washing clothes, and the yogin's secret is the ultimate bath, a cleansing in the water of immortality that makes the ritual convention, the relative or symbolic truth, dispensable. The Guru's three secrets are no hidden precepts; they are the principal means of purification and propitiation, the means of transforming saṃsāra into nirvāṇa. Mudrā, mantra, and samādhi, can be considered as physical, auditory and mental pegs upon which to hang aids to awareness along the path; first aids to concentration (*śamatha*), then to heighten vision (*vipaśyanā*), and finally to ultimate insight into reality (*prajñā*). But the different forms of hand gesture and posture, innumerable variations of mantra, and the many deities in union, yab-yum, give the Tantra its great facility to satisfy all psychological types. Initially the aim is the same—to attain the center of the maṇḍala, and with it release from all attachments, and erasure of all karmic stains; but, thereafter, manifestation of compassion as any facet of the whole gamut of human potential is the tantric Bodhisattva's function, each shade of feeling and meaning wrapped up in a mudrā, mantra and samādhi, so that its attainment can be expedited by magic.

The fire mudrā is a single gesture of the right hand; the vowels and consonants of mantra are represented by female and male deities respectively, each with a purificatory function. Such a bald statement as "the union of father and mother deities" is open to prurient misinterpretation, although the synonymous phrase "the union of creative and fulfillment modes of meditation" leaves little room for the left-handed tantrika's interpretation. Dhobīpa's interpretation avoided even visualization of Cakrasaṃvara and Vajra Vārāhī in union.

Historiography

Dhobīpa is sometimes confused with Ḍombipa due to corruption of his name; Dhombhipa and Dhombipa are further variants. The text has Saliputra for Paṭaliputra. We have no further information concerning Dhobīpa, the eternal washerman.

29

THE SIDDHA KAṄKAṆA
THE SIDDHA-KING

The wish-fulfilling gem of realization
Emanating the radiance of peak experience
Provides all wants through its magical activity.
He who knows the one taste is totally fulfilled.

The King of Viṣṇunagar ruled a prosperous kingdom, enjoying the fat of the land, indulging his every whim. One day a yogin came to him begging alms, and the king magnanimously offered him food and cake, and he received some unsolicited advice in return.

"King and kingdom are hollow words," said the beggar-yogin. "It matters not at all what your temporal state may be, since every living being is born into the same suffering, and birth follows birth in an endless cycle like a treadmill. There are innumerable forms of suffering, enough to fill an aeon of rebirths; even the seeming happiness of the gods in paradise is suffering when they learn that they too must soon die. If the Universal Emperor himself must eventually fall into an inferior state, what of you? Leave your illusory pleasures, those brief joys that are like the morning dew, and practice a sādhana."

"That's all very well," responded the king, "but can you imagine me begging alms and wearing rags? If I could practice a sādhana without abandoning my pleasures I would do so."

"To renounce all this and live like me would definitely be the best decision," insisted the yogin.

"Even the thought of skull-cups, rags and left-over food sickens me," said the king, turning away his head in disgust.

"If you don't change your attitude, your pride and abuse of power will lead you to a low rebirth," the yogin warned. "I have gained inexhaustible pleasure from living the way that I do, for we are both kings in our different ways. However, I do possess secret precepts that you can practice without need to renounce your way of life."

"Then I promise to practice them, if you would be so kind as to give them to me," vowed the king.

The yogin gave him this instruction: "You must mentally relinquish your pride in, and attachment to, the great stone in the bracelet on your wrist; then visualize the light of the jewel and your desireless mind as one."

Gaze into the light of your bracelet's jewel
And see the delight in the nature of your mind:
From your clothes and ornaments and the room
about you
Many colors are reflected in the jewel,
But the jewel's nature is immutable.
From the endless diversity of phenomenal appearances
Many thought-forms arise in your mind,
And the mind itself is like a blazing jewel.

The king concentrated on the jewel in the bracelet on his right hand, and he gained initiation into the real nature of his mind by insight into the sensual pleasure of his gaze. He gained *siddhi* after only six months. One day his servants peered into his chamber through a crack in the door and saw their master sitting on his throne surrounded by innumerable goddesses. Later his household approached him and begged him to tell them the secret of his power. He taught them in this way:

Realization of mind's nature is the king
And pure pleasure is the kingdom;
The king in his kingdom is perfect consummation.
Practice this sādhana if you would be kings.

The king became known as Kaṅkaṇapāda, The venerable Yogin of the Bracelet. Five hundred years later Kaṅkaṇa, his court and the people of Viṣṇunagar bodily attained the Ḍākinī's Paradise.

Sādhana

This king had the sort of karma that is the result of innumerable successive lives of increasing virtue and awareness. When adversity arose he retained equanimity and balance and communicated with love and understanding; when easy times returned he accepted his good fortune without pride of accomplishment or greed for more, sharing with modesty. Comprehending the efficacy of virtues like moral conduct and patience, and realizing the pain accompanying vices such as lying and cursing, his wealth of merit must have increased until his balance in the karmic bank was a monk's dream. His karmic fruit were ripe to the touch, and when the yogin appeared at his door time was for plucking. Merely six months of practice of combined creative and fulfillment meditation upon sensual pleasure gave him *mahāmudrā-siddhi* and total fulfillment. Now he possessed the wish-fulfilling gem of mind,[171] and there would never again be any question of pleasure and pain, right and wrong, profit and loss. Everything that arose would be the manifestation of a Buddha in a Buddhafield. Kaṅkaṇa's story is too good to be true. (See *2* for comparison.)

Historiography

Kaṅkaṇa, derived from Kaṅkaṇapāda (T. gDu bu can), has been corrupted into Kakani and Kikipa. We have no other record of him unless he was Prince Meghavedin of Koṅkaṇa, the teacher of 'Gos Lhas btsas in the lineage of Vajrāsana's method of Guhyasamāja technique.[172] 'Gos lived in the eleventh century. Alternatively, if Viṣṇunagar is the city in which Tilopa taught before his renunciation, there is the possibility of a connection between Kaṅkaṇa and Tilopa.

30

THE MAHĀSIDDHA KAMBALA THE BLACK-BLANKET-CLAD YOGIN

The ocean's vast breadth and depth is treasure-laden;
How marvelously rich, the enjoyment of the Nāga Kings!
From the beginning all light and sound is the
  dharmakāya*;*
How incredibly high, the enjoyment of realized adepts!

There was once a king of Kaṅkarama with two sons. When he died the people elected the eldest son, who was of virtuous disposition, to succeed his father. The prince was crowned, and his virtue brought great prosperity to the eighty-four thousand households of his kingdom. They became so wealthy that they ate from golden dishes.

However, during the first year of his reign the young king did not see his mother. His courtiers told him that she was in mourning. Another year passed before his mother finally arrived at court, weeping. The king was distressed and asked her the cause of her sadness.

"I am weeping to see you on the throne engaged in the wretched business of government," she told him.

"I will abdicate in favor of my brother and take orders," the king declared at once.

He was as good as his word. He took up residence in a monastery with a retinue of three hundred monks. But after some time his mother again appeared before him, weeping. He prostrated before her and again asked her the cause of her distress.

"I am weeping to see you still living like a king, surrounded by a court, even though you are a monk," she told him. And in reply to his request for advice she continued, "Leave this monastery and your sumptuous living and go alone to the jungle."

He did as she advised, and finding a suitable tree in the forest took up residence beneath it. Due to the reverberations of his past generosity his needs were supplied by the local villagers. But again his mother came to him and wept, and again he bowed to her and asked the cause of her sadness.

"What need has a holy man for all these trappings," she moaned.

He discarded his fine robes, his silver hand basin and all his possessions, and taking the path of a yogin he set out to wander from land to land. Before he had gone far his mother appeared in the sky before him, and he recognized her as a Ḍākinī for the first time. She gave him the Saṃvara initiation and taught him how to meditate. Then she vanished, and he continued on his way. He wandered for twelve years from town to town, sleeping in cremation grounds and practicing his sādhana. When he eventually gained *mahāmudrā-siddhi* he levitated into the sky, and suddenly he was faced with his mother and her retinue of Ḍākinīs.

"Why are you indulging your power in this way," she chided. "It would be better if you worked for the benefit of people below."

The master came down to earth, and intent upon selfless service he traveled west to the land of Oḍḍiyāṇa, to Maṅgalapur, a city of two hundred and fifty thousand households. In the area of Karabir he found the isolated Panaba Cliff in which was a cave called Talatse, or Palm Tree Top Cave, and there he decided to stay. When the local *ḍākinī*-witches heard of the master's arrival in their territory they plotted with their leader, Padmadevī, to obstruct his meditation. One day on his way to town wearing his black woolen blanket, a crowd of young *ḍākinī*-witches accosted him.

"Please come to our house for a meal," they implored him.

"I do not take my food from any single household," he told them politely, refusing their offer. But when they begged to be entrusted with his blanket-cum-robe while he was in town, importunately pressing for this favor, he could not refuse. He gave the blanket to Padmadevī and went on naked.

The *ḍākinī*-witches held council. " A siddha's possessions all have power," they declared. "We must eat this blanket." They divided it up and swallowed the pieces, throwing a remaining fragment into the fire, and when the master returned they told him that they had decided to offer him a new blanket. He insisted that they return his

Lwawapa (Kambala) realized the *vajra*-heart.

own, so they offered him gold, but to no avail. He was angry. He preferred to approach the king to protest.

"You are king," he charged the monarch. "Why can't you protect your subjects from thieving witches?" After he had explained his case the king summoned the *ḍākinī*-witches and ordered them to return the blanket. They pleaded that it was no longer in their possession.

The master returned to his cave naked and continued his meditation. He offered a sacrificial cake (torma) to Heruka's Ḍākinī consort, and when one of the witches caused the spring in his cave to dry up he commanded the earth goddess to send water, and she complied immediately, the spring flowing forth again.

An opportunity to curb the *ḍākinī*-witches arose when their sisters came to Oḍḍiyāṇa from Mt. Meru and the Four Continents for an assembly. It was a vast convocation of mean-spirited *ḍākinī*s. The master turned them all into sheep, and when the queen, Padmadevī, prayed that he return them to their original shape he sheared the fleeces of the entire flock, so that when they found themselves again in human form their heads were shaved, and they wept.

Cutting their hair had little effect, for it was then at Palm Tree Top Cave that the goddesses of sensuality attempted to murder him by rolling a huge boulder down upon his head. He raised his hand in a gesture of threat, and the rock's descent was checked. It remains there perched precariously until this day.

Finally the king decided to intervene. "There is not one amongst you," he told the witch-girls," that has not harmed some man at some time. You must beg forgiveness and vow to follow the path of virtue."

Unrepentant, they refused to heed the king, until the master added his threat. "You *ḍākinī*-witches must be controlled. If you refuse to follow my instruction and refuse to vow to protect the Truth, I will send you to Dharmarāja, Lord of Death; and if you break your vow to refrain from evil doing, I will turn you into horses."

They feared the master's power, so they took refuge in the Buddha and swore to protect his Word. Then purified, they vomited up the blanket that they had swallowed previously, and the master collected the pieces and sewed them together again. But the blanket was slightly smaller.

This great yogin became known as Kambala or Lwa ba pa,

Master of the Blanket, and also as Śrī Prabhata, Glorious Light. After serving countless people he bodily attained the Ḍākinī's Paradise.

Sādhana

Kambala's legend, full of female energy, reflects this siddha's preoccupation with the mother-tantra. With Saroruha (see p. 345) he is credited with bringing the mother-tantras, particularly the *Hevajra-tantra*, from Oḍḍiyāṇa, the Land of the Ḍākinīs, to eastern India, though such an assertion raises chronological problems;[173] and his reputation as a master of the *mantrayāna* was so high that some considered him the original authority on the tantras. Although his Ḍākinī-mother gave him the Saṃvara initiation in the legend, in the Tibetan Saṃvara lineages his Guru was either Ḍeṅgipa or Ghaṇṭāpa and he taught Indrabhūti, Lakṣmīṅkarā, and Aciṅta (*38*). But his Ḍākinī-Guru did give him initiation into two other tantras: the *Mahākarūṇikā-tantra*, which he transmitted to Virūpa, and *Vajra Vārāhī's Six Topics* (T. *Phag mo gzhung drug*), which he gave to Lakṣmīṅkarā (*82*). Nāropa's consort, Niguma, said of Kambala that only he could equal her in knowledge of *Vārāhī's Six Topics*.[174]

If Kambala was assisted by the Ḍākinīs in many ways, he was also troubled by negative female energy, as portrayed in the legend. The Tibetan tradition recalls other *ḍākinīs* who attempted to steal his power in Oḍḍiyāṇa.[175] After initiation from an anonymous preceptor he realized his own pure awareness (*jñāna*) and travelled to a town in Oḍḍiyāṇa called rGyu ma sthira. Here he was accosted by a *ḍākinī*-witch who pleased him by presenting him with a flower, but his pleasure was short-lived, as a *ḍākinī* ally told him that the flower signified the giver's power over him. To protect himself he entered into the samādhi of his creative meditation, and at midnight, when the aggrieved flower-bestowing witch showered him with stones, the protective circle of his creative meditation maṇḍala saved him from harm. Happy with that result he decided to explore the powers of fulfillment meditation, and he entered a samādhi in which all attributes dissolved into the infinite space of the *dharmadhātu (alakṣaṇa-samādhi)* and, also, stones materialized out of the sky. Thus is explained the precariously perched boulder at Palm Tree Top Cave.

In the episode of the legend in which the witches cause Kambala's stream to dry up, most versions of the text have Ten Heruka Deities as the recipients of Kambala's offering of ten sacrificial cakes,[176] which are consecrated alchemical preparations imbued with the power that identifies them with the deity to whom they are initially offered. What would appear to be the correct version,[177] translated herein, has Kambala offer one torma to Heruka's Ḍākinī consort. Heruka is a form of Saṃvara, and his consort, Vajra Vārāhī, is the ultimate female archetype, emptiness devoid of ego, who controls all ramifications of *anima* energy. Thus the earth goddess, a female elemental power (*yakṣī*), immediately did Kambala's bidding.

Historiography

The location of Kaṅkarama (or Kaṅkarova), Kambala's birthplace, is not indicated in the legend; it may have been in Orissa.[178] Maṅgalapur, is the ancient capital of Oḍḍiyāṇa on the Swat River. One journey Kambala undertook to Oḍḍiyāṇa is remembered for his contest in magic with Lalitavajra, who had just gained mundane *siddhi.* Arriving before the Muruṇḍaka Mountain Lalitavajra took the form of Yamāri (Yamāntaka) and cleft the mountain with a sword to make a passage. On the return journey they approached the mountain at night, and Kambala caused it to disappear, surprising Lalitavajra in the morning when he found the mountain behind him.[179]

In Oḍḍiyāṇa Kambala and Lalitavajra had visited King Indrabhūti (*42*), the brother of Lakṣmīṅkarā (*82*), and the king who was hassled by the witches that Kambala subjugated. Further, Kambala honored this king by sleeping outside his palace for three (or twelve) years. Whoever neglected to make obeisance to the siddha would become rigid in the calf, while those who bowed down could pass on.[180] This gained him the sobriquet The Sleeping Bhikṣu, although he is best known in Tibet as Lwa wa pa (Lwa ba pa, Ba wa pa) because he habitually wore only one piece of cloth. He is also known as Kamaripa and Śrī Prabhata.

The inevitable problem of identification concerning Kambala arises with those Tibetan historians who identify Kambala, or Lwa wa pa, with Indrabhūti the Younger, son of King Dza/Indrabhūti II.[181] The basis of this identification is a statement made by Kambala himself in his own commentary on the *Śrī-sahaja-siddhi* of Ḍombi Heruka.[182] Another lineage that places Lwa wa pa in the eighth century is the *rDzogs chen anuyoga* lineage, which makes him a Guru-bhai of a Kukkuripa, and Indrabhūti's disciple. Clearly, if a Lwawapa/Indrabhūti lived in the eighth century, Lakṣmīṅkarā's brother would be Indrabhūti IV, and his Guru Kambala. It is possible that the sobriquet Sleeping Bhikṣu was applied to an eighth century Indrabhūti in addition to the ninth century Kambala. There is no doubt that our Kambala was active in the middle and end of the ninth century.

Kambala's place in the Guhyasamāja lineage is confused by the identification with Indrabhūti; one lineage has him receive initiation from Lakṣmīṅkarā. However, he also obtained Jñānapāda's Guhyasamāja tradition from Buddhajñāna and transmitted it to the Līlavajra who must be the disciple of Anaṅgavajra. Yamāntakarāja also initiated him into the *Guhyasamāja*; was his companion, Lalitavajra, who had proved himself "King of Yamāntaka/Yamāri" at Muruṇḍaka Mountain, this Yamāntakarāja?

31

THE MAHĀSIDDHA ḌEṄGIPA THE COURTESAN'S BRAHMIN SLAVE

Great happiness is like a horse, an elephant, and
the ocean;
Realization is like a monkey, a child, and writing
in water;
Indivisibility is like a river, the sun, and medicine;
Attainment is like a hair-knot, an eye, and a wheel.

Ḍeṅgipa was the brahmin minister to the King of Paṭaliputra. King Indrapāla, whose initiatory name was Dārikapa, had been awakened to the karmic misery of his situation by the yogin Lūipa, and when he decided to renounce his kingdom and the world, Ḍeṅgipa echoed his master's decision. Together they went down to the cremation ground to meet Lūipa. The Guru welcomed them, and gave them the initiation and empowerment of Saṃvara. They had nothing to give the Guru as the customary initiation offering, but he accepted the offering of their bodies as slaves, which he intended to sell. He took them first to Orissa, where they stayed some time, begging their food. The story of how the king was sold is related in the legend of Dārikapa (77).

Lūipa and the brahmin journeyed seven days to reach Jayantipur, a country with a Buddhist king, and there they went straight to a brothel, where Lūipa asked for an audience with the chief courtesan. "Is your mistress interested in buying a male slave?" he asked the door-keeper.

"I will buy!" came a voice from within. "What is your price?"

"One hundred ounces of gold," Lūipa told her.

The deal was concluded after the courtesan agreed to two conditions: first that the brahmin should sleep alone, and second that he should be released as soon as he had earned the equivalent of what had been paid for him. The brahmin was led away, and the Guru departed.

The brahmin slave pleased his mistress and was respected by her servants. They called him Swamiji, Honorable Sage. One day when his work was finished, the courtesan forgot to send him his evening meal. He went out into the garden, where it was his custom to retire, but later his mistress remembered him and sent out servants with food, and to their amazement they found him served by fifteen girls, his body radiating light. When the courtesan was informed she was ashamed that she had not recognized her slave's holiness. "I have done wrong in treating you as a slave for twelve years," she said contritely. "Now let me serve you as my priest."

Ḍeṅgipa refused her offer, but taught the Buddha's message to her and to the people of Jayantipur. He initiated them into the maṇḍala of Vajra Vārāhī and instructed them in her sādhana, and eventually he went to the Ḍākinī's Paradise with seven hundred disciples.

The brahmin minister became renowned by the name Ḍeṅgipa, The Rice Thresher, since threshing was one of the tasks he performed. This was the song he sang of his experience:

I am Ḍeṅgipa, the vedic priest,
And absorbed in the rice thresher's samādhi
I thresh rice in the pestle as my yoga.
I sweep together the scattered grains
And thresh it with the Guru's precepts;
Ignoring other people's work
I beat the black grain pure;
I beat out sin with virtue first,
Threshing with the pestle of vajra-*knowledge,*
And the grains of rice are the sun and the moon;
In the essential empty nature of the mortar
I beat giving and taking to a unity.
When thought, like milk, is churned by the mantra HŪṀ
Pure pleasure congeals as fine butter,
And that is the taste of non-duality.

This high-minded brahmin was humbled,

Sold to reduce his pride of caste—
Ḍeṅgipa sold to a courtesan!

Sādhana

Ḍeṅgipa's song of realization introduces images that could be dream omens, analogies of four states of mind, or metaphors. A horse is wild and free; an elephant is all-powerful and immovable; and the ocean is all-embracing: the ecstasies of release create a mind that manifests in uninhibited freedom, that cannot be altered by external pressures, and that embraces every situation. A monkey steals what it wants; a child's innocence is without discrimination; and writing in water vanishes as soon as it is written: a realized mind is like a wish-fulfilling gem; perceiving the one taste in all things there is no virtue or vice; and whatever arises as thought dissolves without trace. A river is a symbol of eternal change; the sun is its own light source; medicine cures disease: in a mind where the knower and known are one there is only the here and now of an instant of the river's flow; all appearances are self-illuminating; and the disease of attachment is cured by equanimity. A hair-knot is the yogin's symbol of unbroken *samaya*; a single eye is the third eye of non-dual awareness; and a wheel is a symbol of eternity: the goal attained is symbolized by the hair-knot; the realized yogin has attained the divine eye; and he lives according to the eight-fold path (an eight-spoked wheel) in a timeless continuum.

Ḍeṅgipa's obstacles to liberation were very similar to those of his Guru Lūipa. Lūipa ate fish-guts to find the one taste of all things and to eradicate a seed of royal pride and racial discrimination; Ḍeṅgipa served a prostitute, and although a courtesan had a certain status in society, to a brahmin, "a high-minded vedic priest," she was "unclean." The situation served to destroy his prejudices and allowed him to discover the sameness in all phenomena. Another virtue of the situation for him was that he could "ignore other people's work" and retreat into an introspective state of absorption in his samādhi. The only obscurity in his verses describing his sādhana is the allusion to the grains of rice as the sun and moon: the pestle, the long heavy stick that husks the rice in a mortar trough, is likened to the *avadhūti*, the central channel, into which the left and right channels, the *rasanā* and *lalanā*, the moon and the sun, are forced to empty. *Vajra*-knowledge[183] is a union of polar opposites—male and female, knower and known, compassion and emptiness, sun and moon. Evidently Ḍeṅgipa's work also included butter-making: the seed-syllable HŪṀ is the euphonic representation of the *dharmakāya*, the Buddha's mode of infinite space and awareness, and when conceptual thought is infused with space and awareness[184] the result is the pure pleasure of a thoughtless trance (*nirvikalpa-samādhi*). Pure pleasure (*mahāsukha*) is the feeling-tone inherent in all experience.

Historiography

Ḍeṅgipa figures prominently in the early Saṃvara lineage that was initiated by his Guru Lūipa. The lineage Lūipa, Dārikapa and Ḍeṅgipa, and Ghaṇṭāpa, comprises a series of anecdotes repeated in various forms by several commentators. Bu ston relates how Lūipa went to the city of Kumārakṣetra in Orissa to convert King Vimalacandra, and assuming the throne at a ceremony at which the king was to preside, shaming the guards and the brahmins sent to remove him, he commanded the king's attention, and by outrageous behavior and verbal gamesmanship converted the worldly king and his brahmin minister. Ḍeṅgipa received his name when Lūipa was inquiring of his converts about their preoccupations, and the brahmin revealed that his mind was fascinated by the sound *ḍeng*, which seems to be the sound of a hammer on an anvil. The disciples' first meditation was to discover the reality of this sound, and in its lack of any substantial existence and its dependence upon a number of interdependent causes the Guru demonstrated the nature of Mahāmudrā. Then Ḍeṅgipa was sent to a liquor-seller in the city to dispense liquor, to serve unclean food, to wipe up vomit, and generally to demean himself, and by discovering the one taste of all things to attain *siddhi*. Eventually he attained the Ḍākinī's Paradise with five hundred barmaids.[185]

The Sakya version of this story reverses the identity of Dārikapa and Ḍeṅgipa. The king is sent to Tsaritrapa in Orissa to hire himself out as a rice thresher, after admitting his chief pleasure was alcohol. In his rice threshing samādhi he visualized his work as a creative and fulfillment yoga, until he gained *siddhi* in a body of light. The sound *ḍeng*, and his name, arose from the pestle in the mortar trough as he husked the rice.[186]

Ḍeṅgipa would have been active in the middle decades of the

ninth century. His name has been treated most cavalierly, corrupted into a host of variants: Ḍiṅgi, Ḍiṅga, Teṅki, Taṅki, Dheṅki, Dhaki, etc. The Tibetans translated it as The Rich Thresher (T.Bras brdungs zhabs). The text has Saliputra for Paṭaliputra, King Indrapāla's city.

32
THE SIDDHA BHANDEPA
THE ENVIOUS GOD

Non-attachment is the highest form of loving kindness;
Realization of the nature of existence is compassion;
Inexhaustible pleasure is sympathetic joy;
And the ubiquitous one taste is perfect equanimity.

Bhandepa was a god living in the sky among the clouds of Śrāvastī. One day to his vast surprise he saw an apparition dressed in a monk's robes, carrying a begging bowl in one hand and a staff in the other, floating past him, radiating a divine aura.

"What is this god-like phenomena floating through the sky," he asked Viśvakārmān, Lord of the Gods.

"It is a saintly *arhat*, one who has cleansed himself of all passion," replied Viśvakārmān.

Bhandepa yearned to emulate such accomplishment, and he descended to our world of the Rose Apple Tree to find a teacher. He found Kṛṣṇācārya and begged him for instruction. The master-initiated him into the Guhyasamāja maṇḍala and taught him the yogin's protection, the four boundless states of mind: compassion as the ultimate vision, sympathetic joy as meditation, loving kindness as perfect action, and equanimity as the goal of his practice. Through his meditation Bhandepa cleansed his mind of all delusion, and he gained *mahāmudrā-siddhi.* He became famous as the yogin Bhandepa.

When Viśvakārmān saw Bhandepa return to the sky above Śrāvastī he demanded to know what he had attained. Bhandepa replied:

I have attained the vision that is without substance,
Meditation that is unremitting,

Action that is like a parent's affection,
And the goal that is like the sky.
When these four are recognized as one,
Where can desire lodge?
How wonderful the Guru is!
The wise man will always serve him.

For four hundred years Bhandepa served the people of the six great towns of Āryāvarta: Śrāvastī, Rājagṛha, Vaiśālī, Vārāṇasī, Paṭaliputra and Kānyakubja. Then with four hundred disciples he bodily attained the Ḍākinī's Paradise.

Sādhana

The irrelevance of sectarian divisions in Tantra is shown in this legend, where the arch-tantrika Kṛṣṇācārya gives Bhandepa, an admirer of the hīnayāna, a tantric initiation and mahāyāna precepts that nevertheless give him *mahāmudrā-siddhi*. From the mahāyāna standpoint, technically, an *arhat*[187] is he who observes impeccable manners, restraining himself from any reaction when reviled, angered, beaten or irritated, possessing few desires, practicing scrupulous modest behavior, eating moderately, and keeping from sleep in the first and last parts of the night. He has meditated upon all phenomena as essentially free of both positive and negative attributes, and as impermanent, sign-less, wish-less, and empty, then analyzing them into the five psycho-physical constituents, the five elements and the five sense-fields; and he has pondered the four noble truths in every way possible. To neutralize the three poisons he has contemplated their antidotes, such as the ugly and repulsive as the antidote to desire. He practices the thirty-seven topics conducive to enlightenment, and contemplates the twelve-fold chain of interdependent origination. He has achieved deliverance from the three realms of saṃsāra, his nirvāṇa is extinction and he will never return to the round of rebirth. If he is a *theravādin* he will attempt to refute the mahāyāna path and he stolidly maintains that the Buddha was merely a human being.[188]

Hīnayāna was the dominant form of Buddhism in India for about a thousand years. In the sixth or seventh centuries it was eclipsed for reasons uncertain, but in Kashmir, Vajrāsana and Nālandā, and in Andhra, ordination could be obtained in the *vihāras* up to the

Muslim conquest. It would appear that the usual Tibetan practice, the vajrayāna ideal of three *yānas* in one, was not given much credence in siddha-Bengal. This doctrine taught that the tantrika should practice the hīnayāna externally, following the strict moral and personal discipline of the *bhikṣu*; internally he should cultivate the mahāyāna attitude of compassion; and in secret he should practice tantric meditation. Amongst the siddhas Śāntipa, Dharmapa, and this Bhandepa, may have followed this system, but Virūpa, for example, is notable for his renunciation of the robe, and both Āryadeva and Nāgārjuna probably wore yogin's dress in their later incarnations.

The four boundless states of mind, or the four stations of purity, taught by Śākyamuni in his discourses, take a central place in all Buddhist sādhana, including Tantra. In Bhandepa's song they are given a mahāyāna interpretation; he does not negate the outer, social virtues, but points at the deeper functions that provoke them. Thus compassion can degenerate into worthless pity, unless it is inspired by an insight that involves empathy; sympathetic joy can become the forced mark of the do-gooder, unless there is an underlying delight in all perceptual situations; while equanimity can become the flat response of an anesthetized mind,[189] rather than awareness of the all-embracing emptiness that is the common denominator of all experience. Thus to reconstruct Bhandepa's practice: through contemplation of all things as emptiness, and realization of an insubstantial vision, he attained compassion; through constant meditation upon that vision with its inherent pleasure, he attained sympathetic joy; through the resulting activity of treating all beings like his own sons, with a detachment arising from meditation on emptiness, he attained loving kindness; and perceiving all things as a union of space and awareness, knowing the one taste, he attained his goal of perfect equanimity.

Historiography

Śrāvastī was the capital of the ancient kingdom of Kośala, which approximates the old Oudh. Śākyamuni spent twenty-five rainy seasons there in the park built by his patron Anārthapiṇḍada. The Jetavana Grove has always been an important place of Buddhist pilgrimage. The other five cities of Āryāvarta, the Aryan heartland, the Holy Land of the Buddhists, were principal cities of Gupta India.

Bhandepa's name is rendered as Bearer of the God of Wealth (T. Nor lha 'dzin), indicating its derivation from *bhandara*, "storehouse." There are other forms of the name such as Bhadepa, Bhadhepa, Bade, and Batalipa. Bhadepa is the Ḍākinī in Kāṇhapa's legend (*17*) who collects herbs from Śrī Parvata. Bhade and Bhandepa are interchangeable in the lists of siddhas' names.[190] Bhade appears in the *nāth* literature as the disciple of Kṛṣṇācārya who saves his Guru from a sexual fall. The musical Bauls of Bengal immortalized this Bhāde as Bāil Bhādāi.[191] If Bhandepa was a disciple of the Kṛṣṇācārya also known as Balinācārya concerned with the *Guhyasamāja-tantra*, he would have lived in the middle eleventh century. If he can be identified with the Bhade of the *nāth*s and Bauls then he would have lived in the second half of the tenth century.

33
THE SIDDHA TAṄTEPA THE GAMBLER

All mental reflections, all concepts, have subsided,
Extinguished in thought-free space;
And every momentary experience of the
phenomenal world
Dissolved, consumed in the continuum of emptiness.

Taṅtepa of Kauśāmbhī was a person of low birth obsessed with the dice. Gambling day and night he lost everything he owned, yet compulsively he continued, living on credit. When his credit was exhausted he was beaten unmercifully by his creditors. At the end of his line, he took to living in the cremation ground and there a yogin found him and asked about his problem.

"I am a gambler," Taṅtepa told him. "I've lost everything I owned, and I've no credit left. I'm beaten."

"Why don't you practice meditation?" asked the yogin.

"Dice is my whole life," said the gambler. "But if there was a meditation that I could practice without giving up gambling, I would do it."

The yogin promised him such a meditation. He gave the gambler initiation and empowerment and taught him this method. "Visualize the three realms—the realms of sensual experience, esthetic form and formlessness—as empty as your pocket after you've lost at dice. Then visualize the nature of your mind as the emptiness of the three realms."

Just as you lost your money at dice
Lose all thought of the three realms
Throwing the dice of thought-free awareness;
Just as you have been knocked down by your creditors

Knock down thought into the sphere of empty space;
And just as you rest in the solace of this cremation ground
Relax in the continuum of pure pleasure.

The gambler meditated according to these instructions, and his concepts of the world on the sensual, the esthetic and the formless planes sank into the empty reality of their own nature, which is like a plenum of space. Further, he understood that the knowledge of his realization was quite without substance. Thus he gained the supreme realization of Mahāmudrā.

His final advice to his disciples was expressed in this verse:

If in the first place I lacked sorrow and remorse,
How could I have entered the path to release?
If I had not placed my trust in a teacher,
How could I have attained the ultimate power?

He spoke these words and levitated, and in his own body he arrived in the Ḍākinī's Paradise.

Sādhana

Taṅtepa's meditation is a simple fulfillment stage method. But his precepts seem too facile to be sufficient, and the gambling metaphors relating the practice to Taṅtepa's own experience only make the instruction more comprehensible to a simple mind. His practice is to relax, watch his mind, and see all experience, the three worlds, and thought, as emptiness. In order for such a practice to be effective, so that the practice is not immediately strangled by distractions and mundane preoccupations, the practitioner must have a very strong intuition of emptiness to start with. In other words his Guru must have given him an intense, durable vision of ultimate reality in his initiation. No doubt his contrition laid an excellent foundation, and his trust expedited the empowerment; but such a simple meditation is the most difficult to perform because there are no aids to keep the attention fixed. It is the barest form of Mahāmudrā meditation. The Guru's induction of the disciple's mind into Mahāmudrā reality is the most subtle form of initiation; it is a revelation of the nature of mind.[192]

Taṅtepa shows the emptiness of all things.

In his song Taṅtepa first claims that his mind is now empty of conditioning, and the mental processes that create a divided world are dead; and second he explains that *dharmas* (momentary experiences) no longer arise. His world is no more an experience of objects and thoughts; it is a continuum of space and emptiness, the content of which is ineffable, because it cannot be objectified. The universe, himself included, has dissolved, and nothing can be said about it except that the yogin is in bliss.

Historiography

We know nothing of Taṅtepa's life except that he lived in Kauśāmbhī, an ancient city in the Ganges Valley. Variations upon the theme of his name are, Tandhepa, Taṅtipa, and Panapa, and in Tibetan The Dice Man (T. Cho lo pa). Thus Taṅtepa is the stereotypal gambler obsessed by the fall of the die in the same way that Khaḍgapa is the obsessive thief and Thaganapa the compulsive liar.

34

THE MAHĀSIDDHA KUKKURIPA THE DOG-LOVER

Ritual worship and offering to the Buddha is futile;
Where conscious effort and striving are present
The Buddha is absent.
Peak experience of the real Guru's grace
Lies within the fortunate man—but can he see it?

A brahmin of Kapilavastu, Kukkuripa placed his trust in the Tantra to solve the problems of existence. He chose the path of renunciation, adopting the life-style of a yogin. Just beginning his itinerant career, slowly begging his way to Lumbinī, he discovered a starving bitch. The dog inspired him to pity, and he carried her to Lumbinī. After a thorough search he finally found an empty cave there, and with the dog he took up residence. He would leave her behind in the cave while he went out begging.

After twelve years of continuous practice of mantra he attained magical power—prescience and divine insight—and the gods of the Thirty-three Sensual Heavens invited him to their paradise. He accepted their invitation, and set out on a ceaseless round of self-indulgent feasting and pleasure provided by the gods.

Meanwhile the dog fended for herself in the cave, rooting around for whatever she could find to sustain life. But she was not forgotten. Even while the yogin feasted on the gods' offerings, he told them of his dog, saying that he must return to guard her.

"How can you think about a dog in a dank cave while you are enjoying this kind of luxury and comfort. Don't be so foolish! Please remain with us here." This kind of divine remark persuaded the yogin to postpone his return, but eventually his love for the dog won, and he returned to her.

He found her in the cave where he had left her, and he patted her on the head in greeting. At that moment the bitch became a Ḍākinī, and the Ḍākinī spoke to him like this:

Well done! Well done! You have proved your worth.
You have overcome temptation,
Returning to receive supreme power.
The mundane power of the gods is delusory
For they retain a notion of self,
And fallible pleasure is not so great.
Now your Ḍākinī will grant you supreme realization,
The immaculate pure pleasure that has no outflow.

Then she showed him the symbolic union of skillful means and perfect insight, and after an irreversible, infallible vision of immutability had arisen in his mind-stream, he attained supreme realization. Thereafter he was called Guru Kukkuripa by all the people of Lumbinī. He lived a life of selfless service, until with an entourage of disciples from the city of Kapilavastu, he attained final release in the Ḍākinī's Paradise.

Sādhana

To perceive the full significance of Kukkuripa's association with his dog, it is necessary to remember that in India the dog is considered an extremely lowly form of life, unclean to the extent that a brahmin will not touch one, and Kukkuripa was born a brahmin. In Tāranātha's narrative of Kukkuripa's story[193] the dog is a metaphor, and also in our legend there is some ambiguity. The dog signifies a very low caste woman, like a Ḍombī or Śavarī, the emanation of a Ḍākinī who could give Kukkuripa initiation through the sexual symbolism of two-in-one union (*yuganaddha*). In this context "sexual union" indicates spiritual integration of skillful means, which Kukkuripa had cultivated by mantra in his practice of the lower tantras, with emptiness and awareness, which in his case seems to have been underdeveloped—the feminine aspect of his being was externalized as a dog. Whether projecting his "anima" upon a dog or woman, the yogin's practice is to achieve spiritual symbiosis by integrating his feminine principle, his awareness of emptiness, with his masculine principle of compassion, and with it to attain supreme success (*parama-siddhi*).

Kukkuripa returns to saṃsāra for the sake of all beings.

Kukkuripa's song expresses one of the revolutionary concepts that set the siddhas apart and made them anathema in the eyes of the brahmins and even certain orthodox mahāyāna Buddhists: "Ritual worship is futile, concealing the truth." Since vedic times the brahmins have taught that proper performance of their rites leads to salvation, and to certain fulfillment of the ritualist's temporal aims. Temporizing to satisfy some critics who practice ritual with success, Kukkuripa's stance could be modified to exclude from futility ritual performed, for example, in a state of non-action,[194] or as a celebration or a healing technique, for he was referring to the futility of ritual as a means of attaining Mahāmudrā. But the anti-ritualist principle is vital insofar as it takes sādhana back to human interaction, back to existential praxis, and back to the internal search. It was the fortuitous appearance of a Ḍākinī that induced Kukkuripa's peak experience of the Buddha-nature. Spurning ritual, he attained enlightenment without even a human Guru.

Historiography

Kukkuripa's name is well known in the Tibetan tradition, and the story of him and his dog is often repeated. But there is very little biographical detail concerning him extant. An exception is Marpa The Translator's remarkable portrayal of him in his biography:[195] Nāropa sends his disciple Marpa to the mother-tantra master to receive the *Mahāmāyā-tantra*, which he, Nāropa, had given to Kukkuripa in exchange for the *Guhyasamāja*. Kukkuripa lives in a swamp of poisonous water in the South. "He has a body covered in hair. His face is like a monkey's. His color is unpleasant, and he can transform himself into anything." Marpa's trip south was anguished, but overcoming his fear of death he finally encountered the Guru: "Under a tree was a human figure covered with the feathers of a bird. His face was tucked into the crook of his arm." The Guru was most generous to Marpa and gave him the precepts of the three yogas of illusion besides the *Mahāmāyā*. These were Nāropa's remarks to Marpa after his return: "Since he has no virtue he lives on an unpeopled island in a lake of poison. As he has the face of a monkey on a human body he has to resort to bitches, for he could find no human consort." Tāranātha evokes the same feeling about Kukkuripa: "He taught a thousand Ḍākas and Ḍākinīs during the day in the guise of a dog, and at night he would perform *gaṇacakra* with them in the cremation ground." He attained *siddhi* by means of the *Śrī Candraguhyatilaka-tantra* (The Moon's Secret Spot).[196]

Kukkuripa's name appears in at least four contexts in the lineal history of the siddhas. First he appears in the Nyingmapa *anuyoga* lineage, particularly as transmitter of the Dupaido, a text that he received from Indrabhūti I and taught to Garab Dorje; this would have been in the eighth century. Then he is identified as the Guru of King Dza of Zahor (8th c.), a disciple of Līlavajra and a Guru of Kambala and Indrabhūti the Younger (late 9th c.), the guru of Mīnapa (early 10th c.), and the mother-tantra teacher of Marpa (11th c.). Those who believe that mahāsiddhas like Kukkuripa attained immortality early in their careers and retained an illusory body of light on earth for hundreds of years, could hardly have a better example of this phenomenon. One source identifies Kukkuripa with Jñānagarbha from whom Marpa received the *Guhyasamāja-tantra.*[197] Marpa also refers to Kukkuripa as Śāntibhadra. Jñānagarbha lived at Talakṣetra in Western India, and most of the contexts in which we find Kukkuripa relate to western India, and to the North-west and Oḍḍiyāṇa in particular. Our legend is an exception, making him a brahmin of the Śākya kings' ancient capital where Śākyamuni grew up; Kapilavastu is eight miles from Lumbinī, where Śākyamuni was born. Associated in this way with the Buddha, the Dog King is given a universality that elevates him above any of the specific lineal relationships. He is indeed the eternal Buddha of the down-trodden and oppressed. The root of his name is *kukkura*, which means "dog;" Kukkurāja (King of the Dogs), is a common alternative form (also Kuṭarāja, Kukuripa).

35

THE SIDDHA KUCIPA THE GOITRE-NECKED YOGIN

Sahaja, *the inborn absolute, brings pain*
When the yogin reacts excitedly,
Quick and irritable, like an elephant's eye;
But relaxed, he enters a sublime trance,
Detached and free of desire.

In the clear light of the Guru's Word
I lost the extremes of affirmation and negation,
But the elusive reality became an extreme;
Realizing that extreme I realized ultimate truth.

Kucipa was a low-caste farmer from Kahari. Due to past karma he was afflicted with a goitre on his neck. When it grew in size he sought solitude out of shame, and he nursed his mental and physical pain alone. One day the venerable Nāgārjuna passed by, and as soon as Kucipa set eyes on him he put his trust in him, and placing his palms together in respect, he said:

Master, you have come at last!
I am tortured by an evil past
And I suffer intolerable pain.
Please show me the way to be free.

Nāgārjuna first gained assurance that the sick man would practice what he taught him, a sādhana that would replace his pain with happiness, but requiring application and diligence. Then he revealed the maṇḍala of Guhyasamāja and guided Kucipa into it. After that he taught him the technique of employing suffering as the path in the framework of the creative and fulfillment modes of meditation.

"Take the goitre on your neck as the object of creative visualization. Imagine it growing larger," the Guru told him.

Kucipa meditated as he was instructed, and the goitre grew larger than before and his pain increased. When Nāgārjuna returned and asked him if he was happy, he was assured that his medicine had worked, so he gave him the fulfillment stage visualization: "Visualize the whole world gathered into your tumor."

Kucipa meditated accordingly and the goitre diminished in size and disappeared, and with health came happiness. When his Guru returned, again assured that his medicine was effective, he gave these further precepts.

Pleasure and pain come from assertion and negation.
Free yourself from these extreme concepts
And what is the difference between pleasure and pain?
Experience the emptiness of every separate situation.

The yogin-farmer understood the meaning of these precepts perfectly. He attained the realization of imageless Mahāmudrā and served the people of Kahari for seven years. He was called Kucipa, The Goitre-Necked Yogin. Finally, with seven hundred disciples, he attained release in the Ḍākinī's Paradise.

Sādhana

It was most fortunate for Kucipa that his intuition served him well when Nāgārjuna passed by. In desperate straits it is not easy to chose one's own doctor, and a bad choice can result in the healer's abuse of the patient's dependency, while in the worst case a quack can turn neuroses into psychoses. Nāgārjuna prescribed visualization techniques in both stages of Kucipa's practice: to visualize the goitre engorging was to focus the form and demonstrate control over it by proving its illusory insubstantial nature; and then in the second part, visualizing the universe in the goitre was to envisage its emptiness (see p. 167). This sādhana thus shows the central importance of the power of positive thinking in tantric technique. Starting with the premise that the body and matter are gross forms of "mind-stuff,"[198] and that the whole universe is mind-created insofar as we only know it through the "creative" functions of sense perception, it is an easy step to believing that it can be altered by eliminating conditioned mental functions and by concentrated attention. Western psychology has, unhappily, tended to separate the body and mind, and consequently western medicine is slow to apply psychosomatics in both diagnosis and prescription. But the cure of Kucipa's disease was merely a by-product in his attainment of *mahāmudrā-siddhi.*

The technique called "employing suffering as the path"[199] takes the first noble truth Śākyamuni taught at Sarnath, suffering itself, as the object of meditation. The creative stage focuses it and the fulfillment stage turns it into emptiness; thus it is the path to its own demise. Kucipa's visualizations illustrate the first line of Nāgārjuna's final precept: pleasure and pain come from assertion and negation (no causal relation between pleasure and assertion and pain and negation is implied). One of the great achievements of Nāgārjuna the *madhyamika* philosopher was to produce a logical formula that places the mind outside the extremes of affirmation, denial, both, and neither, the place that Kucipa sees as the extreme of no extreme. This place is reached by experientially realizing the elusive, indeterminate nature of every situation (*dharma*), because the elements of every situation are empty in their own nature.[200]

Kucipa's meditation achievement is qualified by the word "imageless."[201] "Image" is the word used to describe an object of meditation. Kucipa's meditation on elusive empty space has no image, for all specific characteristics of his existential situation dissolve into the continuum of space. "Imageless Mahāmudrā" has another connotation: the successful adept is ignorant of his attainment because his "self," the observer, has vanished.

Historiography

Kucipa is probably derived from the Sanskrit *kubjika*, which means "bent" or hump-backed" (T. lTag ba can). Variations of his name are Kusūlī, Cubji, Kujipa, Kutsipa and Kubjipa. There are no other references to the siddha Kucipa, but like many siddhas he has namesakes in an earlier period, one at Aśoka's Second Council and another who assisted in the preparation of the *Vibhāṣa.*[202]

36

THE SIDDHA DHARMAPA THE ETERNAL STUDENT

Susceptible to the venom of dualistic thought,
Intellectual minds are poisoned by analysis;
The ultimate grace of the Guru's Word
Cures the malaise of deluded samsaric vision.

Dharmapa was the eternal student who read ceaselessly and always listened attentively to his teachers, studying with perpetual diligence. But he lacked both analytic and meditative insight, so he was unable to assimilate or practice his knowledge. He was a brahmin scholar at the tantric academy of Vikramaśīla in Bengal, and much was expected of him. One day when a yogin visited him and kindly suggested that he was in need of assistance, he frankly confided in the yogin that although he had received a vast amount of instruction he had no teaching to offer. As he put it, he "forgot" whatever he was taught. He begged the yogin for a method to overcome his forgetfulness. The yogin granted him an initiation that transfers the Guru's power and insight to the initiate and then instructed him in the one flavor of all things, in the unity in multiplicity.

As the smith melts fragments of metal,
Fusing them into a single ingot,
Dissolve the fragments of your knowledge
In the vast expanse of your mind's nature.

Through the insight that his initiation had given him, the scholar understood the meaning of this instruction and also what it implied; he realized that the ultimate unifying factor in all the doctrines that he had learnt was the nature of his mind. He attained the power and realization of Mahāmudrā, and he became known as Dharmapa. He set innumerable converts on the path to liberation, and finally attained ultimate release in the Ḍākinī's Paradise in his own body.

Sādhana

The Buddhist student is urged to cultivate three types of wisdom: the wisdom of learning, the wisdom of critical analysis and meditative wisdom. The first consists of intelligent methods of study such as listening attentively, reading closely, and obeying the teacher. The second, critical analysis, is an intellectual discipline involving sifting information received, relating it to the student himself, evaluating, comparing, analyzing form and content; students are encouraged to think for themselves, not accepting the teacher's doctrines blindly except when secret precepts are transmitted. The third is application in meditation and in daily life of what has been learnt and analyzed. The principal danger inherent in scholarship lies in the second of these functions, where the intellect can become fascinated by the material, its form, its logical nicety and the power of its content, and where it is easy for the intellect to deceive itself into thinking that analytic understanding is realization: arrogance results. Further, the intellectual function of dualistic analysis can become a veritable disease of the mind, an insuperable obstacle to gnostic realization. But Dharmapa lacked even analytic insight. He was stuck with fragments of information that he was unable to assimilate, and it appears that he hardly deserved the title of scholar. The Guru's blessing enabled him to see the nature of his mind, and to realize that knowledge was not different from mind-in-itself—a continuum of empty space. Immediately achieving the effect of the third type of wisdom he could teach directly out of experiential realization, guided by extra-sensory perception of his disciples' needs.

Historiography

There are two Dharmapas amongst the eighty-four siddhas of our legends, although other lists make the second (*48*) Gharbaripa. This legend's own etymological definition of Dharmapa is "one endowed with the ability to study and listen" (*paṇḍita*, T.*thos ldan*), and not the literal definition, which is "practitioner of *dharma*" or "Buddhist student" (T.*chos pa*), the definition given for the second Dharmapa. Another source calls our eternal student, "The Grammarian" (T.sGra sbyor zhabs), which would explain his function at the academy.[203] The same source asserts that his Gurus were Kāṇhapa and Jālandhara, which would place him in the first half of the tenth century. If "Dharmapa" is the contraction of a *paṇḍita-siddha's* name, the Ācārya Dharmapāla is an obvious possibility, and his disciple, the siddha and scholar Dharmakīrti, is another; the name Dharmapāpataṅga appears in a fourteenth century list,[204] and finally the mahāpaṇḍita Dharmākaraśānti is a possible candidate. Two meaningless variant spellings of Dharmapa's name are Dhamapa and Damapa.

37

THE SIDDHA MAHIPA "THE GREATEST"

A mountain of ignorant pride
Hid my wish-fulfilling gem of realization.
Now the magic of enlightened action provides
all my wants,
For he who knows the one-taste is totally fulfilled.

Mahipa of Magadha was a vain man of low caste. He had an incredibly powerful physique, and he never stopped adoring himself. "I am the greatest," he would think. "There's not a man alive who can defeat me." He lived by the strength of his arm and bathed in his glory.

One day he was confronted on the street by a yogin, who stopped and stared at him. "And what are you thinking?" the yogin asked.

"Nothing, nothing at all," said the strong man, taken aback.

"Then what's this 'I am invincible!' going on in your mind?" the yogin demanded.

The proud man was humbled, and paid homage to the yogin, bowing down before him. "Get rid of your demeaning pride," said the yogin.

"Then please show me the way," the strong man responded.

The yogin gave him the initiation that transfers grace and these instructions:

Understand appearances as mind,
And meditate with unwavering attention
Upon mind as unborn and unceasing emptiness.
Perfect control is your goal.

"I do not understand," said the strong man.

The Guru tried again:

Identified with your strength's emptiness
You are truly invincible.
Rivet appearances, energies and cognition
To the vast expanse of the sky.

The strong man thought that these instructions would present no problem, since the obstacles to his meditation were used as the path. But when he tried to grasp the object of his meditation he could not find it, and when he tried to locate consciousness, the knower, that too remained elusive. In this way he gained the realization that is like the unlimited expanse of the sky. For three hundred years he instructed the people of Magadha, showing them real strength in the indeterminate, ultimate nature of being. Finally he attained the Ḍākinī's Paradise in his body with two hundred and fifty disciples.

Sādhana

Mahipa was instructed in the same type of meditation that Taṅtepa performed so effectively; but Mahipa's intellect could not grasp the meaning, and he asked for an alternative meditation. Conditioned preconception of appearances as a concrete, substantial reality, is fixed inviolate in the minds of people of this materialistic age, apart from those with psychedelic experience or those scientists on the frontiers of physics and mathematics. Mahipa's Guru gave him short-cut precepts that utilized his chief obsession as the object of meditation[205] in this fulfillment technique. But to bind the object of meditation, in this case Mahipa's physical strength, to emptiness, or rather to the plenum of infinite space, is a skillful device both self-defeating and self-fulfilling, because the object of meditation *is* emptiness and is realized to be so when it dissolves in a meditator's relaxed and attentive mind. The same applies to energies (*prāṇa*) and consciousness (*citta*), where "energies" are both breath and subtle psychic forces that energize and control the psycho-organism, and consciousness is the cognitive element in the six sensory processes. Mahipa is asked to do the equivalent of suspending a lump of sugar in a glass of hot water.

Incidentally Mahipa was taught the essence of the martial arts, which were never as highly developed in India as in China and Japan. The contender who identifies with his manifest strength is at its mercy, weakening with it and failing with it; identified with the emptiness of physical strength he is in touch with an infinite reserve of power, and detached he has perfect self control. Mahipa, however, does not apply his realization to physical competition. No matter how the ultimate nature of being[206] is discovered, its realization is applicable to every situation and to all personality types.

Historiography

Elsewhere Mahipa's Guru is identified as Kāṇhapa,[207] which places Mahipa in the tenth century. Mahipa may have been Vīṇāpa's Guru,[208] an assertion that is chronologically consistent. *Mahipa* is derived from *mahiṣa*, which means "strong" or "mighty." Mahilapa, Kakipa, Mardila, are variations of his name. Mahipāda is rendered The Great Man or The Proud Man (T.Chen po zhabs, Nga rgyal zhabs) in Tibetan.

38

THE SIDDHA ACIṄTA
THE AVARICIOUS HERMIT

In image-free, objectless Mahāmudrā,
The ten thousand delusive thoughts are empty.
Since all phenomena are knowledge and pure awareness
I see my reality as Mahāmudrā.

There was once a poverty-stricken woodsman of Dhanirūpa who dreamed of riches night and day. He had no other thoughts in his mind but wealth and how to acquire it. Tormented by this obsession he sought refuge in solitude, where he was discovered by the yogin Kambala.

"You have managed to retreat from contact with men and their talk," commented Kambala, "but what of your mind?"

"I am obsessed by thoughts of material wealth," the hermit confessed. "If it wasn't for this obsession I'd have an empty mind. How can I be rid of avarice?"

"There is a method of overcoming greed, "Kambala told him. "If you promise to practice it, I will teach you."

The hermit vowed to follow the Guru's instruction, and Kambala gave him the Saṃvara initiation and these instructions upon the profound fulfillment process of meditation:

What is to be gained by desire?
Desire is like the son of a barren woman,
So free your mind of it.
Visualize your body as the heavens
And your thoughts as stars in the sky;
Then the God of Wealth himself will appear,
And with his actual manifestation
All your desires will be fulfilled.

The disciple meditated upon his Guru's instruction. His avaricious thoughts vanished into the radiance of stars, the stars vanished into the boundless expanse of the sky; and he became thought-free. He returned to his Guru and told him that his mind had become empty. Kambala gave him further instruction:

What is the nature of the sky?
Can you make an object of that?
That which is devoid of color and shape—
How can you desire it? How can you meditate upon it?

When the hermit realized the significance of this verse, he gained *mahāmudrā-siddhi.* He became known as Guru Aciṅtapa, The Thought-free, and he taught the ultimate nature of being to his disciples. For three hundred years he served others selflessly, and then with countless disciples he attained the Ḍākinī's Paradise in his very body.

Sādhana

After Aciṅta had fulfilled his meditation, after he had transformed his body into a body of clear light and the thoughts that arose dissolved into the light as stars at dawn, it appears that he failed to realize his success. Hovering on the brink, a blind man with a million dollar cheque in his hand, Kambala had to shake his mind to make him realize what had happened. With his final precepts Aciṅta finally woke up to the fact of identification with space—the blind man could see. The twelve year sādhana is a lengthy process of the disciple awakening to what is obvious to the Guru from the first, and the problem for the disciple is how to realize the obvious. Of course reality is not the sum of our petty thoughts and emotional projections; and of course if only we stopped day-dreaming and obstructing the natural play of things, we could get what we need. What we want most is obstructed chiefly by our desire. Desirelessness is irresistible; it creates a vacuum into which all objects of desire must rush. Thus an empty mind is the throne of the God of Wealth, who takes his seat as soon as thought stops. Propitiation of the Deity Kubera, the God of Wealth, is performed by visualization of the deity and recitation of his mantra in the creative stage, and then realizing him by emptying the mind in the fulfillment process, as in the sādhana of any Buddha. Kubera is the Buddha himself with a different face, for only the Buddha can offer whatever is desired like the wish-fulfilling gem. The gods of wealth who are not Buddhas are black powers of the mind, manipulating and controlling for petty egoistic purposes; they may bring wealth but at a heavy karmic cost. Kambala used the carrot of wealth to induce Aciṅta to practice Mahāmudrā meditation, but after Aciṅta had attained a thought-free state (*nirvikalpa-samādhi*) culminating in *mahāmudrā-siddhi*, it appears that he abandoned his dreams of wealth.

Historiography

Aciṅtapa, The Thought-free, may have been this siddha's personal name but it is also an epithet applied to several siddhas, who presumably were adept in attaining thought-free states (*nirvikalpa-samādhi*). Mīnapa was called Aciṅta, and so was Maitripa, Marpa's Guru. As a disciple of Kambala Acintapa would have lived in the second half of the ninth century.

39

THE SIDDHA BABHAHA THE FREE LOVER

Pleasure! pleasure! unconditional pleasure!
Unconditional desireless pleasure!
Every thought-form perceived as pleasure!
O what unattainable secret pleasure!

Babhaha, Prince of Dhañjur, was intoxicated by the thrills of sensual pleasure. One day he spoke with a wise yogin who had come begging at the palace. The yogin inspired faith in him, and he asked for precepts to assist him in his sexual practice.

"Consummation, the *samaya*, is the fountain of all mystical experience; the Guru is the source of all success," were the precepts the yogin gave him. He then bestowed the initiation that transfers grace upon the prince, and instructed him in the fulfillment yoga technique of psychic channels, vital energies and seed essence:

In the lotus maṇḍala of your partner,
A superior, skillful consort,
Mingle your white seed
With her ocean of red seed.
Then absorb, raise and diffuse the elixir
And your ecstacy will never end.
Then to raise the pleasure beyond pleasure
Visualize it inseparable from emptiness.

After twelve years of profound experience in this technique, the prince found that the obscurations of his vision had vanished, and he gained *siddhi.* He sang:

As the king of geese
Separates water from milk
The Guru's precepts
Draw up the ambrosial elixir.

He served his disciples well before eventually attaining bodily the Ḍākinī's Paradise.

Sādhana

Babhaha is taught the fulfillment process technique called Eternal Delight in the *Six Yogas of Nāropa.* The same result can be achieved with or without a partner, using someone else's body or using one's own body.[209] The practice for the celibate yogin is described in Nalinapa's legend (*40*), and such use of sexual energy is considered more desirable in the Tibetan tradition. But the well known axiom "No *mahāmudrā* without *karma-mudrā*," where the female consort is the *karma-mudrā*, and the central place that this yoga holds amongst the fulfillment stage topics, indicates its significance. The tradition defines "the superior consort" in physical terms, employing the criteria of the Indian science of erotics as explained in texts such as the *Kāmasūtra*: the *padminī* is the best partner. Regarding the yoga itself, psychic channels carry the vital energies that consist of seed-essence; and the essence of the yoga is the skill in controlling the subtle energies. First, energy is sent downward to the sexual center; second, with perfect control, male and female energy is intermingled under the power of retention; third, the elixir of pleasure and emptiness united is raised, like a goose drawing water out of milk, up the central channel; and fourth, it is diffused throughout the psycho-organism by the constantly bifurcating "capillary" channels.[210] With the withdrawal of "pleasure and emptiness indivisible"[211] up the central channel, the four levels of joy are experienced at the four main *cakra*s, and by saturation of the body-mind, eternal delight[212] is achieved, and ultimately rainbow body is possible. The technical description of the technique should not obscure the *sine qua non* of a "spiritual relationship" between the yogin and his consort. Although the female body is being used as a source of "nectar," without a totally open, empathetic and responsive relationship, the yoga will fail. Further, desirelessness is the key to success, and insofar as such a state cannot be attained by striving, the pleasure that results from consummation is "unattainable." Finally, as Babhaha's Guru implies at the beginning, this practice is physically and mentally dangerous and requires a skillful guide. The *samaya* he mentions can be interpreted in several ways, all of them equally vital: it may be maintaining the relative vows and commitments of the vajrayāna, or of this specific practice; it may be the *samaya*, the body, speech and mind union, of Guru and Ḍākinī where Vajrayoginī is the Ḍākinī; or it may be the fully empathetic responsiveness of yogin and yoginī in their sexual encounter.

Historiography

The meaning of *Babhaha* can only be inferred from the Tibetan translation "He who draws water from milk" (T.Chu las 'o ma len), referring to the yogin's ability to suck up the essential female *bodhicitta* from the intermingling of nectars in the *bhaga* maṇḍala into the central channel. There is an eastern belief that geese have the facility of sucking out water from milk, thus keeping the milkman honest. Babhaha, which could be onomatopoeic, is also spelled Bhalaha, Bhaṁva, Babhahi, Baha and Bapabhati. His home town of Dhañjur is unidentified, as is his Guru.

40

THE SIDDHA NALINAPA
THE SELF-RELIANT PRINCE

In the swamp-born lotus at my fontanelle
Lie germinating seeds of joy;
In my throat center is supreme joy,
In my heart center detached joy,
And in my gut center—innate, sahaja *joy,*
And the unsurpassable attainment.

There was once a prince of the land of Paṭaliputra who was reduced to dire poverty. He was forced to gain his livelihood by gathering lotus roots from a lake. One day he met a yogin who spoke to him of the frustration and suffering of existence in saṃsāra and the great bliss of nirvāṇa. Revulsion against existence on the wheel of rebirth began to grow within him, and he asked the yogin to guide him on the path to freedom. The yogin gave him the Guhyasamāja initiation and empowerment together with instruction concerning "reliance upon one's own body."

Visualize upon the crown of the head
The immaculate white HAṀ of pure pleasure
And in your gut the translucent syllable BAṀ,
Blazing with light and melting the HAṀ on your head.
The four levels of joy will then gradually arise—
Joy, supreme joy, detached joy, and innate joy.
Thus leave the frustration of saṃsāra
And attain the pure pleasure of liberation.

Nalinapa meditated in this way, and by virtue of the successive stages of joy produced in his four focal points of psychic energy he became free of delusive imagination and the frustration of existence, like a lotus that grows up from the slime of a lake uncontaminated by its source. After nine years he realized the ultimate truth, and the defilements of his mind dissolving, he attained *mahāmudrā-siddhi*. He worked for the people of Paṭaliputra for four hundred years, before bodily attaining the Ḍākinī's Paradise with four hundred and fifty disciples.

Sādhana

Nalinapa's instruction of reliance upon one's own body[213] is the celibate's practice corresponding to Babhaha's fulfillment yoga with a consort. Most beneficial in a person with strong sexual desire, the essence of the practice is to sublimate lust into fierce undiscriminating awareness that overwhelms or "burns out" the functions of the relative mind that create a sense of ego, that create the conceptual filter through which we normally perceive sensory stimuli, and, in a word, that create saṃsāra. The monosyllabic, euphonic equivalent of the nature of the navel or gut cakra (*nirmāna-cakra*) varies according to the tantra. Nalinapa is told to visualize the seed syllable BAṀ; this could be a corruption of RAṀ, the euphonic nature of fire.[214] In the siddhas' *caryāgīti* and *dohās* the deity arising from this seed-syllable is a yoginī—Ḍombī, Caṇḍālī, Nairātmā or Prajñā—whose nature is the emptiness of divine passion (*mahārāga*). Thus the fire of the yoginī in the gut center blazes up to melt the HAṀ in the head center, which is the seed syllable of the Five Dhyāni Buddhas, representing the five psycho-physical constituents. The HAṀ "melts" and "drips down" as the ambrosia of the male principle, the white ambrosia that the yoginī is represented as carrying in her skull-cup. With the interfusion of the red (female) and white (male), the four levels of joy arise successively, each level associated with a *cakra*. Joy, in the head center, is described as the highest physical pleasure attainable through the senses. Supreme joy, in the throat *cakra*, is the pure spiritual joy of supra-sensual, esthetic pleasure. The joy of the heart *cakra*, the focal point of the *dharmakāya*, and the essential nature of mind, is detached or desireless joy, literally "freedom from joy" or "beyond joy;" this joy has no object, either sensual or mental, associated with it—it is the joy of emptiness. In the gut *cakra*, the *cakra* of integration, is innate joy, and as *sahaja* indicates, it arises coincident with every moment of experience. It is indistinguishable from pure pleasure (*mahāsukha*) and it is united with emptiness, which is the yogin's nature of being at this final stage of attainment of Mahāmudrā. Many variations of this technique of reliance upon one's own body are described in different traditions and tantras; each one is a complete and efficacious vision described in terms of the fulfillment stage, and comparison serves no practical purpose. A Guru's transmission and guidance is indispensable in this as in all fulfillment practices.

Historiography

The root of *Nalinapāda* is *nalina,* which is a lotus or waterlily, known to the Tibetans as The Divine Flower (*T. lha yi me tog*). The Saliputra of the texts has been rendered Paṭaliputra.

41
THE MAHĀSIDDHA BHUSUKU (ŚĀNTIDEVA) THE IDLE MONK

Until my time of realization I savored various tastes,
And in saṃsāra I was alienated from the Buddha;
Upon realization saṃsāra and nirvāṇa united in
pure pleasure,
And I became like a flaming jewel in the vast ocean.

During the reign of King Devapāla the seven hundred monks of the great monastic academy of Nālandā were well provided for by the king's generosity. Food, cloth and all the necessities of life were freely available. During this period a prince of pious disposition was ordained in the *mahāsāṅghika* order, the largest of the four orders represented at Nālandā. The Abbot was satisfied with the progress of all his three hundred students in their study of the five arts and sciences except the prince. While his fellow monks were studying, the prince kept to his bed, warming his stomach so that he might better digest his morning meal of five measures of rice. The king, informed of the prince's behavior, called him The Idler, Bhusuku, the monk who did nothing but eat, sleep and stroll for the sake of his digestion.

Now it was the custom at Nālandā to maintain constant recitation of the scriptures. Each monk would take his turn in the rota, reciting a sūtra that he had learned by heart. Bhusuku memorized nothing, so he missed his turn on the rota. This was resented by his fellow monks, and the Abbot warned him that unless he did his duty he would be expelled from the monastery.

"I have broken no vow," Bhusuku protested. "It would be unjust of you to expel me. I am simply not a scholar."

Bhusuku (Śāntideva), the great poet, vanishes into space.

However, the Abbot insisted that if he missed his turn again he would be expelled. The monks awaited for that event, eager for Bhusuku's humiliation, and they spread the word of his impending shame. The night before the prince's turn on the rota came about, the Abbot came to Bhusuku's cell intent upon giving him some saving advice.

"You have been eating and sleeping while you should have been studying," he said. "You are certainly incapable of reciting a sūtra. You will be expelled if you fail, you know," the Abbot continued when Bhusuku demurred. "Tonight you should recite the mantra of Mañjuśrī, the Bodhisattva of Intellect. Repeat the ARAPACANA mantra throughout the night."

He gave Bhusuku the secret precepts of Mañjuśrī's sādhana and the blessing of the mantra, and Bhusuku tied his collar to the ceiling to prevent himself from falling over and falling asleep, and he began to recite the mantra that he had been taught. Towards morning his cell was suddenly filled with light and the Bodhisattva himself appeared.

"What is your purpose?" asked Mañjuśrī.

"Tomorrow I must recite a sūtra and I am invoking Mañjuśrī to aid me," Bhusuku replied.

"Do you not recognize me?" Mañjuśrī exclaimed.

"I have no idea who you are," Bhusuku replied.

"I am Mañjuśrī himself!"

"Then I beg you to grant me the power and realization of every quality of perfect insight," Bhusuku implored.

"Consider it granted," the Bodhisattva said. "Recite your sūtra in the morning!" and he vanished.

The next day at the time of Bhusuku's recitation, the king, his court, the people and the pundits gathered together with flower offerings and incense to await his arrival, everyone expecting to laugh at his expense. When Bhusuku appeared he requested the monks' canopy, and most confidently he mounted the temple throne. At once he rose, levitating above the cushions, his body glowing and pulsating with light. Those who had come to mock became apprehensive. The temple door was closed.

"Shall I recite a traditional sūtra or my own composition?" he asked the king.

The pundits glanced at one another, and the king and court began to smile again. "Your eating habits are most unusual," said the king, "and your sleeping and strolling habits are rare indeed. It is fitting that you maintain your standards of originality and recite a sūtra of your own."

Then Bhusuku recited extempore the ten chapters of *The Path to Enlightenment*, the *Bodhicāryāvatāra*, and having delivered this most sublime and profound discourse he rose into the sky. The five hundred pundits, King Devapāla and all the people were amazed, inspired to great heights of faith. They strewed flowers up to his knees, saying, "This is not Bhusuku, The Idler, this man is surely a sage." And they renamed him Śāntideva, Divine Peace, for he had reduced their pride.

Afterwards, the pundits requested a commentary, which Śāntideva gave them, but when they entreated him to become their abbot he refused. Offering his robes, his begging bowl and all his sacred artefacts to the altar in the temple, unknown to the Abbot and the monks he left for another country.

Slowly he made his way to Dhokiri, a town of some two hundred and fifty thousand households. In Dhokiri he made himself a sword out of a piece of wood and painted it gold, and then presenting himself before the king he asked for a position as swordsman in the palace guard. The king agreed to employ him at the handsome rate of ten *tola*s of gold per day. Living comfortably on this wage Śāntideva remained in the palace guard for twelve years, constantly attentive to the ultimate nature of reality. During the great autumn festival of the Great Mother Goddess, Umādevī, he accompanied the guards to the temple as though he too were a devotee. But on one occasion, when the guards were cleaning their swords, one of them noticed that Śāntideva's weapons appeared to be made of wood, and he reported this to the king. Śāntideva was called to the throne.

"Show me your sword, guard!" ordered the king.

"It will do you harm if I unsheathe it," Śāntideva warned.

"Do as I say!" the king commanded. "I will take responsibility for whatever happens."

"Then please cover one eye," Śāntideva pleaded, finally. When the king and his attendants had done as he asked he unsheathed his sword, and its brilliant glare blinded their uncovered eyes, and they fell upon their knees, entreating his forgiveness and mercy. Śāntideva rubbed spittle on their blinded eyes, and their lost sight returned. The king asked him to remain as his palace priest, but Śāntideva declined.

Śāntideva then left Dhokiri and retreated to a mountain cave. Here he was seen killing deer and eating venison, and after this had been reported to the king, His Majesty arrived at the cave with his entourage.

"You taught the King of Nālandā a lesson and here you restored the sight of the blind. It you have that kind of power, why do you harm living beings?" the king asked aggressively.

"I am no butcher," replied Śāntideva. "I am a healer." And opening the door of his walled-in cave, animals streamed out into the sunshine, seeming to multiply as they ran, covering the hills and valleys, until finally they vanished into nothing. "You fortunate people should realize that all elements of experience are merely dream and illusion," he taught them. "The reality of phenomena can never be established. With an understanding of all things as insubstantial figments of the mind, enter the path of liberation." Then he spoke these lines:

The deer I took for venison
Never came into existence,
Never lived on earth,
And will not cease to be.
If no entities of experience have substance,
What is the reality of hunter and victim?
Alas, you pitiful people,
You called me Bhusuku!

Thus Śāntideva converted the king and his court, setting them upon the path of truth. Devoted practice of his sādhana had given Bhusuku an encounter with Mañjuśrī, and realizing the unity of Body, Speech and Mind he was instantaneously endowed with the talents of a Buddha and *mahāmudrā-siddhi.* As Śāntideva he lived for one hundred years before he attained the Ḍākinī's Paradise.

Sādhana and Historiography

We have uncovered no evidence that settles the question of whether there were one or two Bhusuku Śāntidevas. The Indian and Tibetan traditions assume that there was one, but this is by no means certain. Both Tāranātha and Bu ston's accounts of Śāntideva weave together the stories of the inspired mahāyāna writer and the tantric siddha, like our legend, adding some interesting details.[215] Śāntideva was born to the throne of Saurāṣṭra (Gujarat) at a time when, according to Huien Tsiang, Buddhism flourished there. He learned the method of propitiating Mañjuśrī from a *kusulu* tantrika and attained a vision of the Bodhisattva, who told him not to ascend the throne. Śāntideva fled to Nālandā where he was ordained by the Abbot Jayadeva (T.rGyal ba'i lha). We have knowledge of two Jayadevas: the first was the preceptor of Virūpa, early ninth century,[216] and the Guru of Atīśa in the eleventh century. The former could well have been the tantric siddha and *caryāpada* singer's preceptor. At Nālandā Śāntideva angered his fellow monks with his slothful exterior manner, and redeemed himself in their eyes by reciting the *Bodhicāryāvatāra*. It was during his recitation of the ninth chapter on the *prajñāpāramitā*, at verse thirty-five—"neither being nor non-being is true reality"—that he levitated and dissolved into the sky, only his voice remaining. The ninth chapter is still considered to be the finest exposition of the difficult topic of perfect wisdom. When he left Nālandā three monks followed him and asked for commentaries on his great work. He directed them to a Nālandā storeroom where he had deposited the *Śīkṣa-samuccaya* and the *Sūtra-samuccaya*, both practical works on the Bodhisattva Path, written on birch bark.

Śāntideva was then elected head of a *pāṣaṇḍika* community, where he performed the miracle of feeding all with a single bowl of rice. King Ariviśana's kingdom, where he became a palace guard, was probably in Orissa, or south of Orissa in Kaliṅga with Triliṅga as its capital (Dhokiri is otherwise Dekira, or rDo kiri in the legend). A final revealing anecdote, probably referring to the siddha Śāntideva, takes him to Śrī Parvata where he took the guise of a Buddhist sadhu devoted to Ucchūṣman (Mahādeva), going naked and living on washing-up water. Here an anti-Buddhist teacher with the name of Śaṅkaradeva threatened to destroy all Buddhist books and edifices if a Śiva maṇḍala that he created out of colored powders in the sky could not be destroyed. Śāntideva destroyed the maṇḍala with a mighty wind that also killed the heretics and created chaos in the land, although he saved the king and queen. This last tale makes a connection between Buddhist and Hindu Tantra at Śrī Parvata, Śrīśailam (see p. 121).

The siddha-poet Bhusukupāda, who may have been ordained by the Abbot of Nālandā, Jayakara, at the beginning of the ninth century, and who wrote in the style associated with Saraha's lineage of siddhas, has a song that echoes Śāntideva's explanation of his flesh-eating habit in our legend: "What is uncreated from the beginning can have neither birth nor death nor any other kind of existence. Bhusuku or Rauta(?) says: this is the nature of all things—nothing comes or goes, and there is neither existence nor non-existence in *sahaja*."[217] In another song Bhusuku sings: "I have steered the thunder-boat through the canal of the lotus and cast off all afflictions after reaching non-dual Bengal. Today Bhusuku has indeed become a Bengali, for he has taken a Caṇḍālī as his wife."[218] This song seems to indicate that Bhusuku was originally from outside Bengal; but although there is no reason why the writer of the ethically immaculate *Bodhicāryāvatāra* should not also write songs about his Caṇḍālī consort, the principle that induced him to write his songs in the vernacular should also have been applied to his popular discourse on the Bodhisattva's path, which was written in Sanskrit. Other lines of Bhusuku that stick in the mind are, "Dark is the night and the play of the rat begins. . . . When the rat's activity ceases all fetters are destroyed."[219] And also, "On seeing and hearing *sahaja* all the senses are destroyed, and the mind within revels in solitude."[220]

The early Śāntideva wrote only the *Bodhicāryāvatāra* and its two commentaries. There is only conjecture as to when he lived. A Singhalese authority gives AD 690–730 precisely, but without evidence;[221] other scholars, however, tend to agree with this seventh to eighth century dating. If the source that makes Bhusukupāda the disciple of Nāgabodhi and the Guru of Sarvabhakṣa is correct,[222] then it is confirmed that the siddha lived during the first half of the ninth century, contemporary with King Devapāla of our legend and the mahāsiddha Virūpa. In Tibet, Śāntideva is also known as Kṣitigarbha, the name of a disciple of Atīśa who accompanied his master to Tibet in 1042. It is of course conceivable that both Śāntidevas were given the epithet Bhusuku due to their incorrigible laziness. One Tibetan source explains the epithet as descriptive of one who is only concerned about the four basic functions of existence: eating and drinking, sleeping and defecation and urination. An etymological attempt makes bhu (*bhuj*) pleasure and *su* (*svap*) sleep, but *ku*? Our legend gives eating, sleeping, and strolling for the digestion.

42
THE MAHĀSIDDHA INDRABHŪTI
THE ENLIGHTENED SIDDHA-KING

At the propitious peak moment
If he lacks spontaneous grace
No internal or external activity
Can induce the yogin's awakening.
Between blissful joy and the Buddha
There is no distinction at all;
Cut the strings of attachment
And realize the blissful nature of being.

The country of Oḍḍiyāṇa was divided into two kingdoms. King Indrabhūti ruled the two hundred and fifty thousand households of Sambhola, while King Jalendra reigned over the same number of households in Laṅkāpurī. Now Indrabhūti had a seven year old sister called Lakṣmīṅkarā, whom King Jalendra wished his son to marry. A proposal of marriage was sent to Indrabhūti, who studied it with his ministers before concluding that despite a difference in religion—one family worshipped Buddha the other Brahmān—since the families were of equal status, an alliance was desirable. The courier returned to Jalendra with the message that since religion was the only obstacle, the prince and princess should be considered betrothed.

The following year the prince came to Sambhola to meet Lakṣmīṅkarā. Indrabhūti gave him horses, elephants, gold and silver before he returned to Laṅkāpurī. His father expressed surprise that the prince had not brought Lakṣmīṅkarā home with him, but he was satisfied with the prince's explanation that she was yet too young to leave home.

Indrabhūti had many wives, all of whom had faith in the

Buddha's teaching. When the Guru Lawapa (Kambala) passed through Sambhola, the women, including Lakṣmīṅkarā, asked him for initiation and instruction. The young princess having received instruction practiced her precepts earnestly. When she turned sixteen her prospective father-in-law, King Jalendra, sent an escort to bring her to her betrothed, but when the young yoginī-princess reached Laṅkāpurī a great loathing for the world overcame her, and she fled to a cave to continue her yoga until she attained *siddhi*. Then from the highest level of attainment she commenced teaching latrine-sweepers and other outcastes, finally attaining the Ḍākinī's Paradise.

Indrabhūti received word from King Jalendra about his sister's behavior, and he was highly impressed by her example. "While my sister has been attaining Buddhahood I have been leading a complacent life of ease and comfort," he thought. "She has fathomed the mystery of existence, and I, too, should strive on that same path. I will relinquish the burden of government, a punishment inflicted by my karma, an unworthy task, and practice a sādhana."

So Indrabhūti abdicated in favor of his son and retreated to a small palace, where he practiced his sādhana for twelve years. He gained *mahāmudrā-siddhi*, but no one knew of his accomplishment. One day his son and some courtiers came to visit him, and about to open the door, his son heard a voice from above, "Do not go in! I am up here!" Looking up they saw their king enthroned in the sky. Overjoyed as if they had reached the first level of the Bodhisattva's path, they paid homage to him. The king remained in the sky for seven days, teaching his son and the courtiers the inconceivable doctrine of "profundity and immensity." Finally, with seven hundred disciples, in his very body he attained the Ḍākinī's Paradise.

Sādhana

Indrabhūti's sister, Lakṣmīṅkarā, plays such an important role in this story that we learn little of the king himself, except that he was a tolerant man, predisposed towards the contemplative life. Yet his song of realization is one of the most instructive, hitting two tantric nails very nicely on their heads. First, he says that no amount of conscientious effort will induce the goal of spontaneity; and second, he defines the Buddha as the pure delight inherent in all human beings. The teaching he gave his disciples after he had attained

Indrabhūti enjoys the dance of sensory awareness.

mahāmudrā-siddhi was the simple, direct teaching called "profundity and immensity,"[223] which is a common expression of Dzokchen *atiyoga* rather than of Mahāmudrā. Profundity and immensity are the two basic dimensions of the *dharmakāya*, the inner space that is all-pervading and encompassing, and the manifest compassionate emanation that is inseparable from it.

Historiography

Indrabhūti is the archetypal tantric king. Indra is King of the Gods, and *bhūti* or *bodhi* means "wisdom" or "enlightenment;" thus Indrabhūti or Indrabodhi is The Enlightened Divine King. But the legends and lineages refer to historical personalities who played vital roles in the development of Tantra, and their kingdoms were Oḍḍiyāṇa and Zahor (also Kāñcī: see *74*). The identification of the various King Indrabhūtis presents the most intractable problem in the history of the siddhas. The two principal early Indrabhūtis are both known as King Dza (or sons of King Dza); the syllable *dza* (Sanskrit *ja*) has no esoteric significance, and may indeed be a corruption of *rāja*.

Indrabhūti the Great, the first Indrabhūti, King of Oḍḍiyāṇa, sometimes called King Dza or the son of King Dza, is called the first tantrika, and he was the initiator of several important tantric lineages. At his birth the hīnayāna was still dominant in north-west India, and it is quite possible that he was the Indrabhūti that the scrupulous Chinese recorded in the *T'ang Annals* as King of Oḍḍiyāṇa in AD 642, although a later date is more credible. In the legends of the *Guhyasamāja-tantra's* origin it is related that from the thirteenth floor of his palace King Indrabhūti watched a strange flight of radiant creatures flying across the sky, and informed that these beings were *arhat*s he invited the five hundred saints to enjoy his hospitality. He asked them for instruction, but was disappointed when he was urged to abandon sensual pleasure. He wanted a way to obtain Buddhahood without renouncing the senses, a way that involved women, he insisted. The *arhat*s were disobliging, but he eventually obtained such precepts, instruction on the *Guhyasamāja-tantra*, the first tantra to be revealed, a father-tantra, from a divine agency, either the Buddha himself,[224] or Vajrapāṇi.[225] The king converted and emptied Oḍḍiyāṇa, and then taught the *nāga*s and *nāginīs*; a *nāginī-yoginī* taught it to the "southern king" Viśukalpa, who taught it to Saraha, the Great Brahmin of Baṅgala. It must have been this same Indrabhūti who revealed the *Vajrakīla-tantra* and taught it to Dhanarakṣita, who initiated Padmasambhava;[226] and the same Indrabhūti who initiated the *rDzogs chen anuyoga* lineage: Indrabhūti, Kukkuripa, Garab Dorje, Śrī Siṅha, Mañjuśrīmitra and Vimalamitra who taught it in Tibet.[227] The ascription of the revelation of the later, *Hevajra-tantra*, a mother-tantra, to this Indrabhūti is more difficult; the early Hevajra lineage is Indrabhūti, Mahāpadmavajra (not Padmasambhava), Anaṅgavajra, Saroruha, Indrabhūti III (late ninth century).[228]

Indrabhūti II, the Middle One, also known as King Dza, is associated with Zahor, the principality in the Upper Kangra Valley with Mandi as capital. A rain of *anuttarayoga-tantra* texts fell upon his palace roof and Kukkuripa explained the texts to him. One of the texts, the *Karaṇḍavyūha*, was blown to Tibet, where King Lhathothori found it upon his palace roof.[229] This last fiction is one of several that seek to inflate Zahor's importance and associate it with Tibet; the fifth Dalai Lama, reputedly of Zahor royalty, was probably responsible for contriving the relationship of Indrabhūti II with the Abbot Śāntarakṣita of Zahor (or Sahor, in Bengal, near Vikramaśīla); with Mandāravā, Padmasambhava's consort, whose father was an early eighth century Indrabhūti of Zahor; and thus with Padmasambhava himself, whose adoptive father was an early eighth century Indrabhūti of Oḍḍiyāṇa, sometimes confounded with Indrabhūti the Great.[230] The eighth century *bLon po bka' thang*, rediscovered in the 14th century, that makes Śāntarakṣita the grandson of Indrabhūti II, renders the salad even less savory; but the great Longchenpa himself asserts the basic fact that Indrabhūti II of Zahor received tantric texts and gained realization.[231]

King Indrabhūti III, the Younger, of Oḍḍiyāṇa, is Lakṣmīṅkarā's brother, the Indrabhūti of our legend, who lived in the late ninth century. When Lalitavajra arrived in Oḍḍiyāṇa with Kambala, it was this Indrabhūti who went to meet them. He had recently gained magical power, and when he sat at the master Lalitavajra's feet to massage them, as custom dictated, he manifested four hands to work on both feet at once. The Guru emanated four legs, the king eight hands, the Guru eight legs, the king sixteen hands, the Guru sixteen legs, but then Indrabhūti could manage no more than the number of hands of the gods, and when the Guru showed him a hundred feet the king's pride was utterly crushed.[232] This was the king that Kambala saved from the hassling *ḍākinī*-witches, and before whose palace The Sleeping Bhikṣu sat for three (twelve) years, though for why is not clear. The mother-tantra was this Indrabhūti's main preoccupation, and the many mother-tantra titles ascribed to Indrabhūti found in the Tenjur are probably the *paṇḍita*-king's work. He received the *Hevajra-tantra* from Saroruha and gave it to Jālandhara; he received the *Saṃvara* from Lawapa and initiated Kacapa and others. Kukkuripa was one of his Gurus. If he was also a great adept of the *Guhyasamāja-tantra*, recipient of the tantra from Anaṅgavajra, whose Guru, Padmavajra, wrote the *Guhyasiddhi*, then he is the author of the *Jñānasiddhi*, another great *Guhyasamāja* commentary.[233]

Two controversies contort this picture. First, 'Gos Lotsawa identifies Lawapa with Indrabhūti the Younger in a Guhyasamāja lineage (see p. 184); second, Dudjom Rimpoche identifies Indrabhūti the Younger as the eldest son of Indrabhūti II/King Dza, also identifying him with Lawapa.[234] The resolution of this conundrum requires further research. However, what is clear is that Indrabhūti/King Dza is the center of a cycle of legends of great importance, and that their significance has been the cause of their loss of historicity.

Sambhola or *Sambhala*, Indrabhūti's capital, may be the root of Sambhalpur Vihāra.[235]

43

THE SIDDHA MEKOPA
GURU DREAD-STARE

The Guru's chief injunction is
"Realize the nature of mind!"
Afterwards, "Do not discriminate between forms,
And accustoming yourself to non-duality
Live in a cremation ground.
When you have realized the principle of sameness
Go into the world as a mad saint."

Mekopa was a Bengali food-vendor. Out of the goodness of his heart, every day he fed a certain yogin. One day the yogin asked him why he fed him.

"I am laying up merit to gain a better rebirth," he replied. The yogin offered to teach him a sādhana that would assure him a better rebirth, and the vendor promised to practice it. He received an initiation that transfers grace and instruction in recognition of the nature of mind:

Your mind is like a wish-fulfilling gem,
Manifesting the variety of nirvāṇa and saṃsāra.
Since knowing and unknowing are a duality
Look into the unchanging space of mind's nature
And discover where mental duality arises.
That non-dual space is without substance,
So all experience must be illusion.
We are bound by delusive desires and misunderstanding!

Mekopa realized that all phenomenal appearances were but figments of his mind, and that mind in reality was a vast space where there is neither coming nor going. He remained composed in that ultimate state of mind for six months. Cognition of the patterns and concepts that his mind usually created was replaced by a realization of the natural disposition of his own mind.

Thereafter he roamed about the cremation ground like a wild animal, sometimes wandering into town and acting like a madman, staring with dreadful eyes. People called him Guru Dread-stare, but he became renowned as Mekopa. He trained many disciples with his profound teaching, and finally expressing his realization he bodily attained the Ḍākinī's Paradise.

Sādhana

Expecting to find a rational metaphysical basis for the siddhas' experiences implies misunderstanding of the nature of Tantra. Tantra is not a philosophy seeking a logical model of the macro/micro cosmos; rather it is a pragmatically-gathered assortment of soteriological techniques where the proof of the pudding is in the one taste. Thus the statement that the mind's nature is "a non-dual space without any substance," and that all entities of experience (*dharmas*) are illusion because no-thing can arise out of nothing, is less a premise and a deduction to be proved experientially than a personal statement about the nature of a mystical experience that cannot be proved or disproved, even if the tantrika could be interested in proof. The common and shared experience of yogins meditating upon the nature of their minds is the discovery of emptiness as the root, and illusory, insubstantial appearances as the branches. It is only for the few to make this discovery, those karmically destined and capable of gazing at the sun without blinking. If the preparation for this experience has not been complete, then naturally enough, when the full force of reality impinges, the yogin can lose his balance slightly. Mekopa was able to teach in the stream of full awareness, but he seems still to have been overwhelmed by the nature of his sense perception, since he wandered about with a crazy gaze, his eyes bulging out of his head, frightening people. The phrase "like a wild animal" implies that he could not act up to the conventional standards of social behavior, and, perhaps, that he could not look after himself properly. This description could equally apply to the behavior of a novice under the effect of a strong psychedelic drug, and the similarity is not accidental. Such yogins are honored and worshiped in India and Nepal. They are accepted as god-knowers merely by the manifestation of such mudrā and mantra. They are known as *pagala-babas,* "crazy saints."

In the thousand years since the Mahāmudrā tradition was formulated, it has undergone minor modification at Tibetan hands. The change has been to improve the course of preparation so that what happened to Mekopa is less likely to happen to the initiates of the Tibetan Kahgyupa sect. Mekopa was thrust immediately to the center of the maṇḍala with the precept "Realize the nature of mind," and then, with the instruction against discrimination in an ultimate sense, he was equipped to act. The very similar tradition which has retained these very direct and efficacious precepts in the way that they are expressed here in a Mahāmudrā context is the Dzokchen or *Mahāsaṅdhi* school. Again, the instructions from Mekopa's Guru express a fundamental Dzokchen view in similar terminology: unconditioned space is the nature of all things, but the mind is capable of imposing an ignorant dualistic structure upon this inchoate space, or alternatively, of dissolving itself in the attainment of gnostic awareness. Although the origin of Mahāmudrā is not clear, it is most likely that it originated in Oḍḍiyāṇa and was transmitted with the mother-tantras by the early siddhas travelling from Oḍḍiyāṇa to eastern India, siddhas who would also have had knowledge of Dzokchen.

Historiography

Mekopa is probably a derivation of *megha*, "cloud;" Megopa is a variation of the siddha's name. Megopa was one of the Five Little Ones, disciples of Maitripa who lived in the eleventh century.[236] Otherwise we know nothing of him. The Tibetans rendered his name Dread-stare (T.'Jigs 'jigs su lta ba).

44

THE SIDDHA KOṬĀLIPA
THE PEASANT GURU

All pleasure and pain arises in the mind,
So obey the Guru and dig mind's nature;
Even a wise man may toil on a mountain of rock
And never realize his natural state of bliss.
Awaken consciousness in the heart's core
And the six sense-fields become a stream of pleasure;
All abstract labeling is futile, the cause of anxiety,
So in and out of meditation, relax in natural ease.

Koṭālipa met his Guru, the master Śāntipa, while he was at work digging a mountain terrace. Śāntipa was on his way back to his own country of Magadha from Śrī Laṅkā, where he had been invited as a missionary by the king, and he encountered Koṭālipa four days out of Rameśvaram. Koṭālipa stopped his work to watch the great man pass, and Śāntipa called him, asking him who he was.

Koṭālipa bowed low. "I am a peasant digging this mountain," he replied in answer to the master's question. "We were driven from our homes by warring kings who continuously plundered the land. Sick of such treatment, we have come to this place to scratch a living out of this poor mountain soil. Here at least we are safe."

"If I had a mantra for digging mountains and instruction to go with it, would you practice it?" Śāntipa asked him.

Koṭālipa said he would indeed practice it, and Śāntipa taught him like this:

Your body is debilitated
Due to the life you lead,
And your karma is inherently hostile,
Karma of six-fold perversity:

Digging the earth as generosity,
Non-violence as moral conduct,
Endurance of pain as patience,
Persistent effort as perseverance,
Unflagging energy as concentration,
And cognition of all this as perfect awareness;
These are the six failings of your karma.
Abandon them for these six perfect karmas:
Devotion to the Guru as generosity,
Guarding the mind as moral conduct,
Constancy of mind's nature as patience,
Meditation upon mind's nature as perseverance,
Undistracted absorption as concentration,
And perception of reality as perfect awareness.
Make these karmas a constant habit.

Koṭālipa asked for more precise instruction.

"Devote yourself to the Guru," Śāntipa said. "And since all pleasure and pain arises from your own mind, preoccupy yourself with the innate purity of your mind. The unchangeable pure nature of your mind is like the unchanging mountain; dig it with the spade that is an unceasing stream of radiant knowledge. As you work in the fields your meditation and your digging must be simultaneous, like the actions of your left and right hands."

Happiness and sorrow are both functions of mind;
Cultivate the mountain of mind with these precepts.
You may dig life-long in this mountain of earth,
But never can you realize the pure pleasure of
mind's nature.

The peasant Koṭālipa meditated according to this instruction for twelve years, and he attained *siddhi*. After performing many selfless deeds, bodily he obtained the Ḍākinī's Paradise.

Sādhana

The master of sūtra, Śāntipa, is calling a literal interpretation of the mahāyāna practice of the six perfections (*pāramitās*) a perverse path. He is telling the peasant to reject an interpretation of the perfections that turns them to poison, that perverts karma, and leads to physical enervation. He is saying that when the object of concentration is physical suffering, the virtues of persistent effort, unflagging energy, and clear perception, devoid of any understanding of mind's nature, constitute a samsaric death-trap. Likewise, non-violence (*ahiṃṣa*), one of the basics of Śakyamuni's teaching, is meaningless unless it is a spontaneous expression of a joyful mind arising out of non-referential awareness. There is no virtue in practicing any meditation that does not work, and if meditation causes suffering instead of curing it, give it up, says Śāntipa.

The repeated statement that pleasure and pain, virtue and vice, all arise from the mind, implies that virtue and pleasure are also a part of the ignorance and delusion of saṃsāra. Virtue must be accompanied by insight, otherwise it is little different from vice. Virtue and insight are the two wings of the Garūḍa, which lives in space and is an insubstantial illusion—a mythical Buddha-bird. Śāntipa also stresses the importance of the Guru by indicating that Koṭālipa's misguided practice has led to his debilitation, and proved to be worse than no dharma at all. A Guru who has mastered skillful means—diagnosis and prescription—was Koṭāli's great need, and also, as Indrabhūti said, no matter how conscientiously the yogin practices external or internal techniques, without the Guru's blessing nothing is gained. We assume that Śāntipa showed his disciple the nature of his own mind (no formal initiation is mentioned), and thereafter he is able to practice the creative mode as the work of digging the fields, using the six perverse karmas as friendly helpers, and the fulfillment mode as absorption in the nature of mind. It is then as if Koṭāli were identifying with the mountain watching the spade turning over each load of earth in a series of non-dual events composed of knowledge and emptiness.

Historiography

Koṭālipāda has its root in *kuṭhāra*, "axe," and therefore "hoe" or "spade," and he is better known to the Tibetans as Tog tse pa, Hoe Man. Kodāli, Kuṭali, Kuṭhāri and Kutṛha are forms of his name. In Śāntipa's legend (*12*) he is the humbling disciple requested to return the precepts necessary to release the old Guru from a life of scholarship and teaching. Koṭālipāda lived in the second half of the eleventh century, and he may have taught Phadampa Sangye

Mahāmudrā precepts. He is one of the few siddhas from the South, and must have lived in our Tamil Nadu. There is little evidence of tantric Buddhism in the far South after the considerable hīnayāna and mahāyāna activity up to the sixth or seventh centuries.

45

THE SIDDHA KAMPARIPA THE BLACKSMITH

In the hearth that was the nature of my body
Lay the coals of preconception and conceptual thought;
Pumping the bellows of lalanā *and* rasanā
Kindling the flame of the avadhūti's *pure awareness*
I melted the iron of thrice poisoned thoughts
And I hammered out the dharmakāya.
Kamparipa became free through this realization.

Kamparipa was born into a family of outcaste smiths of Paṭaliputra. He grew up to follow the family trade. One day a yogin came into his smithy and began to talk, inquiring about his work.

"I'm doing the same work as my father and my grandfather before me," said the blacksmith.

"Are you happy?" asked the yogin.

"How can I be happy?" retorted the smith. "I'm always being burnt by sparks and hot coals. I only endure it to make a living."

"Would you be so kind as to give me some food?" the yogin asked finally.

The blacksmith and his wife were surprised and pleased that a yogin should ask for food from such untouchable people as themselves. After the yogin had eaten he asked them if they practiced the Dharma.

"Who would teach such people as us?" replied the smith.

"If you have faith and promise to practice what I teach you, I will instruct you," the yogin told him.

Joyfully they prostrated before him, and presented him with the best offerings they could provide. He gave them the initiation that transfers grace and then instructed them in the three psychic channels as objects of meditation.

"Internalize the bellows, coal, fire, molten iron, and so on, through process of visualization. The bellows are the *lalanā* and *rasanā*, the hearth is the *avadhūti*, sensory consciousness is the blacksmith; pure awareness is the fire, and conceptual thought is the coal. Beat the iron of the three poisons into the finished product that is the pure pleasure of the non-dual *dharmakāya.*"

Transform your daily task
Into an internal meditation.
Pumping the two arms of the bellows,
Lalanā *the right arm and* rasanā *the left,*
To ignite the coals of conceptual thought
Lying in the hearth that is the avadhūti,
Kindle the flame of knowledge and awareness
To melt the iron, the three poisons and the five passions.
The result is the immaculate dharmakāya.

Attuned to his work, after six years of meditation Kamparipa attained *mahāmudrā-siddhi.* His fellows remained ignorant of this achievement until the products of his craft began to appear spontaneously in the hearth. "Our blacksmith has attained the qualities of a Buddha," the astonished people of Paṭaliputra whispered one to another. Henceforth the blacksmith was known as Guru Kamparipa, and having lived for the sake of all beings, eventually he expressed his realization and attained the Ḍākinī's Paradise in his very body.

Sādhana

As Kamparipa's meditation was his craft, to outside eyes his life proceeded normally, without change. The only alteration was in Kamparipa's view of life. In his practice of creative and fulfillment modes united, the principal symbolic elements in his visualization were the three psychic channels. *Lalanā, rasanā* and *avadhūti* are figurative terms (*saṅdhyābhāṣa*) for the three psychic channels: *lalanā* means "tongue," *rasanā* means "woman," and *avadhūti* means "*yoginī*" or "the central channel." The *lalanā* carries consciousness and the male aspect of the psyche, and the *rasanā* carries emotional energies and thought-forms and the female aspect. Watching the bellows pumping into the hearth that is the *avadhūti*, the blacksmith visualizes the perceptual duality of subject and object, self and other, resolved in the flame of pure awareness and knowledge[237] that consumes preconception and conceptual thought. "Pumping the bellows" is to work the lungs and concentrate upon breathing, for the energies of the *lalanā* and *rasanā* are only the subtle form of breath breathed in and out of the nostrils. But no amount of breathing will "ignite the coals" until the transfer of grace at initiation has induced recognition of the nature of mind and brought pure awareness into consciousness. However, once lustful and acrimonious thought is burnt up in that flame, passion becomes malleable, and the blacksmith watches the iron soften before he beats it on the anvil. The three poisons are desire, aversion and ignorance, and the five passions are lust, hatred, pride, envy and sloth.

Clearly there is sympathetic magic operative in these meditations, where the meditative process can be watched and experienced in an external analogy. Actually *seeing* thought go up in smoke, as the *lalanā* and *rasanā* empty into the *avadhūti*, can empty the mind of all distracting thought and concepts, besides providing an effective object of concentration. Likewise, physically beating the passion out of iron, after its reinforcing thought has been eliminated and one step towards detachment has been achieved, the sublimated energy of passion is used to destroy itself. If visualization is considered to be a high form of sympathetic magic, then the entire creative stage could be given that label; and insofar as man is only what he thinks he is, our every day reality can be defined by the anthropologist's "sympathetic magic." Only the Buddha is free from such magic; the process of transforming illusion would be better described as divine magic. But magic is the relevant word, and debased as it has become, the connotations that the siddhas lend it should rehabilitate it and give it a new respectability. Certainly Kamparipa would have known what it meant. His finished products were not simply pieces of iron, they were the *dharmakāya* itself.

Historiography

Kamparipa has at its root *karmara*, "artisan," and the principal variant of his name is Karmāri or Karmāra. In Tibetan he is The Blacksmith (T.mGar pa). His Guru may well have been Avadhūtīpa otherwise known as Maitripa,[238] who lived in the later eleventh century. Saliputra is the text's rendition of his home town.

46

THE MAHĀSIDDHA JĀLANDHARA THE ḌĀKINĪ'S CHOSEN ONE

To invoke blessings in yourself,
Every thought and concept of the three realms
Gathered into body, speech and mind,
Bind them in the lalanā, rasanā *and* avadhūti.

Jālandhara was a brahmin of Turkhāra City. One day, disgusted by what he saw about him, he retired to a cremation ground and sat down beneath a tree. There he entered a state of blissful, heightened consciousness, and he heard the voice of a Ḍākinī coming out of the sky, saying, "Noble Son, may you know the absolute truth!" In great joy Jālandhara prayed to the Ḍākinī again and again, until she actually appeared before him. She gave him the Hevajra initiation and empowerment together with these instructions on fulfillment meditation:

"Gather all inner and outer phenomena, the three realms, the world of appearances and all its possibilities, into the planes of your body, speech and mind. Then concentrate the conceptual structure of body, speech and mind into the three psychic channels. Empty the *lalanā* and *rasanā* into the *avadhūti*, and then eject all the constructs of your mind through the 'gate of purity' on the crown of your head. Thereafter, meditate upon the indivisibility of appearances and emptiness."

All entities of experience, inner and outer,
Gathered together in body, speech and mind,
Right and left channels emptied into the avadhūti,
Eject everything through the gate of purity.
Arisen in the space of pure yoga,
That emptiness is the highest form of pleasure.

Try to sustain the inseparable union of pleasure and emptiness.

Jālandhara meditated upon these instructions on the fulfillment process for seven years and gained *mahāmudrā-siddhi*. Then after expressing his realization and working selflessly for untold beings he attained the Ḍākinī's Paradise with three hundred disciples.

Sādhana

Repetition of a precept does not necessarily clarify it, as Jālandhara's instruction proves. The basic idea of emptying the psycho-organism of its concepts and preconceptions of the universe is evident, but the details of the meditation are omitted. Three successive sets of three concepts are given: the three realms, the three gates, and the three psychic channels. These three planes are increasingly subtle forms of what must be purified, and a quantitative transformation of "mindstuff" occurs from one level to the next. In reverse, evolution from one plane to the next describes the process of manifestation of our delusory universe. The first stage clarifies the mind and sets the world in harmony as all experience is analyzed according to the three realms: the sensual, esthetic and formless realms—all entities of experience can be subsumed under these three heads. Phenomena and noumena having been classified accordingly, the universe is seen as an extension of the psycho-organism as body, speech and mind. "Body" indicates the plane of visual appearances; "speech" the plane of sound, vibration, vision and pure form; and "mind" indicates thought and degrees and modes of consciousness. Body, speech and mind also compose the entire universe. The symbology of the three psychic channels cuts across the above classifications; *lalanā* represents the "subjective" pole, the male aspect and the five "subjective" principles of the psycho-organism, the five psycho-physical constituents; and *rasanā* represents the "objective" pole, the female aspect and the five materiality-producing forces that are the five elements. The final analysis probes to the root of our universe, to its basic unconscious, dualistic structure and the subject/object dichotomy that informs our entire world view and is thus the basis of our ignorance and alienation. Emptied into the *avadhūti*, which represents the purified, all-embracing mind, or pure awareness, our world, which proves to be composed of preconceptions and concepts, is visualized

Jālandhara unites compassion and emptiness.

ejected through the gate of purity, and what remains, as the doors of perception are opened, is non-dual experience of space.

But these precepts elaborated above do not constitute the meditation. The practice involves watching the mind, classifying experience as it arises, seeing the dualizing process at work, penetrating every entity of experience to its emptiness as mental constructs are ejected as flotsam and jetsam. The "gate of purity"[239] and the ejection are not merely metaphors. It is at the fontanelle, at the exit of the *avadhūti*, where "the thousand petalled lotus" grows. In some techniques of this nature a mantra is given to open the "gate," and the affect of this mantra is to open the soft patch of skin that covers the fontanelle so that a stalk of *kuśa* grass can be inserted: more sympathetic magic?

Historiography

Jālandhara is an important siddha in the mother-tantra tradition and Buddhist sources make frequent reference to him. But he is also a founder of the *nāth* lineages and the *nāth* literature and oral tradition is a more fertile source of anecdote. Tibetan sources sketch his life like this:[240] he was born a *śūdra* in Sindh; he was taught and performed his sādhana in Oḍḍiyāṇa and in Jālandhara, both in northwest India; he then visited Nepal and thereafter travelling to Avantī in Mālava he met Tantipa and Kṛṣṇācārya; only then did he go to Bengal, where known as Hāḍipa he performed many miracles and where Mayanāmatī made her son, King Gopīcāṇḍ, his disciple, the disciple who was to bury his Guru alive for ten years until, finally, he was rescued by Kṛṣṇācārya. The tradition that he was born in Turkestan can be supported by our legend if Nagara-thod-tha is taken as a corruption of Thogar (of Turkhāradeśa or Tochārestān), on the Upper Oxus below the Pamirs. There is no doubt that he was initiated into the mother-tantra lineages in Oḍḍiyāṇa; but the place where he practiced his sādhana, and which gave him his name, does present a problem. Outside contemporary Jullunder in the east Punjab is a complex of ruins that Huien Tsiang visited between AD 680–720, when fifty monasteries stood there inhabited by two thousand monks of both hīnayāna and mahāyāna sects. Kaniṣka's great council had convened there and the *Mahāvibhāṣa* had been compiled there by five hundred monks in AD 300.[241] But just as we have distinguished between a tantric and an orthodox Śrī Parvata, a Jālandhara tantric *pīṭhasṭhāna*, older than the monastic complex, is to be found on the River Beas in the Kangra Valley near Nagarkot, or more precisely, near Jvālāmukhī.[242] With Oḍḍiyāṇa, Pūrṇagiri, and Kāmarūpa, Jālandhara was one of the four principal power-places of the *Hevajra-tantra*, which was our siddha's major tantra; it is also an ancient *śākta pīṭha* where the *devī* is worshipped as Caṇḍī with Mahādeva.[243] It was this power-place that gave Jālandhara his name.

Jālandhara is one of the nine original *nāths*, five of whom are counted amongst the eighty-four siddhas: Kāṇha, Mīna, Gorakṣa, Cauraṅgi and Jālandhara (Hāḍipa). He is one of the twelve apostles of the *kāpālikas*' founders, and he is one of the nine *nāth* incarnations of the nine *narāyāṇas*.[244] In the *nāth* lineage he is *guru-bhai* of Matsyendra, and disciple of Adi-nāth, and he founded one of the two major *nāth* lineages including the Phā and Augharī sects. His principal disciples are Kṛṣṇācārya, Gopīcāṇḍ and Bhatṛhari (Bairāga or Bhatṛnāth). In the earliest *nāth* texts, like the *Gorakh-bodh*,[245] Jālandhara and the other Buddhist siddhas can be discerned as the personalities of Buddhist legends, but in the later oral tradition they become practitioners of *haṭhayoga* intent upon mundane siddhi, and their stories are full of magical display. Hāḍipa, as Jālandhara is more often called in the *nāth* literature, has the gods and goddesses at his beck and call and the syllable HŪṀ (more associated with the Buddhist tantras) is the all-fulfilling spell that accomplishes desires magically.

The cycle of stories involving Hāḍipa, his disciple Gopīcāṇḍ and Gopīcāṇḍ's mother, Mayanāmatī, is very popular among the *nāths*. Like Kambala, Gopīcāṇḍ was induced to abdicate his throne by his *ḍākinī*-mother, who feared the curse that her son would die unless he became Hāḍipa's disciple. Mayanāmatī convinced her son through demonstration of miraculous powers under conditions of extreme suffering. Hāḍipa's burial under the king's stables for ten years further convinced Gopīcāṇḍ. Then trekking through the jungle as Guru and disciple, Gopīcāṇḍ lagged behind Hāḍipa and he was stolen by Yama's legions. Hāḍipa descended to the city of the dead in a great rage—a common passion amongst the *śaiva* siddhas but rare amongst the Buddhist—and severely chastised Yama and his officers, demanding Gopīcāṇḍ's return. Thereafter Gopīcāṇḍ received the split-ear initiation, thus becoming the first of the *kānphaṭa-yogins*. He was then sold to a prostitute who abused him as a menial for refusing to make love to her. This comprised his twelve year sādhana. Hāḍipa turned the whore into a bat, while the enlightened yogin was reinstated as king.[246]

In most of the vernacular stories about apparently futile magical powers there is a hidden meaning relating to *kāya-sādhana*, perfection of the body leading to immortality, a common practice amongst the *nāth*s, or demonstrating wisdom (*mahājñāna*). But whereas the same term, *mahājñāna*, is used by both Buddhists and *śaiva*s, in Mahāmudrā it means pure awareness of space while in the *nāth*s' stories it has been debased to mean the faculty of divining solutions to practical and spiritual problems. This anecdote[247] illustrates another distinction between the Buddhist and *śaiva* traditions: initially the Five Nāths practiced ascetic yoga successfully, but after Adi-nāth, Śiva, had taken Gaurī as his consort, and Gaurī had failed to persuade Śiva that the life of a married householder tantrika was the superior mode, she stooped to low levels of seduction to prove to her Lord that his disciples were still capable of lust. All fell victim to her except Gorakhnāth, who was the Sir Galahad of the *nāth* stories. To atone, Hāḍipa set himself a self-imposed sādhana as sweeper of Mayanāmatī, where he enjoyed the company of Queen Maya. He took his name, Hāḍipa, from *hāḍi*, "sweeper," in this story; or, at the time of the creation of the world when each of the Five Nāths was born out of a part of the Primal Lord's body, Hāḍipa was born from the Lord's bone (*hāḍa*).

Ten of the eighty-four siddhas are amongst Jālandhara's disciples: Kāṇhapa and Tantipa are taught by him in our legends; Mīna (*8*), Cauraṅgi (*10*), Anaṅga (*81*), Carpaṭi (*54*), Dharmapa (*36*), Campaka (*60*), Kukkuripa (*34*) and Khaḍgapa (*15*) are mentioned as his disciples in other sources. In the Tibetan Hevajra lineage Indrabhūti III is his Guru and Kāṇhapa his disciple;[248] in one Cakrasaṃvara lineage Kacapa is his Guru and Kāṇhapa his disciple, and in another Kurmapa is his Guru and Kāṇhapa his disciple,[249] the same as in his Kālacakra lineage. These lineal relationships place him in the late ninth and early tenth century, while his Hāḍipa persona associates him with the tenth century *nāth*s. Both Jālandhara and Kṛṣṇācārya must have lived very long lives, unless the *nāth*s of these same names were separate individuals. Doubt has indeed been expressed that Jālandhara and Hāḍipa are the same person. An attempt has been made to date Hāḍipa/Jālandhara by associating his disciple-kings, Bhatṛhari and Gopīcāṇḍ, with historical figures, kings of Ujjain and a Bengali principality, without sufficient evidence.

Jālandhara is also known as Jālandharipa. The Sanskrit root is *jāla*, "net," and the Tibetan translation, "Net-bearer" (T.Dra ba 'dzin pa).

47

THE MAHĀSIDDHA RĀHULA
THE REJUVENATED DOTARD

The celestial Rāhu, the dragon planet,
Eclipses the light of the moon;
The Rāhu of non-dual space and knowledge
Eclipses the lunar circle of relative phenomena.

The low-caste Rāhula was born, grew up and grew old in Kāmarūpa. In his dotage he was unable to control his bodily functions, and his senility caused his family to curse and abuse him, and he was miserable. He became worried about his rebirth, and he would wander through the cremation ground in hope of meeting a Guru. One day a yogin stopped him and asked him what he was doing.

"The full moon of my youth had been eclipsed by the planetary dragon of old age," he told the yogin, sadly. "My sons and relatives abuse me, and I can only hope to find peace in death."

"As you have grown old," the yogin replied, "the three torrents of birth, sickness and old age have ravaged you. Now the torrent of death rises up to carry you away. Don't you want to make provision for death?"

"Indeed I do," replied the old man fervently. "But who would teach an old man like me?"

And the yogin sang:

The pristine nature of the mind is unaging,
And faith—true wealth—is never diminished.
If you can practice a sādhana with devotion,
You should follow me.

He gave the initiation that transfers grace and this instruction on the mystic seed: "Visualize the seed syllable A: on the crown of your head and emanating from it a lunar disc that surmounts it. Imagine that the mental constructs of all phenomenal creation enter the moon."

When the dragon of non-dual realization
Eclipses the subject/object circle of constructs,
At the pure pleasure spot of your fontanelle
A stream of pleasure and emptiness united
Flows from the essence of the mystic circle,
Destroying such enemies as the body-mind sheath;
And then the qualities of the Buddhas arise.
Ehma! Immortality is so wonderful!

By means of this meditation the moon of subject/object duality was gradually eclipsed by the non-dual circle of realization. The ambrosia of non-duality flowed through the gate of purity filling and saturating the old man's body, which was transformed into the body of a sixteen year old youth. Thus he gained *mahāmudrā-siddhi*, and after training the people of Kāmarūpa he expressed his realization and bodily attained the Ḍākinī's Paradise.

Sādhana

In Rāhula's fulfillment stage visualization, out of empty space (*dharmakāya*) arises the A: that is the "unborn" or "potential" sound, the basis of all sound; it represents the empty essence of the Buddha's mode of being as vibration and visionary pleasure (*saṃbhogakāya*). Out of the A: appears the lunar disc that represents the emptiness of phenomenal appearances (*nirmāṇakāya*). The magic of the meditation depends greatly upon the power of these symbols. At a glance they are meaningless, but after years of practice, and after success has endowed the symbols with the power of evoking their reality, when the yogin begins his meditation, simply by visualization of these symbols the Buddha's *trikāya* is evoked and the function of "Rāhu" begins."The mental constructs of all phenomenal creation" are the three realms, body, speech and mind and, basically, the subject/object duality. The basic dichotomy of the mind can be expressed as "I" and "mine" or the knower and the known, and also as the ego and the enemy, the executioner and the victim (or *vice versa*), us and them, good and evil, right and wrong, good and bad, knowledge and ignorance, assertion and denial, being and non-being, and so on. The lunar disc, or mystic circle,[250] into which all concepts and constructs must enter, is "eclipsed" by *rāhu*, which symbolizes the pure awareness of the *dharmakāya*. *Rāhu* belongs to the tantric trinity of sun, moon and *rāhu*, which are directly analogous to the *lalanā, rasanā* and *avadhūti*. Thus *rāhu* as the dragon planet that eclipses sun and moon symbolizes the union of sun and moon. The creative energy of pure awareness dissolves the polarized, karmic energies of sun and moon;[251] non-dual awareness eclipses the dualistic constructs of mind.

To induce the moon on the crown of the head to shower down its nectar is the aim of several techniques. It may be melted by the fire of the yoginī in the gut center, or it may be activated by *kuṇḍalinī* rising from the sexual *cakra*, or by the white seed syllable OM. One way to understand the release of the flow of nectar is to conceive of the moon as fixed ideas and preconceptions, constructs and concepts, dissolving and flowing down into the psycho-organism. The nectar is pleasure and emptiness coincident, the nature of experience in the head *cakra* after the dissolution of mental rubbish. As the nectar floods the body four hostile powers are destroyed. These powers are functions of karmic, genetic, racial and cultural conditioning. The first is the psycho-physical aggregate—form, sensation, perception, motivation and consciousness; these five psychosomatic components define the ego's "island." The second of these powers is passion—desire, hatred, pride, envy and sloth; it is an unreliable but powerful ally to the tantrika. The third is death, which implies constant fear of cessation. The fourth is cupidity, the basic desire for sensual and sexual satisfaction that cannot be assuaged. These four are conceived as devils: the first two bedevil thought, and the other two are "non-human devils" or "spirits"—fear and lust are instinctual impulses outside, or basic to, the normal neurotic confusion of the mind.[252] When these four hostile powers have been destroyed the qualities of the Buddhas spontaneously arise. Further, since the notion of the body together with the mind's dualizing functions have been destroyed, the psycho-organism is transformed into an immortal body of light (see p. 135).

Historiography

Rāhula, or Rāhulabhadra, is a common Buddhist name. The first Buddhist Rāhula was Śākyamuni's son, a monk, who was born at the time of an eclipse. The great mahāyāna Rāhulabhadra was also called the Great Brahmāṇa Saraha, who taught the first Nāgārjuna, and to whom that Second Buddha may have been indebted for the principles of his *madhyamika* philosophy and the ethos of his entire vision. This Rāhula wrote one great piece of philosophical verse, *Praise to The Goddess of Wisdom* (*Prajñāpāramitā-stotra*), which alone brought him immortality.[253] He was alive in AD 119 during the reign of Kaniṣka II.[254] Another Rāhulabhadra has been identified with the mahāsiddha Saraha; he ordained the siddha Nāgārjuna while he was Abbot of Nālandā. But Saraha himself had a preceptor called Rāhulabhadra. During the same period Buddhaśrijñāna, the founder of a Guhyāsamāja lineage, had a *kṣetriya paṇḍita* Rāhulabhadra as disciple;[255] and Āryadeva had a *śūdra* disciple of the same name whom he taught at Nālandā, and who later received his blessing as the lineage holder.[256] Finally, the last abbot of Nālandā was called Rāhulaśrībhadra. The Tibetan monk Dharmaswamin found him hiding from Turkish soldiers in the ruins of the monastery in the thirteenth century.

Rāhu (T.sGra-gcan) was an *asūra* (anti-god) who disguised himself as a god and joined the line of gods waiting to receive a portion of nectar (*amṛta*) after the great churning of the ocean. The Sun and Moon revealed the fraud to Viṣṇu who cut off the demon's head; but immortal he lives in the sky, intermittently wreaking vengeance on the sun and moon by swallowing them. He is a dragon's head, the ascending node of the moon, the eighth planet, an important luminary in the demonic sky. Rāhula (T.sGra-gcan 'dzin) is the destroyer of Rāhu; it is an appellation of Buddhist monks. Rāhula's song has Rāhu(la)bhadra in the first line, and Rāhula in the third; there is no evident explanation for the discrepancy.

Kāmarūpa, where our Rāhula was born, is one of the four great Ḍākinī *pīṭhasṭhānas*, and an ancient center of *śākta* worship, located in Assam near Gauhati. It is said to be the only power-place in India where the original Buddhist tantric rites are still performed. We have no evidence of the association of any other Rāhula with Kāmarūpa.

48

THE SIDDHA DHARMAPA/GHARBARI THE CONTRITE PAṆḌITA

Pour the oil of responsive sensibility
Into the lamp of phenomenal existence;
Lighting the wick of the six sense-fields
The flame of non-dual pure awareness
Destroys the oblivion of delusory thought.

Dharmapa was a *paṇḍita* of Bodhinagar. He spent his entire life reading and teaching at the expense of his sādhana. When he grew old and lost his sight he felt the need for a relevant existential praxis and bemoaned his lack of a Guru. A Ḍākinī answered his need. Appearing in a dream she gave him an intuition of her as his Guru and spiritual friend. The *paṇḍita* prayed to her with all his heart, and she appeared to him in manifest form to give him initiation and this instruction:

Visualize phenomena as a lamp-bowl,
Mental constructs as butter-oil,
Your sensory perception as wick,
And knowledge as the burning flame.
Pour the butter of conceptualization
Into the lamp-bowl of every experience,
And lighting the wick with the flame of knowledge
Behold the wish-fulfilling gem of mind.

For five years he meditated on these instructions concerning the transformation of concepts into pure awareness. Just as poison is transmuted by the sound of mantra, the *paṇḍita*'s concepts became pure awareness, and his decrepit body was transformed into the form of an eight year old boy. The people of Bodhinagar were astonished, but he answered their amazement with this verse:

> *With positive causes and conditions*
> *How can a negative result occur?*
> *The man with clear intelligence*
> *Must exert himself conscientiously.*

Thereafter, reading and teaching, he worked selflessly for others, until, finally, expressing his realization, he attained the Ḍākinī's Paradise.

Sādhana

Like Lūipa and Jālandhara, Dharmapa received a visitation from his Ḍākinī-Guru quite fortuitously. Lūipa met his embodied Ḍākinī while begging at a brothel, and she taught him with a symbolic act; Jālandhara's Awareness Ḍākinī appeared as a result of involuntary contemplation. Dharmapa's Ḍākinī came to him in a dream due to his deeply felt need for a Guru. Perhaps the Awareness Ḍākinī can be conceived as a female archetype, a selfless anima, arising out of Jung's collective unconscious. In the case of Dharmapa's dream, since dream belongs to the plane of visionary enjoyment where vibration takes instructive form, the Ḍākinī is a *saṃbhogakāya* emanation, the principle of perfect insight into emptiness in anthropomorphic form. Although the *paṇḍita* had spent his life engaged in intellectual pursuits, he had accumulated sufficient karmic impetus in the direction of perfect insight for that ideal to appear to him as the Ḍākinī when he needed her and when he prayed to her. He had also achieved a sufficiently responsive mind so that when he named the object of his desire and visualized her, his prayer was answered. The mind in its deluded state is always a wish-fulfilling gem in potential, otherwise prayer would never work. The yeshe-norbu (*cintāmaṇi*) is a state of being that always and immediately responds to a conceptual wish, or prayer, by manifesting that actuality (see p. 89). The wish-fulfilling gem, or responsive emptiness and space, is what answers prayer, no matter what the faith of the supplicant.

The allusion to the power of mantra to transform poison may refer to the specific mantras used in healing to neutralize a snake's venom, or other natural poison, or it may refer to the mantras that transmute the poisons of the mind into their inherent awareness. In either case the principle is the same: absorption in the emptiness of either gross material or subtle mental, poison, using sound as the medium, transforms the poison into mind's nature. According to some, the specific resonance of combinations of vowels and consonants has an effect independent of the samādhi of the yogin or healer who recites the mantra. In theory this hypothesis is valid; in practice it is unproven.

There is an important discrepancy between the Guru's meditation instruction and Dharmapa's song of realization. In the first case the "oil" is conceptualization and mental constructs, and in the second it is responsive sensibility.[257] Thought is the raw material for the novice; thought is the path; thought is the object of concentration; thought is what must be penetrated by insight and transformed into empty awareness.[258] After mental constructs dissolve, the conceptual wish to obtain Buddhahood becomes the responsive sensibility that reacts to fulfill the Bodhisattva Vow. Thus the "oil" is whatever arises to do, say or think for the sake of others. Virtually every siddha spent years, sometimes decades, using selfless service as the oil to keep his butter-lamp lit. The siddhas who performed this kind of meditation never abandoned their sensual pleasure while practicing their sādhanas or performing their selfless service; the other constant, besides the oil, is the wick, which is the six sense-fields, or in full, "cognition of the six sets of three elements of perception—stimulus, sense organ and consciousness."[259]

Historiography

If indeed an error lies behind the inclusion of two siddhas of the same name, Dharmapa, there is no way to discover when it was made, although it certainly came before the various texts of the legends now available were put into their final form. Saṅkṛtyāyana gives Gharvari (or Gharbhari) instead of Dharmapa,[260] and other Tibetan lists give Gharbari and Gharma-pāda; an Indian list gives Garbaripa. Obviously a Gharbaripāda was counted amongst the eighty-four siddhas, and in some lists at Dharmapa's slot. Saṅkṛtyāyana gives Śavaripa as his Guru, without his source; the compiler of the *Songs*, Vīra Prakāśa, asserts that he lived three Guru-disciple generations after Virūpa; and Tāranātha asserts that Ḍombi was Garvarīpa's Guru.[261] If Dharmapa was Gharbaripa and he was in Virūpa's lineage he would have lived in the late ninth century. But there are too many unknowns in this equation to be able to make any definitive statement about Dharmapa's lineage.

49

THE SIDDHA DHOKARIPA THE BOWL-BEARER

In the vast space that is the nature of the bowl
Place the knowledge that is the nature of all things;
The result is inseparable space and knowledge,
And knowledge is realization for the happy yogin!

Dhokaripa, a low-caste beggar of Paṭaliputra, carried a bowl with him wherever he went. In it he placed whatever he could beg or scavenge. One day, after he had found nothing to put in his bowl, he sat down under a spreading tree, and there a yogin approached him and asked him for something to eat. The beggar apologized for his inability to provide for his brother in need, and the yogin responded by offering to teach him the Dharma. The beggar promised to practice what he was taught, and he received the Hevajra initiation and empowerment together with instruction in the creative and fulfillment processes of meditation. The yogin said:

Listen, Dhokaripa!
Put knowledge of all forms
Into your bowl of pure space
And visualize the two as one.

Dhokaripa realized the meaning of this instruction through his meditation, and after three years he gained *siddhi.* He still carried his bowl, and when the people of Paṭaliputra would ask him the reason he would reply:

This is the bowl of emptiness
And I beg the alms that give me pure pleasure—
Pure pleasure is Dhokari's desire.

Do you lucky people understand my secret,
The secret of Dhokari whose desire is fulfilled?

Dhokaripa worked selflessly for others, and after expressing his realization he bodily attained the Ḍākinī's Paradise.

Sādhana

In the Mind Only school of mahāyāna metaphysics,[262] a practical philosophy that the tantrikas drew heavily upon, one experientially-derived premise that was heavily criticized by *madhyamika* opponents was that mind is self-aware. Since all entities of experience (*dharmas*) are dependent upon mind for their existence in the same way that a tree falling in a forest only falls if it is seen to fall, all things are "only mind." Further, since the emptiness of mind that is pure awareness and clear light is also the emptiness of all mental events, phenomena are self-aware. This intrinsic awareness that is inseparable from the light-form of appearances is called "knowledge."[263] Dhokaripa calls knowledge "things-in-themselves" or "thingness."[264] His bowl is space and its contents are knowledge; the bowl is the universe and its contents are siddhas; the bowl is the *dharmadhātu* and its contents are the *dharmakāya*; the bowl is mind and its contents are mental events. Man and his environment, mind and mental events, space and knowledge, are inseparable. Dhokaripa, the simple beggar, gained *mahāmudrā-siddhi* equal to any of the sophisticated siddhas with their complex sādhanas.

50

THE SIDDHA MEDHINI
THE TIRED FARMER

Through the perfect insight of our innate knowledge
And the skillful means of our usual heightened
perception,
Out of the ground that is our actual nature of being
Pure pleasure spontaneously arises—the goal achieved.

Medhini, a low-born farmer of Paṭaliputra, met his yogin-Guru when he sat down one day to rest from his exhausting work. The yogin divined that Medhini was sick of his miserable life and offered to teach him a yoga if he would promise to practice it. Medhini was enthusiastic, and the yogin gave him initiation and then instructed him in creative and fulfillment meditation. The farmer tried to meditate, but thoughts of his farmwork interfered with his concentration, and he could not continue. Confiding his difficulty to his Guru the yogin gave him instruction in images that harmonized with his thoughts.

With consciousness as the plow
And feelings of pleasure and pain as the oxen,
Plow the field of your conditioned being.
Then scattering the seed of cognitive experience
Harvest an endless crop of pure pleasure,
The pleasure of a continuous stream of reality.

After twelve years of meditation the farmer's conventional notions of things had dissolved, and he gained *siddhi*. He levitated to the height of seven palm trees and expressed his realization. After working for the people of Paṭaliputra in many ways, he bodily attained the Ḍākinī's Paradise.

Sādhana

Medhini's meditation is peculiar in that it lacks any explicit transformative Buddha-quality, any function that dissolves or unites dualities. One explanation could be that this function is inherent in the image of the yoked oxen representing the duality of pleasure and pain. The etymological root of the word yoga is "to yoke," and the fundamental "yoga" in all tantric practices that have liberation from saṃsāra as their aim, is the "yoking" of the subject/object dichotomy of the relative mind. In practice, unifying one pair of opposites is to resolve them all. When the sting is taken out of pleasure and pain by discovery of the unifying factor, the emptiness, the one taste that is their common denominator, every experience whatsoever is experienced as pure pleasure, "the pleasure of a continuous stream of reality."[265] With pleasure and pain yoked together, "plowing" the notion of the psycho-organism is to dissolve or illuminate it, so that all experience arises as flashes of instantaneously released, self-aware, entities of experience with the feeling-tone of bliss, The text has both "consciousness" and "mental constructs" as the plow, but if Medhini's visualization is to be consistent with similar techniques, like Dhokari's for example (see p. 000), the plow should be, or become, knowledge or awareness. Otherwise Medhini may yoke his oxen, but until the flash of illumination transforms consciousness into pure awareness he waits in saṃsāra.

Historiography

Other sources[266] give Hālipa as an alternative name of The Farmer (T. *Shing las can*) and assert that he belongs to Līlapa's lineage: Līlapa, Guṅḍhari, Medhini; or Līlapa, Guṅḍhari, Dharmabodhi, Medhini. It is uncertain who this Līlapa is. Lākhapuya or Lākhapum are given as Hālipa's birthplace instead of Saliputra.

51

THE SIDDHA PAṄKAJAPA THE LOTUS-BORN BRAHMIN

Alone in the world and lacking realization
A wish-fulfilling gem and glass trinkets are
indistinguishable;
But with realization and guided by a Guru, they
are as alike
As the sun and moon's radiance is to a fire fly's glow.

Although Paṅkajapa was the son of a brahmin, he was born from a lotus in a lotus garden in a solitary place. Not far away from the pond where he was born was a shrine containing an image dedicated to the Bodhisattva Avalokiteśvara, and mistaking the Bodhisattva for the god Mahādeva, the brahmin worshiped him. It was the custom in that country for a devotee to make threefold offerings of flowers to an image and then to take a flower and place it on top of his own head. One day the mahāsiddha Nāgārjuna passed by the shrine and stopped to offer flowers to the Bodhisattva. Avalokiteśvara appeared in person, and after accepting the offering he placed a flower upon the master's head.

Paṅkajapa witnessed this scene and was incensed with jealous anger. "I have worshiped this image for twelve years," he told Nāgārjuna, "but I have never received such a sign. You make a single offering of flowers and receive the deity's blessing!"

"Your thoughts are impure," Nāgārjuna told him. "I am faultless."

The brahmin recognized his mistake and was repentant. He placed the master's feet upon his head, asking to be accepted as his disciple. Nāgārjuna gave him initiation and instruction upon the unity of vision and action:

Through compassion, pleasure in sensual fulfillment
And our original indeterminate nature are made one,
For in perfect vision there are no distinctions:
That is Avalokiteśvara's understanding.

The disciple understood this instruction, and after only seven days of meditation he reached his goal. Looking upon everyone with compassion his instruction in enlightened action brought great happiness. He finally attained the Ḍākinī's Paradise in his very body.

Sādhana

Paṅkajapa's story is one of the several legends that illustrate the non-sectarian ethos that characterized the siddhas' praxis. Although the Tibetans' traditional antagonism towards the brahmins, and their brahmanic philosophy, has no doubt slipped in to color some of the legends in anti-brahmin shades, that does not explain away the mutual antipathy of brahmin and Buddhist implicit in Virūpa's encounter with the King of Indra (p. 46) or the feeling of vast superiority that the Buddhists felt for the ancient *devī* cults whose *ḍākinī*-witches harassed Virūpa, Kambala, Kṛṣṇācārya and others. But generally it is reasonable to assume that within the tantrika community Buddhists and *śaivas* lived in non-sectarian harmony, sharing each other's shrines, symbols, lineages and also teachers Avalokiteśvara and Mahādeva are still worshiped as one god—Triloknāth, Lord of the Three Worlds—in Nepal. Mahādeva, Śiva, is not then The Destroyer, but the Great God in whom birth, life and death combine, and Avalokiteśvara is not just the Bodhisattva of Compassion but the beginning and end of creation as he is depicted in the *Karaṇḍavyūha-sūtra.* Just as Buddhist and *śaiva* Tantra still co-exist in Nepal with mutual respect and with no disparity in the minds of the secular, Newari devotees, so it must have been in the era of the siddhas in India.

Paṅkajapa, a lotus-born brahmin (this unique paradox remains unexplained), worships Avalokiteśvara for twelve years, and after seven days of meditation upon the unity of vision and action[267] he attains *mahāmudrā-siddhi.* In Hindu Tantra the difficulty of propounding a consistent non-dual vision is that the absolute principle of being, Brahmān, always hovers above as a transcendent cosmic ego. Only in Saṅkarācārya's *advaita-vedānta,* based on the metaphysical principles of his Buddhist Gurus, is it done successfully. But in practical yoga, it was the *śaiva*s who developed the practice of indiscriminate activity as a path to liberation; the *kāpālika*s took this principle to an extreme in their "dung-eating," flesh-eating and allied practices, practices that nevertheless are quite efficient in destroying the last vestiges of prejudice, preconception and notions of ritual purity. As an alternative to the debasement that accompanied the *kāpālika*'s undiscriminating activity, Nāgārjuna's precepts make compassion the liberating factor. Compassion, an undiscriminating empathetic feeling of love and a sensitive responsiveness to the needs of all beings, must be united with the activity that leads to sensual fulfillment, and the emptiness of our original indeterminate nature perceived in compassionate vision is then perceived in every action whatsoever. In other words, do whatever you will, provided that you are responding with love and see the emptiness in it. Paṅkajapa's seven day sādhana, something of a record in the legends, had as path and goal the unity of compassionate vision and sensual activity. The legend implies that it was merely the recognition of the deity as the Bodhisattva of Compassion that made all the difference to Paṅkajapa; it could also be inferred that he had been practicing undiscriminating sensual *śaiva* Tantra, and that could be the significance of his name.

Historiography

Paṅkaja (T. *'Dam skyes*) means "swamp-born," and that is a generic name for lotuses, since they grow in the slime of a lake bottom, but it is also the name of a particular species of lotus. The chief variant of Paṅkaja's name is Saṅkaja. There is no evidence that can determine which siddha Nāgārjuna was Paṅkajapa's Guru; if it was Saraha's disciple, Paṅkaja lived at the beginning of the ninth century.

52

THE MAHĀSIDDHA GHAṆṬĀPA THE CELIBATE BELL-RINGER

To bless oneself bind tight the three channels:
Lalanā, rasanā *and* avadhūti.
Bent on realization the wise attend to three things:
The Guru, mind and phenomena.

Ghaṇṭāpa was a monk of the great monastic academy of Śrī Nālandā. He kept exemplary monastic discipline and became learned in the five arts. He then left Nālandā and wandered here and there, putting his wisdom into selfless practice, and repute of his learning spread far and wide. At that time the Emperor Devapāla, master of the incalculable wealth of his kingdom by virtue of his accumulated merit, reigned over the one million eight hundred thousand households of his own kingdom, the nine hundred thousand households of Kāmarūpa and the four hundred thousand households of Bengal—three million one hundred thousand in all. It was to the king's city of Paṭaliputra that the master Ghaṇṭāpa came to teach, begging alms for subsistence and taking up residence under a spreading tree.

One night the pious Devapāla, the patron of innumerable monks and yogins, asked for his wife's advice. "All composite creation is impermanent; all living creatures suffer; all experience of life is essentially meaningless," he began. "My royal responsibilities extend to both this world and the next, so shouldn't we two, husband and wife, provide support for those monks, ascetics and priests in need, and thus accumulate merit for our next rebirths?"

"In the past you have provided for many, many holy men," his wife replied. "Today another monk arrived in this capital city of Paṭaliputra. He is a strict observer of moral conduct, a great saint.

He has placed his mat under a tree on the outskirts of town, and possessing nothing but his robes and other bare necessities he begs his food. We could offer him a feast—eighty-four main dishes, fourteen kinds of sweetmeat, grape wine and the five kinds of beverage, and so on. We could replace his lamp with the sparkle of jewels and offer him every pleasure that the kingdom can afford."

The king agreed to his wife's proposal, and the following morning he sent his servant to invite Ghaṇṭāpa, for it was none other than he, to the palace. But the master declined the invitation, and the servant returned alone. The next day the king himself, with a great retinue, went to the master's tree. He prostrated before Ghaṇṭāpa and then submitted many reasons why the saint should accompany him to the palace.

"You should not have bothered to come here," Ghaṇṭāpa answered.

"With great faith I have come to offer you my charity," the king responded.

"Your kingdom is full of vice," Ghaṇṭāpa told him. "I shall not come."

"Please stay with us for just one year," the king insisted.

Ghaṇṭāpa refused. He also refused to visit the king for six months, three months, two weeks and, finally even for one day. "You cannot stand, walk, sit or lie down without sin," the master told him. "I refuse."

The king returned every day for forty days to beg Ghaṇṭāpa to change his mind, but without success. Finally he and his consort became angry, and hatred burnt in their hearts. "Whoever can destroy this monk's virtue and chastity can have half of my kingdom and one hundred weight in gold," the king decreed, and he sent out criers to proclaim his offer.

Now in Paṭaliputra lived the most cunning whore that ever existed, and seeing a way to gain great wealth and power, certain that she could seduce Ghaṇṭāpa, she went to the king's palace and gave him confident assurance that she could undo the monk.

"Do your utmost," said the king.

The whore had a twelve year old daughter, a virgin, unspoiled by the world. The girl had a radiantly beautiful face, a seductive gait, sweet intelligent speech, a voluptuous body and fine shapely breasts. When the sun caught sight of her it stopped in its tracks. "I will send my daughter to bring back this saint to the world of desire and

Ghaṇṭāpa is favored by his *vajra*-queen.

destroy his virtue," she decided. On ten consecutive days she went to see Ghaṇṭāpa, each time circumambulating him and prostrating before him. On the tenth day she said, "Please allow me to be your patron during the summer monsoon retreat."

Ghaṇṭāpa was uninterested in her offer. But day after day for a month she pleaded to be allowed to serve him, and finally he agreed. The whore, whose name was Darima, was delighted and gave a feast to celebrate her success. This refrain was constantly on her lips:

A girl's deceits fulfill her desires,
And her sex is her unfailing weapon.

"With my guile I can deceive and seduce the world," she thought to herself. "One monk presents no problem!" And volubly she boasted of her abilities. When the monsoon retreat began Ghaṇṭāpa told the woman to send only man-servants with his food and on no account to sent maids. Darima agreed. For the first two weeks she sent waiters carrying rice and spring water, but on the fifteenth day she prepared a feast. She dressed her daughter like a princess, ornamenting her in sparkling jewels, and then sent her to the master with fifty waiters to carry the food, instructing her to send the men back at the edge of the clearing where the master's hut stood. The girl followed her mother's instruction, and remembering the tricks that her mother had taught her she entered the master's hut. Coming from the jungle the monk noticed that his usual waiters were absent, and he was amazed to find an exquisitely dressed and ornamented virgin inside the hut.

"What happened to the waiters?" he asked her.

"They had not time to stay," the girl replied. "I am here to serve you."

Ghaṇṭāpa ate his meal, and the girl lingered on until she was told sternly to leave.

"There are five-colored clouds in the sky," she responded. "I think it will rain. I will wait here awhile." So she remained until sunset. "The sun is setting," she said finally. "I have no escort and I am afraid of robbers along the path who will covet my clothes and jewels and kill me."

This was undeniable, and Ghaṇṭāpa allowed her to sleep outside the hut. But during the night she became frightened and cried aloud, and Ghaṇṭāpa permitted her to come inside to sleep. The hut was small, and inevitably their bodies touched, and then intertwined, and eventually united in love. Passing through the four levels of joy they traversed the path of liberation to its end. In the morning Ghaṇṭāpa asked the girl to stay with him, and they became yogin and consort. A year later a child was born.

Meanwhile the king was becoming impatient. Frequently he would ask the whore if she had been successful, but she was constantly evasive. Three years passed, and only then did she go to the king to tell him of her success.

The king was content. "Tell your daughter that I will come to visit her and the monk in three days time," he said.

On the appointed day the king gathered the people of Paṭaliputra and set out to visit Ghaṇṭāpa. The master consulted his wife on the appropriate course of action. "Should we stay here or go to another country?" he asked her.

The girl wanted to go elsewhere, as she was afraid of the people's scorn and abuse. So Ghaṇṭāpa hid their child in his robe, took a pitcher of liquor under his arm and set out with his wife. On the road they met the king on his elephant.

"What is that under your robe?" demanded the king balefully. "And who is this girl?"

"I am carrying a jug of liquor, there is a child under my robe, and this is my consort," replied Ghaṇṭāpa, looking the king in the eye.

"When I invited you to my palace you refused to come," said the king. "You told me that I was a sinful man. But now you, a monk, have a wife and child. It is you who are evil!"

"I am faultless," replied Ghaṇṭāpa. "You insult me!"

When the king repeated his accusation, without warning Ghaṇṭāpa suddenly flung his child and the liquor to the ground, and the earth goddess, becoming frightened, let forth a flood of water that gushed out of a fissure in the ground. The child and the jug floating in the water changed into a thunderbolt (*vajra*) and bell (*ghaṇṭā*); the yogin and his consort were transformed into the deities Saṃvara and Vajra Vārāhī in father-mother union, and the two of them rose into the sky above the king and his attendants who were floundering in the flood. The drowning people stared up in deep fear, crying, "We take refuge in the master!" praying to him fervently. But Ghaṇṭāpa remained firm in his samādhi of immutable wrath. The people were on the point of drowning when the

Bodhisattva Avalokiteśvara appeared and stopped the flood with his foot where it issued out of the ground, and they were saved. Then they bowed down, begging the master's forgiveness. A stone image of the Bodhisattva Avalokiteśvara magically appeared at that place, and even today from under the statue's foot a spring spurts out like a fountain to a height of six feet.

Ghaṇṭāpa taught the supplicant people with these precepts:

Although medicine and poison create contrary effects,
In their ultimate essence they are one;
Likewise negative qualities and aids on the path,
One in essence, should not be differentiated.
The realized sage rejects nothing whatsoever,
While the unrealized, spiritual child,
Five times poisoned, is lost in saṃsāra.

Through this illumination the king and his people lost their self-righteous prejudice and bias, and in one accord they found faith, and a countless multitude of people entered the path. They called the master Ghaṇṭāpa, Holder of the Bell, and his fame reached the corners of the earth.

In six previous incarnations the girl had caused the monk to break his vow, but in this lifetime all the monk's dualistic mental constructs dissolved in the infinite expanse of emptiness inherent in all things, and by virtue of a fully developed mindstream he gained the true path. Ghaṇṭāpa called his son Vajrapāṇi, Vajra-in-hand. As for the girl, his consort, as a result of her service to him in past lives, in this life the defilements of her mind were purified. Thus Ghaṇṭāpa, possessing the power and virtue of a Buddha, finally attained the Ḍākinī's Paradise in his very body with his consort.

Sādhana

Another version of Ghaṇṭāpa's legend sheds some light on the obscurities of this story, besides telling us more of Ghaṇṭāpa's life.[268] Son of Nālandā's king he renounced the throne and was ordained at the monastery by Jayadeva Subhadra (see p. 227). After achieving renown at Nālandā, becoming Guru to the king, he met Dārikapa who initiated him into the Saṃvara maṇḍala and sent him to the jungle to meditate. Later he was instructed to go to Oḍḍiyāṇa by a voice in the sky. His Guru in Oḍḍiyāṇa was a female swineherd, whom he rejected at first due to her extreme unattractiveness, but after he had recognized her as a Ḍākinī she gave him the Saṃvara initiation again, and told him to go to Orissa to complete his sādhana. In the Orissan jungle he offended the king by refusing to accompany him to the city, his Mahāmudrā practice being his justification. The whore's daughter sent to seduce him was the element lacking in his sādhana and he initiated her and took her as his Ḍākinī. Although the king intended to ridicule the yogin, it was Ghaṇṭāpa who himself went to the city to convert the people. He emanated a boy and girl, took a ladle himself to take liquor from his consort's pot to give to the children who filled the pitchers of every family in town. Finally, he threw the ladle on the ground, water gushed forth, the boy and girl became thunderbolt and bell, and the master and his consort became Saṃvara and consort in union. Thereby Orissa was established in the vajrayāna.

Our legend has as its dominant theme the stupidity of the sort of self-righteous mind that insists upon its own limited moral virtue and condemns others for practicing a life-style that transcends moral discipline. The Ḍākinī-girl had seduced Ghaṇṭāpa in previous lives, but each time, as a monk, he had been bound by the moral imperative. In this lifetime his mind was sufficiently mature to accept the Ḍākinī's teaching and to attain liberation after progressing through the four stages of joy. Thereafter his purity was sealed in Mahāmudrā, but the king, who failed to understand that "the soul of sweet delight can never be defiled," rejected Ghaṇṭāpa's claim of faultlessness. The kind of self-righteous mind that condemns a man and woman for "living in sin" cannot accept the possibility of a dominant streak of purity in all other people. If our legend had made it clear that Mahāmudrā meditation prevented Ghaṇṭāpa from accepting the king's invitation, it would appear less like karmic retribution when the king tried to humiliate him. In his teaching to the king and people, Ghaṇṭāpa taught them what he had learnt: "Do not cultivate virtue and renounce vice, but accepting everything as it arises, penetrate the essence of the experience to obtain the one taste." After the vision that he had shown them, perhaps they were ready for such instruction; but he had failed to understand it in his six previous lives, and the two sets of moral standards that he demonstrated first as a monk and then as a yogin showed two separate and valid paths. It is certainly dangerous, as Tibetan Gurus never tire of telling, for the man who clings to the moral imperatives of dualistic ethics to practice activity that gives the siddha pure pleasure and awareness, for he quickly finds himself in a hell of doubt and confusion. But it is no coincidence that outcastes lacking all moral and social conditioning gained initiation into the Inner Tantra and had a distinct advantage on the tantric path after having gained insight into emptiness. Moral concepts can be the most intractable obstacles to spontaneous fulfillment of the Bodhisattva Vow of uncompromising compassion.

Historiography

It is certain that Ghaṇṭāpa was a contemporary of the second great Pāla Emperor Devapāla (AD 810–830), but less likely that Devapāla was the king whom he offended. Devapāla patronized Nālandā munificently. Bengal was called Baṅgala in those days and comprised present East and West Bengal besides parts of Bihar. Kāmarūpa was the contiguous state in the Brahmaputra Valley. His own state with its capital city at Paṭaliputra (Saliputra) must have comprised eastern and southern Bihar. The Tibetan word rendered throughout as "household" (*grong khyer*) is more strictly "town" or "village;" but even the translation "village" has no credence as there are only six hundred thousand villages in the whole of overpopulated India today. "Household" implies the collection of dwellings comprising the quarters of an extended family.

Ghaṇṭāpa is known in Tibet for his inception of the *Pañcakrama* Saṃvara lineage. His *Pañcakrama*, treating the five limbs of fulfillment yoga, is the best known of his seventeen works, most of which relate to the *Saṃvara-tantra*.[269] He received his Saṃvara revelation from Vajrayoginī, who may have been the swineherd (T.Phag rdzi ma) he met in Oḍḍiyāṇa, and who may have been the yoginī Vilasyavajra who had been taught by Ḍombi Heruka.[270] In the Tibetan lineages Ḍeṅgipa is sometimes given besides, or instead of, Dārikapa as his other Saṃvara Guru. Kurmapāda, Jālandhara and Kāṇhapa and Kambala, are given as his disciples. The disputed association of Jālandhara and Kṛṣṇācārya with Ghaṇṭāpa (in Mar mdo's Saṃvara lineage) gives them a very early date unless Ghaṇṭāpa had a very long life and was teaching through the second half of the ninth century. Dharmakīrti was also a disciple of Ghaṇṭāpa. The *Kālacakra-tantra* lineage includes Ghaṇṭāpa, which makes him one of the earliest Indian initiates of that tantra that must, therefore, have reached eastern India in the ninth century.

Ghaṇṭāpa (T.Dril bu pa) is frequently called Vajraghaṇṭā, "Bearer of the Bell and Thunderbolt." He is often depicted carrying bell and *vajra*, particularly in the well-known icon showing him floating in the sky in union with his consort.

53

THE SIDDHA JOGIPA THE SIDDHA-PILGRIM

Constantly focusing the light of the mind,
Bright and subtle, like the tip of a flame,
All phenomena, static and kinetic,
Melt into their inner space, the dharmadhātu.

Jogipa was an outcaste *caṇḍāla* of Oḍantapurī. He had great energy but little insight. The Guru Śavaripa granted him the initiation and empowerment of Hevajra and instructed him in creative and fulfillment meditation. But when Jogipa attempted to meditate he found that he had not understood his Guru's instruction, and returning to Śavaripa he asked him for devotional exercises of body and speech instead. His Guru told him to recite the mantra of Vajra Heruka while making pilgrimage to the twenty-four sacred power spots. Jogipa did as his Guru instructed, and after twelve years of pilgrimage the defilements of his mind had been eradicated, and he gained *mahāmudrā-siddhi.* After expressing his realization he worked for others for five hundred years, using many different skillful means, before rising bodily into the Ḍākinī's Paradise.

Sādhana

Nāropa denigrated "simple fools who wander about the country from power-place to power-place"[271] interpreting the twenty-four power-places literally, as geographical locations. Nāropa knew these power-places[272] as twenty-four focal points of energy in the psycho-organism, each ruled by a Ḍākinī, and comprising the body of Vajrayoginī, which should be illuminated in meditation. But Jogipa showed in his attainment of *mahāmudrā-siddhi* by the exoteric practice of pilgrimage and recitation of mantra that *kriyāyoga* leads

Jogipa makes pilgrimage to the twenty-four power-places.

to the same goal as the higher tantric paths. Tantra provides skillful means for every personality type and level of ability.

Historiography

There are only a few variations in the lists of power-places found in various mother-tantra contexts as diverse as the *Saṃvara-tantra* and the Longchen Nyingtik. This is the standard list:[273] PŪRṆAGIRI (Paurṇagiri, Puliramalaya, etc.) in the Bijapur region of Karnataka in South India;[274] OḌḌIYĀṆA (Uḍḍiyāṇa, Oḍiyāna, Urgyan), the Swat Valley in North Pakistan; JĀLANDHARA in the Upper Kangra Valley, H.P.; KĀMARŪPA, near Gauhati, Assam; ARBUDA (Arputa, Arbuta), Mt. Abu, Rajasthan; GODĀVARĪ, as the source of the major Deccan River; RĀMEŚVARAM in Tamil Nadu; DEVĪKOṬṬA, south of Dinajpur, West Bengal; MALAVA, ancient Avantī, modern Mālwa including Ujjain, M.P.; OḌRA (Oṭre, Oṭi), North Orissa; TRIŚAKUNE, Trisrotah, the Tista River (?); KOŚALA, ancient Oudh with Śrāvastī as capital; KALIṄGA, ancient South Orissa and North Andhra, with Daṇṭapurī as capital; LAMPĀKA, capital of Oḍḍiyāṇa, near Mardan; KĀÑCĪ (Kāñcīka), Conjeevaram or Kāñcīpuram, south-west of Madras; HIMALĀYA (Himādri, Himavat), Mt. Kailāśa, or Bhīmāsthān in Peshawar Dist., or Nandādevī Peak in Garhwal Dist., U.P.;[275] PRETAPURĪ TSARITRA (Tsari), in Tibet near the Arunachal border; GṚHADEVA (Nepāla), Paśupati near Kathmandu;[276] SAURĀṢṬRA (Sourakhta), an ancient kingdom including Surat, Cambay and Kathiawar; SUVARṆADVĪPA, Sumatra; NAGARA, Nagarkoṭa or Jvālamukhī?[277] near Jālandhara q.v.; SINDHU, the Indus, Nagara Ṭhaṭha, east of Karachi;[278] MARU (Maro, Marobarlaraste), East Rajasthan; KULĀNTA (Kulāta, Kupānta). The haphazard list given in the *Hevajra-tantra*[279] is consistent with the above list in all but five unidentifiable instances.

Many of the names in the list of the twenty-four power-places are simply names of kingdoms or districts, but these places were so well-known that there would be no doubt as to their identity. Most of them were *śākta-pīṭhas*, worshiped since pre-Aryan times. The original *devī* goddess would have acquired a consort, usually a form of Śiva, as the *śaiva*s came to dominance, and then as tantric Buddhism gained sway, the *devī* would have been identified with Vajra

Vārāhī and Śiva with Saṃvara. The first four in the list are the four major power-places representing the four major *cakras* treated in the *Catuṣpīṭha-tantra.*[280] The twenty-four are divided into three groups of eight places forming maṇḍalas relating to the head, throat and heart *cakras*, to the Body, Speech and Mind of the Ḍākinī, and, in theory, creating geographical maṇḍalas in which the power-places are located in the cardinal and intermediate directions. In the *Hevajra-tantra* the places are also classified according to their significance as meeting places for the initiate community, but the terminology employed is obscure (see also *71*).

Jogipa, or Yogipa (T.rNal byor pa), is a descriptive epithet rather than a personal name, but there are references to Jogipāda in our sources. Śavaripa was his Guru.[281] If Śavaripa was Saraha's disciple then Jogipa would have been a contemporary of King Dharmapāla, and he would have lived around the turn of the ninth century. If this Śavaripa was Maitripa's Guru, he would have lived in the middle of the eleventh century. Oḍantapurī is the name of a monastery north of Nālandā.

54

THE MAHĀSIDDHA CELUKAPA
THE REVITALIZED DRONE

Following my True Guru's injunction, year after year,
Earth and water and fire and air gradually dissolved,
And all spontaneously arisen appearances became
Mahāmudrā.

Celuka was born of low caste in Maṅgalapur. He was forever listless, idle and overpowered by lethargy. Oppressed by the nightmare of samsaric existence, he was sitting beneath a tree one day when the yogin Maitripa passed by and asked him what he was doing.

"I am thinking how I could obtain a sādhana so that I can escape from this abject condition," he replied. "My problem is that I have met no master who could teach me an appropriate method. I am so lazy that I could not even begin to search for a teacher. Can you teach me how to overcome inertia?"

"If you take initiation you will sleep less and eventually gain release from saṃsāra," Maitripa told him. He granted Celuka the initiation and empowerment of Saṃvara and instructed him in the profound fulfillment meditation upon psychic channels and energies: "Concentrate the whole of phenomenal existence into the fields of your body (senses), speech (psychic energies) and mind (consciousness), and injecting the *lalanā* and *rasanā* into the *avadhūti*, visualize your body and the *avadhūti* as a lake, and cognition as a swan upon the lake. By keeping your psychic energies in the *avadhūti* you will overcome fatigue in a state of thoughtlessness and mental quiescence."

Celuka meditated like this for nine years, and dispelling the defilements of his mind he attained *mahāmudrā-siddhi.* He expressed his realization in this way: "All experience of the phenomenal world is gathered into the fields of my body, speech and mind. The two poles of dualistic mentality, the two psychic channels, are united in the *avadhūti*, the third channel, and the space of mental quiescence, non-conceptualization, itself the *avadhūti*, is visualized as a lake from which the swan of cognition feeds upon the nectar of immortality inherent in all things." He rose bodily into the Ḍākinī's Paradise.

Sādhana

One of the immediate and self-evident effects of release from saṃsāra, an effect that can be sampled in even a short course of meditation, is a rise in the energy level of the psycho-organism. Lethargy is swept away and diligence and perseverance need no longer be wilfully and conscientiously applied. The yogin becomes capable of superhuman tasks, calling upon an unending supply of energy; in retreat he can sustain months of practice without sleep. Technically this effect is described as "uniting the *lalanā* and *rasanā* in the *avadhūti*," or uniting the objective and subjective poles of mentality. When this union has been achieved, an introspective mind is thrown out into the sensual realm wherein the deeper layers of being are experienced in ordinary sensual perception. The *avadhūti* (the central channel) is then the etherialized psycho-organism (see Celuka's song) and its phenomenal awareness, and it is likened to a placid lake; in mental terms the *avadhūti* is a thoughtless state of mental quiescence,[282] and the stream of awareness of sensual perception of the empty space of "material," or rather "immaterial," phenomena is likened to a swan floating calmly upon the lake. This vision of reality as a swan on a lake became a constant mode of being and perception for Celuka; there was no difference between his life and his practice.

The adjective descriptive of this level of fulfillment meditation, "profound," is a translation of the Tibetan word literally rendered as "superficial" or "elementary." It would appear that the Tibetan translator rendered the Sanskrit word too literally.[283] Such is an example of the fallacy of linguistic translation.

Historiography

Celuka (also Celuki, Cilupa; T. Tsi lu pa, Tshim bu pa, Tse lu ka) was Kālacakrapāda Senior, the Great. The Tibetan tradition tells us that while still a boy his *ḍākinī*-mother took him to Śambhala, where after receiving the blessing of an extraordinary faculty of memory, a monk who was an emanation of Avalokiteśvara taught him the root *Kālacakra-tantra*, the *Sañcaya-tantra* and the *Vimalaprabha*, the principal commentary. Alternatively, this devotee of Tārā may have received the *Kālacakra-tantra* doctrines directly from Avalokiteśvara, after travelling to Śambhala in a vision. His teaching career began at Pulahari, where he taught Nāropa, his disciple Bodhibhadra and Piṇḍo Ācārya, the disciple who was to become Kālacakrapāda Junior (see Kālapa, *27*). Then in Orissa, patronized by the King of Kaṭaka (Cuttack) he stayed in the great Ratnagiri Vihāra. After war had led to interment of the texts and subsequent loss of a part of them, Celuka moved east to Kusumpara where he taught Upāṣaka Bodhi (Bodhibhadra?).[284]

Celuka and Piṇḍopa, Kāla-pāda Senior and Junior, are the central figures in an eleventh century renaissance of the *Kālacakra-tantra* tradition, which had begun in the early ninth century (AD 806 was the date of the first year of the first Kālacakra cycle). Virūpa, Dārikapa and Ghaṇṭāpa were masters of the system; from Ghaṇṭāpa the lineage included, Kurmapa, Jālandhara, Kāṇha, Bhadrapa, Vijayapāda, and Tilopa before Nāropa,[285] who also heard the system from Kāla-pāda Senior. If Celuka did indeed teach Nāropa, and if he was alive to see the Turks reach Orissa (where they ignored the great and ancient *vihāra* of Ratnagiri, near Bhubaneswar),[286] then he must have lived well over a hundred years, seeing the latter part of the twelfth century. Rather than a *kṣetriya* of Madhyadeśa, our legend makes Celuka a *śūdra* of Oḍḍiyāṇa; thus it is easy to speculate that he was responsible for a latterday transmission of the *Kālacakra* from the North-west (where Śambhala is believed to lie) to eastern India. Further, it is tempting to identify Indrabhūti's land of Sambhola (*42*) a near homophone of Śambhala, with the origin of the Kālacakra tradition.

Celuka's Guru Maitripa (Maitrigupta, Avadhūtipa, Advayavajra) who lived circa AD 1010–1089, received Saṃvara initiation from Śavareśvara and Virūpa II. Nāropa, Śāntipa and Ḍamarūpa were also his Gurus.

55
THE SIDDHA GODHURIPA THE BIRD-CATCHER

All inner and outer phenomena perceived as mind,
Realizing the reality of mind's nature as light,
Sleeping, waking, dreaming and meditating in the
dharmakāya,
Fully awakened, I realized perfect Buddhahood.

Godhuripa, a bird-catcher of Ḍisunagar, was trapping birds in a net one day when a yogin stopped him and asked him what he was doing.

"The accumulated evil of my past lives has led to my present rebirth as a bird-catcher," Godhuripa told him. "I am forced to do violence to life in order to live. It is a miserable existence, but I see no way out."

"If you compound your bad karma, in future lives your misery will be greater still," the yogin told him. "Why not practice a Buddhist sādhana and find constant happiness?"

"If a Guru would take pity on me, such a miserable sinner, why would I refuse?" said Godhuripa.

The yogin granted him initiation through a transfer of grace, and instructed him in the meditation that employs a single object of contemplation consistent with a dominant image in the mind. "Visualize all temporal sound as the sound of birdsong, and the birdsong and your image of the sound as one."

Lose your mind in sound, again and again;
Then listening to the sweet sound of the koïl
You hear its every note the same in essence.
Visualize each sound and the hearer of the sound
As an all-embracing field of reality.

Ghoduripa meditated according to these instructions, and he realized the unity of sound and emptiness. After nine years the defilements of his mind had vanished, and he gained *mahāmudrā-siddhi*. He revealed his achievement, and remaining in the world for one hundred years he worked for countless beings before bodily attaining the Ḍākinī's Paradise with three hundred attendants.

Sādhana

Godhuripa's practice of uniting birdsong with its mental image is identical in principle to Vīṇāpa's practice (*11*) of uniting the image of the notes struck on the *vīṇā* with the actual sounds themselves. Vīṇāpa's instruction to listen to the unstruck sound translates in Godhuripa's meditation as visualization of the sound and its hearer as an undifferentiated field of emptiness,[287] which is what occurs when subject and object are united in a gnostic experience of reality. The first part is creative meditation and the second part is fulfillment meditation. First the auditory sense-field is purified by ridding it of preconceived images of sounds; residual echoes of sound, like visual images and ideas, are stored to be projected upon similar forms that arise in perception. It was the *memory* of the koïl's song (*koïl* or *kokilā*, the nightingale of the cuckoo family, see p. 366) that Godhuripa forgot by absorbing himself totally in the bird's song. Gaining a direct perception of sound, the sound of silence was heard in every sound. Discovering the one taste, it was an easy step for Godhuripa to universalize that insight and visualize it in every entity of experience, and visualization is the preliminary step to recognition of what is there in reality.

In his song of realization Godhuripa explains it differently. Taking external objects and their internal counterparts as equally unreal entities, he detaches himself from them by conceiving them as projections of mind's nature, and then realizes the nature of both inner and outer phenomena as light. Thus desubstantiating the universe—material objects as well as the ego and its forms—appearances are perceived inseparable from emptiness, and in each of the four states of being,[288] pure pleasure and space obtain as ultimate reality.

Historiography

Tāranātha tells a story of a bird-catcher whose name was Vyāḍhalipa. His Guru was Virūpa the Younger. His remarkable sādhana consisted of first sharpening his concentration into sāmadhi by contemplating cutting the throats of model birds, and then traveling the villages killing birds in order to provoke compassion and *ahiṃṣa* (non-violence) in his audience before restoring the creatures to life. Such action is called "wise penitential activity."[289]

The question of Godhuripa's identity arises. *Vyāḍhipa* (Vyāḍhalipa) is derived from *vyāḍha*, the bird-catchers' caste name, and both Godhuripa and Vyāḍhipa are rendered "Bird-catcher" (T.Bya rnon pa) in Tibetan. *Godhuri* (and Gorura, Vagura, Godura) may be derived from *vāgura*, "net." Our oldest source[290] identifies Godhuripa with Guṇḍaripa, who was a singer of *caryāpada* songs, whose Guru was Līlapa, and whose disciples were Dharmapa (Dharmabodhi) and Hādipa (Medhini, *50*).[291] Vyādhipa's disciple was Kuśalibhadra.[292] Thus Guṇḍaripa and Vyāḍhali belong to different generations. Ḍisunagar is unidentified.

56
THE SIDDHA LUCIKAPA THE ESCAPIST

From beginningless time, for ever,
We struggle in the ocean of saṃsāra.
The true Guru is the surest vessel
To make the difficult crossing
And bring us to freedom, now!

Lucika, a brahmin of Bengal, sickened by the sight of so many people dying around him, turned his mind away from this confusing maelstrom of existence and fled to a hermitage. He wished to practice a Buddhist sādhana, but he could find no Guru to instruct him. One day a yogin passed by his hermitage, and Lucika immediately fell down in homage before him.

"Why are you paying me homage?" asked the yogin.

"I have turned my back upon the world and wish to follow the Buddha's path. But I have found no one to teach me. Today I have found my Guru. Please instruct me!" Lucika pleaded.

The yogin granted him the initiation and empowerment of Saṃvara and instructed him in creative and fulfillment meditation. Lucika meditated according to the yogin's instruction for twelve years, and after uniting creative and fulfillment meditation he achieved his goal. He expressed his realization in this way:

Saṃsāra and nirvāṇa are two,
Yet I see no distinction.
Liberation is pure pleasure
And clinging to anything less
It is difficult to cross over.

Then he vanished, rising bodily into the Ḍākinī's Paradise.

Sādhana

Faced with death all around him, Lucikapa lost interest in the mundane world. On Śākyamuni's third excursion out of the seclusion of the sensual domain that was his palace, he saw a single corpse. So refined was his sensibility that merely by the realization of the fact of death, which had been kept hidden from him, his reaction was like this: "This is the end that has been set for all of us, and yet the world forgets its fear and takes no heed. The hearts of men are surely hardened to fear for they feel quite at ease while traveling along the road to the next life. Turn back the chariot! This is no time or place for pleasure excursions! How could an intelligent person pay no heed at a time of disaster, when he knows of his impending destruction?"[293] For some, like Lucika, this is the only possible reaction to the fact of death, and the principal function of all sādhana has been called "preparation for death motivated by the fear of death." Certainly if death is understood as a metaphor for life, all tantric sādhana can be described in that way.

In his verse of realization, indirectly Lucika gives two important indicators about Tantra. First he indicates the unstated *mahānirvāṇa*, where both saṃsāra and nirvāṇa are states of mind, saṃsāra the state where desire is rife, and nirvāṇa the hīnayāna goal of cessation of desire. Saṃsāra and nirvāṇa are not different because they are both states of pure pleasure and emptiness indivisible. Secondly, he implies that in Tantra the Buddha's being with its feeling tone of pure pleasure, experienced in initiation and at peak experience of meditation, should be assumed to exist even though it is temporarily occluded by the veils of emotional or conceptual ignorance. Only by visualizing and assuming the highest is the highest made possible. Accepting any lesser state as "reality," condemns the yogin to that lower level of achievement. Possessing the Buddha-nature, we *are* Bodhisattvas and reality *is* a continuum of delight and emptiness. The elementary principles of positive thinking are not only relevant but imperative when applying the Guru's precepts.

Historiography

In Tibetan Lucika's name is rendered as "He who sitting down, stands up" (*Tsog 'dug kog langs mkhan*). Further, *lucika* is probably derived from the Sanskrit *luñcaka*, "One who pulls out," thus, "The Escapist." There are no references to Lucikapa in other sources.

57

THE SIDDHA NIRGUṆAPA
THE ENLIGHTENED MORON

Our True Guru's precepts show the peaceful center,
Pacifying violent emotions and conflicting thoughts.
Stilling those wave-like disturbances in meditation
We conduct ourselves with attention and poise.

Nirguṇa was born into a family of low-caste householders in Pūrvadeśa. His birth was attended by a great feast and celebration, but as he grew up, unable to perform even the simplest tasks, his parents became disillusioned and disappointed. Their son was stricken by a moronic lassitude.

"This moron can do nothing, neither good nor bad," his family would say. "It were better had he not been born."

Unutterably depressed after being reviled in this way, one day Nirguṇa moped off, and eventually laid himself down in a lonely place, where a yogin found him.

"Get up and beg alms in town," the yogin told him.

"I can't get up," Nirguṇa replied, unwilling to stir.

Out of pity the yogin gave him food. "Do you have any skill?" he inquired.

"Venerable sir, my name is Moron," he said as a matter of fact. "I have no skill whatsoever."

"But you need to eat and drink," insisted the yogin. "Aren't you afraid of death?"

"Yes surely," Nirguṇa admitted. "But what can I do?"

"If you can practice it I will give you a sādhana," the yogin offered.

"If I can practice it lying down, please teach me," Nirguṇa responded.

The yogin initiated him and instructed him in the indivisibility of appearances and emptiness:

> *Both "the knower" and "the known" are delusory,*
> *And those who fail to realize that*
> *Suffer hopeless anxiety and should be pitied.*
> *Yet even this anxiety has no basis in reality.*
> *When the mindstream has become clear light,*
> *The indivisibility of appearances and emptiness,*
> *Free of inhibition, you can wander*
> *In the villages as a crazy saint.*

Nirguṇa followed these instructions, begging his food and practicing his sādhana, until he realized the unity of appearances and emptiness as clear light, and attained his goal. People who met him roaming about the country would ask him who he was, whereupon he would gaze into their eyes and weep, and seeing the depth of compassion in his heart people would weep with him. Those who were fit vessels he made his disciples, teaching them the unity of appearances and emptiness. Thereafter, gradually, like a boat sinking into the ocean, all their delusions dissolved, and, like Nirguṇa, they gained *mahāmudrā-siddhi.* He bodily attained the Ḍākinī's Paradise.

Sādhana

Nirguṇa is another siddha who was rescued by his Guru from an abject fate. The principal characteristics of these miserable siddhas-to-be, their despondency and *weltschmertz*, their loathing of life and inadequacy, color these short legends in a uniformly depressing way. However, the siddhas' magical attainments are high-lighted by contrast to their miserable pre-initiation conditions, and the point that initiation and sādhana is successful in direct proportion to the intensity of despair, contrition, and desire to be free of samsaric suffering, is repeatedly and effectively instilled. In Nirguṇa's case, the absence of those qualities rewarded in society, and also those talents required to survive in a competitive world—energy, creativity and mental alertness—had no bearing on his capacity to meditate and no effect on the quality of his gnostic awareness and *mahāmudrā-*

siddhi. This follows logically from the mahāyāna premise that the Buddha-nature is innate in us all, that it is in fact the nature of our being, and the light of Buddha's awareness shines out from the man or woman who has emptied his mind of gratuitous conceptualization, preconception and mental constructs, quite independent of physical or mental capacity or attainment. What is more important than intelligence and talent is sharp and complete sensory faculties; it is an odd paradox that the one-eyed, or partially deaf, lack the doctrinal admission requirements for entry into the Ḍākinī's Paradise.

What depends upon intelligence, social grace and endowment of skillful means, however, is the nature of enlightened conduct. Nirguṇa seems to have lacked the "attention and poise"[294] he mentions in his song of realization, and this inadequacy resulted in behavior judged by his social critics to be "crazy." Nirguṇa, Mekopa (*43*), and Kālapa (*27*) were not *paṇḍitas*, nor even worldly-wise, but they were crazy gnostic saints.[295] Lacking any subtlety or diversity of skillful means to express deep empathetic responsiveness, Nirguṇa could only gaze at the indeterminate absolute in another man's heart, and weep. Not that this method was ineffective, on the contrary he would have destroyed the defenses of many a cold-blooded, hard-hearted materialist he met on the road, inducing them to join him in tears of compassion, the tears of the Bodhisattva Avalokiteśvara, whose eyes are constantly awash with the nectar of compassion for mankind. The Goddess Tārā was manifest as one of those tears.

The instruction that Nirguṇapa gave to his disciples, precepts upon the indivisibility of appearance and emptiness[296] would be creative and fulfillment meditation techniques leading to the basic insight of the *Prajñāpāramitā-hṛdaya-sūtra* that emptiness is form and form emptiness, and to its corollary that all phenomenal existence is *illusory*, and that dualistic mental constructs reinforcing perception of discrete entities and a substantive ego, are *delusory.*

Historiography

Nirguṇapāda (T.Yon tan med pa) is derived from *nirguṇa*, "without quality." Pūrvadeśa means East India, Bengal. Nirguṇa's Guru may have been Kṛṣṇācārya.[297] Naguṇa is a common alternative form of his name.

58
THE SIDDHA JAYĀNANDA CROW MASTER

In the samādhi of pure awareness and knowledge,
I abide in our innate purity, free from distinctions;
With such realization I have total conviction
And an absence of preconception and discursive thought.

There was once a brahmin minister of a brahmanical king of Bengal who converted to the Buddhist Tantra. He practiced the tantric mysteries in secret and received blessing without anyone's knowledge. In the course of time he threw out many sacrificial cakes, and another brahmin minister, who had no sympathy for the Buddha's teaching, reported the matter to the king. The king had the Buddhist minister cast into a dungeon and put into irons.

"It is no sinful waste to make offerings to the gods," the prisoner asserted, "Release me from these chains!" But the king was adamant.

At the time the brahmin usually performed his worship and threw out offerings, crows gathered to receive their customary feast. When they found that this was not forthcoming, a vast array of the birds flocked to the king's palace, and began to dive and peck at the people's heads. A crowd gathered, and one man, who knew the language of birds, was told by the crows that the king had imprisoned a brahmin who was their father and mother. The king realized that the brahmin was innocent of crime, and begging Jayānanda's forgiveness he requested him to send the crows away. When the birds dispersed at the brahmin's command, the king was impressed and found great faith. He ordered twenty loads of rice to be scattered, and otherwise distributed, daily.

The brahmin became known as Guru Jayānanda, and he sang:

By the grace of the Guru I gained perfect realization,
Innate, spontaneously arising, pure awareness.
Now that I am minister of pure pleasure
I no longer attend the court of saṃsāra;
The king, the naturally radiant nature of being,
Defeating the hostile powers of duality,
Has detached himself from worldly pleasures.
Listen, you ignorant people!
Listen to Jaya's words of victory!

After seven hundred years of selfless service to others, he attained the Ḍākinī's Paradise.

Sādhana

We are not informed about the nature of Jayānanda's sādhana, but his statement of realization is quite clear. The terms he uses are all words representing aspects of the unitary gnostic experience: "innate, spontaneously arising, pure awareness"[298] describes the experience as awareness alone, awareness graphically represented as a Ḍākinī performing an endless dance, passing effortlessly from one *mudrā* to another. "Pure pleasure"[299] is not only the feeling tone of the experience but the content of it—the paradise of Sukhāvatī is an extension of a mind that is nothing but pure pleasure. "The naturally radiant nature of being"[300] is not only the inherent nature of all being, but also its manifestation; what is clear light in its nature, cannot be anything but clear light in its manifestation.

At the center of offering rites, and also the *gaṇacakra-pūja*, sacrificial cakes are tasted by the participants to attain transfiguration in a process very similar to the Christian eucharistic sacrament; the cakes are then thrown out for the benefit of lower life forms—dogs, birds, *preta*s and spirits of various kinds. These tormas are composed of numerous symbolic ingredients, the basis being roasted and ground grain; modelled as *yantra*s, they are consecrated as the deity itself. The Sanskrit word *bali* originally indicated sacrifice of any kind, including blood sacrifice; the Tibetan form, torma (*gtor ma*), is derived from the verb "to scatter," indicating how the nature of sacrifice within the Buddhist context evolved. To the Tibetans, crows are birds of ill-omen; the shadow of a crow passing over a human being causes instant neural upset, and when the victim is highly susceptible to such influences, epilepsy and similar fits.

Historiography

There is only one Jayānanda mentioned in Tibetan sources, and he was a great *paṇḍita.* He traveled as far as Shan-su in China, stopping at many Tibetan institutions along the way, where his visit was recorded in the texts he translated, and he impressed the Tibetans sufficiently for them to nominate him as an incarnation of their great king, Srong btsan sgam po—a high accolade indeed. He was also known as Kha che pan chen and Kha che dgon pa pa, The Great Kashmiri Paṇḍita and The Kashmiri Hermit. He was, principally, a student of the *madhyamika.* He was a disciple of Atīśa and Kālacakrapāda Junior, and lived, therefore, in the eleventh century, although he was alive well into the twelfth.[301] The king in the legend would have been a Pāla *rāja* had he ruled Bengal, but some authorities consider Baṅgala to be a corruption of Bhagalpur, an ancient city-state located on the Ganges east of Patna.

Jayānanta is the chief variant of his name, which means Rejoicer in Victory. Jayānandī-pāda was a poet-siddha.[302]

59

THE SIDDHA PACARIPA THE PASTRYCOOK

Looking nowhere, gaze at the center—
Supreme joy, detached joy, pure pleasure!
Practicing the magic of the tantric mysteries
Gather the yogin's intuitions.

Pacaripa was a vendor of chapatis, unleavened bread, in the country of Campā. Clothed only in a loincloth, for he was very poor, he would take chapatis from a businessman and hawk them in the streets. In this way he could make a small profit and support himself. One day after he had been unable to sell any of his wares, bitten by hunger, he began to eat a chapati, but before he had eaten half of it a monk, who was an emanation of Avalokiteśvara, appeared in front of him. Pacaripa's faith was aroused by this apparition, and after prostrating before the monk he offered him the remaining half of his chapati. Then responding honestly to the monk's enquiry, Pacaripa told him to whom the bread belonged.

"Then we are priest and patron," the monk said. "I should give you instruction in return."

Pacaripa prepared a maṇḍala of thanksgiving and offered flowers to the monk. In return he received Refuge in the Triple Gem, the Bodhisattva Vow, and the Six Syllable Mantra of Avalokiteśvara. Thereafter Pacaripa practiced his sādhana, sustaining himself by begging.

One day he encountered his previous employer, and the man demanded the money that was owed him. When Pacaripa told him that he had nothing to give him, the man began to strike him in anger.

"I didn't eat the chapatis alone," cried Pacaripa. "Both master and disciple ate it!" These words resounded loudly, echoing from wall to wall in a marvelous way, and the rich man stopped, frightened.

"The chapati was yours! Now, go!" he said.

Pacaripa went to the temple of Avalokiteśvara and asked for the price of the chapati from the image, and thirty ounces of gold materialized. This he took to his previous employer, and he was absolved from his guilt.

"Ārya Avalokiteśvara must be my Guru," he thought to himself. So he set off for the Potala Mountain where the Bodhisattva lives. On the way he passed through a thick forest of thorns, which pierced his feet and hurt him. He let out a great cry to Avalokiteśvara, who appeared to him in his reality.

"I am indeed your Guru," the Bodhisattva told him. "Now give up your intention to go to the Potala and return to Campā to lead your disciples."

Pacaripa was overjoyed, and floating in the sky he returned to his own country. The people there were overcome with astonishment and begged instruction from him. He taught them the indivisibility of appearances and emptiness. Thereafter he was known as Guru Pacaripa, and finally he rose bodily into the Ḍākinī's Paradise.

Sādhana

Pacaripa was a simple man and he received a simple Mahāyāna sādhana to practice. Refuge in the Triple Gem—the Buddha, Dharma and Sangha: enlightened being, vibration and embodiment—formulated liturgically as "I take refuge in the Buddha, Dharma, and Sangha,"[303] recited thrice at the beginning of each and every devotional occasion, is the essence of the Buddhist creed, common to all vehicles, sects and schools. Exegesis upon the Refuge encompasses the whole of the Buddhist doctrine. The Bodhisattva Vow, or more strictly, the aspiration towards an enlightened mind, has been formulated quite differently by various schools. In the basic mahāyāna form it is a pledge to renounce nirvāṇa and serve others at any cost; in *atiyoga* it is an assertion of the yogin's essential identity with the Buddha-nature and recognition of the inalienable process of emanation of a compassionate, apparitional sensual level of being. Recitation of the Six Syllable Mantra, OṀ MA ṆI PAD MA HŪṀ, accompanied by a visualization, is the method of invoking the Bodhisattva Avalokiteśvara and identifying with his compassionate nature and assuming his attributes. In his innocence, Pacaripa attempted to reach the Bodhisattva's physical abode, a mythical island mountain in the south-western Indian Ocean, or the Dalai Lama's residence in Lhasa, both named Potala. Previously the Bodhisattva had appeared to him in the guise of a monk; to instruct him to return to his town of Campā, answering his cry of pain, he must have appeared in his visionary form, *saṃbhogakāya*.

Like Jayānanda, Pacaripa taught the indivisibility of appearances and emptiness. No matter what the approach to *mahāmudrā-siddhi* the result is the same, and the most obvious quality of that *siddhi* is the visual effect—phenomenal appearances have been desubstantiated, dematerialized. No longer living in an environment of discrete entities, solid and seemingly immutable, the siddha finds himself in a metamorphosing phantasmagoria of vivid color and form—light-form. Recognition of the emptiness (*śūnyatā*) that is the nature of all things, all-penetrating and all-encompassing, the essence that is inseparable from the manifest apparitional manifestation, transforms the environment into a fairy castle in the sky, a reflection of the moon in water, an hallucination, a visionary world where the siddha can fly through the sky, walk through walls and manipulate the elemental balance. This experience is shared only if people close by are highly susceptible to the vibration, and gain a "contact high." Unbelievers are still trapped in a delusive world of concrete things.

Historiography

There is an ineluctable question of identification associated with Pacaripa. Although his name is probably derived from the Sanskrit *pacala*, "cook," translated into Tibetan as Pastry-seller (T.'Khur ba 'tshong pa), because one text has Carpaṭi listed as siddha *59*[304] Pacaripa has been identified with Carpaṭī, the more famous Buddhist-siddha and *nāth*, who may have been a Guru of Mīnapa. There is little evidence for this identification, less than the case for identification of Carpaṭi with Carbaripa (*64*). Pacaripa is not mentioned elsewhere.

Campā, or Campāvati, was capital of the ancient state of Aṅga, and a river-port at the confluence of the Ganges and Campā Rivers. Emigrants departed from Campā for the colony of Campā in Indo-China, which thrived until the Khmers destroyed it. It was one of the Six Great Cities of Mauryan North India, where Buddhism and Jainism flourished, but not to the neglect of Brahmānism. By the early seventh century it was greatly diminished; Huien Tsiang found the Buddhist monasteries desolate. Campānagar, or Campāpur, in east Bihar, is its contemporary form, while the Buddhist site at Patharghat attests to its former glory. (See p. 300.)

60

THE SIDDHA CAMPAKA THE FLOWER KING

Like the clear light of means and insight united,
The Guru's constant flow is all-embracing;
Sahaja *is a spontaneously arising wish-fulfilling tree,*
Its fruit the trikāya, *naturally radiant, perfect in itself.*

The king of Campā was himself called Campaka after the delicate white and yellow flower of that name. His kingdom was fabulously wealthy, and pleasure came to him easily. But in his youthful pride, intoxicated by the thrill of power, he gave no thought to his future life.

In his garden of *campaka* flowers he had a summer house containing a throne of the sweet-smelling yellow variety of the *campaka* flower. He was reclining on his throne one day when a yogin came to him begging alms. The king washed the yogin's feet, and after giving him cushions to lie upon and food to eat he listened to his discourse. The king and his court asked the yogin to stay with them as their priest, and the yogin agreed.

"You have travelled through many countries," said the king. "Have you ever seen flowers such as these, or a king such as I?"

"The scent of the *campaka* flowers is incomparable," replied the yogin. "But your body odors are not so agreeable. Indeed your kingdom is superior to all others, but eventually you too must pass away empty-handed."

This conversation inspired the king to begin an analysis of himself, and in so doing he destroyed attachment to his body. Then he went to his Guru for further instruction. First the yogin taught him the laws of cause and effect that govern all human activity. Then he initiated him and taught him the path of creative and fulfillment yoga. But the king was too preoccupied with thoughts of his flowers and his power to be able to meditate attentively. The yogin taught him how to make his mental activity into the path itself:

Know the nature of appearances to be emptiness:
That is the flower of the Guru's instruction,
Wherein the mind must settle as a bee
To suck the pollen that is endless ambrosia.
"Flower," "bee" and "pollen" are essentially one,
And the honey is pure pleasure itself.
Such is the word of the Sixth Buddha,
Mahāvajradhara. Meditate without doubt.

Campaka meditated for twelve years and reached the realization that the Guru's instruction, which is the emptiness of appearances, the underlying reality of his own mind, and his peak experience, these three, were inseparable, and he attained his goal. Thereafter he was called Guru Campakapāda, and he taught the Dharma to his consorts and large court, before bodily arising into the Ḍākinī's Paradise.

Sādhana

What is the point of learning the principles of karma, "the ineluctable laws of cause and effect," if the goal of sādhana is a supralogical space where spontaneity that leaves no trace in the ether (*akāśa*), and supercedes karma, is the nature of the siddha's activity? *Dhyāna, chan* and *zen* (but not Dzokchen), the uncompromising "quietist" schools, do not teach cause and effect. But the Bodhisattva schools following the gradual path maintain that the mind must be disciplined over whatever period is necessary to accumulate the habit of gnostic awareness and virtuous conduct, so that when enlightenment occurs the mind is perfectly conditioned to virtue, and spontaneous action is exclusively virtuous. An understanding of the laws of karma gives facility in calculating and assessing virtue, and distinguishing right from wrong; these laws also teach the means of skillful travel through the six realms of saṃsāra and the three realms of existence. But the sudden schools would argue that a siddha has no need to learn such information, as his knowledge is the be all and end all.

The Sixth Buddha, Mahāvajradhara, is the *adi-buddha*, who rules the Five Dhyāni Buddhas, Vairocana, Amitābha, Ratnasambhava, Amoghasiddhi and Vajrasattva, and contains their maṇḍala. Iconographically, he is depicted sitting in lotus posture, with arms crossed over his heart-*cakra*, both hands holding *vajras*, and he is colored blue, symbolic of the all-encompassing *dharmakāya*; he wears the Bodhisattva's ornaments to indicate that the three modes of the Buddha's being are contained in him. In Mahāvajradhara's instruction, objective appearances, subjective mind and unitary pure awareness, are symbolized by flower, bee and pollen; the union of Guru and Ḍākinī creates the nectar of immortality.

Historiography

The *campaka* flower, a kind of magnolia, grows on a shrub or a small tree (*michelia champaca*) throughout India. It is sacred to all Hindus, who offer it to their gods and rub it over their bodies at marriages. Its scent is strong to the point of oppression. Shelley knew it: The wandering airs they faint / On the dark, the silent stream; /And the chumpak's odors fall / Like sweet thoughts in a dream.[305] Campā was famous for it. In the days of Śākyamuni Buddha an artificial lake surrounded by *campaka* shrubs was a favorite resort for wandering monks. Campā took its name from King Campā of the Mahābharāta; and the city was a thriving metropolis by the time of the Buddha.

61

THE SIDDHA BHIKṢANAPA
SIDDHA TWO-TEETH

Following the elusive path of the pure pleasure union
To the incomparable, inaccessible shrine of gnosis,
The superior yogin *with the faculty of perfect balance*
Attains realization by the grace of the Guru's precepts.

In Paṭaliputra there once lived a man of low caste who squandered his inheritance and was reduced to begging from town to village. One day, after his begging had proved fruitless, he retired to a lonely place, his misery pressing his mind in on itself. While he sat there alone, a Ḍākinī appeared before him and asked him what troubled him. The beggar told her of his troubles and anxieties.

"I have the means to fulfill your desires," she said.

"Then please teach me," he implored.

"What will you give me in return?" she asked him.

He bit together one upper and one lower tooth, and the others he extracted and gave to her. Knowing then that he was capable of superior thought, she gave him initiation and instruction in the two-in-oneness of skillful means and perfect insight. After seven years of meditation he saw the truth of his union, the inexhaustible virtue and power of the Buddhas arose in his mindstream, and he expressed his realization. He continued roaming from village to town, but only for the sake of those ready for his instruction. He was known as the Guru Bhikṣanapa, and after many years he rose into the Ḍākinī's Paradise.

Sādhana

The slightly ludicrous nature of Bhikṣanapa's offering to the Ḍākinī is obviated if his two remaining teeth are understood metaphorically in the light of the Ḍākinī's offer to fulfill his desire. His instruction was "the union of skillful means and perfect insight."[306] One of the superior tantric vows is the pledge never to divorce pleasure and emptiness from the symbolic Guru/Ḍākinī union; means and insight are interpreted as pleasure and emptiness in the *anuyoga* context. The primary interpretation of skillful means as compassionate activity is not thereby rejected; Bhikṣanapa is the Ḍākinī's compassionate partner spontaneously creating her apparitional dance. The balance and harmony of union, implied in the metaphor of Bhikṣanapa's two teeth, is the same balance, or lack of bias,[307] that he sings of in his song of realization. There is no union of means and insight, Guru and Ḍākinī, without perfect equanimity, implying supreme balance. To walk the path of Tantra is to risk falling off into the adamantine hell, the *vajra nāraka*, and safety checks do not exist. Like a tight-rope walker performing without a thought in his head, fully concentrated upon the present moment, the siddha concentrates totally on the ultimate *samaya*, the absolute specific; acting without inhibition, thoughtlessly and spontaneously he sustains the unity of intuitive knowledge of emptiness and the appropriate skillful means. He falls when he forgets his *samaya*, when objective thought arises, when one selfish thought destroys the union of means and insight. To employ a sexual analogy: this balance is like sustaining a sexual relationship so finely tuned that both partners are on the verge of the consummation that is always denied yet constantly experienced in the pure pleasure of expectation and continuous creative peak energy. All this is implied in the beggar's gesture to the Ḍākinī, who had good enough reason, therefore, to infer that he was capable of superior thought and was ready for instruction.

Historiography

Bhikṣanapa (or Bhikhanapa, Dhikṣana, Bhakana, and so forth) rendered into Tibetan as Alms-taker or Beggar, has its root in *bhikṣa* "to wish to share or partake," which is the root of *bhikṣu*, "a Buddhist monk." Also, *viṣana* means "tusk" or "horn." *Bhikṣanapa* is also translated into Tibetan as Siddha Two-teeth (T.So gnyis pa'i zhabs).

62

THE SIDDHA DHILIPA THE EPICUREAN MERCHANT

When I realized my original nature as the Buddha,
The Buddha became the nature of every reality;
Through the empowerment of sahaja, *the innate absolute,*
I am permeated by the unborn Vajradhara.

In Satapuri there lived an oil merchant called Dhilipa, whose trading brought him immense profit. He was as rich as Kubera, the god of wealth, and he indulged himself to the full. At each meal he would consume eighty-four main dishes, twelve kinds of sweetmeat and five kinds of beverage—indulgence customarily reserved for the king. But the king remained in ignorance of the merchant's habits.

One day the Paṇḍita Bhahana visited Dhilipa. He spoke to him of the pain and frustration of the wheel of existence and the means to escape it, and the merchant gained faith in him and asked him to become his household priest. Sometime later, while the *paṇḍita* was watching Dhilipa extract oil from sesame seeds, he remarked that such work may lead to greater and greater profit, but that it was no way to attain liberation. The oil merchant responded by asking for instruction, and he received initiation and instruction on the inherent radiance of seemingly concrete objects:

Extract from the sesame oil of your body
The oil that is conceptual thought,
And pour it into the vessel of mind's empty nature;
Then the wick of appearance and emptiness united,
Lit by the flame of knowledge and pure awareness,

Dispels the gloom of ignorance.
Abide in inexhaustible pleasure,
The incomparable pleasure of liberation.

After nine years of meditation the merchant had united creative and fulfillment meditation, and he reached his goal. Effulgent light radiating from his body filled the sky in all directions, and the king, hearing of this merchant's achievement, sent a witness to verify it. "If wealth is measured in terms of inexhaustible bliss, then I am a king without equal," Dhilipa sang. The people gained faith in him, and to each one of them he gave instruction consistent with his disposition and capability. After many years, with a vast retinue, he attained the Ḍākinī's Paradise.

Sādhana

Sesame seed is sometimes used as a metaphor for "seed-essence,"[308] the empty, sub-atomic building block of appearances, and thus it is the substance of pure awareness; it has the same relation to *bodhicitta* as spermatoza has to seminal fluid. In the context of this legend the crushing of sesame seed is a metaphor for extracting subtle dualistic concepts from the delusion of substantial materiality that is sustained by them, or for extracting the concepts of name and form that give substance to differentiated entities of reality, in particular the body. Dhilipa is instructed to visualize the oil as these mental constructs that are to be dissolved in mind's empty nature,[309] a process otherwise described as emptying the *lalanā* and *rasanā* into the *avadhūti*; then from the union of appearances and emptiness, the interfusion of *lalanā* and *rasanā*, the gnostic flame of pure awareness and knowledge is ignited. Thereafter, what appeared to the conditioned mind as concrete entities[310] is now irradiated, self-illuminated, inherently luminescent light-form,[311] appearances and emptiness united, where the ontological element of light is also the epistemological element of cognition.

The rationalist's objection, "But objects are solid. They have weight and density!" is answered by indicating the delusory functions of the other senses, particularly the tactile sense and the mental constructs that predetermine tactile reactions. Remove the concepts of gravity, density and weight and the siddha can "walk through walls" and "mould rock like butter." A totally illogical mixture of metaphysics and myth? Mind has made the world as we know it in the image of conventional, conditioned concepts, and to decondition mind is to destroy the conventional world; what remains—naked reality, raw energy and light—can be interpreted in any way the mind is capable of conceiving it. Such is tantric doctrine and such is the experience of siddhas who have gained control over the elements after accomplishing their *magnum opus*; and the analogy of Dhilipa's instruction demonstrates how it is done.

Historiography

The name Dhilipa (Delipa, Teli, Telopa, Tailopa, Bhalipa) is derived from the Sanskrit *taila*, "sesame seed oil," and Tailopāda. Thus it has the same root as Tilopa (*22*), Nāropa's Guru. Tāranātha identifies the oil-pressing siddha as Nāropa's Guru. Born in Caṭigharo in the East, educated as a brahmin, attaining renown as a scholar, he became a wandering mendicant. Attracted by the Buddha's teaching he was ordained; only to be unfrocked for associating with a mundane Ḍākinī whose work was extracting oil from sesame seed. Later he moved in with her. Finally he flew up into the sky in union with his consort, still pressing sesame seed. He attained *sahajāvidhyā*, knowledge of the innate emptiness that accompanies every moment of experience.[312] In our legend, the Paṇḍita Bhahana (Bhana) is unidentified, as is Satapuri.

63
THE SIDDHA KUMBHARIPA THE POTTER

The accelerating wheel of habitual action
Created the song and dance of existence;
But now the fire of knowledge and pure awareness
Has consumed all my mental obscurations.

Kumbharipa, the potter, lived in Jomanaśrī, working continuously at his craft. But his mind was oppressed by tedium, and he felt the need of a change of heart. One day a yogin visited him, begging alms; and after offering him food, the potter confided his problems.

"Guruji, I gain little benefit from this hard work. It is endless toil, endless tedium, and I am becoming increasingly depressed."

"Benefactor," replied the yogin, "don't you understand that all beings on the wheel of rebirth never find a moment of true happiness. From time without beginning until time without end there is only suffering. Do not be depressed by your own little misery!"

The potter was impressed and asked the yogin for a sādhana. He received initiation and instruction in creative and fulfillment meditation:

The clay of passion and thought is prepared
From the soil of unknowing and ignorance;
On the wheel of greed and grasping
The six kinds of pots are fashioned from this clay.
Fire the pots in the flame of pure awareness.

The potter understood these instructions in the recognition of conceptual thought, and he meditated for only six months before the defilements of samsaric delusion were eradicated and he attained his goal. Then as he sat in meditative composure, the potter's wheel turned automatically, and the pots sprang from the wheel like the joy from his heart. When the towns-people discovered that he had gained the power of the Buddhas they called him Guru Kumbharipa. After expressing his realization, he bodily attained the Ḍākinī's Paradise.

Sādhana

There is an immediate hostile reaction to the statement that all life is suffering, that we are never happy. Happiness, however, must be understood as the Buddha's eternal, pure pleasure (*mahāsukha*). All our temporal, human joys and pleasures, and the gods' long-lasting but passing ecstacies, are suffering simply because they are temporal and passing. Only Buddhahood deserves effort; ephemeral sensual pleasure is not worth the candle. Although all temporal existence is suffering, since nirvāṇa is found only in saṃsāra, eternal pure pleasure is to be found within suffering, even if it is only an ephemeral flash.

Kumbharipa's instruction is on recognition of thought,[313] thought being defined as all objects of the sixth sense—the mind. Evolution of the conditioned mind is described according to the doctrine of conditioned co-production (*pratītya-samutpāda*). Ignorance, or the inability to perceive the emptiness of phenomena, is the root of saṃsāra; out of ignorance arises passionate reaction and conflicting dualistic thought, mental chatter interpretive of other people's actions, for example, all toned by emotion. The six types of mental syndrome, each characterized by a different emotion and thought-pattern, are represented by the six realms of saṃsāra (the realms of gods, men, antigods, hungry ghosts, beasts and denizens of hell). After his initiation into the nature of thought from his Guru, the potter's practice was to remain attentive to thought, constantly penetrating its form to its empty essence—"firing the pots in the flame of gnostic awareness." Six months of practice indicate one month for each of the six kinds of mental syndrome. Although there is no attempt to avoid the mind's creation, or to change it or eliminate it, as the practice continues the mind empties by itself, or rather it ceases to produce the thought and emotion that is the meat of the meditation, and finally the mind is a Buddhafield. Instead of other people's actions and words provoking proud, jealous, hateful or desirous thoughts, all beings are seen as gods and goddesses, Ḍākas and Ḍākinīs, performing an endless dance of pure pleasure.

Historiography

The name of the eternal potter, Kumbharipa (or Kumaripa, Kumara, Kumbaripa, etc.), is derived from *kumbhakara*, a potter. (T.rDza mkhan). His home town, Jomanaśrī, is unidentified. The name Kumbharipa is not found in any of the Tibetan lineages.

64

THE NĀTH SIDDHA CARBARIPA (CARPAṬI) THE PETRIFIER

The supreme vow of all the Buddhas
Is nothing but self-realization.
Whoever realizes the innate purity of his mind
Gains the same vision as all the Buddhas.

In a certain district of Magadha there lived a wealthy herdsman. He owned a thousand water buffalo and vast herds of sheep and horses. When his aged father died he gave a great feast for the entire district, a feast lasting many days and remembered thereafter for the fine food and delicacies that were served. Early one morning before the feast ended, the family and guests went down to the Ganges to bathe, leaving the herdsman's young wife and her child in charge of the house. During her family's absence the Guru Carbaripa materialized before the young woman and asked for food, but the wife was afraid of her husband's wrath.

"If your husband or mother-in-law are angry with you for entertaining me, come to my forest hermitage on the hill over there. You can see my fire from here," the yogin reassured her. "If they are not angry, so much the better. Please give me some food."

Then the woman gave him food and listened happily to his conversation. Shortly after the yogin departed, the mother-in-law returned, and seeing the remains of a meal and little food remaining in the house, she began to berate her. The young wife in her turn became angry, and she fled to Carbaripa's hermitage with her child.

"Well done!" said the yogin in welcome. And he sprinkled her and the child with consecrated water that miraculously turned them into stone images of the Buddha. Thus they were no longer in need of food or provisions.

Meanwhile the husband returned home and asked for his wife. "She has simply vanished," they told him. But persevering in his enquiries, he discovered where she had gone and pursued her to the yogin's retreat. There he received the same consecration by sprinkling of water, and he too was changed into a Buddha image. The Guru placed the three of them together on a single couch. When their family and friends began to arrive in search of them, some alone, some in pairs, they all received the same treatment. As many as three hundred people arrived, like lost buffalo calves, and all were transformed into Buddha images.

The herdsman's young son gained the eight great *siddhis*: from his testicles came *khecari-siddhi*; from his penis (*vajra*) came the nectar that transmutes base metal to gold; from his lower gate (anus) came the ambrosia of deathlessness; and from his eyes came the power of flight, and so on. He became famous throughout the land, and the King of Campā and many buffalo folk came to pay respect. The king had great faith in him and built a temple for him and his parents, and a larger temple for the three hundred smaller images. He became known as Dumapa.

This temple became a popular power place for the practice of sādhana, and it is said that when the minds of the yogins meditating there became bedeviled by intractable evil thoughts, they were beaten or otherwise chastised by the images. Dumapa quickly attained magical powers; but he remains there still awaiting the coming of Maitreya, the Buddha of Loving Kindness, whereupon he will work for all mankind.

Sādhana

Unlike any other legend amongst the eighty-four, Carbaripa's legend is evidently an accretion of anecdotes that became associated with an un-named power place. If we ignore the mention of Magadha, the legend's internal evidence supports the identification of Carbaripa with Carpaṭi, the *nāth* siddha, one of the nine founding fathers of the *nāth* lineages, and one of the twelve disciples of the twelve original *kāpālika* Gurus. In our legend the king of Campā (text: Campaka) would be King Sāhila of Chambā, in Himachal Pradesh; a Chambā chronicle mentions Carpaṭi as a contemporary and Guru of the tenth century king.[314] The buffalo herdsmen would be the Gujars who have wintered in Chambā with large buffalo

Carbaripa (Caparipa) is at one with the sky.

herds from time immemorial. Like Gorakṣa and Mīna, Carbaripa/Carpaṭi, or his disciple Dumapa, only attained mundane *siddhi*. The description of the boy's attainment is in the terminology of the *nāth* tradition, although the relation between the *siddhis* and their anatomical places of origin is not clear. *Khecari-mudrā*, which produces *khecari-siddhi*,[315] involves turning the tongue up and back into the hollow above the throat (where a channel that brings *soma* or *amṛta* from the moon at the *sahasrāha-cakra* on the crown of the head has its exit) and fixing concentration of sight at the space between the eyebrows (where the "third eye" has it location in the subtle body).[316]

In this most confused of legends, it is clear that the boy attained the *siddhis*, but it is not clear who is named Dumapa (or Dhu ma pa). If it is not the boy, Dumapa could be Carbaripa who brought the petrified people together under one roof: one edition of *The Legends* has Du ma pa, The Gatherer. Dhu ma with Dha ma are two disciples of Kāṇhapa, while Carbaripa is Kāṇhapa's disciple.[317] Further, it may have been either Carbaripa or Dumapa who was to await Maitreya before practicing the Bodhisattva Vow. The *siddhi* of "petrification," which allows a Guru to transform a previously worldly person into a yogin sitting as still as a rock for long periods of time, is particularly relevant in the *nāth* tradition where *haṭhayoga* demands such practice, but Tibetan Lamas also certainly have this power to "freeze" their devotees in meditation. Thus meditation in the Guru's presence is sought after eagerly. One text explains the metaphor by the statement: "he entered the Buddha's self-existent *vajra* mode of being."[318]

Historiography

Siddha number sixty-four is variously called Carbaripa, Javari, Caparipa, Cavaripa, Capalipa, Cārpaṭi. If he can be identified with Carpaṭi, his Guru was Jālandhara and his disciples Mīnapa, Kukkuripa, and Khaḍgapa. If Carbaripa was Javari, the only information we have is that he was a disciple of one of Kāṇhapa's disciples[319] or of Kāṇhapa himself. In the first case he would have lived at the end of the ninth and beginning of the tenth century; in the second case he would have lived in the ninth or tenth century. The root of *carbaripa* is probably *carpaṭa*, meaning "ear;" thus the case for Carpaṭi being the correct form of the name is strengthened.

65
THE YOGINĪ SIDDHĀ MAṆIBHADRĀ THE HAPPY HOUSEWIFE

When my mind was enshrouded in ignorance
Critical thought attended every sound;
When reality was revealed as my own nature
The nature of whatever appeared was reality itself.

In the town of Agarce there lived a wealthy householder, who had a thirteen year old daughter. She was betrothed to a man of her own caste, and as was the custom the young woman lived in her parents' house until she was old enough to be her husband's wife. During this period the Guru Kukkuripa came to her house begging food.

"What a fine handsome man you are!" the girl told him. "Why do you wear patched robes and beg your food when you could take a wife and live comfortably?"

"I am terrified of the wheel of rebirth, and I am trying to find the great joy of liberation from it," Kukkuripa told her. "If I do not take this opportunity, in my next life I may not be so lucky. This human birth is really a precious chance, and if I break my vows of chastity by taking a wife, all my hopes and aspirations will be shattered and I'll be afflicted with many kinds of grief. When I realized that, I gave up the pursuit of women."

The girl was impressed by Kukkuripa and trusted him. After she had offered him good food, she said, "Please show me the way to liberation."

"I live in the cremation ground," Kukkuripa replied. "If you so desire, come to me there."

Preoccupied with the significance of the Guru's words,

Maṇibhadrā, for that was her name, neglected her work for the rest of the day, and then at nightfall she went to the cremation ground. Kukkuripa recognized her spiritual maturity and gave her the Saṃvara initiation and empowerment together with instruction in the union of creative and fulfillment meditation. Thereafter she remained in solitude for seven days, establishing herself in the practice of her sādhana. But when she returned home her parents beat her and reviled her. Maṇibhadrā defended herself, "There is no one in the universe who has not been either father or mother to me," she said. "Besides, a pure blood line and a good family upbringing does not free a girl from the grip of saṃsāra. So relying upon a Guru I have decided to practice a sādhana that can bring me liberation. I have already begun."

Her words mollified her parents, who could find nothing to answer her with, and putting all thought of her housework out of her mind, Maṇibhadrā began to practice her sādhana one-pointedly. After a year, when her betrothed came to take her to his own house, she accompanied him without demur. In her new home she performed everything that was expected of her cheerfully and uncomplainingly, always speaking modestly and sweetly, thus controlling both her body and speech. In good time she gave birth to a son and a daughter and brought them up in an exemplary manner.

Twelve years had passed since she met her Guru and formed her aspiration, then one morning as she returned from the stream with a pitcher full of water, she tripped over a root and fell down, breaking her pot. In the afternoon, after she had been missed from the house, her husband came looking for her and found her gazing fixedly at the broken pitcher. When he asked her what was the matter, she continued to stare, evidently not having heard him. All her family and neighbors came to try to distract her, but she remained silent and unmoving until nightfall, and then she expressed her realization in these words:

Sentient beings from beginningless time
Break their vessels, their lives ended,
But why do they return home?
Today I have broken my vessel
But abandoning my saṃsāra home
I go on to pure pleasure.

The Guru is truly wonderful!
If you desire happiness, rely on him.

So saying, Maṇibhadrā floated into the sky and taught the people of Agarce for twenty one days. Thereafter she attained the Ḍākinī's Paradise.

Sādhana

The moral of Maṇibhadrā's tale is that a woman can practice a sādhana while performing her duty as a model wife and mother. Throughout their history, the Hindus have never relaxed their view that the woman belongs in the home. Rāmacandra's wife Sītā, who burned herself rather than suffer the disgrace of even slight suspicion that she betrayed her husband, is the Hindu woman's paragon. The third and fourth stages of life, withdrawal and complete renunciation, apply to a woman as much as a man, but until the children are mature a woman is bound by tradition to fulfill domestic roles. Female *bhikṣuṇīs* and tantrikas certainly existed from the time of the Buddha, but in tiny numbers; perhaps the proportion of male siddhas to female siddhas (four) and siddhas' consorts (four) amongst the eighty-four reflects the actual ratio of male to female tantrikas in siddha India (10:1), although in Tāranātha's tales of the siddhas there is a higher proportion of yoginīs, involved either as teachers or consorts.[320] Anyhow, just as a king can practice his sādhana while sitting on a throne, and craftsmen can attain *siddhi* while performing their craft, a housewife can attain *mahāmudrā-siddhi* while doing her daily round. She need not be a sexually promiscuous outcaste to attain *siddhi*.

The metaphor of the broken pot is most apposite. Crushing sesame seed or breaking a pot, the meaning is the same; except that with a broken pot the space inside immediately joins the space outside, like a river running into the sea—thus Maṇibhadrā's immediate *nirvikalpa-samādhi*. Fear of the indeterminate nature of being is what induces beings to return to their homes, to saṃsāra, again and again, at death and also when a moment of revelation destroys the sense of finite identity and habitual dualistic modes of perception. Our legend is not clear as to whether Maṇibhadrā actually returned to her children after her enlightenment.

Historiography

We know the name of Maṇibhadrā's Guru, but there is no indication as to which Kukkuripa it was. There was a Dog King Guru alive throughout the entire siddha period. If this Kukkuripa was a siddha involved with the mother-tantra, then he may have been Marpa's Guru, who gave him the *Māyāmayurī-tantra*; if this guess is correct, Maṇibhadrā lived in the eleventh century. Agarce (Ag rtse, Agce, etc.), her town, is unidentified. Maṇibhadrā is also known as the Yoginī Ghahurī (Bhahuri), which is a corruption of Gaurī. Gaurī, originally Mahādeva's consort, is one of Hevajra's retinue of fifteen yoginīs; she represents the essential purity of form as a sense object, in the east of the maṇḍala. But there is no point of association of this yoginī with the Maṇibhadrā in the legend.

66

THE YOGINĪ SIDDHĀ MEKHALĀ THE ELDER SEVERED-HEADED SISTER

All inner and outer phenomena perceived as mind,
Meditating with detachment, all has the same flavor.
In supreme meditation without effort or striving,
I found non-dual pure pleasure and perfect
Buddhahood.

A householder of Devīkoṭṭa had two daughters, Mekhalā and Kanakhalā. He married them to the two sons of a boatman. But their husbands abused them verbally, and the neighbors, too, gossiped about them maliciously, although they were innocent.

"Let's fly from this injustice and go to another country," the younger sister suggested one day.

"We are abused because of our lack of virtue," replied Mekhalā. "It will be no different anywhere else. We must stay here."

Just then the Guru Kṛṣṇācārya passed by in the street below. Seven hundred Ḍākas and Ḍākinīs attended him, a canopy floated unsupported above his head, *ḍamaru* skull-drums sounded in the sky about him, and many other signs of his realization could be seen and heard. The sisters decided to go to him and tell him how everyone, including their husbands, maligned them, and to ask him for a sādhana to practice.

They went to his house, told him their problem and requested instruction. Kṛṣṇa initiated them and gave them the Vajra Vārāhī instruction on the union of vision, meditation, action and goal, and sent them away to practice. They practiced diligently for twelve years and were successful in their meditation. Then they went in search of their Guru. They found him in his hermitage, and prostrating before him they worshiped him. The Guru spoke to them kindly, but he did not recognize them, and asked them who they were. They reminded him of their previous meeting.

"Then you should have brought me offerings," the Guru told them.

"What can we give you?" the sisters asked.

"Give me your heads!" demanded the Guru.

"We give what the Guru asks," they replied. Then with the keen-edged sword of pure awareness, which they drew from their mouths, they severed their own heads and offered them to their Guru. They sang:

Through the grace of the Guru's instruction,
Uniting creative and fulfillment meditation,
We destroy the distinction between saṃsāra and nirvāṇa;
Vision and action united in co-incident harmony
We destroy the distinction between acceptance and rejection;
In the union of vast space and pure awareness
We destroy the distinction between self and others.
As tokens of the indeterminate, we offer these gifts.

The Guru exclaimed:

Behold these two great yoginīs!
They have reached their goal in joy!
Now forgetting your own peace and happiness,
Live for the sake of others.

Kṛṣṇācārya replaced their heads on their shoulders without leaving so much as a scar. The people who observed this were delighted, and called the two sisters the Severed-headed Yoginīs. When the two yoginīs touched their Guru's feet, they attained *mahāmudrā-siddhi.* They worked selflessly for many years before expressing their realization and attaining the Ḍākinī's Paradise.

Sādhana

First, Mekhalā's admission that the two sisters were not so innocent is borne out by their names: *Mekhalā* (derived from *mahākhalā*) means Elder Mischievous Girl, and *Kanakhalā* likewise, Younger Mischievous Girl. The Guru's failure to recognize the girls upon their second visit, and his demand that they give him their heads, may have been skillful devices to allow them to prove that their previous self-centered conceit had now vanished, that they understood the unity of all things and, even more significantly, the oneness of all things. The kind of mental chatter that creates and reinforces the view that "Due to my superiority I can manipulate others to my own advantage" defines the girls' head-centered personality deficiency, a syndrome dominated by vanity belonging to the female stereotype that the girls represent. The yoginīs' demonstration of egolessness, the proof that subject/object, self/other dichotomy had been resolved, was performed with verbal acuity showing their non-dual awareness. Further, the head is "crowned" by the moon which is the source of the Ḍākinī's ambrosia, and this constitutes a suitable offering to the Guru.

The Guru's failure to recognize the girls may have been a ploy to examine their realization, but as Śāntipa's failure to recognize Koṭālipa indicates, in the Indo-Tibetan tradition proximity to the Guru is no prerequisite for successful sādhana, and after the imperative initiation encounter the disciple may vanish to his retreat and the Guru may forget all about him. One of the many invaluable functions of intuition of the First Noble Truth, the truth of suffering, is a confession of spiritual insufficiency, if not sickness. The encounter with the doctor-Guru should be profoundly intimate, but thereafter, with medicine in hand, the disciple-patient need have no further recourse to the Guru to achieve the cure of Mahāmudrā. Clinging to the doctor indicates either a continuing failure on the doctor's part, or hypochondria, or some similar neurotic attachment, or a misunderstanding of the doctor's role, on the part of the patient.

The compendium of Buddhist sādhanas called the *Sādhanamālā*[321] contains a description of Vajrayoginī as Sarvabuddha Ḍākinī standing in aggressive stance (*pratyālīdha*) holding her head in her left hand and a knife in her right. On her right and left stand the Ḍākinīs Vajravarṇanī and Vajravairocanī holding skull and knife. Three jets of blood spurt from Vajrayoginī's neck into the mouths of her own head and the mouths of her two attendants. This tradition is attributed to Śavaripāda (*5*). In the Hindu *Tantrasāra* the same vision is described with the same detail, but the yoginī is called Chinnamastakapa and her attendants Ḍākinī and Varṇanī. Chinnamastā is one of the ten *mahāvidhyās*, aspects or modes of Śakti, Śiva's consort, usually depicted standing upon Kāma and Ratrī in sexual union. In this context the image of Chinnamastā represents the *śaiva* yogin's female energy fulfilling the function of ego-destruction. Chinnamastā(ka) means Severed-headed, or Severed-headed Mother (T.dBu bcad ma). The identity of Vajrayoginī with Śakti and the identical symbolic meaning of the severed head—death of the ego—demonstrates the concurrence of Buddhist and Śiva-śakti traditions. In Nepal this icon is still worshiped by Buddhists as Vajrayoginī and by *śaiva*s as Chinnamastā.[322]

Historiography

The Guru of our legend is easily identified. His *ḍamaru*s mark him as the son Kṛṣṇācārya (Kāṇhapa,*17*) who was sent to Kāmarūpa (not far from Devīkoṭṭa, in Bengal) to obtain the drum that was to keep his retinue of Ḍākinīs dancing. He taught Vajra Yoginī's Severed-head sādhana on his death-bed (see p. 127). Thus the girls Mekhalā and Kanakhalā would have lived in the late ninth century. This Kṛṣṇācārya was a lineal descendent in the Saṃvara lineage of Śavaripa, the putative originator of the Chinnamastā/Vajrayoginī tradition. It is also interesting to note Kṛṣṇācārya's strong mother-tantra leanings and that a Kāṇhapa was one of the Five Nāths.

If uniting vision and action was the girls' sādhana, as it was Paṅkajapa's (*53*), as they indicate in their song, then the passage in the text that describes their instruction as "the pairing of vision, meditation, action and the goal" should be amended to read "Vajra-Vārāhī's instruction on uniting vision and action."[323]

67
THE YOGINĪ SIDDHĀ KANAKHALĀ THE YOUNGER SEVERED-HEADED SISTER

Donning the impregnable armor of patience,
Crowned with the virtue of diamond-like fortitude,
I embarked in the vessel of my own mind,
And with confidence possessed the human corpse.

Kanakhalā was the younger of the two sisters from Devīkoṭṭa, called The Obedient Severed-headed Yoginīs, disciples of Kṛṣṇācārya. Her story is told in Mekhalā's legend (*66*).

68

THE SIDDHA KILAKILAPA THE EXILED LOUD-MOUTH

In the immaculate sky of the dharmadhātu
The thunder of pure potential rumbles through space;
All experience of the delusive phenomenal world is transformed,
Beautified by the attainment of the trikāya*'s pure awareness.*

A man of low caste called Kilakila from Bhiralira was notorious for his loud mouth and argumentative behavior. His previous actions had determined an inherently quarrelsome disposition, and the people of the town found him insufferable. Eventually they told him to leave. He went to the cremation ground in a very melancholy state, and in this depressed condition a yogin found him. The yogin asked him how he came to be there, and when Kilakila told him truthfully he was offered a sādhana to release him from the wheel of rebirth. The poor man fell on his knees, imploring the yogin to teach him. He received the Guhyasamāja initiation and empowerment, and instruction in self-liberating appearances:

Your own and others' speech is only sound:
Meditate upon all sounds as one undifferentiated sound;
Then visualize the sounds you utter yourself
Emerging from the unobstructed emptiness of the sky
Rolling like thunder,
And then falling like a rain of flowers.

With diligent meditation the quarreler gradually lost his delusion of angry, spiteful tones in others' voices. Then he lost the sound of his own voice in a rain of flowers in the vast space of unobstructed emptiness. Then all phenomenal appearances and sound arose as Mahāmudrā, and he achieved the goal of self-liberating appearances. Renowned as The Quarreler, he worked selflessly for his followers, before proclaiming his realization, and with three hundred disciples attaining the Ḍākinī's Paradise.

Sādhana

Kilakila's meditation was eminently practical; he was seeking clear light in emotional darkness. Meditating upon another person's words as the echo of emptiness, the mind-created image projected upon the sound by a paranoid mind dissolves, and the ego, no longer feeling threatened by its own projections, ceases to react with competitiveness, aggression, argumentation and fighting, the overt forms of anger. In order to penetrate the sound, and to perceive its nature rather than its ephemeral form, the method concentrates upon the sameness of sound, its empty identity. First discovering the emptiness of external sound, and then the hollowness of one's own sound, all phenomena are seen as insubstantial, self-less, lacking an *ens*,[324] lacking any pantheistic or personal soul. When Avalokiteśvara was asked by the Buddha what object of meditation he preferred, he chose sound and the ear as most suitable to this age; his mantra OM MAṆI PADMA HŪṀ became the most popular of all tantric practices in Tibet. To seat consciousness at the door of the auditory sense, and to listen to the sound of silence, is a meditation that can be practiced anywhere, and its rewards are immediate and amazing. Kilakila's goal achieved, the personality problem that had ruined his life was resolved, and he was left with the pure pleasure of listening to all sound as the goddess Sarasvatī herself, a lady of infinite sensuous beauty, intelligence and compassion. Every perception arose spontaneously as the liberated goddess.

Such an unpretentious meditation technique can be transposed easily from its Tibetan cultural milieu to the West. Some tantric forms are conspicuous and some tantrikas immediately identifiable as such. This is not desirable unless by advertising the fact of one's attachment to a Guru by wearing peculiar garb a technique of meditation is being practiced whereby heavens are raised higher and hells dug deeper by other people's response—admiration or scorn, for example—and the resultant mental states taken as objects of meditation. In the context of *anuttarayoga-tantra* "meditation" invariably implies the function of re-cognizing the absolute specific. Choice of meditation technique is determined by the Guru or by personal karma.

Historiography

The word *kilakila*, or any of Kilakila's variant forms (such as Kilikili, Kalakala, Kalaka and Kalakama), are onomatopoeic expressions of joy; it is also a name of Śiva. The Tibetan rendering, The Quarreler, is no translation; nor does the name derive from *kīla* (*phur ba*), a magical dagger. Kilakila's birthplace is either Bhiralinga or Bhiralira, neither identified. This siddha represents a personality type, paranoid and argumentative, tending toward rebirth as a beast, belonging to the *vajra* family where aversion is the mind's dynamic.

69

THE SIDDHA KANTALIPA THE RAGMAN-TAILOR

With the True Guru as needle
And compassion as thread,
I stitched the three realms together.
Look at this yogin's wonderful cloth!

An outcaste of Maṇidhara, ignorant of wealth and pleasure, Kantali was a stitcher of rags. One day at work he jabbed his finger with the needle, drawing blood. Finally, driven beyond endurance of the pain and misery of existence, he ran to a lonely place and rolled on the ground in torment. The Ḍākinī Veṭālī in the form of a woman, finding him in this condition, kindly asked what ailed him. Kantali told her honestly about his circumstances.

"This means that you have suffered some great pain in your last life," she told him. "In your next life you will be afflicted by a similar pain, and in all successive lives pain will follow you. There is nothing but pain on the wheel of rebirth."

"Please show me how to avoid it?" Kantali begged.

"Could you practice a sādhana?" she asked him.

Kantali told her that nothing would stop him if she would teach him, and so she gave him the Hevajra initiation and empowerment, together with instruction upon the four boundless states of mind, the yoga of identification with the Guru, and fulfillment yoga. However, when the rag-stitcher tried to meditate, his thoughts reverted constantly to his work. The Ḍākinī told him to make his discursive thought into the path itself:

See your scavenged rags as empty space;
And with the needle of mindfulness and knowledge

Use the thread of compassion to stitch your clothes
And cover all beings of the three realms.

Through this technique of meditation Kantali realized the emptiness of all elements of experience, and a great compassion for all benighted beings arising within him, realizing coincident compassion and emptiness, he gained Mahāmudrā-siddhi. He became renowned as Guru Kantalipa. Working selflessly for all beings he finally revealed his realization, and bodily he attained the Ḍākinī's Paradise.

Sādhana

The verse of Veṭālī's instruction to Kantalipa has been edited to make metaphysical sense and to accord with the song of realization; the verse originally identified the needle as compassion and the thread as mindfulness.[325] Kantali's sādhana is to unite skillful means with perfect insight. When his rags have been visualized as emptiness they become a unity of form and emptiness. The needle of mindfulness and knowledge[326] is the means by which the apparently concrete appearance of the rags is perceived as emptiness. The thread of compassion is the skillful means by which the rags of emptiness are given meaning and purpose. Perfect insight into emptiness is analogous to the rags, and compassionate skillful means is analogous to the thread. The needle of mindfulness and knowledge, referred to as the True Guru[327] in the song, is the means of intuiting the emptiness of appearances and of uniting "objective" perfect insight and "subjective" skillful means. Any defectiveness in this analogy lies in the corrupt text.

Kantali's Ḍākinī Guru, Veṭālī, is one of the fifteen yoginīs of the Hevajra maṇḍala. These yoginīs are personifications of the emptiness of the elements (5), the psycho-physical constituents (5), and the objects of the senses (5); in their emptiness, they are all Buddha Ḍākinīs. Veṭālī was originally a blood-drinking, flesh-eating goddess, Mistress of the Ghouls[328] or animated corpses. At her once popular temple in Bhubaneswar, Orissa, the *kāpālikas* worshiped her as Kāpālinī.[329] The temple is now dead.

Tāranātha has a story of a yogin initiated into the *Tārā-tantra* by Nāropa. He gained *siddhi* through the Nine Herukas of the *tantra*. The yogin happened to sew together a rag-robe at the same time as a

Kantalipa (Tsembupa) attained *vajra*-fearlessness.

Mongolian king finished building his castle, and by function of sympathetic magic the castle fell down when the robe fell apart. This happened thrice, and when the king summoned the yogin the latter obtained his pledge that he would serve the Dharma. The yogin was called Kandhapa (or Kandhari).[330]

It was customary for yogins to wear robes sewn together from rags, the better to emulate the most humble of mankind, so it is probable that there were many yogins called Kantalipa or its variants (such as Kanthapa, Kantapa, Kaṇtālipa, Kanālipa and Kandipa). *Kantha* means rag, *kānthā* is "an outer garment of patched cloth," and *kanthadi* is a rag-wearer; *caṇḍāla*, an outcaste untouchable, may be cognate to *kanthadi*. Kāṇha's disciple Kantalipa was from Maihar,[331] which may be a corruption of Maṇidhara (or Maṇibhadra), our Kantalipa's birthplace, which is unidentified.

70

THE SIDDHA DHAHULIPA THE BLISTERED ROPE-MAKER

The treasure trove of knowledge, two-in-one,
In non-dual space, cannot be found by seeking;
Let the mind abide in a state of non-action
And in such samādhi true pleasure arises.

In the town of Dhokara lived a low-caste rope maker called Dhahuli. He sold his products in the market-place. One day hard at work, rolling the *kuśa* grass into a rope, great blisters erupted on the palms of his hands. In great pain he ran weeping to a lonely place, and there a yogin found him and asked him what was the matter. Dhahuli told him the truth.

"If you break down over such a trifling pain, what will happen when you suffer the intolerable agony of the lower realms?" the yogin asked him.

"Please show me how I can avoid that pain," Dhahuli begged. The yogin initiated him through a transfer of grace, and instructed him in a method of making conceptual thought into the path:

Visualize both the apparent form of your rope
And your notion of it existing in all-embracing space.
Then meditate with incessant energy
Upon the one, original, insubstantial essence.

Persevering in meditation on the meaning of these words of instruction for twelve years, the rope-maker understood that the conventional, nominal concept of "rope" had no substantial basis; that the relative, sensorily perceived phenomenon of rope was a constituent part of a field of relativity comprising the totality of the universe; and that the absolute verity of his experience of the rope was a vast expanse of pure space without boundary or center. He realized that concept and appearance are essentially one in the *dharmadhātu*, and he gained *siddhi*. He became well-known as Dhahulipa, and for seven hundred years he wandered through India working selflessly for other people, before proclaiming his realization and attaining the Ḍākinī's Paradise.

Sādhana

Dhahuli's Guru taught him a simple meditation using the categories of the *yogācāra* school of practical metaphysics. The *yogācāra* "idealists" recognized three principles of reality, three "absolutely specific constitutive principles of reality."[332] The first, name and concept, or "the notional-conceptual," is considered unreal and redundant; it is the conceptual filter that detracts from the possibility of gnostic awareness; figuratively it is the snake into which mental functions transform the rope. The second principle is "the relative," which indicates the sensually perceived phenomenon as a union of consciousness, sense organ and sense object; it is an "illusionary reality" because although it certainly exists it has no substantial basis, and it is part of a field of relativity in which all constituents are inter-related. Finally, "the absolute principle" is synonymous with emptiness, ultimate reality, the *dharmadhātu*. Thus the essence of Dhahuli's rope is the absolute constitutive principle of reality, the *dharmadhātu*, which is his object of meditation. Since the concept of the rope and the rope's conventional, relative form are both insubstantial and baseless, by assuming the absolute, visualizing it and cultivating the intuition that penetrates illusory, concrete appearances, the absolute soon becomes the customary mode of perception—particularly when meditation upon it is unceasing! The warning in Dhahuli's song of realization is very important: knowledge of the absolute rises by a process of relaxation into it, and not by forced concentration of any kind. Whatever can be forced is a dualistic mental function that obstructs gnostic awareness. When the rope has become an hallucination, or like the reflection of the moon in water, all appearances will have become the same, and all things arise as Mahāmudrā.

There is considerable similarity between Dhahuli and Kantali's meditation. Both craftsmen meditated upon the objects of their daily work as space. The distinction between their meditations defines the subtle difference in meaning between the terms "thought" or "discursive thought" and "mental constructs" or "conceptual thought."[333] Often these terms are used interchangeably, but there Kantali's meditation is called "transforming discursive thought into the path," whereas Dhahuli's meditation is called "transforming mental constructs into the path,"[334] where "mental constructs" refers to the nature of thought and to the mental images that are projected upon objects of perception.

Historiography

Dhahuli is also called Dhaguli, Dhahuri, and Dharuri (T. rTswa thag can—The Ropemaker), and the root of the words is uncertain. His birthplace Dhokara (Dhekara, rDe ka ra) Deśa, is also unknown.

71

THE SIDDHA UDHILIPA THE BIRD-MAN

Following after wandering thought is madness;
Resisting that tendency habitual karma *is restrained.*
Abiding nowhere, mind is centered;
Nothing is to be found by seeking elsewhere.

By virtue of his previous generosity, an aristocrat of Devīkoṭṭa possessed a vast fortune. In the luxury of his palace he enjoyed every pleasure that his imagination could conjure. Gazing from his window one day, he watched five-colored clouds forming into various animal shapes, and continuing to look he saw a swan appear and fly across the sky. "What a joy it would be to fly!" he thought to himself, and he became obsessed with the idea. When the Guru Karṇaripa came to his palace to beg alms, he offered him the best food he could provide and then entreated the yogin to teach him to fly. He made prostration to him and offered him the price of the teaching.

Karṇaripa gave him initiation into the *Catuṣpīṭha-mahāyoginī-tantra* and told him to visit the Twenty-four Great Power Places to collect the twenty-four panaceas of the twenty-four Ḍākinīs, reciting the mantras of the Ḍākinīs ten thousand times each.

The pilgrim accomplished that task, and then he went back to Karṇaripa and asked him how to prepare the elixir. "First place the panaceas in a copper pot, then in a silver pot and finally in a golden pot. Then you will be able to fly," the yogin told him.

After twelve years the elixir was perfected, and through his arduous preparation he could fly through the sky. He became known as Udhilipa, The Flying Siddha. After proclaiming his realization he bodily attained the Ḍākinī's Paradise.

Udhilipa (Ḍiṅgipa) unites with all-pervasive space.

Sādhana

We cannot be sure whether Udhilipa was given an exoteric or esoteric interpretation of Karṇaripa's precepts. He may have criss-crossed India in an extended pilgrimage, and as a method of maturing the mind-stream such a *kriyāyoga* practice is incomparably effective, but *anuttarayoga-tantra* purists would despise such a course, insisting on a *hathāyoga* interpretation. The *Catuṣpīṭha-mahāyoginī-tantra*,[335] a *sahajayāna* text, treats the four power places (*catuspītha*) as the four upper *cakras*, naming them *atmāpīṭha, parapīṭha, yogapīṭha* and *guhyapīṭha*. The twenty-four *pīṭhas*) are the minor junctions or *cakras* in the Body of Saṃvara (Heruka). Each of the eight spokes of the heart *cakra*, which carry the materializing energies of the five elements and the five sense objects, divide into three—red, white and blue—channels, connecting the heart center with the twenty-four *pīṭhas*. The twenty-four *pīṭhas* are divided into three maṇḍalas of eight each, maṇḍalas of Body, Speech and Mind. From each of the twenty-four *cakras*, three channels diverge, each of those seventy-two channels dividing into a thousand capillary channels; thus the twenty-four internal power places are control boxes for the entire psycho-organism. At the essence of each of the twenty-four *cakras* is a red and white seed,[336] which is the *cakra*'s panacea, and each *cakra* is represented by a Ḍākinī or yoginī who may be propitiated by her mantra and her panacea thereby obtained. "Gathering the panaceas" through recitation of mantra is a process of purification of body, speech and mind, and an identification with the absolute reality of being in its separate parts. "Pouring the panaceas" from copper to silver to golden pot is to transform the maṇḍalas of body, speech and mind into the *nirmāṇakāya, saṃbhogakāya* and *dharmakāya*. With attainment of the *dharmakāya* not only can a yogin fly and perform the eight great *siddhis*, but he has also attained *mahāmudrā-siddhi*.[337]

Historiography

The external references of the four principal power places according to the *Hevajra-tantra* are Jālandhara (North), Oḍḍiyāṇa (West), Pūrṇagiri (South), and Kāmarūpa (East) (see p. 278 for locations of the entire twenty-four *pīṭhasṭhānas*).

Udhilipa, with its root *uddiya*, "flying," or "soaring," has been corrupted in many ways (for example, Otili, Odhali, Udheli, and Udhari). To the Tibetans Udhili is The Flier (Phur pa). If Karṇaripa (*18*) is Nāgārjuna's disciple, Udhilipa lived in the ninth century; but if he is Gorakṣa's disciple, known also as Vairāgi, and certain elements of the legend, particularly the *haṭhayoga* terminology and concepts, not least the *siddhi* of flying, indicates *nāth* associations, then Udhilipa will have been alive in the eleventh century and will be found in *nāth* lineages.

72

THE KAPĀLI SIDDHA KAPĀLAPA
THE SKULL-BEARER

The non-dual Vajradhara that is all phenomena,
The adventitious ornaments and skull,
The delusory ego itself:
One cannot find them by seeking.

There was once a low-caste laborer of Rājapurī who had a wife and five sons. His young wife died at her appointed time, and he carried her body to the cremation ground. While he was still bewailing his loss beside her corpse, he received news that his sons had also died. Returning to the cremation ground with their corpses he laid them down beside his wife. He was weeping and wailing when the Guru Kṛṣṇācārya appeared.

"Yogiji, my wife and sons are all dead," he told the yogin in response to his query. "I'm desolate, and I cannot tear myself away. So here I sit."

"All beings of the three realms live under a cloud of death," the yogin told him. "You are not alone in this suffering. Since your misery has rendered you useless, unable to work or play effectively, you are no use to anyone. Why not practice a sādhana? Doesn't this continuous round of existence make you afraid?"

"I am afraid," replied the bereaved man. "If you know of a way to rid me of fear, please teach me."

Kṛṣṇācārya initiated him into the maṇḍala of Hevajra and instructed him in the creative and fulfillment stages of meditation. To aid his practice, the Guru carved the yogin's six ornaments out of his sons' bones for him to wear and, cutting off the head of his wife's corpse, he made a skull-bowl.

"Visualize the skull as creative meditation and the emptiness within it as fulfillment meditation," instructed the Guru.

The disciple meditated upon all his activity for nine years and achieved the goal of uniting creative and fulfillment meditation. He revealed his realization to his disciples in this way:

I am the yogin of the skull!
I have realized the nature of all things
As the nature of this skull.
My activity is now completely uninhibited!

They called him Guru Kapālapāda. After this revelation of his realization he worked selflessly for others for five hundred years before attaining the Ḍākinī's Paradise with six hundred disciples.

Sādhana

The precise relationship between the Buddhist tantrikas, the *nāths* and the *kāpālikas* has yet to be defined, but what is clear is that the Buddhist *kapālis* and the *kāpālikas* shared outer forms, although metaphysical interpretation may have differed. The *kāpālikas* were one of four *śaiva* sects (with the *paśupatas*, *śaivas*, and *kālāmukhas*) that had evolved parallel to Buddhist Tantra. The *kāpālikas*' ethos was derived from their antecedents, upper-caste brahmin-slayers called *kapālins*. The *kapālins* were compelled to take the Great Vow (*mahāvrata*), a twelve year vow of renunciation to absolve their sin. They lived in the jungle naked, begging according to strict rules, subjecting themselves to ascetic behavior that had a purificatory effect despite themselves. What inspired the *kāpālikas*, yogins who gave the Great Vow a soteriological twist, was the knowledge that refuge in this most shameful of human states, where they discovered the essential nature of filth, physical and moral, was the path to the non-dual, one taste of all experience, pure pleasure, and the heights of Śiva's Paradise.

The *kāpālikas*, like the *kapālins* before them, gained their name from the skulls they carried. The *kapālins* often carried the skull of the brahmin they had killed; the *kāpālikas* sometimes carried skulls of saints or siddhas to extract the virtue of the previous user while maintaining the *kapālin* guise. The symbology of the skull for the Buddhist tantrika is described in the legend (see also *49*). In the *kāpālika* tradition, "He who knows the six insignia, who is proficient in the highest mudrā, and who meditates on the Self in the vulva attains nirvāṇa."[338] The six insignia (*mudrikā ṣaṭka*) are necklace, neck ornament, ear-ring, crest-jewel, ashes and sacred thread. The *Hevajra-tantra* prescribes these six insignia, and its commentaries explain their significance to the wearer, the yogin who takes the vow to Śiva. "He . . . who meditates on the Self in the vulva attains nirvāṇa," on the contrary, is a Buddhist statement. The *Hevajra-tantra*'s six bone ornaments are crown, ear-rings, necklace, bracelets (armlets, wristlets and anklets), a belt and the sacred thread. The bone ornaments symbolize the Five Dhyāni Buddhas.[339] *Khaṭvāṅga* (trident), symbolizing the Ḍākinī and *kapāla* are also objects carried by both Hevajra tantrika and *kāpālika*; the ear-rings, common to all, are the principal insignia of the *nāth*s, the *kān* (ear) *phaṭa* (split) yogins.

There is a tendency to paint the *kāpālika*s as ghoulish exotericists, as their contemporary brahmin detractors portrayed them in their anti-tantrika literature, but assuredly they practiced an esoteric interpretation of their vows. This is Kāṇhapa (the Father?): "It is only the Kapāli who can realize Nairātmā." "I have become a Kapāli without aversion." "The yogin Kāṇha has become a Kapāli, entering the practice of yoga, sporting in the city of the body in a non-dual form."[340] It cannot be said to whom precisely Kāṇha referred with his "Kapāli," but indubitably our Kāpālapa was embraced by that term. One obvious formal distinction between Kapālapa and the *kāpālika*s is that the former worshipped Hevajra while the latter worshipped Bhairāva and Bhairāvī, the wrathful Śiva and Consort. While the *paśupata*s, for instance, took only the male deity as their *iṣtadevatā*, the *kāpālika*s could worship the Devī, like the *śākta*s. Finally, the highest definition of The Skull-Bearer (Kapāli) is given in a *Hevajra-tantra* commentary: "He who cherishes pure pleasure is a Kapāli."[341]

Historiography

Kapālapa (or Kapālipa, T.Thod pa can) is every skull-bearing tantrika; the name is too general to find a Guru for him. He was a *śūdra* from Rājapurī in the legend. In siddha-India Rājapur was a prominent place of pilgrimage near present Jammu, and Rājapura was the ancient town, now called Rajaor.

73
THE SIDDHA KIRAPĀLAPA (KILAPA) THE REPENTANT CONQUEROR

So long as ignorance enshrouded me
I was bound by the concept of self and others.
At the moment of realization all concepts foundered,
Even "Buddha" became a meaningless label,
And the mind caught in its own empty nature
Reality became indeterminate and unstructured.

The King of Grahara ruled a vast and prosperous kingdom. He reveled in the pleasures of Kubera, the god of wealth, but yet he was not satisfied. He plundered the cities of neighboring states and enjoyed their wealth also. However, he was ignorant of the horrors of war. Once when his army was raiding a nearby city, he followed close behind it, and was appalled to find women, babes, the sick and aged, left fainting and weeping in the streets, their men-folk fled before the invading army. When his minister explained the situation to him, he became profoundly repentant and deep compassion welled up in his heart. After arranging for the men of that city to return, restoring each to his own family, he went back to his own city and rang the great bell of charity. He distributed his immense fortune to the poor, and decided to devote himself entirely to sādhana. When a yogin came begging at the palace gates he offered him the best food he had and asked him for instruction.

The yogin taught him how to take refuge in the Triple Gem, and how to practice the Bodhisattva Vow and the four boundless states of mind. The king was not satisfied with this, and asked the yogin to teach him the Dharma that leads to Buddhahood in one single lifetime. The yogin gave him the Saṃvara initiation and empowerment and established him in creative and fulfillment meditation. However, the king's previous preoccupation overwhelmed his concentration, and his meditation was shrouded by thoughts of government and his army. The Guru gave him instruction in self-liberating thought:

Visualize all beings of the three realms
As a host of proud warrior heroes.
The infinite sky of mind's nature
And the untold heroes that arise therein,
Inseparably united, defeat your enemies.
Then Great King, bask in the bliss of victory,
The peak of existence. Meditate like that.

After twelve years of meditation King Kirapāla gained enlightened vision and attained *siddhi.* When his queens and ministers saw his palace bathed in light one day, they realized that he had reached his goal, and they worshiped him. He taught them like this:

With your lust aspire to relate to all beings
In the four boundless states of mind;
And with your warrior's rage
Destroy every demon that enters your mind.

He was called Kirapālapāda. After revealing his realization he worked selflessly for seven hundred years before attaining the Ḍākinī's Paradise with six hundred disciples.

Sādhana

King Kirapāla's sādhana was similar to that of Dhahuli and Kantali. In his practice of "self-liberating concepts,"[342] after he had established the nature of his mind as emptiness in the fulfillment stage, whatever arose immediately dissolved back into its own nature, which is like the sky.

Historiography

Kirapāla's legend is a latter-day facsimile of the Mauryan Emperor Dharma Aśōka's conversion story. Aśōka had enlarged his kingdom of Magadha to include Afghanistan in the west to Assam in the East, but starting his victorious march south, he was so appalled by the terrible loss of life and by the wounded at the fearfully bloody battle against the Kingdom of Kaliṅga, which stretched from Puri to the Kṛṣṇa Delta, that he vowed to forgo war forever. His rock edict, still visible near Bhubaneswar, memorialized that decision and encouraged his subjects to emulate him and to practice the Dharma. However, we have no historical record of King Kirapāla (Kirbala, Kirava, Kirapa, Kiraba, Kirabala, Kilapa), a name which suggests a scion of the Pāla dynasty, and it is impossible to identify his kingdom, Grahara (Prahara, Sahara), unless like Grahura (see also *7* and *81*) it is a corruption of Gauḍa, a Ganges principality on the Bihar/West Bengal border. In Tibetan the king's name is rendered "He who abandoned concepts" and "He who abandoned all things" (T.sNa tshogs spangs pa). Without evidence, one source makes Kilapa the disciple of Lūipa.[343]

74

THE MAHĀSIDDHA SAKARA (SARORUHA) THE LOTUS BORN

The Nāga King Basūka overpowered
Showered gifts upon the suffering people.
In the great power place of Tathatā! Just That!
The Nāga King of Knowledge propitiated
Showers knowledge of the tantric mysteries
Upon fortunate male and female Knowledge-bearers.

Indrabhūti, King of Kāñcī, ruler of one million four hundred thousand households, had no son. He invoked both worldly and heavenly gods, and eventually a being entered his wife's womb. The pregnant queen's thoughts became increasingly pacific, and after six months she dreamed that she ate Mount Meru, drank the ocean dry, and suppressed the three realms with the sole of her foot. The king was unable to interpret these dreams for her, and he offered large rewards to his astrologers and priests for an interpretation.

"The dreams portend the birth of a Bodhisattva king who will rule the Kingdom of Truth," the pundits finally declared. "Your worldly subjects will be displeased, but to placate them a fountain of wealth will rain down material riches at his birth."

At midnight on the tenth night of the ninth month after his conception, the child was born. By virtue of his previous karma and merit, he was born in the center of a lotus in the middle of a large lake. His birth was attended by a shower of riches over the country. The people wondered what this downpour of wealth portended, but at midday the following day they discovered the lotus-born child, and they called him Saroruha Kumāra. Through his merit the people remained prosperous and contented.

Later the queen gave birth to another child. When the old king died Saroruha refused to rule, the younger brother acceding to the throne. He became a monk instead, and set off for Śrī Dhānyakaṭaka. On the road he found his Guru. Ārya Avalokiteśvara, in the guise of another monk, tested Saroruha's honesty and then offered to reveal to him the Buddha's mode of consummate enjoyment, the *saṃbhogakāya*, but first the disciple should show his faith and devotion to the Guru and admit his incapacity to manifest the *saṃbhogakāya* himself. Saroruha prostrated before the Bodhisattva, who then revealed the reality of Hevajra and his retinue. After the initiation Avalokiteśvara vanished.

Saroruha proceeded to Śrī Dhānyakaṭaka where he began his sādhana of realizing the initiatory revelation. After some time a man who looked like a yogin came to his hermitage to discover the master's intentions, and impressed by him he offered to serve him on the condition that he receive instruction when the master gained *siddhi*. He moved into an empty cave and tended Saroruha's needs for the duration of his twelve year sādhana.

At the beginning of Saroruha's retreat a famine struck the land, and many people died of hunger. Fearing that knowledge of the famine would distract his master's meditation and postpone the date of his own initiation, the servitor kept silent, preferring to subsist off the master's leavings. One day towards the end of the twelve years, after begging had proved fruitless, the servitor went to the king's palace where he was given a bowl of uncooked rice, which he carefully brought back to the cave. However, on the threshold, his strength failed him and he fell down, spilling the grain.

"Are you drunk?" the Guru enquired.

"Where could I possibly find liquor?" replied the servitor. "No I am weak from hunger."

"Have you been unable to find food?" asked Saroruha.

Then his servitor admitted that he had refrained from telling his master about the famine and its dire consequences upon the people.

"Why did you not tell me?" his master rebuked him. "I have the power to bring rain. Now leave me!"

Saroruha gathered up the spilt grains and took them to a nearby stream, where he made offerings of sacramental cakes to the *nāga* guardians. Then with mudrā, mantra and samādhi, he coerced the Eight Great Nāga Kings, torturing them until their heads were about to burst. Finally they came begging to serve him.

"This famine is your doing," the master reproached them. You are to blame for the deaths of so many people. Today you will send a shower of food, tomorrow a shower of grain, the following day a shower of provisions, and the succeeding three days showers of gold and jewels. On the seventh day send a shower of rain."

The Nāga Kings obeyed this difficult command, and the people's suffering was alleviated. Knowledge of the master's power spread throughout the country and many people were inspired with faith. Then the master gave his servitor, whose name was Rāma, initiation and empowerment, and Rāma obtained magical powers. At that his Guru instructed him in the creative and fulfillment meditation of Hevajra, warning him, "If you fail to act selflessly for the sake of others, you will never attain the Ḍākinī's Paradise. Go to Śrī Parvata and practice your sādhana there." Then the master rose into the sky.

Rāma went to Śrī Parvata and won a princess for his consort. They remained together in the jungle and built a temple to the god Rāma. Finally they attained the Ḍākinī's Paradise.

Sādhana

There is little didactic content in the legend of Sakara apart from the precept enjoining the yogin to put others before himself, even at the expense of his sādhana, which is an appropriate precept from a disciple of the Bodhisattva of Compassion. Avalokiteśvara made the great vow before Amitābha that if he ever turned his back on saṃsāra before all beings were first released from it, then his head should be split into a thousand pieces. He did free all living beings, he did turn his back on saṃsāra, and his head was split into a thousand pieces, for the instant he turned his back saṃsāra was again repeopled with suffering beings. He became Mahākarūṇika (T.Thugs rje chen po), the eleven headed, thousand armed form of Avalokiteśvara.

Historiography

The main point of interest in this legend is the identity of the principal. Sakara is mentioned only in the title; in the story the siddha is called Tsokye (T.mTsho skyes), literally Lake Born, a synonym of Lotus (Padma), and the identification problem arises from the plurality of compound Sanskrit names of which Padma, or a synonym, is a part: Padmasambhava, Padmakara, Saroruha, Padmavajra (T.mTsho skyes rdo rje), and Paṅkaja (*51*), are a few of them.

Padmasambhava, Tibet's Great Guru, was the son of a King Indrabhūti, but he had no connection with any of the events of this legend. Further, he was virtually unknown outside of Tibet, and he had no influence on the eastern Indian mahāsiddha lineage. Mahāpadmavajra (8th-9th century) was initiated by the Great King Indrabhūti (*Hevajra-tantra*) and also by the Ḍākinī Sukhalalita (*Guhyasamāja-tantra*), and he taught the Swine-herd Ḍākinī and Anaṅgavajra. Born a brahmin in Maru (Rajasthan), he worked in Oḍḍiyāṇa. He is sometimes called Saroruha the Elder. But we cannot identify him with our mahāsiddha.[344]

Padmavajra, Saroruha the Younger, who was adopted by the king of Kāñcī,[345] is our most likely candidate. His main sphere of activity was Oḍḍiyāṇa, where he learnt the tantras and became royal priest. He gained his experience of the mysteries from the Swine-herd Ḍākinī; but the king was so offended by this alliance that he had them burnt together, although when they emerged from the flames unharmed the king was converted. The subsequent appearance of Turkish troops in this version of Saroruha's legend is consistent with a lifetime lived in the middle to late ninth century.[346] Tāranātha specifically identifies Tsokye as The Middle Padmavajra, and also as Saroruha, and in the same passage is found the statement, "the two *ācāryas* Lwa wa pa and Saroruha brought the *Hevajra-tantra*."[347] The word "brought" has been translated with the sense of "brought forth" or "revealed," but it is possible that these two yogins could actually have brought the tantra from Oḍḍiyāṇa, where Indrabhūti had revealed it, to Baṅgala, during the reign of Devapāla, whose patronage stimulated intense interest in the tantras. Here, Anangavajra is Saroruha's Guru, and Indrabhūti of the late ninth century is his disciple. Most of Saroruha's works in the Tenjur concern the *Hevajra-tantra*.

Saroruha was an initiate of the Guhyasamāja by the Swine-herd Ḍākinī, but was he the Padmavajra Guru of Anaṅgavajra who wrote the famous commentary, the *Guhyasiddhi*? Anaṅgavajra's disciple Indrabhūti was the author of the *Jñānasiddhi*, another famous *Guhyasamāja* commentary, but if Saroruha was not as adept in the *Guhyasamāja-tantra* as the *Hevajra*, we have two Padmavajras contemporary in the second half of the ninth century. Farmer Padmavajra, another link in the tantra's Oḍḍiyāṇa history, lived in the early ninth century.[348] Yet another Padmavajra was a disciple of a Kukkuripa and Guru of Tilopa in the tenth century.

It is assumed that Sakara, as a synonym of Saroruha, is a corruption of Puṣkara (T.Pu sa ka ra), Blue Lotus, like the other variants of this name (Pukara, Sagara and Sugara). But when Maitripa was en route to Śrī Parvata to meet Śavari (the Younger), he encountered a siddha Sakara on the road and invited him to join him. They discovered Śavari in a compromising situation, dallying with women. Maitripa in his sutric innocence was profoundly shocked, but Sakara prostrated in full confidence in the Guru and gained instant enlightenment.[349] Maitripa and this Sakara's contemporaneity is confirmed elsewhere.[350]

From the *nāth* standpoint Sakara (or Saṅgāri) is none other than Gopīcāṇḍ, the Malva king and disciple of Jālandhara and Kṛṣṇācārya.[351] Influenced by his Ḍākinī mother, the king sought a Guru that he might gain immortality; but he failed to fathom the arcane precepts of his mother's Guru, Jālandhara, who told him to put his hand inside an empty pot and what he would grasp would be the essence of the teaching that would lead to immortality. Lacking a sense of humor, the skeptical king had the Guru buried in a pit underneath the royal stables. Kṛṣṇa came to his rescue somewhat tardily, and when the king found the Guru still alive after twenty years of interment he gained faith, renounced his kingdom and became the renowned siddha Saṅgāri.[352] But Jālandhara could not have lived to meet Maitripa's contemporary, Sakara, and Gopīcāṇḍ probably lived earlier than Maitripa.

The odd appendage to our legend concerning RĀM has no explanation. Viṣṇu's *avatār* Rāmacandra has no place in the *vajrayāna* pantheon, and this essentially layman's archetype is spurned by the *nāths*.

Śrī Dhānyakaṭaka, the great *stūpa* at Amarāvatī, where the Buddha is said to have taught the *Kālacakra-tantra*, was prominent in early Buddhism. It was eclipsed by the Śrī Parvata at Vijayapurī (now under the Nāgārjunakoṇḍa Lake) during the Ikṣvāku period, regained supremacy after Vijayapurī's downfall and then declined with Buddhism in Andhra during the sixth and seventh centuries. Its tenuous association with the *Kālacakra-tantra* forms its only significance for the siddhas.

75
THE SIDDHA SARVABHAKṢA THE GLUTTON

In ignorance different flavors are quite distinct;
With realization all flavors are essentially the same.
Likewise, in ignorance saṃsāra and nirvāṇa appear
separate,
But with realization they become a pure pleasure union.

Sarvabhakṣa, a man of low caste with an exceedingly large belly, was a subject of King Siṅghacandra of Ābhira. He would eat anything he could lay his hands on. One day after he had failed to fill his stomach he retreated to a cave, obsessed with food. The Guru Saraha found him there and asked him what he was doing.

"The heat of my stomach is so great that I can never satisfy it," the glutton told him. "Today I have found nothing to eat, and I am in pain."

"If you cannot endure such a small hunger," asked the Guru, "what will you do when you are reborn as a hungry ghost?"

"What is a hungry ghost?" asked Sarvabhakṣa.

Saraha pointed one out and described its nature. Then the glutton wanted to know the cause of such a rebirth, and the Guru told him.

"How can I avoid it?" asked Sarvabhakṣa, shaken to the roots of his being.

Saraha initiated him and taught him the method of Bhusuku, the embodiment of indolence:

Visualize your belly as the empty sky
And your digestive heat as the final conflagration;
Regard food and drink as all phenomena,
And in eating, consume the universe.

The glutton practiced this meditation with devotion. He swallowed the sun and moon and devoured Mount Meru. Deprived of light, the people were frightened and the Ḍākinīs sought the Great Brahmin Saraha for help.

Saraha gave the glutton further instruction: "Visualize everything you eat as nothing."

With continued practice the glutton realized the identity of appearances and emptiness, and attaining his goal the sun and moon appeared again and everyone was happy. After fifteen years he attained *mahāmudrā-siddhi.* Then he revealed his realization and worked for humanity for six hundred years before attaining the Ḍākinī's Paradise with a thousand disciples.

Sādhana

Hungry ghosts[353] are spirits, or psychological projection, created by the karma of unmitigated greed and avarice, and their suffering is the result of a vast accumulation of demerit. They can never get what they want. Their mouths are like the eye of a needle; their throats are as thin as a hair; and their stomachs are like mountains. Some have no flesh or blood, consisting only of skin and bone. Their mouths belch fire, for if they should find some putrid morsel to eat, it turns to flame in their mouths. The lowest form is reduced to fighting for pus issuing from tumors on each others' throats. Even the moon heats them in summer, and in winter the sun is cold. Their glances make trees barren and rivers dry up. Longevity of five to ten thousand years is assured.[354] Generosity is the antidote to a hungry ghost's karma; but Saraha uses the initiate's temporal, relative aspiration to escape from rebirth as a hungry ghost to free him from saṃsāra altogether, and to lead him to absolute *mahāmudrā-siddhi.* In the vehicle of multiple means any of the six realms of saṃsāra can be used as grist for the mill of meditation that effects liberation from transmigration; even hell can be transcended by appropriate skillful means, for even the denizens of hell have the Buddha-nature. In fact, the stronger the poison the easier release can be; complacency and self-delusion are the most difficult of states to escape.

Sarvabhakṣa (T.Thams cad bza' ba), The Indiscriminate Glutton, demonstrates the power of visualization. Or is the metaphor of his swallowing the sun and moon simply a metaphor parallel to "emptying the *lalanā* and *rasanā* into the *avadhūti*," the sun and moon eclipsed by Rāhu in the central channel? In support of the more literal interpretation there is the case of the old and apprehensive woman in Banares who visualized herself a tigress to such effect that she emptied the city, the inhabitants fleeing from her transmogrified form. But for the yogin to effect change in his vision is one thing; it is quite another for him to alter the "objective" reality of people around him who have no faith. An example of the efficacy of "spell" (mantra) to effect the kind of alteration that led to the evacuation of the city of Banares is demonstrated, for instance, by the power of the Nazi's black magic that created the mass hallucination permitting the holocaust; their "spell" altered an entire nation's perception of reality so that genocide could occur in its midst. With the Allied conquest of Germany the democratic spell effected another alteration of illusion, a change to the liberal norm. Christian cults' creation of "the Kingdom on earth" is no more a fool's paradise than any self-serving ideal illusion, like "the American Dream." Life is very literally what we make it, and no one individual's vision has any greater ontological validity than any other. Some visions however, have greater efficacy in producing happiness, or liberation from the hold of all relative visions, than others. The Tantra's creative stage visions have built into them a factor that destroys attachment to them, and that ingredient is emptiness. Sarvabhakṣa's attachment to form caused the power of his visualization to "destroy the universe;" visualizing all things as emptiness they became mere illusory light-form and Sarvabhakṣa lost all attachment to them.

Historiography

Sarvabhakṣa, a *śūdra* from Ābhira[355] (or Mahar, Sahar, Sagara—none located) is clearly identified as a disciple of Saraha in our legend. Other sources identify his Guru as Saraha the Son, Śavaripa, or as Bhusuku. Bhusuku was the indolent monk who did nothing but eat, sleep and stroll for the sake of his digestion; thus Bhusuku will have been his spiritual Father. Saraha's disciple would have lived in the late eighth, early ninth century. King Siṅghacandra of our legend is identified as a King Harischandra, but neither are found in the dynastic lists.[356]

76

THE MAHĀSIDDHA NĀGABODHI THE RED-HORNED THIEF

It is good fortune for us all to live on the earth;
We free ourselves from poverty in the ocean's depths;
There is great enjoyment in wielding a sword;
And we meet friends when we meet the Aimless Ones.

When Ārya Nāgārjuna was residing at the Suvarṇa Vihāra, a brahmin from western India who had turned thief came to his door. From the threshold the thief saw the master eating delicacies from golden plates. As the thought of stealing the gold arose in his mind, Nāgārjuna read his thoughts and threw him a golden chalice.

"What is he doing," wondered the thief. "Can he read my mind?" Aloud, he said, "Why did you do that? Now I don't need to steal it!"

"I am Ārya Nāgārjuna," the saint replied. "My wealth is yours. You do not need to steal here. Eat and drink, stay as long as you wish, and when you are ready to go take as much as you want."

The thief was very impressed by this attitude, and with awakened faith in the Guru, he asked him for instruction. Nāgārjuna initiated him into the *Guhyasamāja-tantra* and instructed him in self-liberating greed.

Abandon all thought of action
And at your fontanelle visualize a large horn,
The horn of concepts, translucent and red,
A red ruby radiating light.

Nāgārjuna then filled the hut with jewels, and the thief sat down content to meditate upon the Guru's instruction. After twelve years a great horn had grown out of his skull, and trembling and shaking he was in a miserable condition. When his Guru came to him asking

Nāgabodhi abides on the Sacred Mountain Śrī Parvata.

how he fared, the disciple revealed his suffering and received this further instruction from Nāgārjuna:

This great horn of fixed notions
Has destroyed your happiness;
Attachment to seemingly concrete objects
Always causes people to suffer.
The things of experience have no real existence,
So how can birth, life or death,
Like clouds gathering and swirling in the sky,
Harm us or profit us in any way?
Likewise, how can the purity of mind's nature
Be affected, positively or negatively,
When both "knower" and "known" are unfounded
from the first?
Both are essentially empty as they stand.

Through these words Nāgabodhi realized the emptiness of the nature of his being. Abiding in meditative absorption for six months he realized the indivisibility of saṃsāra and nirvāṇa, and reached his goal. He was called Nāgabodhi.

Nāgārjuna appointed Nāgabodhi to succeed him as master of the lineage and empowered him to give his disciples the eight great *siddhis* as they were required. The eight magical powers were passing through the earth beneath, wielding the sword of awareness, destroying and annihilating, creating and enriching, dispensing the treasures of the pill of divine vision and the eye salve of omniscience, speedwalking, and performing the alchemy of deathlessness.

The master commanded him to remain on Śrī Parvata, working selflessly for others until he received the revelation of Maitreya, The Buddha of Loving Kindness. It is said that he will remain there for twenty thousand years.

Sādhana

The premise underlying Nāgārjuna's instruction to Nāgabodhi is that greed, avarice and attachment[357] are a function of the notional-conceptional[358] mind. First, conceptual thought separates "the knower" from "the known," and with this initial alienation of the ego from the environment a subtle craving for desirable objects develops to compensate for feelings of doubt, hesitancy and insecurity. This craving reinforces and focuses the notional-conceptional function of isolating the specific sensory stimulus belonging to a desirable object, naming it, conceiving of it as a discrete entity with a substantial essence that can be grasped and possessed. Since desirable objects are delusory, being merely concepts, mental pictures arbitrarily composed out of various sensual stimuli, they can never be possessed in a way that brings satisfaction, but the constantly reinforced karma of avarice results in the compulsive acquisitiveness of the miser and the repetitive crimes of the petty thief or kleptomaniac (not the professional thief).[359]

Nāgabodhi's ruby horn, the horn of avarice and lust, is explained as reified names and concepts, and this is what causes suffering to the thief as it does to all mankind. A thief differs from the upright citizen in that his moral conditioning has been ineffective or that it has been thrown off by some emotional or intellectual force. Nāgabodhi's horn, like all desirable objects, is a reification of a name and concept, here manifested under the controlled conditions of meditation. The horn vanishes when delusions of desirable objects dissolve, when subject and object are realized as essentially empty and when the nature of being[360] is realized as emptiness; Sarvabhakṣa's actualized visualization dissolved for the same reasons. With this realization the fear that arose from original alienation, the dualization that is *vajrayāna*'s original sin, is dissolved, and with the confidence that nothing whatsoever can touch one's essential nature of being, just as the sky remains unaffected by the black or white clouds that gather in it, saṃsāra and nirvāṇa are unified, and *mahāmudrā-siddhi* results.

Nāgabodhi's song of realization employs common mahāyāna metaphors. Between heaven and the netherworld, on earth, we are endowed with the precious human body; the *nāga*s guard treasure in the ocean depths; the sword of awareness destroys dualities; enlightened yogins are our guides and initiators.

Historiography

Tāranātha ascribes Nāgabodhi's meditation to a Siṅkhipa.[361] This Sinkhipa (Siṅghipa) visualized horns that reached the roof of his cave; fulfillment meditation dissolved them. A similar legend is related in Nepal about the Buffalo Buddha (T.Ma he sangs rgyas), a moronic herdsman who visualized horns that grew to the roof of his cave (on Nāgārjuna Hill, outside Kathmandu). When he achieved *mahāmudrā-siddhi*, he shot through the roof of his cave straight to the Ḍākinī's Paradise.[362]

Tāranātha's Nāgabodhi came from a Baṅgala family patronized by Nāgārjuna. He was ordained, became a master of the *Tripiṭaka* and a devoted disciple of Nāgārjuna. Later he became a *rasāyana siddha* and an *ācārya*, obtaining *mahāmudrā-siddhi* on Śrī Parvata. Even here the ninth century Nāgabodhi may be confused with Nāgārjuna's second century disciple of the same name, known also as Tathāgatabhadra and Nāgāhvaya. The early Nāgabodhi wrote a massive work called the Twenty Five Thousand, a *prajñāpāramitā* work extant only in Chinese that related the mahāyāna sūtras to his master's *madhyamika* philosophy, proving himself a great master of the *Tripiṭaka*. Although there is very little biographical material on the siddha Nāgabodhi's life, we know that he wrote four commentarial works on the *Guhyasamāja-tantra*, giving him high status amongst the commentators on Nāgārjuna's school of *Guhyasamāja* exegesis.[363] This work was probably accomplished at Śrī Parvata (Śrīśailam), where Virūpa met him and received Yamāri mantras. Nāgabodhi may also have travelled to the North-west; he became a target of polemical abuse for teaching the *anātman* doctrine in Kashmir;[364] and he was Guru-bhai of King Indrabhūti, both receiving *anuyoga* precepts from King Dza. But another Nāgabodhi may be indicated here.

The only Suvarṇa Vihāra of which we have notice is a monastery near Krishnagar in Bengal.

77

THE MAHĀSIDDHA DĀRIKAPA
SLAVE-KING OF THE TEMPLE WHORE

Sukhāvatī lies within us, but delusion veils it;
Accumulate virtue and mystical awareness to reveal it.
Although we strive to gather both for a hundred lifetimes,
Without a Guru we will never realize Sukhāvatī's pure pleasure.

Indrapāla, the King of Paṭaliputra, went hunting one day. Returning through the market-place at midday, when all the people bowed down before him he recognized the siddha Lūipa in the crowd.

"You are a fine and handsome man," the king told Lūipa. "Give up eating those rotten fish guts. I will provide you with good food and the necessities of life. Indeed, I will give you your every desire. I will even give you my kingdom if you want it."

"If you are offering me the way to deathlessness and eternal youth, I will accept it." Lūipa replied.

"I offer you my kingdom and my daughter's hand in marriage," the king insisted.

"What good are they to me," Lūipa retorted.

King Indrapāla felt a sudden revulsion for this life. "It is true that the crown is of no great significance and that wearing it has many evil repercussions," he said. "I will renounce it!" And to his brahmin minister, he said, "I have had enough of this world. The luxury of good food and fine clothing is superfluous. I am going to practice the Dharma."

His minister agreed with his abdication in favor of his son, and after the son had been crowned, the king and minister set out together for the cremation ground where Lūipa lived. They knocked on the door of the hermitage and were invited inside. Lūipa granted them initiation into the maṇḍala of Saṃvara, but having nothing to offer as fee, perforce the king and minister were compelled to offer him their bodies as slaves. Then they accompanied their Guru to the land of Orissa, where they remained for some time, begging their food. From Orissa they went on to the country of Bhirapurī, to Jaṅtipur, a city of three hundred thousand families. In that city was a great temple wherein seven hundred dancing girls performed worship, and Lūipa sought their mistress, Darima. He was stopped by the three hundred guards protecting her chamber. "Will your mistress buy a male slave?" he asked them.

"If I like what I see, I will buy him," came a voice from within.

Darima liked the look of the king and offered a sum of one hundred *tolas* of gold for him. The deal was sealed after Darima agreed to the conditions that the king should sleep alone, and that he should be freed after he had earned the price that was paid for him. Lūipa received payment and departed with the brahmin minister.

The king served Darima for twelve years. He washed her feet, massaged her body, and served her in every way. But he never forgot his Guru's instruction. He endeared himself to the other servants by performing their tasks for them, and he became the highly respected master of servants. One day a king called Janapa, or Kuñci, came to the temple with five hundred *tola*s of gold to spend on worldly pleasures. The slave-king acted as intermediary, receiving seven *tola*s of gold for every service he provided. After many days of debauchery, one night Kuñci's stomach troubled him, and he went outside for a stroll. Smelling some delightful perfume and seeing light radiating from a shrubbery, he investigated and was amazed to find Darima's slave sitting upon a throne, served by fifteen girls. He called Darima, who was immediately filled with remorse at her treatment of her slave, and she prostrated and circumambulated him.

"We are human beings and therefore err," she said to him. "We failed to recognize the saint that you are. I have abused you and I have sinned. Please forgive me. I beg you to become our priest that we may venerate you for twelve years."

The king refused Darima's request, but Darima, Kuñci and the dancing girls became his disciples. Levitating into the sky he gave them instruction called Emptying the City:

The heritage of kings of the mundane world
With their canopies, elephants and thrones,
Palls beside my exalted state.
I am shaded by the canopy of liberation,
I ride the great vehicle of the mahāyāna,
I reign on the throne of the three realms:
That is Dārikapa's pleasure!

The master became known throughout the world as Guru Dārikapāda, The Prostitute's Slave. Finally with seven hundred attendants, he attained the Ḍākinī's Paradise.

Sādhana and Historiography

There is clear evidence in the minister Ḍeṅgipa and the king Dārikapa's legends that the two stories have become confounded and confused. Both king and minister are sold to prostitutes, one secular and one sacred; they are both sold in the city of Jaṅtipur (Jayantipur, Jintapur, and so on);[365] in Ḍeṅgi's song of realization within the legend, he describes himself as a rice-thresher, only the appended couplet mentioning the courtesan. It seems certain that Ḍeṅgipa was a farm laborer, a rice-thresher, and Dārikapa was the courtesan's slave; further, it is likely that Ḍeṅgipa was previously the king and Dārikapa the minister, contrary to our legends.

The Tibetan Sakya sect's versions of the king and minister's stories are most extensive, entertaining and given most historiographical credence.[366] A king had sought Lūipa after his renown as the fish-gut eater had spread abroad. When the time was propitious Lūipa sought the king, who was expecting a lesser potentate to come to pay tribute the day after Lūipa arrived in his town. The town had been decorated, cleaned and beautified for the occasion, and Lūipa slept on the throne that had been erected for the king in a public garden. A brahmin who came to purify the way before the king came forth was surprised by a naked, dishevelled, fish-gut-eating character with a greenish complexion sitting on the throne. Lūipa played world emperor, defying all attempts to move him. With discretion tempered by valor the king finally came with troops to confront Lūipa, but Lūipa's gaze paralyzed the king's entire entourage. The minister realized who Lūipa was, and, admitting reverence, one by one the entourage was released from paralysis. Then the king and Lūipa began a dialogue "Who are you?" "I am king." "No, I am king!" "I am the real king." "Prove it!" And with a song, Lūipa reduced the king and minister to devotional awe. They begged for instruction, but Lūipa refused them until they had renounced their status and possessions. Then Lūipa performed an *abhisamaya sādhana* and anointed them, before sending the king to Tsaritrapa in Orissa, where he became known as Ḍeṅgipa (see p. 189), and the minister, admitting a fondness for betel nut, was sent to Kāñcī City in Ḍākinaba in the South, where he was to serve a beautiful whore. His duties consisted in attending to the lady's clients, young bloods and travellers, all of whom would provide for his betel addiction. After constantly attending to the "absolute specific" he achieved *mahāmudrā-siddhi.* He stayed and taught in Kāñcī, and became known as Dārikapāda.

Bu ston has Lūipa send the king to the city of Khur in Odapurī (in Orissa), to a courtesan who was an incarnation of Vajrayoginī, and there he washed the feet of drunkards and lechers by day and meditated by night. Previously his vice had been fornication, and after his attainment of *mahāmudrā-siddhi* he gained courtesans as disciples. Upon the evening of his enlightenment he assembled fourteen thousand women with the sound of his *ḍamaru* to participate in his *gaṇacakra-pūja.*[367]

There is an ambiguity in the Sakya story which implies that it was Dharmapāla of Bharendra himself, the previous employer of Lūipa the scribe, who became the master's convert. Bu ston identifies the king as Vimalacandra of Kumārakṣetra in Orissa. Our legend has Indrapāla of Saliputra (Paṭaliputra), which indicates a scion of the Pāla dynasty (the Indra—King of the Gods—of the Pālas).

To support the identification of Dārikapa with the minister, in the Fourth Kālacakra Lineage he is called the Southern Brahmin.[368] In Marpa Dopa's Saṃvara lineage he is Ghaṇṭāpa's Guru. Antara is also given as his disciple, together with the Ḍākinī Cinta, who associates him with the North-west. But in the Tibetan lineages Dārikapa and Ḍeṅgipa are apt to be confused, and confirmation of their lineal relationships is required. The Tibetans called him The Prostitute's Slave (T.sMad 'tshong ma'i g-yog) or Whore's Man (T.sMad 'tshong can).

78
THE SIDDHA PUTALIPA THE MENDICANT ICON-BEARER

The Buddha-nature exists in all beings.
Leave the perverse path paved by the intellect
To strive on the essential path of the heart,
And inevitably you will reach the ultimate goal.
Whoever takes empowerment from the True Guru,
He is permeated by sahaja,
The taste of the innate absolute,
And the unborn Vajradhara is sealed in him.

A low-caste householder of Baṅgala, a married man, was approached one day by a mendicant yogin begging alms. He prepared the yogin a feast, and through the yogin's presence real faith was awakened in him. He asked the yogin for instruction and was granted the empowerment of Hevajra, receiving teaching upon Hevajra's spiritual path. The yogin gave him a painted scroll, an icon of the deity Hevajra.

"Hang this from your neck and beg your way from town to village," he was instructed.

He followed this injunction, and after twelve years, unknown to anyone, he attained *siddhi*. Later, when he was begging at a king's palace, the king noticed that the Hevajra in the icon was depicted standing upon his own deity. He was incensed.

"Is it right that your deity should use my deity as a throne," roared the king.

"I am not the artist," the yogin told him. "The painting was done by a professional artist, and although it may give offense it is definitely correct."

"That rings true," thought the king, mollified, and to Putalipa he said, "It may be painted correctly, but how did your deity come to use my deity as a throne?"

"My deity is your god's deity," said Putalipa simply.

"Show me a token of your god's superior power," the king demanded.

"If you have an icon painted with your deity seated upon mine, their positions will be reversed in the night," Putalipa averred.

"If that happens, then I will follow your creed," promised the king. He summoned an artist, and the new painting was made.

During the night Putalipa visualized the gods' positions reversed, and in the morning, on the new painting, it was so. The king was amazed, and begged for teaching. His entire kingdom was converted, and the yogin named Putalipa became famous. He served beings for five hundred years, and after revealing his realization, with six hundred disciples he attained the Ḍākinī's Paradise.

Sādhana

The most common icon of Hevajra shows him with eight faces, four arms and legs, embracing his consort Nairātmā who has one face and two arms and legs. He is invariably colored blue and she white. Their stance is a dancing posture, one leg raised and the other bent (*ardhaparyaṅka*). He is often seen carrying sixteen skulls in his sixteen hands, while Nairātmā carries skull and curved-bladed knife; in other forms he holds sixteen different symbols. In the sixteen-armed form he stands upon the four obstructive powers in the form of four brahmanical deities: the four psycho-physical constituents (*skandha-māra*) are yellow Brahmā; the power of emotional defilement (*kleśa-māra*) is blue Viṣṇu; the power of death (*mṛtyu-māra*) is white Maheśvara (Śiva); and the power of divine pride and lust (*devaputra-māra*) is white Śakra. The two, four and six armed Hevajras or Herukas stand upon a corpse (*veṭāla*).[369]

Thus, since the king's deity is not named in the legend, it is impossible to discover which deity he worshiped. Several Buddhist tantric deities stand upon brahmanical gods: Saṃvara and Vajra Vārāhī stand upon Bhairāva and Kālaratrī; Vighnāntaka stands upon Ganeśa, their son. This iconographical convention may memorialize a time when the Buddhists converted *śaiva*s in large numbers, making their shrines into Buddhist power places and renaming their images as Buddhist gods. Śiva and Umā at Paśupatī in Nepal, for instance, are *liṅgam* and *yoni* worshiped as such by Hindus, but Tibetans worship them as Cakrasaṃvara and Vajra

Vārāhī and believe that in historical time Heruka came to Paśupatī and overcame Mahādeva and his Consort, turning them into slaves.[370] It is reasonable to assume that all or most of the twenty-four *pīṭhasṭhānas* suffered the same transformation.

Historiography

The root of *putalipa* is uncertain, so Sutali could be his name (or Satapa, Purali, Tali). The Tibetan form is "Ornament Beggar" (T. rGyan slang ba). The text of the legend is corrupt, phrases and sentences disarranged; but the sense is always clear.

79

THE SIDDHA UPANAHA THE BOOTMAKER

The designs of an inherently pure heart
Merely by the thought are actually manifest.
Thus reality is fluid and responsive,
And my every desire is completely fulfilled.

In Seṅdhonagar there lived a man of low caste called Upanaha, a bootmaker by trade. One day the bootmaker watched a yogin-magician begging alms, and with awakened faith he followed him to his hermitage and asked for instruction in the Dharma. The yogin taught him the causes and conditions of life's frustrations and the benefits of freedom from saṃsāra. Filled with disgust for existence and its delusiveness and confusion he begged the yogin to show him a way out of it. He was initiated by a transfer of grace from the yogin and was instructed in turning attachment into the path of liberation:

The ornamental bells on the shoes you make
Jingle pleasantly on people's feet;
Gathering all sound into that sound,
Visualize sound and emptiness as indivisible.

The bootmaker followed these instructions, and for nine years he meditated accordingly. He dispelled the defilements that clouded his intuition and marred his ability to destroy obstacles to his progress, and he reached his goal. He became known as Guru Upanaha. After expressing his achievement he worked selflessly for mankind for nine hundred years, and finally he attained the Ḍākinī's Paradise with eight hundred disciples.

Sādhana

In Upanaha's meditation the creative stage is concentration upon the specific sound of jingling bells—perhaps the bootmaker made shoes for dancing girls—and the fulfillment stage is to visualize that sound as all sound, or conversely to gather all sound into that sound. Like visualizing all phenomena in a sesame seed at the tip of the nose (*26*), to find the emptiness in form, to visualize all sound as identical, is to realize the sound of silence, the emptiness in sound. Then sound and emptiness are indivisible, and when attachment to one sense-field is destroyed, attachment to all sense-fields dissolves. So long as intuitive insight into objects of attachment perceives the emptiness, attachment is the path to liberation.[371] The emphasis lies on the subjective element rather than the object of sensual attachment; the conceptual mind is the villain of the piece, not any inherent quality of the object. Mahāmudrā precepts always return to "What is mind?" and "How can it be returned to its primordial, pristine state of emptiness and clear light?"

Regarding Upanaha's song of realization, the siddha's mind is an instrument upon which he can play existential symphonies, or it is a stage upon which players dance and sing according to his direction. If Hollywood is the metaphor: producer, director, stars and actors, camera, screen and audience, are all functions of his mind. The Bodhisattva Vow is the producer, creating the momentum and setting the parameters in which life and death, good and evil, function. But what happens when two directors, two conceptual minds capable of creation and destruction, two siddhas, or an entire coven of siddhas, gather together? If a black thought arises then a magical contest is staged, as is described in many of the old legends. If all siddhas have taken the same refuge they form a celestial orchestra, each playing a different instrument in harmony to create great existential music just for the sheer joy of it.

Historiography

Upanahapāda—otherwise Panahapa, Pahana, Sanaka—is probably derived from *upanahi*, "He who ties together," ambiguously implying that he stitches leather together and also unites sound and emptiness. *Upānah* means "sandal" or "shoe," and for the Tibetans Upanahapāda is The Bootmaker (mChil lham mkhan) as distinguished from The Cobbler (Lham mkhan, *14*).

Upanaha's city of Seṅdhonagar (Saiṅdhonagar) may have been the origin of the fervid anti-tantric *seṅdhopa*s or *saiṅdhava*s who held authority at Vajrāsana during the siddha period. Tāranātha refers to them as the Siṅghala *śrāvaka*s or *śrāvaka seṅdhopa*s (*saiṅdhava*s) (see TARA IIA:n.144), and while it is unlikely that the Śrī Laṅkān Buddhist monks held authority in Northern India it is possible that the strongly hinayanist North-west had privileges in Vajrāsana. The Kingdom of Siṅghala was located south-east of Oḍḍiyāṇa and north of Siṅdh (from which Seṅdho/Saiṅdha is derived). Takṣila was the ancient capital of this area.

80

THE SIDDHA KOKILIPA THE COMPLACENT ESTHETE

Non-action is the secret precept,
Non-attachment is realization,
Non-referential pleasure is meditation,
And non-attainment is the supreme goal.

The King of Campārṇa, finding his palace intolerably hot in the summer months, would retire to the shade of his mango grove to enjoy the cool water running nearby, and the various flowers and fruits, the fragrance and the rich colors. He reclined upon the silks and satins of his cushions and divans while many young girls attended him, some fondling him, some fanning him, some singing, some dancing, and others strewing flowers about him, tending to his every whim and to the desires of his entourage. One day while he was wasting his precious human opportunity and the bounty of the kingdom in this orgy of self-gratification, a perfected monk approached the three hundred palace guards to beg food. They turned him away, but the king noticed him, and chiding the guards he called to the monk to enter, inviting him to share refreshments.

"Which of our two life-styles gives the most joy?" he asked the monk complacently.

"A child would say your style," responded the monk. "But the wise man knows that your way of life is poison to the mind."

"Whatever do you mean?" asked the king.

The monk described the three poisons, and continued, "If you mix temporal power with the three poisons, you end up in a bad state. It is like eating good food and drink mixed with arsenic."

The king was a highly discriminating man, and receptive to this intelligence he took refuge in the monk. He received the initiation and empowerment of Saṃvara and was shown the path he should follow. He abdicated in favor of his son, so that he could be totally free of the old dispensation. Yet sitting in his mango grove, his mind still clung to the sound of the *kokilā* bird, and he was unable to concentrate. His Guru showed him "the sudden dissolution of whatever constructs arise in the mind:"

Like thunderclouds gathering in an empty sky
Pouring down rain upon fruit trees and crops,
After the kokilā's *thunder in your empty ear*
Clouds of conceptual thought-consciousness gather,
Constantly precipitating poisonous emotion
To generate a harvest of lust and hatred.
This is the way of the fool.

Out of the empty space of mind's nature
Inseparable sound and emptiness thunder,
With gathering clouds of inexhaustible pleasure
Sending sweet rain of self-radiant reality
To ripen a harvest of fivefold awareness.
That is the wise man's miracle.

The king followed this instruction, and within six months he had reached his goal. He was called Kokilipa after the birds whose song he meditated upon. He worked indefatigably for others before attaining the Ḍākinī's Paradise.

Sādhana

The *kokilā*, or Koïl, with its cry *ku-il ku-il* or *ho-whee-ho ho wee-ho*, belongs to the cuckoo family and lays its eggs in other birds' nests, particularly the crow's nest. But it is known as the Indian nightingale and is respected as such in sentimental poetry and songs. Its melodious and rich liquid call is rhythmically repetitive, and therefore an excellent object for meditation (see also *55*). The incentive to practice meditation that a *yogin* can offer a complacent esthete, whether in a *rāja*'s India or, say, Huysman's *fin de siècle* Paris, is heightened perception and direct sensation unencumbered by mental chatter. "Pure pleasure" (*mahāsukha*) does not refer to other-worldly rapture or onanistic mystical bliss, but to the rarified, and at the same time existentially intense, pleasure, dormant in ordinary perception; in the same way "the nature of being" is not only an abstract metaphysical concept, it is the "authenticity" palpably perceptible in the vibration of a man or woman who fortuitously or by practice has discovered the emptiness in the suffering of existence.

The three poisons that, mixed with power, send Authority to the lower realms are desire, aversion and ignorance. From these three basic emotive reactions to every moment of perception, the various forms of emotivity arise, subsumed under five heads: lust, hatred, pride, jealousy and sloth. Meditating upon the empty essence of these emotions, the five modes or aspects of a siddha's awareness are discovered: the awareness of sameness, discriminating awareness, mirror-like awareness, all-accomplishing awareness and awareness like the sky. The key element in virtually all the legends is the initiation that first introduces the man eaten up by disgust with himself, or the world, to the essential nature of being, or *sahaja*, the inborn absolute, that arises co-incident with every moment of perception. Thereafter, by practicing the meditation that induces that same state of knowledge, whatever constructs arise in the mind are immediately liberated,[372] which is to say that they dissolve without producing any karma of body, speech or mind; they are like bursting bubbles.

Historiography

Kokilipa (Kokilā, Kokala) was king of Campārṇa (Campārana, Campara), which must be Campā (see *60*), famous for its pools and flower groves in ancient times. It should be made clear that the Tibetan word translated as "king" (*rgyal po*) renders the Sanskrit *kṣetriya*, a member of the second caste, the ruling, warrior caste. Thus this "king" Kokilipa could have been only a local land owner, "squire," or "lord of the manor." Since Kokilā is such an unusual name, it is possible that our Kokilipa is Vidhyākokilā (Rig pa'i khyu byug), who was a disciple of Candrakīrti and the Guru of Kuśulu the Younger in a Guhyasamāja lineage.[373] He also appears in the list of Atīśa Śrī Dipaṅkara's "fourteen other teachers," so we cannot be certain of his dates.[374]

81

THE MAHĀSIDDHA ANAṄGAPA THE HANDSOME FOOL

Saṃsāra is insubstantial like a dream,
This body iridescent like a rainbow;
But poisoned by nescience, desire and vanity,
We cling to illusion, believing it to be real.
Awaken from the poison-trance of attachment
And saṃsāra itself becomes the dharmakāya.

There was a low-caste man of Gauḍa, who due to his practice of patience and tolerance in past lives, was endowed with a particularly beautiful body. Comparing himself with others, he became very conceited. One day a gentle and courteous monk accosted him and graciously begged alms. Anaṅga, the handsome youth, invited him to his house, asking him to accept his hospitality for a few days. The monk accepted, and Anaṅga washed his feet, prepared a couch for him, and offered him good food.

"Why do you beg and mortify yourself like this?" he asked the monk.

"To free myself from the fear that the wheel of existence has instilled in me," the monk replied.

"What is the difference between the basis of your character and mine?" Anaṅga asked him.

"There's a great deal of difference," replied the monk. "Conceit is the basis of your character and pride is devoid of creative potential. The basis of my character is faith, and faith creates immense capacities."

"What kind of capacities?" Anaṅga asked.

"In this lifetime the capacity to practice Dharma, so that the problems of men and gods are resolved," the monk told him. "But ultimately the capacity to obtain the Body of a Buddha, which depends on faith." The monk elaborated upon the various mundane and supra-mundane qualities and powers.

"Is it possible for me to obtain this capacity?" Anaṅga asked him.

"Have you any skill at craft or trade?" enquired the monk.

"I can do nothing of that sort," Anaṅga replied.

"Then can you sit still and meditate?" asked the monk.

"That I can do," Anaṅga asserted.

The monk bestowed upon him the initiation and empowerment of Saṃvara and instructed him in the inherent lucency of the six sense-fields.

All the multiplicity of appearance
Exists as nothing but the nature of your mind.
Let the objects of your six sense-fields alone
And abide in a state of freedom and non-attachment.

Anaṅga meditated accordingly, and within six months he had reached his goal. As Guru Anaṅgapāda he worked selflessly for others, and finally in his very body he attained the Ḍākinī's Paradise.

Sādhana

The faith of a Bodhisattva is not the faith of evangelical Christianity, for example. It is "confidence" rather than blind faith. The Buddhist is taught to examine, question, and take nothing on trust in doctrinal matters. The Buddhist cannot believe in a Creator-Father God in the sky until he has direct experience of him; all the gods of the Buddhist pantheon are meta-psychic realities of whom he has intimate knowledge through meditation. Faith to Anaṅga's Guru was divine confidence in the truth of his own insights, the power of his attainments, the efficacy of his practice, and knowledge[375] of the meta-psychic realities of Guru, Deva and Ḍākinī substantiated and reinforced by every instant of intuition into the nature of experience as empty space. Such faith is inviolable, indestructible *vajra*-faith.[376]

The instruction the monk gave Anaṅga is a modified form of the basic *vipaśyanā* meditation technique. *Vipaśyanā*, "heightened perception," is otherwise known as "guarding the doors of the senses." Lodging consciousness at the doors of perception, in the sense organs themselves, whatever objects arise are watched without interference. Such a technique can be practiced throughout one's waking hours, and the immediate effect is a heightening in the intensity, vividness and clarity of perception. With practice, insight into the emptiness of the sense-fields should arise, and then "freedom and non-attachment" occurs. "Freeedom" is space free of obstructions—prejudices, preconceptions, emotional attachments—that tie up, construct and block the free-flow of energies. "Non-attachment" is the result of intuition of emptiness.[377] When sense objects are perceived to be nothing but space they cease to be desirable, and the one flavor of pure awareness replaces the variety of positive and negative feelings that are the result of attachment.

Historiography

Anaṅgapāda can be identified with Anaṅgavajra, an important link in the Hevajra lineage, the disciple of Padmavajra and the Guru of Saroruha (*74*). He was born in Gauḍa (Gahura, Ghahuri),[378] a city-state on the Ganges in eastern Bihar and western Bengal, and he travelled to the North-west to receive his training, like several of his contemporaries from eastern India. Padmavajra sent him to the Kotamba Mountain (?), and after twelve years he attained *siddhi*. To cap his training he then sent Anaṅga to the Swine-herd Ḍākinī, who also taught Saroruha, and keeping pigs he became identical to Vajrasattva. Still in Oḍḍiyāṇa, he performed Bodhisattva service.[379] The Swine-herd Ḍākinī gives us intimation of Vajra Vārāhī, the Sow-headed Consort of Saṃvara; but there is also significance in her untouchable caste and the uncleanliness of her work.

One tradition makes Anaṅga a son of the founder of the Pāla dynasty, Gopāla (AD 735-761).[380] The Pālas were of low caste like Anaṅga, a *śūdra*, and Dharmapāla and Devapāla, Gopāla's successors, were known as Gauḍiśvara, Lord of Gauḍa. Gauḍa was Anaṅga's birthplace, but his royal ancestry is not confirmed. Besides Padmavajra, Kambala and a disciple of Ḍombi Heruka are mentioned as his Gurus, and Virūpa, Līlavajra and the last Indrabhūti as his disciples. These siddhas place him in the middle of the ninth century. Saṃvara and Hevajra were his principal absorption, but he was also an initiate of the *Guhyasamāja-tantra*.

Anaṅga (T.Yan lag med pa), "Limbless," is a name of Kāmadeva, the Indian Cupid; but in the *nāth* tradition, the name describes a yogin who has withdrawn his "limbs" like a tortoise, dead to the world, totally introspective, all his consciousness concentrated in the sixth sense.

82

THE YOGINĪ MAHĀSIDDHĀ LAKṢMĪṄKARĀ THE CRAZY PRINCESS

Firstly, the wise man creates enlightened vision,
Secondly, he meditates unswervingly upon empty being,
Thirdly, with constant intuitive, mystical experience,
He does what he must with modesty and grace.

Lakṣmīṅkarā was the sister of King Indrabhūti of the Oḍḍiyāṇa kingdom of Sambhola. Since childhood she had been blessed with the qualities of the elect, and listening to the teaching of Kambala and other masters she had gained a full understanding of many tantras. But her brother had betrothed her to the son of Jalendra, King of Laṅkāpurī, and now an escort had arrived to conduct her to her husband's palace. She left Sambhola accompanied by a retinue of Buddhist friends, loaded with a vast dowry, but upon arrival at Laṅkāpurī she was refused admittance to the palace.

"It is an inauspicious day," she was told. "You must wait."

She languished outside, her depression deepening when she saw that the people of the city were not Buddhists. Her despondence turned to sickness of heart when some time later a prince and his party cantered by, obviously having returned from the chase, as many animals' carcasses hung over their saddles. Then someone told her that the prince who had just passed by was her husband. She received this information like an over-fed guest pressed with yet more food, and her heart turned over.

"My brother, a prince who cherishes the Buddha's doctrine has sent me amongst impious worldlings!" she cried, and then fainted.

When Lakṣmīṅkarā revived she began to distribute her dowry amongst the poor of the city. She gave it all away, including her jewelry, which she presented to her attendants before sending them back to Sambhola. She then locked herself in the chamber that her husband had provided, refusing to admit anyone for ten days. She tore off her clothes, covered herself with oil and coal dust, mussed her hair and feigned insanity, all the while unswervingly concentrating upon the essential truth in her heart. In despair the prince sent doctors to treat her, but she attacked them and threw things about whenever they approached. A messenger was sent to Indrabhūti, but her brother was untroubled, realizing that his sister was demonstrating her revulsion for saṃsāra.

Henceforth Lakṣmīṅkarā was to all appearances insane. Escaping from the palace she scavenged food thrown out for dogs, and slept in the cremation ground, but all the while she was deepening her experience of the essential nirvāṇa. After seven years she attained *siddhi.* Then she instructed a sweeper of the king's latrines, who had served her, and this man quickly gained the capacity of a Buddha, without anyone's knowledge.

At about this time King Jalendra went hunting with his court. He became separated from the party and dismounted to rest. He fell asleep, and awakening when evening was upon him he could not find his way. When he stumbled upon Lakṣmīṅkarā's cave his curiosity was aroused, and approaching quietly, peering inside he saw the yoginī, her body radiating light, surrounded by numerous goddesses worshiping her. Perfect faith arising in his heart, he remained there the night, and although he found his way back to the city the next day he could not keep from returning to the cave. He prostrated before Lakṣmīṅkarā, and in response to her doubtful enquiry as to his motives he affirmed his faith in her as a Buddha and asked her for instruction. Lakṣmīṅkarā taught him these verses:

All beings on the wheel of rebirth suffer,
For in saṃsāra there is not a moment of bliss.
Even superior beings, men and gods, are tormented,
While the lower realms are pain itself,
Where ravenous beasts constantly devour each other,
Some beings ceaselessly tormented by heat and cold.
Seek the pure pleasure of release, O King!

She continued, "You are not to be my disciple. Your Guru is one of your latrine sweepers, one of my disciples who has attained *siddhi.*"

"I have many sweepers," replied the king. "How shall I know him?"

"Put your trust in the man who feeds the people after finishing his work," she told him. "Go to him at night."

The king sought and found the good sweeper. He invited him to his throne room, sat him upon the throne, prostrated before him, and requested instruction. He received initiation by transfer of the Guru's grace, and he was taught the creative and fulfillment stages of Vajra Vārāhī's sadhana.

Lakṣmīṅkarā and the sweeper performed many miracles in the town of Laṅkāpurī before she bodily attained the Ḍākinī's Paradise.

Sādhana

Unlike Maṇibhadrā (*65*), who married after she had received initiation, becoming a model wife, Lakṣmīṅkarā took the hard path, although she was quite unprepared for it by her upbringing. No doubt the approaching trauma of the nuptials of an otherworldly and delicate sixteen-year-old with a mature warrior prince, whom she had not met since she was a child of seven, was a strong factor in favor of her renunciation. Still today in India both men and women, but more frequently men, opt out of the horror of the first night of an arranged marriage and take *brahmācārin* vows of celibacy in an *āśram*. Such individuals have fine potential for sublimating their sexual energy in an internal *kuṇḍalinī* yoga, and the price they pay, which is some degree of social ostracism, and in Lakṣmīṅkarā's case complete rejection as an idiot, assists in providing a totally undemanding environment. This is a harsh path, and after seven years Lakṣmīṅkarā's associates and converts were of the lowest social caste; no doubt many who take this path do not attain their goal. But those women who do make it through are certainly of a most extraordinary type and, more than their male counterparts, deserve every respect for their success.

Historiography

The name Lakṣmīṅkarā is known chiefly for the yoginī's association with the tradition of the *Six Topics of Vajra Vārāhī* (T.*Phag mo gzhung drug*); she wrote a manual describing the methods of fulfillment stage meditation similar to the *Six Yogas of Nāropa* (T.*Na ro chos drug*). The identity of this Lakṣmīṅkarā is in some doubt. It would appear that Indrabhūti's sister, the Lakṣmī of our legend, received the teaching on Vārāhī from the Guru Kambala/Lwa wa pa, a renowned authority on the *yoginī-tantra*, and upon the Saṃvara fulfillment stage in particular (see p. 183), and it is possible that she was responsible for formulating the *Six Topics* as a separate entity. In this way the discrepancy in the lineages, some of which begin with Lakṣmī and others with Kambala, is explained.[381] But there is another problem stemming from the lineages: her disciple was Virūpa, who taught Avadhūtipa (Maitripa) and Paiṇḍapātika, younger contemporaries of Nāropa. The great Virūpa, born in the eighth century, could hardly have taken initiation from a yoginī at the end of the ninth, when Indrabhūti, his sister and Kambala were still alive; that must have been another Virūpa, probably the disciple of Anaṅgavajra who received the *Mahākarūṇikā-tantra* from Kambala. Otherwise, if it was Virūpa III at the beginning of the eleventh century who received the *Six Topics*, it could have been Śrī Lakṣmī the Great of Kashmir (who could also have been the Lakṣmī who taught the *anuttarayoga-tantra* to Karopa, a disciple of Maitripa) who initiated the tradition. Kashmiri Lakṣmī's Guru was the brahmin scholar Bhadra (Sūryaketu) who taught her in Kashmir during Nāropa's lifetime.[382] This problem is yet to be resolved.

Indrabhūti and Lakṣmīṅkarā, brother and sister, were also Guru and disciple. Lakṣmī received the Guhyasamāja from Cittavajra (also described as her brother), and taught it to Indrabhūti.[383] Here the identification of Indrabhūti with Kambala is important (see p. 184), as Lakṣmī's Saṃvara and Hevajra Guru would have been her brother. Anaṅgavajra is another of her Gurus.

Finally, another Lakṣmī should be mentioned. The nun Śrī Lakṣmī, also of Kashmir, initiated the tradition of fasting to propitiate Avalokiteśvara (T.*smyung gnas*).[384] This lineage has no recorded Indian succession, and it is probable that from Śrī Lakṣmī the teaching was transmitted directly to Tibet. Śrī Lakṣmī lived in the eleventh century, when Kashmir was on the point of destruction by the Muslims.

In Tibetan Lakṣmīṅkarā, Provider of Fortune, is sometimes rendered as the Well-matured (T.Legs smin kara), or as Glorious Creatrix (T.dPal mdzad ma) or Glorious Goddess (T.dPal lha mo), confounded with the epitome of beauty and bounteousness that is the Goddess Lakṣmī, consort of Viṣṇu.

83

THE SIDDHA SAMUDRA
THE PEARL DIVER

With realization of the unborn, but without meditation
training,
The yogin is like a cannibal with a baby in his arms.
If his meditation is dissociated from the nature
of his being,
He is like an elephant stuck in the mud.

In the land of Sarvaṭira there lived a man of outcaste family who was a pearl diver by trade. He dived for pearls in the ocean and sold them in the market-place. One day, unable to find a single stone, and therefore unable to feed himself, he wandered to the cremation ground in despair, bemoaning his fate. The yogin Aciṅtapa found him there, and receiving an honest reply to his enquiry as to his state, the Guru gave him some advice.

"All beings bound to the wheel of life suffer untold pain. In your past lives you have endured severe, intolerable suffering, and in your present life you have more of the same, without even a moment of pleasure."

"Guruji, please show me the way out of this mess," Samudra begged. Aciṅtapa initiated him and gave him instruction in the four boundless states of mind and the four internal joys:

Neutralize the eight mundane obsessions
Through loving kindness and compassion,
Sympathetic joy and equanimity,
Then visualize to perfection in reality
A stream of delight descending from the head center:
The four joys induced in the four psychic centers,

Indivisible pleasure and emptiness obtains everywhere,
And inexhaustible pleasure alone
Precludes even a moment of suffering.

With an understanding of this meditation instruction, meditating for three years, the pearl diver attained *siddhi*. He became known as the Guru Samudrapāda. After expressing his realization and working selflessly for others, he attained the Ḍākinī's Paradise with eight hundred disciples.

Sādhana

Again in Samudra's story we are overwhelmed by the assertion of universal and unmitigated misery. There is no moment of real happiness in saṃsāra; man has created a mental prison that is unalleviated pain. Such statements, from an ultimate standpoint, are no more true than their opposite, but like all tantric doctrine they are skillful means with a definite purpose. In order to gain the siddhas' freedom it is first necessary to confirm the prison from which escape is to be made. So long as our beliefs about the human condition are equivocal and uncertain, permitting callow notions like, "It's really not so bad, is it?" and "There *are* compensations!" and "Love is happiness," then aspiration will not be sufficiently intense, or focused, to achieve release. Thus it is at times of profound despond that the Guru's message is met with acceptance, and then confirming the prison by thinking of the key the prison is destroyed once and for all.

The way to destroy the prison is to destroy the mental constructs, the conceptions and discursive thought derived from those constructs—the notion of an ego, the division into subject and object, the belief in external, discrete entities and an objective, concrete reality—that are created by knotted channels and contaminated energies originating in the head center. The Ḍākinī's fire in the gut center melts the moon in the head center and the nectar flowing down the central channel creates the four levels of joy—joy, superior joy, detached joy, innate joy—in the head, throat, heart and gut centers respectively. The pleasure that finally suffuses the organism is inseparable from emptiness, the ineluctable element that renders it "inexhaustible,"[385] or more literally, "without outflow;" it is an ultimate pleasure, non-referential, dependent upon nothing, and therefore indestructible. This is a yoga of Vajra Vārāhī belonging to her *Six Topics* (T.*Phag mo gzhung drug*), and it is the central practice of the fulfillment stage.

The eight mundane obsessions are praise and blame, ignominy and fame, loss and gain, pleasure and pain.

Historiography

Samudra means ocean; the Tibetan translator rendered Samudrapa as "He who draws wealth from the sea" (T.rGya mtsho las nor bu len mkhan). His birthplace, Sarvaṭira (Sarvadideśa, Sarbadi, Sarvāra), oddly has been placed near Gorakhpur.[386] His Guru could be Aciṅtapa (*38*), or Mīnapa (*8*), or Maitripa, but since Aciṅtapa is an epithet of the liberated siddha it is impossible to be sure.

84

THE SIDDHA VYĀLIPA
THE COURTESAN'S ALCHEMIST

A vision of ultimate reality is a vision of your peerless Guru;
Supreme solitude is to contemplate all-embracing space;
Perfect harmony is to realize the nature of every experience;
And when you quaff a draft of etherial milk, then you are truly alive.

A very wealthy brahmin called Vyāli, who lived in the land of Apatra, coveted immortality. He purchased a large quantity of quicksilver, prepared it and added herbs to complete the potion. But he lacked one ingredient, and the potion had no effect. In anger he threw his alchemical manual into the River Ganges. This was the thirteenth year of his sādhana, and he was now penniless. He became a wandering beggar. One day he found himself in a village on the banks of the Ganges near a Rāmacandra temple, and there he met a courtesan, who showed him a book that she had found while bathing. Vyāli laughed, for it was the very same book that he had thrown away. He told the courtesan the story, and so impressed was she that she offered him thirty pounds of gold to continue his work. Vyāli was skeptical, but the courtesan encouraged him to proceed. Again he bought a large quantity of quicksilver, and for one year he worked at his alchemical sādhana, but still no sign of success appeared. The ingredient that was missing was red emblic myrobalan.

It happened, however, that when the courtesan was bathing one day a flower adventitiously adhered to her finger, and when she shook it off a droplet of its nectar fell into the potion. Immediately signs of success appeared. When she informed Vyāli, his only concern was whether she had told anyone else, and he remained anxious until he confirmed that nobody else knew. That evening the courtesan sprinkled some *chirāītā* upon Vyāli's food. Previously he had been unable to taste this most astringent of herbs, but now he could taste it, and the courtesan interpreted this as a sign of success.

"The principal sign of success is a circle of the eight auspicious symbols turning clockwise in the sky—a precious canopy, two golden fishes, the pot of treasure, a *kamala* flower, a white conch, an eternal knot, a victory banner, and an eight-spoked wheel," he told her. "Certainly we have been blessed with extraordinary fortune."

The brahmin Vyāli, the courtesan, and a mare, partook of the potion, and all of them attained the *siddhi* of deathlessness. But out of jealousy, Vyāli decided to deny the fruits of their labor to everyone else, keeping the recipe to themselves. When they went to the heavens they were, therefore, spurned by the gods, so they went to live in the land of Kilampara. They made their home in the shade of a tree on the top of a rock that was one mile high, ten times the distance sound will travel in width, and surrounded by a swamp.

Ārya Nāgārjuna, who had accomplished the power of flight, vowed to recover the secret of immortality that had been lost to India. He flew to the top of the rock, and after hiding one of his shoes he prostrated before the brahmin. Admitting that it was by the power of his shoe that he had gained the top of the rock, Nāgārjuna agreed to give Vyāli the shoe in return for the recipe, and after Vyāli had given him instruction he returned to India with the remaining magical shoe. On the mountain Śrī Parvata he continued his practice for the sake of all beings.

The moral of this story is that it is very difficult to obtain the Guru's secret instruction if the mindstream is possessed by a compulsive attachment to gold and material wealth. Emotional attachment precludes evolution of positive talents and qualities and the ultimate capacity of Buddhahood.

Sādhana

The relevance of the moral to this final legend is as obscure as parts of the legend itself. Despite the brahmin's emotional immaturity, he obtained the power of immortality, although it was the courtesan who added the missing ingredient. The story indicates that merely by following the mechanical instructions of alchemical theory (*rasāyana*), the *sādhaka* can obtain relative, mundane *siddhi*, but that Buddhahood, to which Vyāli did not aspire, is then still as far away as the earth is from the sky. The element that has been repetitively stressed in most of the legends, and which is lacking in this story, is the aspirant's world sickness, contrition, and a turning around in the seat of consciousness that purifies the mind-stream and opens it to the Guru's initiation and instruction. Thus the legends' final message is that without purification of the mind the path to Buddhahood is blocked.

The brahmin's missing ingredient, emblic myrobalan, is highly extolled in India by ayurvedic, homeopathic and naturopathic *materia medicas* alike. Myrobalans are dried plum-like fruits, their kernels of diverse species all known by their excessive astringency. They have been exported from India since Roman times for dying cloth and for their curative properties. European pharmacopeias of the middle ages attest to their miraculous properties. In both India and Tibet emblic myrobalan is combined with cherubic myrobalan and beleric myrobalan to form the highly regarded panacea and giver of longevity and potency called The Three Fruits.[387] Synonyms of emblic myrobalan in Tibetan indicate the attributes of the drug: Source of Youth, Sustainer of Youthfulness, The Glorious.[388] It is an important ingredient in the magical substance called "ambrosia-medicine"[389] distributed during long-life empowerments by the Lamas. We have no information concerning the specific red variety of the drug mentioned in the text; perhaps the adjective has a purely symbolic connotation. The ground stalks of *chirāītā* are also known for their excessive astringency;[390] perhaps the obscurity of the function of *chirāītā* in the legend can be clarified if *chirāītā* is understood as a generic term for astringents, and the bitter potion of immortality as the more bitter condiment that Vyāli's jaded palate could taste.

Historiography

While Nāgārjuna was refectory servitor at Nālandā a famine occurred in Magadha, and concerned for the wealth of the monks the master went to The Medial Isle[391] to secure the elixir that produces gold so that food could be purchased. Nāgārjuna was expelled from the monastery for such impious conduct.[392] In Tāranātha's account a happy ending absent in the earlier legends is appended to the Vyāli story.[393] After Nāgārjuna left with the secret precepts to prepare the elixir, Vyāli returned to the world, and encountering the siddha Carpaṭi (*64*) he became his disciple, and out of gratitude for the master's Mahāmudrā precepts through which he attained *mahāmudrā-siddhi* he gave Carpaṭi the secret of his elixir. Vyāli became a renowned composer of songs of realization. In the famous Muslim chronicler Al-beruni's account of the Vyāli legend, Vikramaditya, a vedic sage, features as the hero. However, if Tāranātha's assertion that Vyāli was Carpaṭi's disciple is credible the Nāgārjuna in the story would have been the tenth century alchemist, and Vyāli would have lived in the tenth century.

The Tibetans identify Kalimpara, where Vyāli retreated with his elixir, with Adam's Peak in Śrī Laṅkā.[394] Apatra may be a corruption of Aparanta, the ancient name of the Western Province of India. Vyāli's name has many variants: Byāli, Bhali, Byari, Bali, Pali, Vyadi. The Tibetan translator rendered his name "Tiger-like Phantom" (T.sTag can sprul can).

Post-Script

Thus the legends of the world renowned eighty-four mahāsiddhas, Lūipa and the others, are completed. I, Mondup Sherab, have faithfully translated these legends according to the oral transmission of Abhayadatta Śrī, who was born into the supreme family in Magadha, adorned with the Buddha's qualities. Through the merit accruing from this my work may those afflicted by the poison of saṃsāra find a healing Guru to cure them, and may they realize that the real nature of poison is the essential medicine.

As spoken from the mouth of Abhayadatta Śrī, the Guru of Campārṇa in India, the *bhikṣu* Mondup Sherab has faithfully translated these legends of the eighty-four mahāsiddhas.

Appendix I

The Texts and Sources

The Tibetan text of *The Legends of the Eighty-four Mahāsiddhas (Grub thob brgyad cu rtsa bzhi'i lo rgyus)* is a part of *The Cycle of Blessings of the Eighty-four Indian Mahāsiddhas (rGya gar grub thob brgyad cu rtsa bzhi'i byin brlabs chos skor)*. This cycle of texts is found in the *bsTan 'gyur* and also in the *sGrub thabs kun btus*. The following sources' editions of *The Legends* form the basis of the adaptations herein: the *sNar thang bsTan 'gyur*, Vol. 86, *lu pa*, reproduced in Khetsun Sangpo's *Biographical Dictionary of Tibet*, Vol. I;[395] the *Peking bsTan 'gyur*; the *sGrub thabs kun btus*, Vol. Śrī (IV), a *ris med* collection of sādhanas compiled by mKhyen brtse dbang po and dKong sprul, republished in Dehra Dun, 1970; the *Grub thob brgyad bcu rtsa bzhi'i chos skor*, published in New Delhi by Chophel Legdan, 1973;[396] the Mongolian Lama Kalzang's edition published by the Elegant Sayings Press in Sarnath, Varanasi; Sempa Dorje's edition in the *Bibliotheca Indo Tibetica*, No. 4, with Hindi translation.[397] The variations in spelling of proper names and in syntax and grammar, which have created some significant differences in these versions, have probably arisen from compounded errors in the writing and carving processes of the various editions and re-editions. The text of the *sNar thang bsTan 'gyur* edition, particularly, is unaccountably corrupt.

The colophons of the various manuscripts of *The Legends* are all similar: "As narrated by the Great Guru Abhayadatta Śrī of Campārṇa in India, the *bhikṣu* sMon grub shes rab has faithfully translated the legends of the eighty-four mahāsiddhas into Tibetan." The identity of the narrator remains uncertain, but it is assumed that he lived in the eleventh and twelfth centuries. We know that Abhayadatta ('Jigs pa sbyin pa dpal) was a native of

Campārṇa, that is, Campā, the ancient city-state on the Ganges near the present Bihar/West Bengal border, and we know that he was a disciple of Vajrāsana (rDo rje ldan pa), one of the last great siddhas, living in the eleventh century.[398] It has been suggested that Abhayadatta Śrī is no other than Abhayākaragupta, one of the last great *paṇḍitas*, a prolific writer attached to the Vikramaśīla Academy, living in the eleventh and twelfth centuries. A disciple of Nāropa, Kālapāda Junior and Bodhibhadra, he taught and collaborated in translation with many Tibetans including gNyan, sGrwa, 'Gos, rMa, and Se Lotsawas (Translators). He wrote commentaries on all the major tantras. The *Niṣpannayogāvalī*,[399] his best known work in the West, is not an iconographical textbook but a compendium of creative stage sādhanas in quintessential form. Abhayākara and the Tibetan Sanskritist and scholar Tsa mi Sangs rgyas grags pa, both disciples of Bodhibhadra, collaborated in a translation of the *Grub thob brgyad cu rtsa bzhi'i rtogs pa gur du bzhengs pa*.[400] If Abhayākara translated one part of the siddha cycle it is quite possible that he translated it all, and is, therefore, Abhayadatta Śrī. However, can Sangs rgyas grags pa be identified with sMon grub shes rab?

sMon grub shes rab and Abhayadatta Śrī also translated the *Songs of Realization* (*Grub thob brgyad cu rtsa bzhi'i rtogs pa snying po rdo rje'i glu*) and its commentary (*Grub thob brgyad cu rtsa bzhi'i rtogs rjod do ha 'grel bcas*), both of which belong to *The Cycle of Blessings*. The "compiler" of the songs was Ācarya Vīra Prakāśa (sLob dpon dPa' bo 'od gsal). Although some of the songs refer directly to the siddha's sādhana in the legend, many others have no bearing whatsoever on the legend, and since the style and vocabulary of the songs is consistent it is conceivable that having immersed himself thoroughly in the siddhas' sādhanas both in theory and practice, Vīra Prakāśa himself "discovered" the songs as revelations of the siddhas' spirit. The significance of the songs as inspired gnostic poetry of an adept in Mahāmudrā is in no way diminished thereby. The translator Mi nyag Tsa mi sMon grub shes rab bzang po lotsawa, or Mi nyag pa, belonged to the Mi nyag tribe. Before their diaspora effected by Genghis Khan in the 11th c., the Mi nyag pas formed a strong kingdom in the Tibetan marches east and south-east of Kokonor. Several Mi nyag pas appeared in early Tibetan Buddhist history. Mi nyag pa had two famous Indian Gurus, Vajrapāṇi from Baṅgala, who taught Mahāmudrā in both

Nepal and Tibet, and Bal po Asu, the son of an Indian refugee to Nepal, also proficient in Mahāmudrā. He wrote a guide book on India, which 'Gos Lotsawa used. Later, he invited the Paṇḍita Sūryaśrī to Tibet. In Tibet, he himself taught many texts written by such siddhas as Lakṣmīṅkarā, Dārikapa, Indrabhūti and Ḍombipa. He was a contemporary of Ye rang pa ("Patan-siddha"), Atulyavajra, Pham thing pa, Zha ma ma gcig, Pha dam pa Sangs rgyas and 'Khon bu pa, who was born in AD 1069. We can guess that sMon grub shes rab was born about 1060, had visited India before 1090 and lived a long life into the twelfth century.

Tsa mi Sangs rgyas grags pa was a well known Sanskritist and a translator of the *Kālacakra-tantra*; sMon grub shes rab may have been one of his initiatory names. As for Vīra Prakāśa, there is a case for identifying him with the narrator of *The Legends*, and here the word narrator is used advisedly as nowhere is it said that Abhayadatta "wrote" (T.*mdzad*) the legends—he "speaks" or "narrates" (*gsung*). In the *sGrub thabs kun btus* (see above) there is a reference to "comprehensive biographies of the mahāsiddhas, written by the *paṇḍita* Vīra Prakāśa, included in the *sNar thang bsTan 'gyur*. Since our legends are the only comprehensive legends in the *bsTan 'gyur*, this reference appears to identify Vīra Prakāśa as the author, if not the narrator of *The Legends*. No other data on Vīra Prakāśa has come to light, although he did write a *Nāmāvalī*, a short synopsis giving name, location, Guru and *siddhi* of the eighty-four mahāsiddhas of the legends.[401] If the evidence of the *Grub thabs kun btus* is found inadmissible due to the collection's late date (19th c.), then the most that can be said concerning the authorship of *The Legends* is that in the late eleventh or early twelfth century Abhayadatta Śrī, possibly Abhayākaragupta, narrated the oral tradition to the monk Mi nyag Tsa mi sMon grub shes rab, who may be Tsa mi Sangs rgyas grags pa, who wrote it down in Tibetan.

Only one Indian source of historical information on the siddhas has been discovered. Prof. Tucci found a fragment of a *Guruparamparā*, a lineage text, in Nepal.[402] In Tibetan there are six works written between the thirteenth and sixteenth centuries with some claim to historiographical notice. Bu ston (AD 1290–1354), the *bKa' gdams pa* compiler of the *bsTan 'gyur*, wrote a *History of the Dharma in India (rGya gar chos 'byung)* including several lives of siddhas,[403] and in his *Collected Works (gSung 'bum)* he gives further biographical clues in legends of his lineage's Indian antecedents.[404] *The Blue Annals (sDeb ther sngon po)*,[405] written by 'Gos Lotsawa (AD 1392–1481), is a lineal history including most of the important Indian lineages, with anecdotes upon important personalities; despite inconsistencies and inaccuracies this constitutes our most valuable comprehensive source. The *Collected Works* of the great, founding Sa skya hierarchs (*Sa skya bka 'bum*), who lived AD 1092–1280, including 'Phags pa's biographical notes on Indian lineage holders, is accorded greatest respect by historians.[406] Last and least is the Tibetan historian Tāranātha (b.1575), who wrote a *History of the Dharma in India* and the *Seven Lineages* (*bKa' 'bab bdun ldan*), a history of seven Indian lineages.[407]

All these Tibetan works suffer from the same faults—or virtues. The religious didactic imperative intrudes everywhere, as it does at every level of Tibetan culture, and wherever historical fact existed invariably it has been subjected to a philosophical or moral argument. Thus historical anecdote has become legend, and history a means to a soteriological end. When considering lineal history, from the Guru's point of view, time is an illusion and human progress a delusion; personality is the detritus of existence and an anonymous embodiment of Buddha nature the reality upon which to focus and which to underscore. Disdain for history is reflected in the lineages' failure to record an exact record of lineal succession, despite the respect for their founders who are worshiped as Buddhas. To establish the original lineages from the Tibetan material is fraught with difficulty. A plurality of names for each siddha and a plurality of siddhas with the same name are the chief problems. Siddhas who were monks received a name at ordination and again at their tantric initiation; then at each successive initiation they would acquire new initiatory names to be used within that community and lineage. Further, many siddhas received sobriquets or nicknames, or were known by an epithet such as Aciṅtapa or Avadhūtipa. Sometimes the Tibetan translators translated the siddhas' Indian names, but generally they transliterated them, and in the process of copying the Sanskrit transliteration generation after generation it became corrupted, sometimes out of all recognition. This corruption coupled with the Apabhraṃṣa dialects' variant forms explains the many variations of the siddhas' names found in different sources and editions of the legends: many are noted in the commentary. James Robinson's work in *Buddha's Lions*[408] has assisted in an attempt to reconstruct the original names by etymological means. But the lineages' greatest historiographical sin was to confound yogins of the same name. During the siddha period it became customary for initiates to take the names of their great mahāyāna forebears (like Nāgārjuna and Āryadeva), and also for a disciple to take the name of his Guru (Kāṇha and Kāla-pāda); further, there was failure to distinguish between siddhas with the same caste name (Vyāḍi, Kumbhari), with names referring to their tribe or color (Śavari, Kāṇha), and with identical sobriquets—a Dog-siddha (Kukkuripa) was active throughout the siddha period. Much work remains to be done on the identification of the siddhas, reconstructing their lineages and placing their lifetimes exactly. The chief chronological problem lies in creating a genealogical tree that takes into consideration the possibility of the extraordinary longevity, if not immortality, attained by those siddhas whose yoga gave them control over their lifespan. The accumulation of our conclusions as to the siddhas' lineages and dates is presented in Appendix II, although this genealogy is only tentative and awaits adjustment and repair by other scholars.

Whatever the identities of Abhayadatta Śrī and Mi nyag pa, their work originated in the late eleventh or early twelfth century, and is, therefore, the earliest extant source of information relating to the siddhas. The narrator and translator could even have known some of the eleventh century siddhas—Kālapa (Piṇḍopa), Celuka, Karmaripa, Megopa, Śāntipa and Nāropa. Why, then, are some legends not historiographically credible? For example, it is our opinion that Dārikapa and Ḍeṅgipa, king and minister in our legends, were actually minister and king respectively; Nāropa, who died in AD 1100, was a great *paṇḍita* at Nālandā before his renunciation according to his biography, yet his legend makes him a woodcutter; and was Nāgabodhi really a thief? The answer must be that the legends were related as legend with total disregard for historical accuracy; they must be appreciated primarily as instruction in the Tantra. It is a telling commentary on the nature of the material at our disposal relating to the siddhas that *The Legends* constitute a major source of historical information.

Appendix II

The Siddhas' Genealogy

The identification and putative dates of the siddhas given in the commentary represents the most obvious conclusions to be drawn from the Tibetan sources—legends and lineages. Few of these assertions, however, are incontrovertible; to make such simple statements, ignoring frequent credible alternatives and intricate supporting arguments, involved highly selective editing. The basic assumption of our chronology is that the eighty-four siddhas, with the exception of Indrabhūti the Great and an early Kukkuripa, lived within the Pāla and Sena period (AD 750-1200). Tantra had flourished for centuries before Gopāla came to power in Baṅgala; the *Guhyasamāja-tantra* may have been written down as early as the fifth century. But it is our contention that Tantra did not become publicly acceptable until the kings of our legends adopted it, the siddha-scholars rewrote and classified the tantras, and the sadhu-siddhas taught it in the villages. Thus, although the *Guhyasamāja* existed before Indrabhūti's time, this great tantric king was responsible for "discovering" it in its final form and boosting Tantra's acceptability by adopting it as his sadhāna. Although the identification of Indrabhūti is the most intractable problem in the genealogy, he probably lived in the seventh century and into the eighth.

The siddhas of the legends belong to the mother-tantra tradition. Nearly forty of the eighty-four siddhas received initiation into the *Hevajra* or *Saṃvara-tantra*, while only seven entered the *Guhyasamāja maṇḍala*, a father-tantra. These seven were Nāgārjuna and his three disciples—Āryadeva, Nāgabodhi and Kucipa—plus Bhande, Nalina and Kilakila. Nāgārjuna and his disciples were also initiates of the mother-tantra, but the *Guhyasamāja* was Nāgārjuna's great literary preoccupation: this

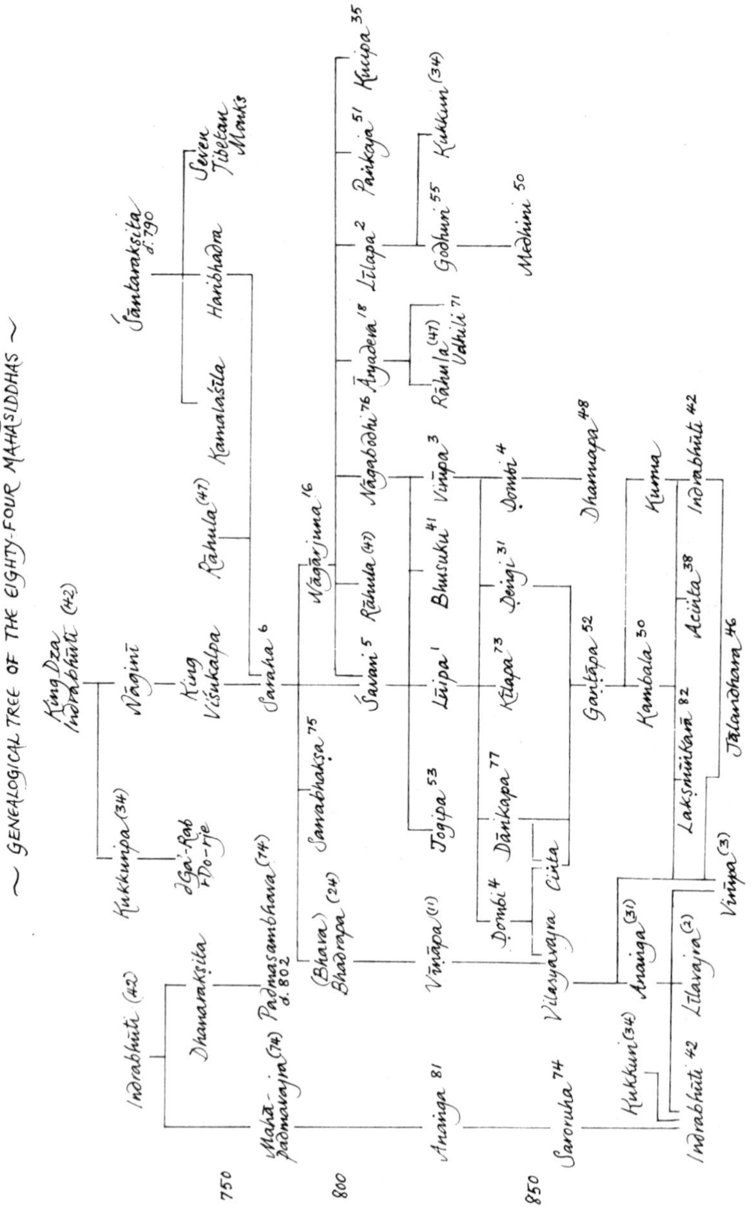
~ GENEALOGICAL TREE OF THE EIGHTY-FOUR MAHĀSIDDHAS ~
750
800
850
Indrabhūti (42)
Dhanarakṣita
Mahā-padmavajra (74)
Padmasambhava (74) d. 802
Kukkuripa (34)
lGa'-Rab rDo-rje
King Dza Indrabhūti (42)
Nāginī
King Viśukalpa
Saraha 6
Sarvabhakṣa 75
(Bhava) Bhadrapa (24)
Nāgārjuna 16
Rāhula (47)
Kamalaśīla
Haribhadra
Śāntarakṣita d. 790
Seven Tibetan Monks
Anaṅga 81
Vīṇāpa (11)
Jogipa 53
Lūipa 1
Śavari 5
Rāhula (47)
Nāgabodhi 76
Āryadeva 18
Līlapa 2
Paṅkaja 51
Kucipa 35
Bhusuku 41
Virūpa 3
Rāhula (47)
Udhili 71
Godhuri 55
Kukkuri (34)
Medhini 50
Saroruha 74
Vilasyavajra
Ḍombi 4
Dārikapa 77
Kilapa 73
Deṅgi 31
Ḍombi 4
Dharmapa 48
Ciṅta
Kukkuri (34)
Anaṅga (31)
Indrabhūti 42
Līlavajra (2)
Virūpa (3)
Lakṣmīṅkarā 82
Kambala 30
Acinta 38
Kurma
Indrabhūti 42
Jālandhara 46

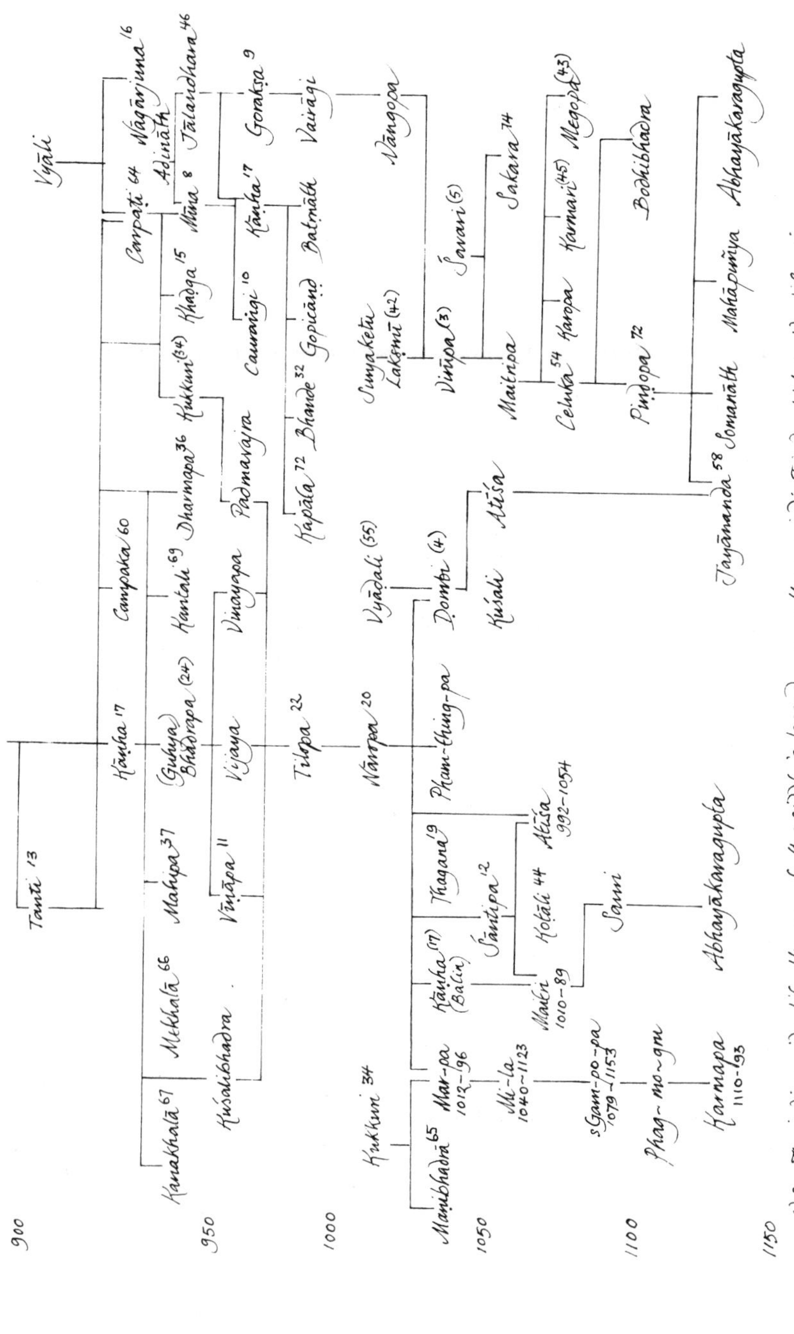

~ N.B. The indices identify the no. of the siddha's legend; parentheses indicate doubtful identifications. ~

Nāgārjuna was Saraha's student. Throughout the legends the accent is on Mahāmudrā, which is associated with the fulfillment stage *yoga* of the *Saṃvara-tantra*, and specifically with Nāropa's practices and Lakṣmīṅkarā's *Six Topics of Vārāhī.* The concept of Mahāmudrā is to be found in *rDzogs chen* works presumably predating Saraha, written in north-west India, but Saraha formulated it as the ultimate path and goal and initiated a lineage that flourished in the monastic academies of Baṅgala, such as Nālandā, Vikramaśīla and Somapurī. If the origins of the *Saṃvara-tantra* were known, the history of Mahāmudrā would be clearer; but it is only conjecture that both the *Hevajra* and *Saṃvara-tantra*s originated in Oḍḍiyāṇa, to be transmitted by pilgrims, and later by refugees, to Āryāvarta, the Holy Land of the Buddhists with Vajrāsana (Bodh Gaya) at its center. Further, before Oḍḍīyāṇa was overrun and destroyed by the Muslims in the ninth century, students from all over India went to this Land of the Ḍākinīs for training, Saroruha, Kambala, Anaṅgavajra, Līlavajra, Lūipa and Saraha himself, amongst them, and the siddhas could have brought back these tantras with them. Finally, if *rDzogs chen* was taught in Vajrāsana, Mahāmudrā may have been the result of *rDzogs chen*'s influence.[409] Whatever the antecedents of Mahāmudrā, it is to be assumed that the siddhas who practiced a Mahāmudrā-sādhana lived after its great proponent Saraha.

Saraha is the cornerstone of the siddhas' genealogical tree. If it is accepted that Saraha was a contemporary of the Pāla Emperor Dharmapāla, that he was both a product and an instrument of the Buddhist renaissance in Āryāvarta and Baṅgala, that he was active in the last part of the eighth century and into the ninth, then the foundation of the genealogy is established, and only the precise dates of the siddhas remain in dispute. It should be emphasized that these assertions cannot be shared by those who accept Tāranātha's chronology as sacrosanct. According to the great Tibetan historian's notions the eighty-four mahāsiddhas' lives were spread out over eight centuries rather than bunched together in a closely knit lineal family, all the siddhas born within a few generations of each other. However, it is probably incorrect to give overwhelming primacy to the Pālas and Baṅgala to the exclusion of other Buddhist tantric kings and principalities. In the South, for instance, where the proto-vajrayāna *nīlapaṭa* cult was first accommodated by Buddhism in the eighth century,[410] Kāñcī, mentioned several times in the legends, and Śrī Parvata, perhaps the most important tantric power place on the sub-continent to both Buddhists and *śaiva-śāktas*, were prominent Buddhist centers, and wherever there were Buddhist monasteries there must have been royal patronage forthcoming. In Śrī Laṅkā, where *nīl-sādhana* was also practiced, *vajiravāda* was responsible for the virtual eradication of the hīnayāna (see p. 98). Tantra was known throughout the Hindu world, and undoubtedly siddhas arose outside the Pāla Empire, and no doubt academies like Vikramaśīla, on a smaller scale, were founded elsewhere. However, forty-seven of the siddhas are associated with the Pāla Empire, compared to nine with the South and the two born in the North-west.

Kālapa has been identified as the last of the eighty-four siddhas. On the assumption that Kālapa is Kālacakrapāda Junior, Piṇḍopa, the disciple of Kāla-pāda Senior, Celuka (whose Guru Maitripa lived AD 1010–1089), he was born in the middle of the eleventh century and survived well into the twelfth. However, Jayānanda, the Kashmiri Paṇḍita, who travelled extensively in Tibet in the twelfth century, was probably born a generation after Piṇḍopa; and there is no greater difficulty in identifying the Kashmiri Paṇḍita with Jayānanda than Piṇḍopa with Kālapa. Supporting the assertion of an early date of composition of *The Legends* is the omission of several of the last great siddhas from the eighty-four. Vajrapāṇi, Vajrāsana, Abhayākaragupta and Mitrayogi, amongst many others who achieved as much as their lineal predecessors, sustained the tradition until the end of the twelfth century. In 1199 AD Mohammed bin Bukhtiar, taking Vikramaśīla for a fort, destroyed the academy and its invaluable library, massacring the monks; thus the Sena dynasty that had replaced the Pālas in 1162 AD was destroyed, and Buddhism in Baṅgala died. Many tantrikas fled north, to Nepal and Tibet, where their salutary influence promoted the Tantra, particularly in the Sa skya monasteries in gTsang. Those who remained, together with the laymen of the conquered Buddhist states, are assumed to have converted to Islam hoping to sustain their internal practice behind a mask of the foreign religion, or they died for their beliefs. Where the decision of Islam or the sword was not forced upon them, without the monasteries that had always been the focal point of Buddhist culture, and deprived of the support of monks, *ācāryas* and yogins, they were reabsorbed into the heterogenous brahmanical religion. It has been suggested that some sects were absorbed into the *nāth-sampradāya*, which as we have seen was a pseudo-Buddhist tradition with non-dual metaphysics, employing many Buddhist originated yogas, strongly influenced by Buddhist thought and method from the time of Mīna, Gorakṣa and Jālandhara. The ethos of Buddhist Tantra emerged in the Middle Ages in the guise of the Dharma Cult of Orissa, for instance, and in the poetic tradition of such mystics as Kabir, and later still Tagore. But when the lineal succession was broken at the end of the twelfth century, as a coherent discipline Buddhist Tantra died in India.

The genealogical tree on page 390–1, representing the siddhas' spiritual lineages, incorporates all the lineal data gleaned from *their* legends, from Vīra Prakāśa's *Nāmāvalī*[411] and from the principal Tibetan lineages. Rāhula Saṅkṛtyāyana's work forms the basis of all research into the siddhas' lineages, and his genealogical trees have been useful in preparing this version.[412] Concerning the deficiencies of this tree the dates in the margin are only indicators of the century in which the siddha lived. The exchange of precepts by contemporaries (e.g. Indrabhūti and Lakṣmīṅkarā) is not shown; where young Gurus taught older disciples, confusing the chronology, there are also omissions. "Kāṇha" embodies both Kāṇha Senior and Junior, whose lives encompassed the entire tenth century. An attempt has been made to gather the *nāth* Gurus in a unified constellation, but at the expense of chronological consistency; and Vyāli's position is most incongruous. The origins of the *Phag mo gzhung drug* lineage have been given twice, in the late ninth century and again in the early tenth. Virūpa's name appears thrice, Kukkuripa's five times, but Indrabhūti's only twice. Since in every relationship in the tree is concealed some academic disputation, the plain, uncomplicated lineages of the principal tantras are given below.

I	II	III	IV	V
SAṂVARA	HEVAJRA	SAMĀJA	VĀRĀHĪ	KĀLACAKRA
Saraha	Śākyamuni	Śākyamuni	(Kambala)	Kulika
Nāgārjuna	Indrabhūti	Indrabhūti	Lakṣmīṅkarā	Celuka
Śavari	Mahāpadmavajra	Nāga-yoginī	Virūpa	Piṇḍopa
Lūipa	Anaṅgavajra	Viśukalpa	Maitripa	Mañjukīrti
Dārikapa	Saroruha	Saraha	lDong ngar ba	Ye rang pa
Vajraghaṇṭā	Indrabhūti	Nāgārjuna	Paiṇḍapātika	
Kurmapa	Jālandhara	Nāgabodhi	Hamu dkar po	
Jālandhara	Kāṇha	Āryadeva		
Kāṇha	Bhadrapa	. . . .		
Guhyapa	Tilopa	Tilopa		
Vijaya	Nāropa	Nāropa		
Tilopa				
Nāropa				
Śāntipa				
Maitripa				
Pham thing				
Bodhibhadra				
Vāgīśvārakīrti				
Marpa				

I. This succession is that adopted by 'Phags pa[413] and identified in the *Blue Annals*[414] as Saraha's Saṃvara lineage of Mar mdo.

II. This Hevajra lineage was originally taken from Tāranātha, and modified by Prof. Snellgrove in the *Hevajra Tantra.*[415]

III. This Guhyasamāja lineage tells the story of the tantra's voyage from Oḍḍiyāṇa to the South and then north again to Nālandā. Tilopa must have received initiation in a vision.[416]

IV. This lineage of *Vārāhī's Six Topics* may omit links between Virūpa and Maitripa. Maitripa taught several Tibetan disciples.[417]

V. This is the short eleventh century lineage of Kālacakra.[418]

Notes To The Commentary

1. *Prajñā*, T.*shes rab*, lit. "superior cognition," perfect insight into the nature of all things as emptiness. *Prajñā* (pronounced "pragya" in India) is pre-eminently a cognitive function that actually militates against intellectualization in that it tends to keep consciousness moving amongst the five sensory organs, and particularly in light and sound, our principal senses.
2. T.*rigs kyi rtog pa.*
3. T.*mnyam nyid kyi ye shes.* See the Five modes of pure awareness in the Glossary of Numeral Terms.
4. *Ekarasa*, T.*ro gcig.* This term appears repeatedly in the songs and legends, and indeed in the entire Mahāmudrā tradition. This one taste does not destroy individual sensations, nor overwhelm shades and nuances of feeling; on the contrary it heightens them through the discriminating awareness of Amitābha. But it does replace the basic sense of dissatisfaction, unease, and "suffering," that accompanies every *dharma* in saṃsāra. *Ro gcig* is the third of the four levels of Mahāmudrā: one-pointedness (T.*rtse gcig*), indeterminacy (*spros bral*), one taste (*ro gcig*) and no-meditation (*sgom med*). Thus only the state of no-meditation, which is the fifth of the Buddha's five paths (*lam lnga*), exceeds the level of one taste.
5. "*Bu ston bka' 'bum,*" KS:401.
6. "*Sa skya grags pa rgyal mtshan gyi gsung 'bum,*" KS:210.
7. TARA IIA:4.
8. VP:35.
9. RS I:112.
10. Das Gupta 1969:384.
11. Rāhula Saṅkṛtyāyana, an explorer of Tibetan and Nepali libraries, from Patna, Bihar, active for the first half of this century, devoted himself to re-establishing Saraha as one of the most significant figures in Indian religious history and literature, as a great poet, yogin and siddha: RS II:intro.
12. BA:385,389.

13. T.*dran pa cig pa'i ting nge 'dzin; dran cig* is here synonymous with *rtse cig*, one-pointedness. *Dran pa* means attention to the nature of mind or the object that is inseparable from it, which for Līlapa was his ring.
14. See the Five constituents of the psycho-organism in the Glossary of Numeral Terms. In the Hevajra maṇḍala, a mother-tantra maṇḍala, it is the female principle of perfect insight that is differentiated iconographically to show the Heruka-yogin the aspects of awareness to be cultivated and the modes of awareness, the metamorphosis of the Ḍākinī, available to his skillful means.
15. TARA I:272ff.
16. RS III:218; TARA I:242ff.
17. RS I:120.
18. T.*nyams su myong ba rang gis rig*. "Existential" is used here and elsewhere to indicate the bare fact of existence; even in the meanest, nihilistic syndrome in meditation, or out of it, there is an intrinsic awareness of clear light in the bare fact of being, which is the lowest common denominator of all experience. Insofar as the path of Mahāmudrā (and of Dzokchen) is concerned with this constant nature of existence, and the initiates who follow that path preoccupied in the fundamental, imperative endeavor to remain aware of the bare fact of being and its potential (T.*rig pa*), Mahāmudrā could be termed Buddhist Existentialism.
19. *Vikalpa,* T.*rnam rtog*. "Thought-forms" or "discursive thought" fail to communicate the significance of the Tibetan word *rnam rtog* (pronounced namtok), which is the meditator's bane and describes any form of thought intruding into the mind during meditation. Preconceptions affirming the context of thought-forms (*mtshan ma*) make namtok impenetrable.
20. *Saṃsāra*, T.*'khor ba*.
21. T.*spros bral*: that which cannot be defined by any logical proposition, particularly the eight extremes (T.*mtha' brgyad*) of Buddhist logic; that which cannot be elaborated upon by any faculty of the conditioned mind. "Indeterminacy" is the second level of Mahāmudrā attainment (see n. 4).
22. T.*sems nyid*, synonymous with *dharmatā*, (T.*chos nyid), tathatā* (*de bzhin nyid*), and *śūnyatā* (*stong pa nyid*). Insofar as form is inseparable from emptiness, the nature of the mind is inseparable from its content.
23. TARA I:266.
24. Sircar 1973:97.
25. Sircar 1973:83.
26. Sircar 1973:15–16.

27. *Pīṭhasṭhāna*, T.*gnas chen*; see *53*.
28. Hindi *ṭhag*, "deceiver" from Sanskrit *sṭhaga*, a "cheat" (see Thaganapa, *19*). The proper designation for these devoted thieves and murderers was *phānsīgar*, from *phānsi*, "a noose," the institution was suppressed in its old form by Capt. Sir W. Sleeman during the presidency of Lord William Bentinck in the Raj of the 1830s. See Yule and Burnell 1979:915.
29. TARA I:214ff.
30. TARA IIA:15-17.
31. TARA I:215.
32. "*'Jam mgon mkhyen brtse'i slob khrid yig*," KS:324ff.
33. BA:390.
34. RS III:218.
35. Ibid.
36. T.*lam 'bras*, pronounced lam-dré. The path of *lam 'bras* begins with the practice of the *Separation from the Four Attachments* (*Zhen pa bzhi bral*), the Sakya school's *sngon 'gro*.
37. But Tāranātha characterized the Ḍombi as "an outcaste living outside the city limits, killing fish, birds and deer and eating them." TARA IIA:20.
38. T.*phyag rgya*. *Mudrā* is a twilight term (*sandhyābhāṣa*) for "consort."
39. T.*gzhan lus*. Babhahi (*39*) used "another body" (*gzhan lus*) and Nalinapa used his own body (*rang lus*) to induce the four joys.
40. Douglas and White 1959:12.
41. *Gośirṣacandana*.
42. *TARA II*, KS:416; TARA IIA:19-22.
43. Rāḍha, or Rāra, consisted of present day eastern West Bengal. TARA IIA:109 n.84.
44. *TARA II*, KS:416; TARA IIA:21-22.
45. VP:35.
46. Only the Peking Tenjur gives Virūpa.
47. RS III:218.
48. BA:243.
49. T.*las kyi rnam smin, byed po rgyu mthun, dbang gi 'bras bu, skyes bu byed po'i 'bras bu*. For further elucidation, and other forms of *karma*, see Guenther 1959:75, 84ff.
50. T.*rnam mi rtog snying rje chen po*.
51. T.*Thugs rje chen po*, pronounced Tujechembo.
52. T.*sems nyid ngal gso*. SD:22.
53. Lorenzen 1972:16; and also Sircar 1973:20.
54. See Mojumder 1967:16 for alternative rendering.
55. In Tāranātha's description of this lineage, Nāgārjuna discovered

Śavaripa when the latter was asked to dance before the master with his two brothers, sons of a dancing master. After initiation and meditation practice he was sent from Baṅgala to Śrī Parvata in the South merely *to act* as a hunter, a Śabara, "for the sake of all beings." "Now as he had combined the hunting of wild beasts with his consecrated practices he was able to get high realization as a result of these unsuitable means." TARA IIA:8.

56. The *King Dohā* or *Royal Dohā* (Guenther 1968:13ff) and the *People Dohā* (Conze 1959:175ff.).
57. T.*mtshan ma rnam rtog*. Saraha's Ḍākinī Guru uses the same phrase as did Lūipa and Virūpa's Ḍākinīs (see p. 34 and 44). "Dualistic concepts and preconceptions" indicate a function of the mind that projects labels, and concrete ideas, upon sensory phenomena reducing them from a flow of illusory forms to substantial discrete entities alienated by the self/other, subject/object dichotomy. See n.19.
58. RS II:1-12.
59. BA:841.
60. RS III:219.
61. *Līla*, T.*rol pa*; also "playfulness," "enjoyment;" T.*rig pa* seen from the "outside."
62. *Jñāna-ḍākinī*, T.*ye shes mkha' 'gro*: she is "the sky," emptiness, but she is known as spontaneously arisen, "self manifest" (T.*rang snang*), pure awareness (*jñāna*, T.*ye shes*). She embodies the tantric mystery of non-dual gnostic awareness. From another perspective, objectively she is the dance of illusory phenomena, and subjectively she is gnostic experience of, for example, empty space and light, empty space and sound.
63. T.*bdag med thig le*.
64. *Bindu*, T.*thig le*.
65. T.*mi gshigs thig le nyag gcig*, a Dzokchen term.
66. T.*klong*. *kLong* is defined as the center of a maṇḍala, and in the same way that the center of a maṇḍala contains the entire circle and encompasses it, because in experience a point has no dimension, a point-instant of awareness is the all-pervading space of the *dharmadhātu* (*dbyings*).
67. *Dhatura*, T.*lang tang*.
68. Lorenzen 1972:10.
69. Das Gupta 1968:382ff.
70. See Locke 1980:423ff. and Das 1981:23ff.
71. TARA IIA:78.
72. Locke 1980:282ff.
73. Any preparatory sādhana is called *sngon 'gro* in Tibetan.
74. The Sempa Dorje edition, p.42.

75. The *nāths* and *kāpālikas* are treated in detail in Briggs (1973) and Lorenzen (1972).
76. RS III:218.
77. TARA I:320.
78. *Ekarasa*: T.*ro gcig*. See n. 4.
79. *Kumbhaka*, T.*rlung bum pa can*. The term *kumbhaka* is understood as "breath control" in Hindu Tantra; in Tibet *rlung bum pa can* refers to the technique wherein breath is inhaled and held for extraordinary periods of time in the lower lungs, which has the effect of bloating the belly. Thus the so-called *sgom chen* or "great meditator" who practices this technique may be recognized by his vast stomach. One such traditional style *sgom chen* lives in a hermitage high above the Dudh Kosi River below Namche Bazaar in Solu Khumbu, Nepal.
80. Tilopa's instruction to Nāropa on Apparitional Body (T.*sgyu lus*) is found in Guenther 1963:61ff.
81. T.*rig pa ye shes*=*ye shes kyi rig pa*, lit. "the knowledge of pure awareness," or "ultimate cognitive knowledge." Ultimate cognition or pure awareness (*ye shes*), is inseparable from its form, the knowledge that is its content (*rig pa*). But this form is unchanging and indestructible; it is the space of the *dharmadhātu*.
82. T.*bden tshig*. "Word" is used in the same sense in the Gospels: "the Word was made flesh;" and "in the beginning was the Word."
83. *Anāhata śabda*, T.*sgra skye med*. In Hindu Tantra *śabda* is sound as a universal, as opposed to *nāḍa* which is the sound created by the vocal chords. No distinction is made in Tibetan, where *sgra* denotes both meanings. As Śabdabrahmā, sound is elevated to the position of Ultimate Consciousness, the "Serpent Power," out of which matter and Śiva and Śakti emerge. Vīṇāpa's sādhana is an analogue for an entire metaphysical substructure.
84. T.*rgyud ma smin pa smin pa'i byed pa'i dbang bskur*.
85. VP:36.
86. TARA IIA:30.
87. SD:47.
88. T.*rnam par mi rtog pa*.
89. *Brahmarandhra*, T.*spyi bo tshangs pa*.
90. *Pañcavidhyā*, T.*rig lnga*. In the non-technical sense *vidhyā*, T.*rig*, is also translated as knowledge, but in the mundane sense of the word.
91. Mudiyanse 1967:1-22. The Siṅghala Chronicles are the *Mahāvaṃṣa* and the *Culavaṃṣa*.
92. There is doubt as to which gate he guarded; Nadou (1980:159-160) gives the options.
93. TARA I:313.

94. TARA I:300.
95. BA:842.
96. T.*rig pa*. In the substantival aspect of its meaning, *rig pa* is "knowledge;" in its verbal aspect it is "all-embracing awareness." See also n.80.
97. T.*gsal stong* = *gsal ba dang stong ba*, lit. "radiance and emptiness." This "radiance" or "luminosity" is composed of *bindus* (T.*thig le*), which are conceived as tiny balls of light like those that float in the field of vision after rubbing the eyes.
98. TARA I:249-251.
99. Das Gupta 1969:202-3.
100. *Vikalpa, vitarka*, T.*rnam rtog*; see nn.19, 57.
101. *Lakṣaṇa*, T.*mtshan ma*; see n.57.
102. *Kleśa*, T.*nyon mongs*.
103. *Avidhyā*, T.*ma rig pa* is an absence of *rig pa* (see n.96) wherein the dualizing functions of mind create the delusions of saṃsāra.
104. T.*shes bya thogs med kyi shes rab*.
105. SD:64.
106. Walleser 1979:23ff.
107. Ibid.
108. Bu ston:122-130.
109. TARA IIA:4-8.
110. Lozang Jamspal 1978.
111. TARA I:120-2.
112. *Gorakṣa-siddhanta-saṃgrāha*, cited in Lorenzen 1972:32ff.
113. Wayman 1977:90ff.
114. Nadou 1980:10.
115. Tucci 1949:214.
116. Sircar 1973:96.
117. TARA IIA:44.
118. *Paramārtha-satya*, T.*don dam bden pa*.
119. *Ekarasa*, T.*ro gcig*. See n.4.
120. *Samatā*, T.*mnyam nyid*. The semantic problems of describing the ineffable are shown by the synonymity of the terminology. The sameness of phenomena is emptiness and knowledge, besides the one taste, suchness and reality (*dharmatā*). It is this sameness that provides the metaphysical rationale for the vulgar dictum "All is One."
121. T.*ma bcos sems*. *Ma bcos* means "unfabricated" and "unelaborated" (*spros med*), and it also means "uncontrived" and hence "without guile" and "innocent." This is the innocence of the saint or siddha who is incapable of discriminating between right and wrong because his mind remains perfectly aware of the sensory perception and does not "elaborate" (*spros*) on a perception with a judgmental

moralistic mind; this is the meaning of "thoughtless samādhi" (*mi rtog pa'i ting nge 'dzin*) and "remaining in the original state of being." Such a state of mind is totally unobstructed and completely fearless, precluding the possibility of rejecting, ignoring or grasping any experience, responding to every situation "for the sake of all beings."

122. Mojumder 1976:44.
123. This definition of *sahaja* (T.*lhan gcig skyes pa*) refers specifically to emptiness as the reality that arises simultaneously with perception of a sensory stimulus; different schools would fill in that blank in different ways.
124. Briggs 1973:68.
125. Das Gupta 1969:392–4.
126. TARA I:268.
127. TARA IIA:44. Here Tāranātha lists Kāṇhapa's disciples.
128. TARA I:247.
129. T.*shing gi lha mo.* Tree spirits, water spirits, rock spirits, etc., are remnants of the animism that the indigenous adivasi tribes keep alive.
130. *Parada-rasāyana,* Tara I:128. For a more extensive description of this *yoga* see Das Gupta 1969:251–2.
131. TARA I:124ff.
132. Tucci 1930:141.
133. RS III:218.
134. T.*rna bar chu zhugs pa 'byin pa.*
135. BA:373.
136. BA:847.
137. TARA I:290.
138. Guenther 1963:50.
139. T.*pho nya.* "courier" or "swift messenger" is the principal meaning of this term, but *pho nya mo,* "female messenger," also means "mistress" or "spiritual friend" (T.*grogs mo* or *phyag rgya*).
140. T.*mtshan ma rnam rtog.* See nn. 19, 57, and pp. 101–2.
141. T.*zag med bde ba.* See Guenther 1963:76ff.
142. T.*ro mnyam drug.* "Experiencing these six forms simultaneously makes us lose our preoccupation with this life and be mindful of death; it makes us think of the suffering of the six kinds of sentient beings, and it makes us renounce the hustle and bustle of this world and gives us mental-spiritual rest . . ." See Guenther 1963:47ff.
143. BA:730–1.
144. Roerich 1959:85.
145. Nadou 1980:152.
146. The Tibetan translation of *Nāropa* is rTsa bshad pa, explained as a

combination of the false etymology of Nāro, *nga ro*, "lion's roar," and the meaning of *nāḍa*, "primal sound:" thus The Roarer, or The Belly Laugher. *Naḍa* also means "reed," "pipe" or "stem," and the reed is a Mahāmudrā image of the Buddha insofar as he is totally responsive to the slightest vibration, and is empty of all preconceptions and critical thought. See Robinson 1979:270.

147. T.*'jigs pas 'jigs spangs pa*. This is a paradigm of the homeopathic method.

148. *Ajāṭa*, T.*skye med*. Since phenomena never come into existence and never cease to exist, because there is no beginning, middle or end to any *dharma*, there is only "pure potential" and all *dharma*s and all sentient beings are "unborn." Semantics force this absurdity; the paradox "born yet unborn" has the same meaning. For the siddha living in the moment, "continuity," the tantra of emptiness, is the only reality; if birth is admitted, death is inevitable, so the notion of *ajāṭa* is born.

149. Guenther 1963:36-7.

150. Nadou 1980:152.

151. *Upāya*, T.*thabs*. "Skillful means" has two distinct levels of meaning: the first refers to the path and the second to the goal. On the path *upāya* is what the aspirant conscientiously practices as his sādhana, the skillful devices that lead to *siddhi* and which become the content of his being as the male co-ordinate of the basic duality of form and awareness; after purification and awakening, whatever arises spontaneously for the benefit of all sentient beings is the skillful means of emptying saṃsāra, the goal.

152. *Prajñā*, T.*shes rab*.

153. T.*mtshan ma rnam rtog*.

154. *Vāsanā*, T.*bag chags*. The complete definition of *bag chags* is Herbert Guenther's "experientially initiated potentialities of experience." These seeds of *dharma*s may be conceived as negative moulds into which patterns of experience will fall; they exist in the ground of being, the seed-bed (*ālaya*, T.*kunbzhi*). The eighth of the eight modes of consciousness is a dim awareness of these negative imprints in this strata of consciousness. Action (*karma*, T.*las*) of body, speech and mind casts the moulds of *bag chags*, although the most intractably ingrained proclivities are those racially and genetically cast "in previous lives." See kLong chen pa, *Yid bzhin rin po che mdzod*, Chapter 1.

155. See Glossary of Numeral Terms.

156. *Ālaya*, T. *kun bzhi*. The *ālaya* is emptiness only after it has been purified by eradication of the propensities that create the dualistic world of saṃsāra and which create the neurotic syndromes that con-

sist of thought forms (*rnam rtog*) and emotions (*kleśa*, T.*nyon mongs*). The entire eight forms of consciousness are then transformed into pure awareness (*jñāna, T.ye shes*). See kLong chen pa, *ibid.*

157. Tāranātha identifies this Bhadrapa as the Guhyapa who slew Kāṇhapa's *dākinī* murderess (TARA IIA:44).
158. BA:803, 745ff.
159. VP:39; RS I:121.
160. TARA I:326.
161. T.*kun rdzob bskyed rim* and *don dam rdzogs rim.*
162. T.*rnam rtog.*
163. T.*rtog pa lam khyer gyi gdams ngag.*
164. T.*stong gsum.* As corollaries of the Hindu's and Buddhist's respective macrocosmic and microcosmic preoccupations, Hindu Tantra dwells more on the universes without, upon the image of our universe as contained in a single speck of dust on the back of an ant living in a universe parallel to this, and upon enormous cycles of time in which human history is a fraction of a second in the mind of a deity, while Buddhist Tantra is concerned with the universes within and the analysis of *dharmas* spanning fractions of seconds.
165. T.*steng sgo.* The lower door is the anus. "The upper door" is also the name of six path of liberation (*sgrol lam*) practices entered into through the mystic initiation (*gsang dbang*) of non-duality.
166. *anāhata-śibda,* T.*skye med.* See p. 92.
167. RS I:122; but also see VP:39.
168. Nadou 1980:152-3 based on BA:757-8.
169. BA:757-8; a *piṇḍa* is a rice ball inserted into the mouth of a corpse on the funeral pyre.
170. "*Bu ston gsung 'bum,*" KS:812ff.
171. *Cintamaṇi,* T.*yid bzhin nor bu,* synonymous with *bden tshig.*
172. BA:360.
173. BA:753.
174. BA:590.
175. KS:253ff.
176. *Bali,* T.*gtor ma*; in Tibet these cakes are made of barley flour, butter and symbolic ingredients.
177. "*sNar thang bstan 'gyur,*" KS:812ff.
178. RS I:122. But Saṅkṛtyāyana and others sometimes interpret corrupt forms of Oḍḍiyāṇa as corrupt forms of Oḍi, Oḍiya or Oḍiviśa. Oḍi was the name of the northern part of Orissa with its capital near the great *vihāra* of Ratnagiri. TARA IIA:33 gives Oḍḍiyāṇa as Kambala's birthplace but admits the possibility of Oḍiviśa
179. TARA I:244-5; and also *DC,* KS:255.

180. *DC*, KS:254.
181. *DC*, KS:253.
182. BA:362 citing *Śrīsahajasiddhipaddhati.*
183. T.*rdo rje rig pa.* The nature of the knowledge that *rig pa* denotes is clarified here by the adjectival *vajra* that implies immutability and indestructibility. This knowledge is awareness of sameness (*samatā*, T.*mnyam nyid*), of unitary relative and absolute, non-referential knowledge that persists whatever, and in spite of, the sensory stimulus.
184. *Dhātu*, T.*dbyings* and *jñāna*, T.*ye shes.*
185. "*Bu ston bka' 'bum,*" KS:401ff. TARA IIA:9 has Lūipa lying on the throne awaiting the king with the appearance of "a bluish man with shaggy locks, looking as though he had been carried there by the wind."
186. "*Sa skya grags pa rgyal mtshan gsung 'bum,*" KS:210ff.
187. *Arhat*, T.*dgra bcom pa*, "Destroyer of Enemies," "The Victor."
188. Guenther 1971:25ff.
189. T.*lung ma bstan*, lit. "not showing afflation," or incapable of divine revelation, lacking inspiration. It denotes a state of pleasant lethargy in which neither happiness nor sadness register and which is easily mistaken for equanimity. Its positive form, afflation (*vyākaraṇa*, T. *lung bstan*), most commonly implies "prophecy" or "prediction."
190. Das Gupta 1969:203; the Java list.
191. Das Gupta 1960:393–4.
192. T.*sems nyid ngo sprod pa.*
193. TARA I:242.
194. T.*byar med.* Insofar as no action has any greater significance than any other when it is non-action, as non-action ritual may be performed and its temporal aims attained; indeed it is only as non-action that ritual is effective. Ritual is futile when it is performed by a *sādhaka* in saṃsāra merely going through the motions, unable to evoke the meaning of the words. Thus "Buddhahood cannot be learned," and it cannot be found by seeking.
195. Nalanda/Trungpa 1982:16–25.
196. TARA I:242. But in TARA IIA:69 Indrabhūti the Middle One (the disciple of Kambala) identified as Kukkurāja, teaches a thousand dogs; he also taught Padmasambhava.
197. BA:400. TARA IIA:67 has a lineage: Kukkuripa, Padmavajra, Tillipa, Nāropa, Śāntipa. This *ācārya* was born in Bengal and became a *paṇḍita* of Nālandā.
198. *Manas*, T.*sems.* The concept of mind-stuff was conceived by the pre-tantric schools of Buddhism and used widely by schools such as the Vaibhāśikas, who saw mind as an existent substance.

199. T.*sdug bsngal lam khyer.*
200. T.*ngo bos stong pa,* lit. "through (its) essential nature, empty." Use of the instrumental case in this phrase introduces the notion that since a *dharma* is essentially empty its manifestation cannot but be empty.
201. T.*dmigs med phyag rgya chen po.* When the ultimate goal is reached there remains no aim to be pursued, and all action of body, speech and mind is spontaneous response for the sake of all beings at once.
202. TARA I:69 n.7, 87.
203. VP:40.
204. Das Gupta 1969:203; The Varṇaratnākara list.
205. T.*'gal ba lam khyer*: "to transform difficulties into the path," to thread all *dharmas*, even though they consist of a series of obstacles and disasters, as beads on the thread of tantric continuity, or immutable knowledge (*rdo rje rig pa*).
206. T.*gnas lugs dngos med. gNas lugs,* lit. "mode or form of being" is a synonym of *sems nyid* or *chos nyid* in Mahāmudrā. *dNgos med* means "insubstantial," "unconditioned" or "unreal." Thus *gnas lugs dngos med* indicates that there is no eternal essence and that the essential nature of being is nothing but the illusory, dynamic form of emptiness that is the dance of the Ḍākinī.
207. VP:40.
208. RS:112.
209. T.*gzhan lus* and *rang lus.* See n.39.
210. The four movements of energy are T. *'babs pa, bskyil ba, bzlog pa* and *'grems pa*. Guenther 1963:79.
211. T.*bde stong zung 'jug.* Guenther 1963:76-80.
212. T.*zag med bde ba. Zag med* literally means "without outflow," or total retention. Like merit (T.*bsod rnams*), happiness (*bde ba*) is conceived as something that can be either expended or retained. "Eternal delight," however, has as its source the yogin's constant identification with pure awareness.
213. T.*rang lus thabs ldan la gdams pa.*
214. SD:142 n.7.
215. TARA I.215-220; Bu ston:162.
216. TARA I:197; Chattopadhyaya 1981:82.
217. Das Gupta 1969:42-3.
218. Das Gupta 1969:109.
219. Das Gupta 1969:37-8.
220. Das Gupta 1969:109.
221. Mudiyanse 1967:65.
222. RS II:21.

223. T.*zab dang rgya*. These two are aspects of unitary awareness rather than the male and female principles that unite to create that awareness.
224. *TARA II*, KS:117; TARA IIA:24-5.
225. "*bKa' gdams glegs bam las jo bo rnam thar*," KS:118.
226. bDud 'joms gling pa, *gNam lcag pu ti*: "*Chos 'byung*," p. 2.
227. Dargyay 1977:38-43.
228. In TARA IIA:25 Śrīsukha or Sahajasiddhi is inserted into this lineage between Indrabhūti and Mahāpadmavajra.
229. Tucci 1949:642 citing the Fifth Dalai Lama's Chronicles; "*Padma gar dbang rtogs rjod*," KS:157.
230. It is interesting to note that in TARA IIA:28 Indrabhūti, the Middle One, of Oḍḍiyāṇa, burns the Ācārya Saroruha with his outcaste consort with the same result as in the story of Ḍombi Heruka and consort's burning and Padmasambhava and Mandāravā's burning.
231. "*bLon po bka' thang*," KS:524-5; and Longchenpa cited in KS:255.
232. TARA I:244-5; *DC*, KS:255.
233. Tāranātha (TARA IIA:29) only distinguishes between an early and a later Indrabhūti, the later being Saroruha's disciple in the Saṃvara lineage.
234. *DC*, KS:253; Dargyay 1977:39-40 for points of style.
235. RS I:125.
236. BA:842-3.
237. T.*ye shes rig pa*. See n.81.
238. VP:42.
239. *Brahmarandhra*, T.*tshangs pa'i bu ga*.
240. *dPag bsam ljon bzang* cited in Das Gupta 1969:391ff; and TARA IIA:36. Tāranātha's extensive narrative of Jālandhara's exploits shows a clear example of material derived from oral sources, probably a *nāth* yogin. He speaks of Jālandhara's "four incarnations" (p.43), and notes that, regarding Hāḍipa, Jālandharipa "adopted the likeness of a street sweeper from Satigrama in Bengal" (p. 00).
241. Nadou 1980:2.
242. Sircar 1973:14; Yule and Burnell 1979:464.
243. Sircar 1973:12, 14.
244. Das Gupta 1969:368, 206-7.
245. Das Gupta 1969:216.
246. Das Gupta 1969:379-380.
247. Das Gupta 1969:377-8.
248. BA:385; see also HT:13.
249. BA:734.
250. T.*zla ba'i thig le* and *thig le*.

251. *Jñāna-vāyu,* T.*ye shes kyi rlung*, the creative potential of pure awareness, is inherent in karmic energy (*karma-vāyu,* T.*las kyi rlung*).
252. See the Four devils in the Glossary of Numeral Terms. The first pair are *rnam rtog bdud* and the second pair *mi ma yin bdud*.
253. Conze 1959:168.
254. TARA I:105.
255. BA:371; TARA I:280.
256. TARA I:126.
257. *Bodhicitta*, T.*byang chub sems.*
258. T.*rtog pa ye shes su slong ba.*
259. T.*tshogs drug rnam shes.* The basic meditation taught by the Buddha Gautama to concentrate awareness upon consciousness of the sensory stimulus in the sense organ is *vipaśyanā* meditation.
260. RS I:123.
261. RS III:218; VP:42; *TARA II*, KS:420.
262. *Cittamatra*, T.*sems tsam pa; "vijñānavāda"* and *"yogācāra"* describe the same school.
263. T.*rig pa.*
264. T.*rdzas nyid*, synonymous with *chos nyid, sems nyid*, etc.
265. *Dharmatā* T.*chos nyid.* Since both delusive and pure sensory perception are conceived as illusory, reality in tantric parlance must refer to the unconditioned nature of being, which is emptiness, *śūnyatā*, synonymous with *dharmatā*.
266. VP:42; RS I:123; RS III:218.
267. T.*lta spyod zung 'jug.* The transformative element in this paradoxical precept is the implied meditation (*sgom pa*); Paṅkajapa is required to meditate upon the imponderable actuation of the sign-less, desire-less and ego-free, non-action.
268. "*Bu ston bka' 'bum,*" KS:383ff; see also TARA IIA:31-2.
269. BA:803.
270. HT:13.
271. *Vajrapādasaraṃgraha xvii, f111b.*
272. *Pīṭhasṭhāna*, T.*gnas chen.*
273. From Kazi Dawa-Samdup 1919 and 'Jigs med gling pa, *kLong chen snying thig mTsho rgyal sgrub thabs.*
274. Sircar 1973:14, 94.
275. Sircar 1973:8ff., 85.
276. Dowman 1981:266-9.
277. Sircar 1973:14.
278. Briggs 1973:103.
279. HT:70, vii v.12-18.
280. Sircar 1973:11.
281. TARA I:290; VP:43.

282. T.*mi rtog pa ngang gi. Ngang*, often synonymous with *dbyings*, can be rendered as "space" rather than "state."
283. SD:185. *Agambhira*, T.*mi zab pa*. The same phrase was used to describe Jālandhara's meditation technique (p. 245).
284. BA:756-7, 762-3; "*Bu ston gsung 'bum*," KS:788ff. for Tsi lu pa, and 811-2 for Mahākālacakrapāda.
285. BA:754.
286. BA:755.
287. T.*kun khyab chos nyid ngo bo.*
288. T.*spyod lam rnam bzhi*: sitting, walking, eating, excreting.
289. T.*rig pa brtul zhugs kyi spyod pa*. The term *brtul zhugs* is used to describe both penitential activity and the paradoxical, apparently crazy skillful means of the yogin with *mahāmudrā-siddhi.*
290. VP:42; RS I:124.
291. RS I:112; RS III:218.
292. TARA IIA:19.
293. Aśvaghoṣa, *Buddhacarita* III, v.60-62 in Conze 1959:39-40.
294. T.*bags kyis* = *bag yod kyis bags. Bag* denotes attentiveness and carefulness with a strong connotation of the contentment and happiness that accompanies concentrated attention to the mind.
295. Hindi *pagala-baba*, T.*smyon pa*. Both the *pagala-baba* and the *smyon pa* are revered and tended by lay devotees in their respective societies.
296. T.*snang stong zung 'jug.*
297. TARA IIA:43.
298. T.*lhan gcig skyes pa'i ye shes.*
299. *Mahāsukha*, T.*bde ba chen po*. Both the Sanskrit *sukha* and the Tibetan *bde ba* serve to describe the feeling-tone of happiness both in mundane existence and meditation. The supreme happiness of Mahāmudrā is simply the superlative form of these words, and the adjective *maha* (*chen po*) indicates the non-referential nature of the experience rather than any qualitative difference in the feeling-tone. "Bliss" and "ecstasy" are words to describe the heightened emotions of trance states rather than the siddhas' pleasure in "ordinary sensual perception" in Sukhāvatī.
300. T.*gnas lugs rang gsal.* See also n.206.
301. Nadou 1980:223, 235-6; BA:219, 284.
302. Mojumder 1976:87.
303. *Buddhanam sarnam gachami*, T.*sangs rgyas la skyabs su mchi'o*, pronounced "sangye la kyap su chiao."
304. The *Sa skya bka' 'bum* list. See also RS I:124.
305. Percy Byshe Shelley, *Lines to an Indian Air* cited in Yule and Burnell 1979:218.
306. T.*thabs dang shes rab zung 'jug gi gdams pa.*

307. T.*phyogs cha bral ba.*
308. *Bindu,* T.*thig le.*
309. T.*sems nyid.*
310. T.*mtshan ma.*
311. T.*rang gsal snang ba.*
312. TARA IIA:45.
313. T.*rnam rtog ngo sprod pa.* The verb *ngo sprod pa* means "to lay bare," "to reveal the nature," and thus "to recognize the nature of." Kumbharipa's object of meditation was thought, and his attainment was realization of the nature of mind.
314. Tucci 1930:137.
315. T.*mKha' spyod dngos grub.*
316. Briggs 1973:298, 338.
317. TARA IIA:78–9. Tāranātha has Campa Carpaṭi as the place where the King of Campa donated two rock temples to the Guru. Vyālipa, who attained the *siddhi* of immortality through alchemy, was both Guru and disciple of Carpaṭi (see p. 382), and Carpaṭi's principal disciple was the siddha Kakkuṭipa, Lūipa's Guru.
318. T.*rang byung rdo rje'i skur song.*
319. VP:44; RS I:124.
320. Tāranātha's *bKa' babs bdun ldan* (TARA II and IIA).
321. Bhattacharyya B. 1924:452. Both the *Sādhanamālā* and the *Tantrasāra* are quoted in Bhattacharyya B. 1932:159–161. The author elaborates the case for a Buddhist origin of the Severed-headed tradition.
322. Slussor 1982:I,307, II pl.544.
323. T.*lta ba dang spyod pa la zung 'jug phag mo'i gdams pa.*
324. *Ātman,* T.*bdag po.*
325. T.*dran dang rig pa'i khab skud kyis/gos dag btsems pa snying rje'i khab.*
326. T.*dran rig. Dran pa* is the means and *rig pa* the end: through application of attention there is memory (*dran pa*) of the nature of mind, and coincident with this "memory" is the perception of phenomena as knowledge (*rig pa*); or, *dran rig* is the function of intuiting the *vajra*-nature of *dharmas* simply by detached attention to their nature.
327. *Satguru,* T.*bla ma dam pa,* the divine Guru as distinct from the human being who transmits mere information. The *satguru* is the incarnate Buddha in whom all tantric initiates go for refuge before the Three Jewels.
328. Ghouls (*veṭāla,* T.*ro langs*) are to be understood as corpses reanimated by the projected spirit of a master (or mistress) of that *siddhi*; but lesser spirits or demons can animate a corpse in the same way.

329. Lorenzen 1972:30.
330. "*Tāranātha'i sgrol ma'i rgyud kyi 'byung khung*," KS:795-6.
331. RS I:125.
332. Guenther 1971:98ff.
333. T.*rnam rtog* and *rtog pa*. *rTog pa* is the process by which subject and object are differentiated inseparable from the constructs that determine the shape of dualistic reality and the concepts that characterize it. *rNam rtog* are the flow of thought-forms that are the product of dualistic mental processes.
334. T.*rnam rtog lam khyer* and *rtog pa lam khyer*.
335. T.*rDo rje gdan bzhi'i rgyud*.
336. The seed (T.*thig le*) is the panacea (*sman*) of the energy center (*'khor lo*).
337. Sircar 1973:11; Kelsang Gyatso 1982:23ff.
338. Rāmanūja quoted in *Śrīharṣa* in Lorenzen 1972:2.
339. HT:64-5, lvi v.11.
340. Mojumder 1976:56, 44-6.
341. Das Gupta 1969:90.
342. T.*rtog pa rang grol*.
343. RS III:218.
344. *TARA II*, KS:236; TARA IIA:26; HT:13-14.
345. DAS 1908:131.
346. *TARA II*, KS:239; TARA IIA:26-9.
347. TARA I:242, 246; TARA IIA:25-6.
348. Wayman 1977:90-6; but TARA IIA:26 has Mahāpadmavajra, Anaṅgavajra's Guru, as the author of the *Guhyasiddhi*.
349. BA:362.
350. Tucci 1930:138.
351. Briggs 1973:69.
352. Das Gupta (1969) ch. IX and appendices B & C treats the cycle of *nāth* legends with sensitivity and insight.
353. *Preta*, T.*yi dwags, mi ma yin* (non-humans).
354. Lozang Jamspal 1978:48-50, v.91-96.
355. *Ābhira* (or *Gomi*), literally means a cattleman, an owner of a herd. The word was applied to various groups of people in Northern India and the Deccan. See Slussor 1982:27.
356. VP:45; RS I:125.
357. T.*mngon zhen*, lit. "manifest desire," hunger for sex, food, wealth.
358. T.*kun tu rtags pa*. The universal labeling function, naming parts of an undifferentiated whole, compartmentalizing and categorizing reality, is performed by the subjective "self," "the knower," for its own purposes, a primary aim being to protect itself in its alienation. Thus the nominal-conceptual function is the ego.
359. This analysis is derived from the *Kun bzang smon lam*, an epitome of

the chapter dealing with the involuntary attainment of Buddhahood in the *rDzogs chen kun bzang dgongs pa zang thal bstan brgyud*, a *gter ma* of rGod ldem can.

360. T.*gnas lugs*.
361. TARA I:127-8.
362. Dowman 1981: 223.
363. Warder 1970:388.
364. Nadou 1980:87.
365. See SD:121, 241.
366. "*Sa skya grags pa rgyal mtshan gsung 'bum*," KS:213.
367. "*Bu ston bka' 'bum*," KS:401ff; TARA IIA:9-10 follows Bu ston.
368. BA:761.
369. Bhattacharyya B. 1959:156-9.
370. Dowman 1981:267.
371. T.*mngon zhen lam khyer*; compare *rnam rtog lam khyer* n.334.
372. T.*rtog pa gang skyes cig car grol ba*.
373. KS:219.
374. BA:243.
375. T.*rig pa*. The "three roots," Guru, Deva and Ḍākinī, may be experienced at the fulfillment of the creative stage practices that bring them to realization in anthropomorphic vision, or as three aspects of knowledge (*rig pa*): Guru is all appearances, sound and thought, the Ḍākinī is the dance of empty awareness, and the Deva is the variety of skillful means.
376. *Śraddhā*, T.*dad pa*. *Vajra*-faith is the third of the three types of faith (T.*dad pa gsum*): pure faith, blind faith (*dang ba'i dad pa, bhakti*), trust and confidence in (*yid ches pa'i dad pa*), and unalterable faith, conviction, *vajra*-faith (*phyir mi ldog pa'i dad pa*).
377. The entire line reads: T.*ma zhen mi 'gegs de la ngang la gzhog*. SD:253.
378. RS:125.
379. *TARA II*, KS:234; TARA IIA:26.
380. Bhattacharyya B. 1924:xliii.
381. BA:390.
382. BA:758; 847.
383. BA:362.
384. BA:1044; also BA:1007-1018.
385. T.*zag med*.
386. RS:125.
387. *Āmlakī*, T.*skyu ru ra, amla* in Hindi, Emblica Officinalis; *heritakī*, T.*a ru ra*, Terminalia Chebulia, a spray of which the Medicine Buddha, Baisajyaguru, holds in his right hand; and T.*ba ru ra*, Terminalia Beleric; these form the threefold preparation *triphala*, T.*'bras mchog gsum*. Yule and Burnell 1979: 608-9.

388. T.*na tsho gnas, Lang tshod bstan byed, dPal ldan.*
389. T.*bdud rtsi sman.*
390. *Kirāta tikta,* T.*tikta,* Gentiana Chiretta; *chirāītā* is Hindi.
391. T.*gLing bar.*
392. Bu ston:122ff.
393. TARA IIA:75-6.
394. SD:261.
395. KS:633-770.
396. Reprinted in Robinson 1979:312-391.
397. See SD in Bibliography.
398. Das 1908:119, 131.
399. Bhattacharyya B. 1924.
400. Listed in *The Catalogue of the Library of the Oriental Institute in Prague.*
401. See VP in Bibliography.
402. Tucci 1930:138-155.
403. See Bu ston in Bibliography.
404. Included in Khetsun Sangpo's *Biographical Dictionary* (KS).
405. See BA in Bibliography.
406. The siddhas' legends are included in Khetsun Sangpo's *Biographical Dictionary.*
407. See TARA I and TARA II in Bibliography. TARA IIA indicates a new translation of the *bKa' 'babs bdun ldan* entitled *The Seven Instruction Lineages* done by David Templeman, published by the Library of Tibetan Works and Archives in Dharamsala during the final stages of preparation of this manuscript. Since this translation is easily accessible, besides bringing further information to light, I have given references to it in the notes besides my translations of, and references to, the Tibetan edition included in parts in Khetsun Sangpo's *Biographical Dictionary.*
408. Robinson 1979:265-283.
409. Dowman 1984:277.
410. RS III:216, 226.
411. Included in SD at pp.35-46 of the appendix.
412. RS I:112; RS II:21; RS III:28.
413. RS III:218.
414. BA:380-5.
415. HT:13.
416. BA:359-362.
417. BA:390-7.
418. BA:754-364.

Glossary of Sanskrit Terms

N.B. The Tibetan equivalent is given after the Sanskrit key-word where applicable. When a colon follows the Tibetan equivalent the literal translation renders both Sanskrit and Tibetan terms; a semicolon following the Tibetan word indicates that the literal translation applies to that word only.

Abbreviations: T. = Tibetan; lit. = literally; syn. = synonym; pron. = pronounced.

Anuttarayoga-tantra: *bla med rnal byor rgyud:* lit. "the matchless or superior *yoga-tantra;*" the fourth of the four classes of tantras (*q.v.*) to which the siddhas' tantras (such as *Saṃvara, Hevajra,* and *Guhyasamāja*) belong and of which Mahāmudrā is the apex. In the Nyingma tradition this class of tantra is divided into *mahā- anu-* and *ati-yoga.* This class is also divided into father, mother and non-dual tantra, the first emphasizing skillful means and the creative stage, the second perfect insight and the fulfillment stage and the third the equality and union of these two pairs.

Arhat: *dgra bcom pa:* lit. "the victorious one;" the *śrāvaka bhikṣu* practicing the hīnayāna Dharma of eradicating the sense of self and extinguishing every flicker of passion and discursive thought, attains the state of *arhat*, who at death achieves nirvāṇa, the extinction of life on the round of rebirth and freedom from transmigration.

Avadhūti: *rtsa dbu ma*; lit. "the central channel," "the medial nerve;" also *kun dar ma,* lit. "the all-pervasive mother." The *avadhūti* runs from the perineum up the spine to the fontanelle through the five *cakras* (*q.v.*) of the subtle body; the *lalanā* and *rasanā*, the right and left channels, running parallel to the *avadhūti,* join it below the navel center. Though represented in linear extension it is the all-pervasive *dharmakāya* (*q.v.*), the plenum of empty awareness; thus Mahāmudrā is achieved when all the karmic energy (T.*las lung*) of the body is injected into the *avadhūti.*

Bhikṣu, fem. bhikṣunī: *dge slong (ma):* the fully-ordained Buddhist monk or nun.

Bindu: *thig le:* lit. "point," "spot;" seed-essence; the energies of the subtle body are fundamentally composed of "relative" seed-essence, which can be described as zero-points, white and red, semen and menstrual blood; the field of sense-perception, which is indistinguishable sense-object, sense-organ and consciousness, is composed of "absolute" seed-essence as a field of "light-form," and this field is Mahāmudrā, unitary awareness. A single *bindu* is a point of emptiness analogous to the cosmic egg (T.*thig le chen po*).

Bodhicitta: *byang chub sems:* "the milk of human kindness;" in the *bodhisattvayāna bodhicitta* is an enlightened attitude, mind-stuff motivated in thought word and deed to seek the Buddha's realization, an attitude created by constant positive thinking, formulating the Bodhisattva Vow in every possible way. In *tantrayāna* the *bodhicitta*, composed of *bindus* (*q.v.*), is synonymous with the red and white energies of yoginī and yogin, *rasanā* and *lalanā* (*q.v.*), symbolized by blood and wine.

Bodhisattva: *byang chub sems dpa':* a being who has determined that life's purpose and pleasure is in coincident satisfaction of self and others through practice of the vow of selfless service. He strives on the path of the ten perfections (*q.v.*), and in Tantra on the path of method, renouncing his own nirvāṇa until all beings can accompany him off the wheel of life.

Bodhisattva Vow: *byang chub sems bskyed:* the vow to liberate all beings from saṃsāra by doing whatever is necessary for whosoever is in need; the arousal of *bodhicitta* (*q.v.*); the creation of an enlightened mind.

Buddha: *sangs rgyas:* the Buddha Śākyamuni, Gautama Buddha; an anthropomorphic representation of the ideal purified (*sangs*) and awakened (*rgyas*) state of being defined by the three modes of being (*q.v.*): absolute empty being; perfectly satisfying, instructive, visionary being; and ubiquitous, compassionate illusory being.

Cakra: *'khor lo:* lit. "wheel;" focal point of psychic energy, energy center; the five principal *cakras* on the *avadhūti* (*q.v.*) are at the head, throat, heart, gut and sexual centers, upon which the structure of energy flows of the entire body is focused. Each *cakra* is represented by a lotus with varying numbers of petals, by a seed syllable and a deity in his or her maṇḍala.

Caryāpapa: *spyod pa'i glu:* syn: *caryādgītī, vajragītī:* "sādhana-songs," didactic, afflated songs sung by the poet-siddhas about their practice and their realization, in the Apabhraṃṣa language, in the *dohā* metre.

Ḍāka: *dpa' bo:* as in India, where the Ḍākinī is a black witch, the Ḍāka, her male counterpart is a wizard, usually practicing mundane *śākta-tantra*; with the Ḍākinī as consort representing the process of enlightened perception, the Ḍāka is the sensory stimulus to the Ḍākinī's pure awareness; as the Ḍākinī's consort the Ḍāka is also the Guru.

Ḍākinī: *mkha' 'gro ma:* Sky-Dancer: where the triad Guru, Deva, Ḍākinī represents the three modes of Buddha's being, the Ḍākinī is the *nirmāṇakāya*, an illusory dance of awareness; in union with the Guru she is the perfect awareness of his compassionate skillful means; as a yidam deity representing the entire psyche as overt female awareness, carrying the trident-with-skulls (*katvāṅga*) to indicate that the Guru is contained within her, she is Vajra Vārāhī, one of the siddhas' favorite deities; incarnate as a mundane Ḍākinī she is guide and ally to the neophyte and a devoted assistant to the adept. There are innumerable forms of the Ḍākinī to represent every aspect and level of female energy. In Hindu India the ḍākinī, or *dāṅkinī*, is a witch, a dabbler in black magic, blood sacrifice and low level Tantra.

Ḍamaru: "monkey-drum," a double-sided drum made out of monkey or human skulls or wood, struck by small balls on cords attached to the central neck, used in practice of *gcod* to evoke spirits, and in other rites to summon deities.

Dharma: *chos:* in the triad of the Three Jewels, Buddha, Dharma and Saṅgha, the Dharma is the Buddha's teaching, his scripture, his word, his message, his vibration and his energy. A *dharma* is a specific teaching and an entity of existence, an instant of sensory experience. Vasubandhu's ten definitions: knowledge, the path, merit, scripture, certainty, nirvāṇa, a mental event, lifespan, becoming, a school of doctrine. Also: existence, reality, meaning, phenomena, and meditation practice.

Dharmacakra: *chos 'khor:* lit. "wheel of dharma;" the auspicious eight-spoked wheel of the teaching; but also synonymous with Dharma-center, or principal place of pilgrimage. It denotes several of the meanings of maṇḍala (*q.v.*).

Dharmadhātu: *chos dbyings:* the all-embracing, ubiquitous plenum of kinetic space that contains the environment, all phenomena, all life, the cosmos itself; the *dharma*-element, the sixth element, the field of *tathatā (q.v.).*

Dharmakāya: *chos sku:* lit. "*dharma*-body;" the absolute mode of a Buddha's being, defined as empty awareness, clear light, or space and knowledge.

Dohā: a metrical form used by the poet-siddhas to compose their songs of instruction and realization (*caryāpadas q.v.*). The word came to denote any of the siddhas' songs regardless of the metrical form.

Gaṇacakra: *tshogs 'khor:* the communion of initiates, the assembly of deities, the accumulation of offerings, at which the *samaya* (*q.v.*) with the Guru, Deva and Ḍākinī is restored by means of a eucharistic rite wherein the participants partake of consecrated offerings. The *gaṇacakra* rite is at the heart of the tantric mysteries.

Haṭhayoga: equivalent to Tibetan *rtsa-rlung*: psychosomatic *yoga*; a corpus of techniques of breathing, visualization and recitation and also body postures (*āsana*), controlling movement of energies within the subtle body. Developed to its highest degree by *nāth* yogins, in Buddhist Tantra it is practiced within the framework of the fulfillment stage; when the stress is on the physical aspect, it belongs to the *kriyātantra.*

Kaliyuga: *snyigs ma'i dus;* lit. "age of degeneracy;" the age of corruption and decay culminating in the final conflagration in which the universe is consumed at the end of a Great Age (*mahāyuga*). Concerning the four ages (*yugas*) comprising a Great Age, no Dharma is necessary in the *satyayuga*, the hīnayāna is taught in the *tretāyuga,* the *prajñāpāramitāyāna* in the *dvāparayuga*, and the vajrayāna in the *kaliyuga.*

Kāpālika: the *kāpālikas* were a left-handed (*vāmācāra*) *śaiva* sect who took their inspiration from the brahmin-slaying *kapālins* forced into drastic penitential asceticism to atone for their sin of killing a brahmin. Their sādhana was defined by their Great Vow (*mahāvrata*), and the token by which they were recognized was the skull used as a begging-bowl (*kapāla*) that gave them their name. They disappeared during the ascendancy of the Buddhist siddhas and it is possible that the *kāpālikas* reformed by Mīnanāth and Gorakṣa and others became the *nāth-sampradāya.*

Karma: *las, 'phrin las:* lit. "action:" karma is no divine, providential force like destiny; it is the direct, observable effect of one's actions: touching a live coal the karmic effects are that one is burnt and that one refrains from repeating the act. But there are types of karmic effect that can only be deduced indirectly, and the sum of karmic effects creates an unfathomable but ineluctable, highly complex pattern of response.

Lalanā: *ro ma;* lit. "the tongue;" the psychic channel on the right side of the *avadhūti* (*q.v.*), and starting at the back of the throat in the right nostril to join the *avadhūti* below the navel; white in color, the absolute aspect, the objective pole, "the sun," carrying creative and procreative energy purified into the skillful means of the Guru.

Madhyamika: *dbu ma'i lam:* lit. "the middle way;" the metaphysical school propagated by Nāgārjuna in the second century, taking emptiness (*śūnyatā*) as the first and last premise; the middle way of indeterminable (T.*spros bral*) reality (*chos nyid*).

Mahāmudrā: *phyag rgya chen po:* lit. "The Supreme or Magnificent Stance, Posture, Gesture;" The Great Seal, The Magnificent Symbol, the non-dual mystic path and goal at the apex of achievement of *anuttarayoga-tantra,* virtually synonymous with Buddhahood and identical to *rdzogs-chen* as the goal. Various didactic, Tibetan etymologies of *phyag rgya chen po* define the nature of this achievement: *phyag* = skillful means, compassion; *rgya* = emptiness, perfect insight; and *chen po* = their union as the ineffable knowledge (T.*rig pa*) and pure awareness (*ye shes*) of the three modes of Buddha's being. Or, *phyag* = the pure awareness of emptiness; *rgya* = release from mundane preoccupation; *chen po* = the union of pure awareness and liberation (*ye shes dang grol la zung 'jug*). See *mudrā.*

Mahāmudrā-siddhi: *phyag chen dngos grub:* syn. *parama-siddhi,* supreme power; Buddhahood; attainment of the three modes of being, the eight great *siddhis* and the six extrasensory perceptions (*q.v.*). See p. 5-6.

Mahāyāna: *theg pa chen po:* lit. "the great vehicle" in relation to the lesser vehicle (*hīnayāna*); its two divisions are *bodhisattvayāna* or *prajñāpāramitāyāna* and vajrayāna or tantrayāna; the principal elements that distinguish it from hīnayāna are the Bodhisattva Vow (*q.v.*), the importance of emptiness, the large pantheon of deities, and the Guru superceding the scripture as the principal source of dharma.

Maṇḍala: *dkyil 'khor*; lit. "center-circumference;" "a circle." A maṇḍala can be defined as a symmetrical *yantra* (q.v.), a two or three dimensional diagram of a meta-psychic reality to be used as an aid in meditation. More specifically: (a) an external, symbolical, ideal representation of the mind; (b) an internal, mind-created, vision of a symmetrical palace with deity and retinue; (c) the body-mind of the Guru or Ḍākinī, etc.; (d) the female sexual organ (*bhaga*); (e) an offering plate; (f) a globe, sphere or disc; (g) a "round-table" conference; (h) a society; (i) a geomantic power-place.

Mantra: *sngags:* in the triad mudrā, mantra and samādhi in the process of evoking a deity, firstly mantra purifies the *sādhaka's* "speech" and energy. Then the seed-mantra (*bīja-mantra*) simulates the deity's sonic essence, the root-mantra (*mūla-mantra*) evokes the specific qualities and attributes of the deity's feeling-tone, vibration and energy, and the *karma-mantra* performs the specific functions of the deity; when "speech" is purified the mantra is the deity's euphonic form—the mantra is the deity himself. When the *sādhaka* has identified himself with the deity through mantra, all his speech is mantra unerringly reflecting or actualizing reality. Thus the Guru's word has the power to transmit the meaning of the goal-path to the mind of the disciple, and it is this function that gives the term "secret mantra," *guhyamantra* (T.*gsang sngags*) its significance as a synonym of vajrayāna. Mantra is of such importance in tantric sādhana that vajrayāna is also known as *mantrayāna.*

Māyā: *sgyu ma:* the color and shape of emptiness moving in a constant stream of metamorphosing light; the dance of the Ḍākinī; the magical display of empty illusion.

Mudrā: *phyag rgya:* lit. "hand gesture;" stance or posture; in the triad mudrā, mantra and samādhi, mudrā signifies the gestures of the hands that represent certain moods, qualities and actions pertaining to the specific deity, and which reinforce the more important mantra and samādhi in the process of invoking the deity. *Mudrā*, syn. T.*gzungs ma*, is the female consort who assists the yogin in certain fulfillment stage meditation practices.

Nāḍī: *rtsa:* lit. "tendons, veins, nerves and psychic channels;" the pathways of psychic energy, psychic nerves; the *avadhūti, lalanā* and *rasanā*, and a constantly bifurcating system of channels that serves the entire psycho-organism, form the structure of energy flows within the subtle body. The structure visualized in fulfillment stage yogas differs from that employed in Tibetan medicine for moxibustion and acupuncture treatment; demonstrably effective, the techniques using this structure do not depend upon a parallel somatic structure.

Nāth(a): an initiate of the *nāth-sampradāya*, an ascetic, *śaiva* order of semi-monastic yogins whose principal sādhana involves *haṭhayoga* techniques similar to many fulfillment stage yogas. The Five Nāths who are the *adi-gurus* of the order, are the mahāsiddhas Mīnanāth, Gorakṣa (Gorakhnāth), Jālandharanāth, Kṛṣṇācārya and Cauraṅgināth.

Nirmāṇakāya: *sprul sku,* pron. tulku; the mode of a Buddha's being that is perceptible to the senses; the Buddha's illusory emanation body, his incarnate form, his body of variegated, rainbow color; the Buddha as all-embracing compassionate manifestation. "Only a tulku can recognize a tulku."

Nirvāṇa: *mya ngan las 'das pa;* lit. "passing beyond suffering;" the hīnayāna nirvāṇa is extinction of individual existence, an end to transmigration; the Bodhisattva's nirvāṇa is simultaneous release of all beings from saṃsāra; the *mahānirvāṇa* of Mahāmudrā is the pure pleasure of uniting skillfully directed compassion and perfect insight in a flow of pure awareness that releases all sentient beings. No matter how it is formulated, nirvāṇa is release from saṃsāra.

Prāṇa: *rlung:* lit. "breath;" psychic energy; psychic energy is extracted from breath, and breathing controls the movements of psychic energy in the channels of the subtle body; strictly, *prāṇa* is only one of the five "breaths" (*vāyus*) relating to the five *cakras*, the energy of the sexual *cakra* called "life force" (T.*srog rlung*) which may rise in the central channel as *kuṇḍalinī.* When awareness-energy (T.*ye shes kyi rlung*) flows out of the *avadhūti* into the *lalanā* and *rasanā,* it divides into two polarized streams of karmic energy (*las kyi rlung*), white and red, objective and subjective, creating the stress and structure of a dualistic universe, saṃsāra. To attain Mahāmudrā, *mahānirvāṇa,* the energies of *lalanā* and *rasanā* must be returned to the *avadhūti.*

Rasanā: *rkyang ma;* lit. "woman;" the psychic channel on the left side of the *avadhūti* and starting at the back of the throat at the left nostril joining the *avadhūti* below the navel; red in color, the relative aspect, the subjective pole, "the moon," carrying passionate energy and mental energy purified into the awareness of the Ḍākinī.

Rasāyana: *bcud len;* lit. "partaking of essences;" alchemy; tantric alchemy is practiced in conjunction with *haṭhayoga (q.v.)* to gain control of the energies of the body in order to attain the highest aim of Mahāmudrā; to inject all energy into the *avadhūti,* obtaining *mahāmudrā-siddhi* and also the secret of immortality, the philosopher's stone, rejuvenation, etc., or to attain the lower aims of sexual potency, health and wealth, etc.; *rasāyana* teaches use of herbs and minerals in healing through sympathetic magic, and also for fasting. The *nāth rasāyana* siddhas are renowned for their *kāya-kalpa,* a process of alchemical purification which in a period of months or years totally rejuvenates the body and induces longevity.

Sādhaka: *sgrub pa po:* a practitioner of sādhana.

Sādhana: *sgrubs thabs;* lit. "the means of accomplishment;" the psychological and meta-psychological techniques of tantric soteriology; sādhana is both a model of the tantric ideal formulated in a manual of instruction in mudrā, mantra and samādhi, visualization and recitation, comprising a ritual meditation, and also the life-praxis of the tantrika intent upon achieving Mahāmudrā or a lesser goal. See p. 5.

Sahaja: *lhan gcig skyes pa:* lit. "produced together," "co-emergence;" The Innate, "the inborn absolute." From the beginning the ultimate and the relative, the male and female principles, form and emptiness, have arisen simultaneously; the inborn absolute is inherent in every instant of sensory experience, and it merely remains for the *sādhaka* to recognize it. However, this is not so easy as the degenerate, latter-day Bengali *sahaja-yoga* school with its concepts of "natural enlightenment" and "no practice" would believe; such notions make mockery of the siddhas' sādhanas.

Samādhi: *ting nge 'dzin:* in the triad mudrā, mantra and samādhi, samādhi indicates the state of mind determined by the technique of invocation; the samādhi of Mahāmudrā is the state of relaxation free of dualistic mental functions in which spontaneous non-action may arise.

Samaya: *dam tshig;* lit. "true or sacred word or pledge;" the ultimate *samaya* is the pledge of commitment to the Guru, Deva or Ḍākinī to maintain the essential union of means and insight continuously, and it is also that union itself; the relative *samaya*s are General, Extraordinary and Superior *samaya*s.

Saṃbhogakāya: *longs spyod sku:* the mode of a Buddha's being that instructs by visionary indication, by vibration and by sound, while the feeling-tone is a constant sense of blissful contentment reinforced by a sense of unlimited potential for enjoyment; this is the realm where most of the tantric pantheon manifests, the realm of the enlightened collective unconscious and its archetypes, and where the qualities and attributes of the Buddha are discovered.

Saṃsāra: *'khor ba:* the wheel of existence, the cycle of transmigration, a cyclic continuity of states of being characterized by one of the six emotional and discursive media described as the six realms of saṃsāra (*q.v.*). In general saṃsāra is sentient existence suffering a loss of awareness (*avidhyā*) and of pleasure in the basic fact of being, due to attachment, aversion and sloth; specifically, the states of dissatisfaction comprising saṃsāra are subsumed under the six categories of being (T.*rigs drug*), each dominated by one of the six emotions (*q.v.*); saṃsāra is characterized as impermanent, unsatisfactory, desire-filled, and seemingly concrete; saṃsāra is the state from which we seek release, while nirvāṇa is that release; saṃsāra is a continuity of suffering including both the agonies of hell and the fleeting ecstacies of heaven, while nirvāṇa is a continuity of pure pleasure. See p. 7–8.

Saṅgha: *dge 'dun:* the community of ordained aspirants in the hīnayāna; the community of human and divine Bodhisattvas in the mahāyāna; the communion of initiates in the vajrayāna; and all sentient beings in Mahāmudrā.

Siddha: *grub thob; grub pa:* an adept who has attained success in his practice, gaining magical power or *mahāmudrā-siddhi.* See p. 4-5.

Siddhi: *dngos grub:* lit. "concrete achievement;" ordinary and supreme, magical power to achieve mundane goals and to employ the eight great *siddhis* (*q.v.*), and *mahāmudrā-siddhi* (*q.v.*) and attainment of the Ḍākinī's paradise. See p. 4-7.

Siddhācārya: a master, adept, teacher, skilled in the techniques of Mahāmudrā meditation; an adept in *sahajayāna.*

Sūtra: *mdo:* lit. "aphorism;" the scriptures of Śākyamuni, both mahāyāna and hīnayāna, but excluding the *agamas* and the tantras which are revealed or traditional scripture. In Tibet, where there was doubt in the case of Nyingma texts, ascription was determined by content.

Tantra: *rgyud:* lit. "thread" "continuity;" syn. *guhyamantra, mahāyāna, vajrayāna.* The three divisions of Tantra in its broadest sense are *śaiva-tantra, śākta-tantra* and *bauddha-tantra*; the division according to right-hand and left-hand (*vāmācāra*) Tantra correlates with the *yogin-yoginī-tantra* division, the left-handed or literally interpreted functions belonging to the mother-tantra lineages. The *bauddha-tantra,* Buddhist Tantra, is divided into four classes (*q.v.*), and the highest of the four (*anuttarayoga-tantra*) include the siddhas' tantras and Mahāmudrā. In another division of "higher" and "lower" the higher Tantra's goal is Buddhahood and the lower Tantra's goals are mundane, such as health, wealth, divination or success in any endeavor. In its esoteric sense Tantra is the continuity of union between the male and female principles, skillful means and perfect insight, which is perceived by the realized siddha as a dance of his Ḍākinī, at one with him though separate. Tantra with an initial capital letter indicates Tantra as a vehicle to a soteriological aim, a spiritual path, a corpus of yoga techniques and the ethos of religion; tantra in its limited, technical sense refers to the original scriptural compilations of meditation techniques and rites associated with the propitiation of a particular deity such as Saṃvara in the *Saṃvara-tantra,* and Hevajra in the *Hevajra-tantra.*

Tathatā: *de bzhin nyid:* lit. "that-ness," "such-ness;" the absolutely specific constituent of every situation (*dharma*) giving meaning, pleasure and illumination to existence; the sole, continuous and fundamental fact of existence, synonymous with emptiness (*śūnyatā*).

Tantrika: *sngags pa:* a practitioner of Tantra. The popular contemporary notion of a tantrika is of a sorcerer, healer, shaman, exorcist, seer, or purveyor of spells, but the tantrika of *anuttarayogatantra* has no distinguishing life-style or occupation.

Vajra: *rdo rje;* lit. "lord of stones;" diamond, the hardest and most brilliant of natural substances provides the best metaphor for the ultimate nature of existence, emptiness (*śūnyatā*), in vajrayāna (*q.v.*); representing the male pole of the basic existential duality, it is the male "scepter" to the female "lotus," skillfully employed compassion to perfect insight.

Vajrayāna: *rdo rje theg pa:* lit. "the adamantine vehicle;" syn. *mantravada, tantrayāna*; little used in Indian tantric literature, the term distinguishes Tantra from the *prajñāpāramitāyāna*, the two divisions of mahāyāna; it indicates that the continuity (*tantra*) of pure awareness (*jñāna*) that is the vehicle of *tantrayāna* is indestructible and immutable.

Vedānta: the school of non-dual (*advaita*) metaphysics, originating from a *madhyamika* lineage of Nāgārjuna, adapted by Śaṅkārācārya, a *śaiva* reformer, who founded the Ten Orders (*daśnāmi*) of *śaiva* renunciates, and gave Hinduism an esoteric, non-dual metaphysic commensurate to Mahāmudrā.

Vihāra: *dgonpa:* residence of monks, monastery; from the time of the Buddha the *vihāra* has consisted of a courtyard surrounded by living quarters with an assembly hall, or temple, in the center or on the east side.

Yantra: *'khrul 'khor:* a blue-print, diagram, magic circle; a *yantra* relates to the visual realm as a mantra relates to the realm of sound and a tantra relates to mind; it is a visual representation and aid to identification with the deity it represents. But a *yantra* is a model of any kind—a maṇḍala, a symbolic physical posture, or a diagram of a charm or talisman for an amulet. An artist trained in the tradition invokes the deity in his being when he draws a maṇḍala, sculpts a Buddha or builds a temple.

Yoga: *rnal byor;* lit. "consummate ease" or "union;" although in the vernacular it has come to mean physical yoga (*āsanas*), in Sanskrit it denotes any mode of meditation in Tantra; thus yoga = meditation technique. In Tibetan Mahāmudrā scriptures *rnal byor* is employed in its literal sense to describe the state of being in pure awareness, identified with the ultimate truth.

Yogi: *jogi* in many dialects of Apabhraṃṣa: synonymous with *nāth* (*q.v.*), a practitioner of *haṭhayoga*.

Yogin, yoginī: *rnal byor pa/ma:* syn. *tantrika, sādhaka*; a practitioner of yoga striving for knowledge of his ultimate nature and for the union of his split mind. The stereotyped Indian yogin is a renunciate, itinerant sadhu, or a cave-dwelling anchorite, but *siddha-yoga* demands no limitation of life-style whatsoever.

Glossary of Numeral Terms

Two veils: *dvyāvaraṇa: sgrib pa gnyis*: the veils of emotivity (*kleśāvarana, nyon mongs sgrib*) and objective knowledge (*jneyāvaraṇa, shes bya sgrib*).

Three gates: *sgo gsum*: body (*kāya, lus*), speech (*vāk, ngag*), mind (*citta, sems*).

Three modes of Buddha's being: *trikāya: sku gsum*: absolute empty being (*dharmakāya, chos sku*), instructive, visionary being (*saṃbhogakāya, long spyod sku*), apparitional being (*nirmāṇakāya, sprul sku*).

Three poisons: *dug gsum*: desire (*rāga, 'dod chags*), aversion (*dveśa, zhe sdang*), ignorance (*avidhyā, ma rig pa*).

Three principles of reality: *trilakṣaṇa: mtshan nyid gsum*: nominal-conceptual (*parikalpita, kun rtags mtshan nyid*), the relative (*paratantra, gzhan dbang mtshan nyid*), the absolute (*parinișpanna, yongs grub mtshan nyid*).

Three psychic channels: *trināḍī: rtsa gsum*: the right hand, *lalanā* (*ro ma*, "tongue"), the left hand, *rasanā* (*rkyang ma*, "woman"), the central channel, medial nerve, *avadhūti* (*dbu ma, kun dar ma*, "the all-pervading mother").

Three realms: *triloka: khams gsum*: the sensual realm (*kāmaloka, 'dod khams*), the esthetic realm (*rūpaloka, gzugs khams*), the formless realm (*arūpaloka, gzugs med khams*).

Three types of wisdom: *shes rab gsum*: wisdom arisen from learning (*śrutimayō-prajñā, thos pa las byung ba'i shes rab*), wisdom arisen from analysis (*chintāmayō-prajñā, bsam pa las byung ba'i shes rab*), wisdom arisen from meditation (*bhāvanāmayō-prajñā, bsgoms pa las byung ba'i shes rab*).

Four aspects of the mahāmudrā doctrine: *bstan pa'i phyag rgya'i rnam bzhi*: vision (*darśana, lta ba*), meditation (*bhāvana, bsgoms pa*), action (*caryā, spyod pa*), and goal (*phala, 'bras bu*).

Four classes of *tantra: catuśtantra: rgyud bzhi: kriyā-tantra (bya rgyud), caryā-tantra (spyod rgyud), yoga-tantra (rnal byor rgyud) anuttarayoga-tantra (bla med rgyud*). In *kriyā-tantra* ritual and formal action has primacy; in *yoga-tantra* practice is interiorized; *anuttarayoga-tantra* teaches non-action.

Four devils or obstructive powers: *caturmāra: bdud bzhi*: the devil of the five psycho-physical constituents or the devil "embodiment" (*skandha-māra, phung po'i bdud*), the devil of emotional defilement, of passion (*kleśa-māra, nyong mongs pa'i bdud*), the devil of death (*mṛtyu-māra, shi'i bdud*), the devil of divine pride and lust (*devaputra-māra, lha bu'i bdud*).

Four noble truths: *chatvāri āryyasatyāni*: suffering (*du:kha, sdug bsngal*), origin of suffering (*samudaya, sdug bsngal kun byung ba nyon mongs*), cessation of suffering (*nirodha, sdug bsngal 'gog pa*), the path to cessation (*mārga, sdug bsngal 'gog par 'gro ba'i lam*).

Four boundless states; the four stations of purity: *caturbrahmāvihāra: tshad med bzhi, tshangs pa'i gnas bzhi*: loving kindness (*maitrī, byams pa*), sympathetic joy (*muditā, dga' ba*), compassion (*karūṇā, snying rje*), equanimity (*upekṣā, btang snyoms*).

Four joys: *caturānanda: dga' ba bzhi*: joy (*ānanda, dga' ba*), supreme joy (*paramānanda, mchog dga'*), detached joy or beyond joy (*vilakṣaṇa, dga' bral*), innate joy or spontaneously arising joy (*sahajānanda, lhan skyes dga' ba*).

Four states of being: *spyod lam rnam bzhi*: sitting, walking, eating, excreting.

Four transformative modes of action or the Guru's four *karmas:*

catuśkarma: 'phrin las bzhi: pacification (*zhi ba*), enrichment (*rgyas pa*), control (*dbang ba*), destruction (*drag pa*). See p. 7.

Five Dhyāni Buddhas: *pañcabuddha: sangs rgyas lnga*: Vairocana (rNam par snang mdzad), Akṣobhya (Mi skyod pa), Ratnāsambhava (Rin chen byung ldan), Amitābha ('Od dpag med), Amoghasiddhi (Don yod grub pa). The adjective "Dhyāni" (Meditation) was applied to the five Buddhas of the basic maṇḍala of the father-tantras, first described in the *Guhyasamāja-tantra*, to distinguish them from other groups of five, by a scholar of the twentieth century.

Five elements or five materiality-producing forces: *pañcadhātu: 'byung mo chen po lnga*: earth (*pṛthvī, sa*), water (*āp, chu*), fire (*tejah, me*), air (*vāyu, rlung*), space or ether (*ākāśa, nam mkha*).

Five focal points of psychic energy, five energy centers: *pañcacakra: 'khor lo lnga*: the head center relates to the *nirmāṇakāya*, Akṣobhya and Body; the throat to the *saṃbhogakāya*, Amitābha and Speech; the heart to the *dharmakāya*, Vairocana and Mind; the gut center to the *sahajakāya*, Ratnāsambhava and Attributes; and the sexual center to Amoghasiddhi, the *svabhavikakāya* and to Action. The extra two centers of the seven-fold Kālacakra system, on the crown of the head and in the anus, are counted as inseparable from the head and the sexual centers respectively. The five-fold system allows correspondence of the maṇḍala of the father-tantra with the *cakra* metaphysics of the mother-tantras.

Five modes or aspects of pure awareness: *pañcajñāna, ye shes lnga*: mirror-like awareness (*ādarśajñāna, me long lta bu'i ye shes*), awareness of sameness (*samatājñāna, mnyam nyid kyi ye shes*), discriminating awareness (*pratyavekṣanajñāna, so sor rtogs pa'i ye shes*), all-accomplishing awareness (*kṛtyānusthānajñāna, bya ba grub pa'i ye shes*), awareness of space, like the sky, (*dharmadhātu-jñāna, chos dbyings kyi ye shes*).

Five passions: *pañcakleśa: nyon mongs lnga*: lust (*kāma, 'dod chags*), hatred (*krodha, zhe sdang*), sloth (*moha, gti mug*), pride (*agra, nga rgyal*), jealousy (*īrṣyā, phrag dog*).

Five psycho-physical constituents: *pañcaskandha: phung po lnga*: name and form (*nāmarūpa, ming dang gzugs*), feeling (*vedanā, tshor ba*), perception (*samjñā, 'du shes*), motivation or conditioned impulse (*saṃskāra, 'du byed*), consciousness (*vijñāna, rnam shes*).

Six extrasensory perceptions: *ṣaḍabhijñāna: mngon shes drug*: the divine eye (*divyacaksur-vijñāna, lha'i mig gi mngon shes*), the divine ear (*divyaśrotram-, lha'i rna ba'i*), thought reading (*cetahparyyāya-, sems kyi rnam grangs shes pa'i*), understanding of illusions and miracles (*ṛddividdhi-, rdzu 'phrul gyi bya ba shes pa'i*), knowledge of one's past lives (*pūrbbanivāsānusmṛti-, sngon gyi gnas rjes dran pa'i*), knowledge of the means to destroy passion (*āśravakṣaya-, zag med zad pa shes pa'i*).

Six great towns of Āryavārta: *grong khyer chen po drug*: Śrāvastī, Rājagṛha, Vaiśālī, Paṭaliputra, Vārāṇasī, Kānyakubja.

Six passions: *ṣaḍakleśa: nyon mongs drug*: the five passions (*q.v.*) and doubt (*vitarka, the tshoms*) or fear (*saṣaṅka, dogs pa*). The six passions relate to the six realms and the six types of being.

Six types of being of the six realms: *ṣaḍakula: rigs drug*: gods (*deva, lha*), anti-gods or titans (*asura, lha ma yin*), human beings (*nāra, mi*), hungry ghosts (*preta, yi dwags*), beasts (*paśu, dud 'gro*), denizens of hell (*nāraka, dmyal ba'i sems can*).

Eight auspicious symbols: *aṣṭamaṅgala: bkra shis brtags brgyad*: precious canopy (*gdugs*), two golden fishes (*nya gnyis*), pot of treasure (*bum pa), kamala* flower (*padma*), white conch with right-hand spiral (*gdung*), eternal knot (*be'u*), victory banner (*rgyal mtshan*), eight-spoked wheel (*'khor lo*).

Eight great siddhis or powers: *aṣṭasiddhi: grub chen brgyad*: power to wield the sword of awareness (*ye shes kyi ral gri*), to pass through matter (*sa 'og 'gro*), to create and destroy (*rtshar bcad dang phan 'dogs*), to dispense the pill of third-eye vision and the eye-salve of omniscience (*ril bu dang mig sman gter rnams*), to speed-walk (*rkang mgyogs*), and alchemical powers (*bcud kyis len*).

Eight mundane obsessions: *aṣṭalokadharma: 'Jig rten chos brgyad*: praise and blame (*praśaṁsā, bstod pa; nindā, smad pa*), ignominy and fame (*ayaśa, mi snyan pa; yaśa, snyan pa*), loss and gain (*alābha, ma rnyed pa; lābha, rnyed pa*), pleasure and pain (*sukha, bde ba; du:kha, sdug bsngal*).

Ten perfections: *daśapāramitā: pha rol tu phyin pa bcu*: moral conduct (*śīla, tshul khrims*), generosity (*dāna, sbyin pa*), patience (*kṣānti, bzod pa*), sustained endeavor (*vīrya, brtson 'grus*), concentration (*dhyāna, bsam gtan*), perfect insight (*prajñā, shes rab*), skillful means (*upāya, thabs*), aspiration (*praṇidhāna, smon lam*), inner strength (*bala, stobs*), pure awareness (*jñāna, ye shes*).

Ten virtues: *dge ba bcu*: not taking life (*srog mi gcod pa*), not taking what is not given (*ma byin pa mi len pa*), to practice sexual purity (*tshangs par spyod pa*), to speak the truth (*bden pa smra ba*), to speak gently (*tshig 'jam por smra ba*), to keep one's word (*ngag mi tshal ba*), to refrain from slander (*phra ma mi byed pa*), to restrain covetous thoughts of other's wealth (*gzhan gyi nor la ham pa mi byed pa*), to avoid thoughts of doing harm to others (*gzhan la gnod pa'i sems mi skyed pa*), to sustain the perfect vision (*yang dag pa'i lta ba*).

Twelve-fold chain of interdependent origination: *pratītyasamutpāda: rten 'brel yan lag bcu gnyis*: ignorance (*avidhyā, ma rig pa*), conditioned impulses (*saṃskāra, 'du byed*), consciousness (*vijñāna, rnam shes*), name and form (*nāmarūpa, ming dang gzugs*), six sense organs (*ṣaḍāyatana, skye mched drug*), contact (*sparśa, reg pa*), feeling (*vedanā, tshor ba*), craving (*tṛṣṇā, sred pa*), indulgence (*upādāna, len pa*), existence or procreation (*bhava, srid pa*), birth (*jāti, skye pa*), old age and death (*jarāmarṇa, rgas shi*).

Abbreviations and Bibliography

BA — Roerich, G.N. trans., 1976. *The Blue Annals.* Second edition Delhi: Motilal Banarsidas.

Bu ston — Obermiller, E. trans., 1931. *History of Buddhism by Bu ston.* Reprint Series 5. Heidelberg: Susuki Research Foundation.

DC — Dudjom Tulku Rinpoche 1976. *rNying ma'i chos 'byung.* Kalimpong.

HT — Snellgrove, D. L. trans., 1959. *the Hevajra Tantra Vol. I.* London: OUP.

KS — Khetsun Sangpo ed., 1973. *Biographical Dictionary of Tibet and Tibetan Buddhism Vol. I.* In Tibetan. Dharamsala: Tibetan Library.

RS I — Saṅkṛtyāyana, Rāhula, 1958. *Puratattva-nibandhāvalī.* In Hindi. Ilahabad: Kitab Mahal.

RS II — ———,1963. *Dohākośa.* In Hindi. Patna: Rashtrabhasa Parisad.

RS III — ———, 1934. "Recherches Boudiques: II. L'Origine du Vajrayāna et les 84 Siddhas," *Journal Asiatique* 225: 206–230.

SD — Sempa Dorje ed. and trans., 1979. *The Biography of the Eighty-four Siddhas by Abhaya Datta Śrī.* Tibetan text and Hindi translation. Sarnath: Central Institute of Higher Tibetan Studies.

TARA I — Lama Chimpa and Chattopadhyaya, Alaka, trans., 1970. *Tāranātha's History of Buddhism in India.* Simla: Indian Institute of Advanced Study.

TARA II — *Tāranātha'i bKa' 'bab dun ldan gyi rnam thar*, extracts in *KS*.

TARA IIA — Templeman, D. trans. and ed., 1983. *The Seven Instruction Lineages by Jo Nang Taranatha.* Dharamsala: Tibetan Library.

VP — Vīra Prakāśa, "*Caurāsi-siddhoṁkī-nāmāvali,*" *SD* app. pp. 35–46.

Bhattacharyya, B. ed., 1924. *Sādhanamālā.* Baroda: GOS CCVI.
———, 1924. *Niṣpannayogāvalī.* Baroda: GOS CIX.
———, 1931. *Guhyasamā-tantra.* Baroda: GOS LIII
———, 1932. *Introduction to Buddhist Esoterism.* London: OUP.
———, 1958. *the Indian Buddhist Iconography.* Calcutta: Firma K. Mukhopadhyaya.
Bhatacharyya, N.N., 1982. *History of the Tantric Religion.* Delhi: Manohar.
Briggs, George, 1973. *Gorakhnāth and the Kānphaṭa Yogīs.* Reprint Delhi: Motilal Banarsidas.
Chang, Garma C.C., trans. 1970. *The Hundred Thousand Songs of Milarepa.* New York: Harper.
Chattopadhyaya, Alaka, 1981. *Atīśa and Tibet.* Delhi: Motilal Banarsidas.
Conze, E. ed., 1959. *Buddhist Scriptures.* London: Penguin Classics.
Dargyay, Eva, 1977. *The Rise of Esoteric Buddhism in Tibet.* Delhi: Motilal Banarsidas.
Das, H. C., 1981. *Tantricism.* New Delhi: Sterling Publishers.
Das, Sarat Chandra, ed., 1908. *Pag Sam Jon Zang.* Calcutta.
Das Gupta, S., 1969. *Obscure Religious Cults.* Calcutta: Firma K. Mukhopadhyaya.
Douglas, N. and White, M., 1976. *Karmapa: The Black Hat Lama.* London: Luzac.
Dowman, Keith, trans., 1980. *The Divine Madman.* London: Rider.
———, 1981. "A Buddhist Guide to the Power Places of the Kathmandu Valley", *Kailash* 8:183-287.
———, 1984. *Sky Dancer.* London: Routledge and Kegan Paul.
Evans-Wentz, W. Y. ed., 1957. *The Tibetan Book of the Dead.* Oxford: OUP.
Guenther, H. V., 1959. *The Jewel Ornament of Liberation.* London: Rider.
———, 1963. *The Life and Teaching of Nāropa.* London: OUP.
———, 1968. *The Royal Song of Saraha.* Boulder: Shambala.
———, 1971. *Buddhist Philosophy in Theory and Practice.* London: Penguin Classics.
Kasi Dawa Samdup ed., 1919. *Śrīchakrasambhāra-tantra.* London: Luzac.
Kelsang Gyatso, 1982. *The Clear Light of Bliss.* London: Wisdom Publications.
Locke, J., 1980. *Karunamaya.* Kathmandu: Sahayogi/CNAS.
Lorenzen, D. N., 1972. *Kāpālikas and Kālāmukhas.* N. Delhi: Thompson.
Lozang Jamspal trans., 1978. *Nāgārjuna's Letter to King Gautamīputra.* Delhi: Motilal Banarsidas.

Mojumder, Atindra, 1976. *The Caryāpadas.* Calcutta: Maya Prokash.

Mudiyanse, Nandasena, 1967. *Mahāyāna Monuments in Ceylon.* Colombo: Gunasena.

Nadou, Jean, 1980. *Buddhists of Kashmir.* Delhi: Agam Kala Prakashan.

Nālandā/Trungpa, trans., 1982. *The Life of Marpa the Translator by Tsang Nyon Heruka.* Boulder: Prajñā.

Robinson, James B. trans., 1979. *Buddha's Lions.* Emeryville: Dharma Publishing.

Roerich, G. N. trans., 1959. *The Biography of Dharmaswamin.* Patna: JRI.

Sircar, D. C., 1973. *The Śākta Pīṭhas.* Delhi: Motilal Banarsidas.

Slusser, M. S., 1982. *Nepal Mandala.* Princetown: Princetown U. Press.

Tucci, G., 1930. "Animadversiones Indicae," *Journal of the Asiatic Society of Bengal* 26:125-155.

———, 1949. *Tibetan Painted Scrolls.* Roma: La Libreria Dello Stato.

Walleser, M., 1979. *The Life of Nāgārjuna from Tibetan and Chinese Sources.* Delhi: Nag Publishers.

Warder, A. K., 1970. *Indian Buddhism.* Delhi: Motilal Banarsidas.

Wayman, Alex, 1977. *The Yoga of the Guhyasamāja.* Delhi: Motilal Banarsidas.

Yule, Henry, and Burnell, A. C., 1979. *Hobson Jobson.* Third edition revised New Delhi: Munshiram Manoharlal.

Index of Sanskrit Names

N.B. The names of the Eighty-four Mahāsiddhas are indicated by bold type, as are the principal references to all main entries.

Index of Tibetan Names

N.B. Ordered according to the Tibetan alphabet

Index of Sanskrit Terms

N.B. Bold type indicates principal references.

Index of Tibetan Terms

N.B. Bold type indicates principal references. Ordered according to the Tibetan alphabet.

Index of Sanskrit Texts